MITANNI

ASSYRIA

NAHARIN

chemish

Haran

Ninive

Keilah

Arrapkha

Ashur   Nuzi

ab

Terqa

Hamath
Qatna   Mari

Kadesh   Tadmor

Eshnunna

ebo-hamath

Euphrates   Sippar

us   BABYLONIA   SUMER   Tigris   ELAM

Babylon   Kish   Shushan (Susa)

aroth   Nippur

n   Isin   Lagash

Uruk   Larsa

bath-ammon   Ur

Eridu

Tema

THE ANCIENT EAST
IN THE SECOND MILLENIUM B.C.E.

Locality mentioned in the Bible...................Hazor
Ancient locality mentioned in other sources.........*Isin*
Modern name .... [Beni Hasan]

PATRIARCHS

THE WORLD HISTORY OF THE JEWISH PEOPLE

FIRST SERIES: ANCIENT TIMES

(PATRIARCHS AND JUDGES)

GENERAL EDITOR

BENJAMIN MAZAR

ASSISTANT EDITOR

ELIYAHU FELDMAN

MANAGING EDITOR

ALEXANDER PELI

JEWISH HISTORY PUBLICATIONS [ISRAEL — 1961] LTD.

PATRIARCHS

VOLUME II

EDITOR

BENJAMIN MAZAR

RUTGERS UNIVERSITY PRESS, 1970

PUBLISHED IN ISRAEL
BY JEWISH HISTORY PUBLICATIONS (ISRAEL – 1961) LTD.

LIBRARY OF CONGRESS CATALOGUE CARD NUMBER 64–15907
SBN 8135–0615–8

PRINTED IN ISRAEL BY PELI PRINTING WORKS LTD., GIVATAYIM

CONTENTS

CONTENTS

AUTHORS

PHOTOGRAPHS

PREFACE

This volume of the "World History of the Jewish People" is devoted to the most ancient period in the nation's annals, from the earliest times to the establishment of the Israelite Kingdom. The origins of the Hebrews, the formation and crystallization of the nation, its history, and the growth of its spiritual culture and social organization are discussed in detail against the backdrop of historico-cultural developments in the lands of the Bible, in the second millennium B.C.E.

The historical fate of the Israelite People was to a large extent determined by the geographical factor. The birthplace and homeland of Israelite culture is located in the Fertile Crescent — a broad region in the great expanse of countries constituting the Near East. Palestine, to which Israelites have been clinging since early antiquity, represents the south-western tip of the Fertile Crescent, separated by only a strip of desert from Egypt. This position between the sea and the desert, with which the small territory on both sides of the Jordan river is uniquely identified, is responsible for the fact that Palestine acquired paramount importance as the locale of major thoroughfares. Visible and hidden threads tied it to nearby or remote neighbors, and its soil served as a perennial arena of contacts among peoples and cultures.

Numerous written documents touching directly or indirectly on Palestine and its close neighbors, and abundant archeological discoveries made at its various sites blend, as so many threads in a large unbroken tapestry, the long periods of the country's history and its culture within the framework of the Ancient East's civilization of the second millennium B.C.E. At the same time, the problems raised by the proper interpretation of the finds are increasing, and it is not seldom that new discoveries cancel out accepted hypotheses and open new horizons for the understanding of phenomena which determined the fate of the country and its neighbors. Nevertheless, despite the great achievements of archeological research and the wealth of written evidence which brought to light data of considerable importance for the history of the period and the various spheres of man's creativity, many extremely difficult and obscure phenomena still require solution.

The problem of primary concern is the evaluation of the traditions and evidence contained in the richest of all sources — both quantitatively and qualitatively — which goes directly to the heart of the matter, and provides a consummate, crystallized expression of Israelite history and culture. This source is the Bible, with its extensive historiographic works as well as other categories of literature which supplement it. Not for nothing are opinions divided as to the methods and means of utilizing the biblical sources for understanding the origins of Israel, the formation of the people and its religion, the conquest of the land, the historical and settlement developments on its soil, its transformation into the crucible in which were forged the nation's cultural, spiritual, and social values until the establishment of the Israelite Kingdom.

The very nature of the Bible's historiographic sections obliges the historian to separate ancient elements incorporated to the compilations from the elements pointing to the time their authors or editors lived in — as expressed by the religious and historiographic views prevalent in their age. The fitting of both those elements within the framework of historic reality determines the relationship between the Bible and the abundant epigraphic and archeological sources. They complement each other, elucidate and explain one another, and open the way toward the clarification of historical processes and phenomena that determined the destiny of the people of Israel from its inception to the establishment of the independent state which emerged in the country, and shaped its destinies for centuries to come.

The present book is the shared effort of many scholars, each of whom contributed one or more chapters. Our purpose being the presentation of the completest picture possible of all the problems involved in the history of the period and its culture in general, and the history of the Israelite People and its social and religious life in particular, the plan of the book includes fields of research varying in nature and content. It was not the editor's intention to give this book the character of a single, undiluted, consistent synthesis. Being a collective enterprise, it presents the results of the research undertaken by various scholars, whose summaries form a single historiographic work. The authors were given the freedom of expressing their views and conceptions both in analyzing and evaluating biblical sources, as well as in their emphasis on the motives, internal developments, and external influences at work in the history of the people and its land, in that ancient and nebulous period. At the same time the book brings out the unique nature of the Israelite People at the time of its beginnings, and its ancient spiritual creativity which found expression in the Bible, thus transforming it into one of the decisive factors in the history of mankind, and into a foundation stone in the world of the spirit, down to our own times.

For technical reasons the volume has been divided into two parts: —
1. Patriarchs; 2. Judges.

It is a pleasant duty to express my appreciation to all those who helped prepare and publish this book — to the authors who made the appearance of the book possible by sparing no effort to write and bring their chapters up to date and correct them in the process of publication; to the translators; to the editorial staff who did not stint work in preparing the book for the press; to the illustrators, and to the compiler of the index. I am grateful to all of them.

BENJAMIN MAZAR

Jerusalem, September 1970.

ABBREVIATIONS FOR BIBLICAL BOOKS

Genesis	Gen.	Habakkuk	Hab.
Exodus	Ex.	Zephaniah	Zeph.
Leviticus	Lev.	Haggai	Hag.
Numbers	Num.	Zechariah	Zech.
Joshua	Josh.	Malachi	Mal.
Judges	Jud.	Psalms	Ps.
I Samuel	I Sam.	Canticles (Song of Songs)	Cant.
II Samuel	II Sam.	Lamentations	Lam.
Isaiah	Isa.	Ecclesiastes	Eccl.
Jeremiah	Jer.	Daniel	Dan.
Ezekiel	Ezek.	Nehemiah	Neh.
Hosea	Hos.	I Chronicles	I Chron.
Obadiah	Ob.	II Chronicles	II Chron.

ABBREVIATIONS FOR JOURNALS
AND SCIENTIFIC LITERATURE

AASOR — Annual of the American Schools of Oriental Research
AfO — Archiv für Orientforschung
ANEP — The Ancient Near East in Pictures, James Pritchard, Princeton, 1954
ANET — Ancient Near Eastern Texts, Ed. James Pritchard, Princeton, 1950
AnOr — Analecta Orientalia (Pontifical Biblical Institute, Rome)
AO — Der Alte Orient
AOS — American Oriental Society
ARM — Archives royales de Mari
.AT — The Alalakh Tablets
BASOR –- Bulletin of the American Schools of Oriental Research
BASS — Beiträge zur Assyriologie und semitischen Sprachwissenschaft
BIES — Bulletin of the Israel Exploration Society
BiOr — Bibliotheca Orientalis (Leiden)
BSL — Bulletin de la Société de Linguistique de Paris (Page numbers preceded by an asterisk refer to the reviews)
HUCA — Hebrew Union College Annual
IEJ — Israel Exploration Journal
JAOS — Journal of the American Oriental Society
JBL — Journal of Biblical Literature
JCS — Journal of Cuneiform Studies
JEA — Journal of Egyptian Archaeology
JNES — Journal of Near Eastern Studies
MSL — Materialien zum sumerischen Lexikon
MSOS — Mitteilungen des Seminars für orientalische Sprachen (Berlin)
RA — Revue d'Assyrologie et d'Archéologie Orientale
RB — Revue Biblique
RT — Recueil de traveaux relatifs à la philologie et l'archéologie égyptiennes et assyriennes
SIL — Studies in Linguistics, ed. G.L. Prager
WZKM — Wiener Zeitschrift für die Kunde des Morgenlandes
ZA 1-44 — Zeitschrift für Assyriologie und verwandte Gebiete
   45 *et seq.* — Zeitschrift für Assyriologie und vorderasiatische Archäologie
ZDMG — Zeitschrift der Deutschen Morgenländischen Gesellschaft

HEBREW-ENGLISH TRANSLITERATION

1. All Hebrew names found in the Bible are given as they appear in the English translation of the Holy Scriptures by the Jewish Publication Society of America, Philadelphia, 1955.

2. Those names that are familiar to the English reader are rendered in their customary, accepted spelling (e. g. Caesarea).

3. All other Hebrew names and words are transliterated as follows:

א   Not noted at beginning or end of word; otherwise by ', e. g. pᵉʾēr or pĕʾēr (פָּאַר), mēʾīr (מְאִיר).

ב   b

ב   v

ג   g

ג   g

ד   d

ד   d

ה   h (unless consonantal, ה at the end of the word is not transliterated)

ו   w

ז   z

ח   ḥ

ט   ṭ

י   y

כ   k

כ   ḵ

ל   l

מ   m

נ   n

ס   s

ע   ʽ

פ   p

פ   f

צ   z

ק   q

ר   r

שׁ   sh, š

שׂ   s

ת   t

ת   t (Except in the word בית – *beth*)

a) The *dagesh lene* is not indicated, save in the letters ב and פ. *Dagesh forte* is indicated by doubling the letter.

b) The Hebrew definite article is indicated by *ha* or *he* followed by a hyphen, but without the next letter doubled, e. g. *ha-shānā*, not *ha-shshānā*.

◌	a	◌	e
◌	ă	◌	ĕ
◌	ā	◌	ū
◌	o	◌	ō
◌	ŏ	◌	u
◌	ē	◌	i
◌	ē, ēi	◌	ī

Sheva mobile (שוא נע) is indicated thus: ͤ or ĕ. Neither long vowels nor *sheva mobile* are indicated in proper names.

ARABIC-ENGLISH TRANSLITERATION

ء	— ' (not indicated at the beginning of a word)	ض	— ḍ
		ط	— ṭ
ب	— b	ظ	— ẓ
ت	— t	ع	— '
ث	— th	غ	— gh
ج	— j	ف	— f
ح	— ḥ	ق	— q
خ	— kh	ك	— k
د	— d	ل	— l
ذ	— dh	م	— m
ر	— r	ن	— n
ز	— z	ه	— h
س	— s	و	— w
ش	— sh	ى	— y
ص	— ṣ		

The Lām of the definite article ال is assimilated before a solar letter. Proper names familiar to the English reader are rendered in their customary spelling.

PART ONE: THE ERA AND ITS SOURCES

CHAPTER I

HISTORIOGRAPHY AND HISTORICAL SOURCES IN ANCIENT MESOPOTAMIA[1]

by E. A. Speiser

A. The Normative Cultural Background

MESOPOTAMIAN HISTORIOGRAPHY, like any other, is in the last analysis a reflection of the underlying civilization. More particularly, it is intimately related to the local concepts of religion and government. The most striking feature of the civilization of Mesopotamia was its essential continuity during the whole of the historic period, in spite of the great diversity of the component ethnic elements; and much of this continuity can be traced back to common ideas and practices in the approach to the cosmos and to society. The cultural ties that linked the Sumerians with the Sargonid Akkadians, the Babylonians with the Assyrians, and the 3rd millennium with the 2nd and the 1st, overcame ethnic, linguistic, and political boundaries. The end product was in effect a joint Mesopotamian achievement.

The role of religion in this intricate process cannot be underestimated. It was a basic tenet of the religion of Mesopotamia that the society of the gods was the prototype and the model of human society. In the cosmos, moreover, no single god was the ultimate source of power and authority; none was really omnipotent. Final authority resided in all the gods as a body. Accordingly, the larger issues of life and destiny were never settled for all time and hence could not be foretold even by the head of the pantheon. Dependent mankind was therefore doomed forever to anxiety and insecurity. Yet as long as there was the chance that things might turn out favorably — by dint of meticulous watchfulness and elaborate ritual — there was little room for apathy and resignation. Mankind was indeed "beclouded," but not altogether without hope.

The authority of the mortal ruler was severely restricted by two factors: first, the king's mandate stemmed from the gods, and it was to them that he was always accountable for the proper conduct of his affairs; and secondly, since even the divine sovereign lacked absolute power, it could not be otherwise with his human counterpart. The ultimate source of authority in the human state was the assembly of the leaders of elders (*puḥrum*).[2] Its deliberations (*mitlukum*) were essential to civilized existence. Without them, and before they had been instituted, there could be nothing but chaos.[3]

Because these concepts were valid throughout the course of Mesopotamian history, they serve as a guide to the native idea of history and constitute a basic feature of Mesopotamian historiography.

B. NATURE OF THE SOURCE MATERIAL

The evidence for the Mesopotamians' interest in their past is both abundant and manifold. The most direct and also the most abundant testimony is provided by such writings as king lists, public building records, chronicles, and annals. A valuable secondary source is furnished by literary histories, in which historical facts, or facts regarded as historical, have been woven into a fabric of myth and legend.[4] Incidental hints are contained also in the omen texts which point back to historical events and allude on occasion to past happenings which chance to be otherwise unknown.[5] Similarly, a ruler with a taste for archeology and chronology may give us in passing a tally of the time that had elapsed between two given events.[6]

One vital reason for the constant preoccupation with the past was the imperative need for maintaining the friendly relations with the gods that had been established by previous generations. A good illustration is this typical statement by the old Assyrian ruler Erishu(m) I: "Should this building grow old with age, and a king like me wishes to rebuild the structure, he shall not displace the nail (*sikkatum*) that I have driven in it, but shall restore it to its place."[7] Contact with the past inspired the assembling of great libraries of ancient records. A letter from Ashurbanipal to his literary agent in Borsippa includes a blanket request for "rituals, prayers, inscriptions of stone, and whatever may be good for my kingship" as well as "any tablet or ritual . . . that is good for my palace."[8] In other words, the past was scrutinized because it might teach the present how to make a success of itself, or at least to get by.

C. TRADITIONAL VIEWS ABOUT THE PAST

Since things on earth were directed from heaven, the Mesopotamian concept of history was fundamentally theocratic. The concrete formulation of this concept derived in large part from the glorious achievements and the subsequent collapse of the celebrated Dynasty of Akkad. The century of Sargon and Naram-Sin stood out for all succeeding ages as a period of unprecedented attainment, which indeed it was. Yet there was also the further fact, at once memorable and awesome, that the seemingly limitless power of Akkad was eventually dissipated. The fate of that dynasty was thus a vivid example of ebb and flow in the fortunes of a great empire and, by extension, of the prospects of other dynasties as well. There thus appeared to be a rythmic regularity in the alternation of good and ill fortune — a plausible basis, in short, on which to found a system of the interpretation of history.[9] A successful ruler, notably Sargon, was the gods' favorite, whereas a Naram-Sin, whose reign began auspiciously but ended in disaster, must have incurred the displeasure of the cosmic powers. The past was thus highlighted by alternating periods of success and failure. The only conceivable reason why the gods would turn against a mortal ruler was that he had offended them somehow (term. techn. *qullulum*), either by transgressing the solemn oath of his office (*māmītam etēqum*) or by overstepping the bounds set for him by his god (*itē ilim etēqum*). Such operation of the law of cause and effect could be adduced from almost any period. Aside from the classic instance of Urukagina and Lugalzaggisi there is, for example, the letter to the god written by Yasmah-Adad of Mari, in which the king affirms that no member of his family had ever "committed an offense against his god";[10] Tukulti-Ninurta I (1243–1207 B.C.E.) brands his Babylonian foe as an *ētiq māmīti* "transgressor of the oath"[11] and has him finally confess, "Most grievous have been the offenses of my land, numerous its sins."[12] There are many similar instances from later times.

The most stilted expression of this view of history is found in the Chronicle Weidner.[13] Its starts out with a didactic warning against those who offend against the gods.[14] But the main concern of the Chronicle is with the pious and successful Sargon and the impious Naram-Sin who brought misfortune upon his own head. In this stereotyped temple view of history, cult and ritual were paramount in the affairs of state. This is an extreme example, to be sure. Other appraisals of significant historical events manage to avoid the extreme mechanism of the Chronicle Weidner and there is sometimes a faint suggestion of ethical principles behind a ruler's misfortune.[15] Sober realism however is both late and rare.

D. OMENS AND LETTERS TO THE GODS

It was noted above that there were two potent checks on the authority of the Mesopotamian kings. One was societal and it stemmed from the role of the assembly. The other religious, in that every major undertaking

required divine approval. Such approval was signified by means of direc-
tions or oracles (*tērētum*) which were obtained through the medium of
omens. The ruler in particular resorted to omens on virtually every conceivable occasion and this fact points up with singular eloquence his abject
dependence in all matters on the will of gods. The omens in turn derived
their answer from events affecting previous kings, thereby emphasizing the
inescapable bearing of the past on present. What is more, the omen texts
frequently dwell on the faults of the older kings, by no means exempting
the most illustrious among them. This common fact should be sufficient to
refute a theory that is still often voiced in our times to the effect that many
of the kings of Mesopotamia were regarded as divine. A god incarnate
would not have to approach his every move with obvious terror, nor would
he need to take his cue from the liver of a sheep.

When the omens turned out to be unfavorable, or when the ruler's
efforts to appease the gods had repeatedly failed, he might address the
deity directly by letter. Such letters to the gods turn up early in the history
of Mesopotamia and they are known to have continued in vogue down to
the later periods. Some of them contain earnest pleas for help. Others,
especially in later times, are dutiful reports designed to show how well the
human ruler had carried out the wishes of his divine master. In this odd
custom we may have an important clue to the gradual development of the
annalistic records in Assyria.

E. Annals and Chronicles

The historical data from the south, and especially from Babylonia, differ
in many ways from the Assyrian accounts. Whether they are in the form of
king lists, building reports, or chronicles, the southern records do not
attempt as a rule to furnish a running account of events year by year. The
Assyrian records, on the other hand, assume the form of annals, starting
shortly after the middle of the 2nd millennium. We know now that the
practice of addressing the gods in writing was current in Assyria as far
back as the age of Shamshi-Adad, a contemporary of Hammurabi and an
acknowledged pioneer in cultural and political matters. We know, furthermore, that some of the later reports in the form of such letters to the gods
came to be reproduced as part of formal annals. In these circumstances
it would not seem too hazardous to assume that the emergence of regular
annals owed much to the example of casual letters, especially since the
contents were often the same in both instances. On this assumption, we
would have a ready and logical explanation for the tone of the annals,

which is often bombastic and immoderate in the extreme. For in that case, the words which the king used were not his own but rather those of the gods' original command which their faithful steward was obliged to carry out. The tone was boastful because the king spoke not in his own name but in that of his divine patron, whose authority and valor were in the last analysis involved.

Given these limitations in recording history, it is not surprising that Assyrian historiography shows a low standard of reliability. Even the so-called Synchronistic History is a markedly chauvinistic product. Babylonia, on the other hand, having never developed formal annals, was in a position to render a more objective performance. And if the Babylonian Chronicle is dry and uninspired history, it is nevertheless a remarkable document in "its sobriety of presentation and its coldly impartial statement of fact."[16]

F. Evidence of the Wisdom Literature

The Mesopotamian idea of history is reflected to some extent in compositions which come under the heading of wisdom literature. The burden of much of it is that since the gods were unpredictable, mankind was doomed to be forever restless and insecure.[17] The king must strive to maintain the existing equilibrium through elaborate efforts at purification and expiation. In special emergencies it may even be expedient to set up a substitute king in order to divert the divine wrath from the established ruler.[18] There are occasions, however, when the land is afflicted even though the king is without blame. This subject is dealt with under the theme of the Righteous Sufferer.

We now have three major compositions on this theme. One is "I Shall Praise the God of Wisdom";[19] another is the Babylonian Theodicy;[20] the third, a recently published version from the Old Babylonian period.[21] All three have this one conclusion in common: even though the ways of the gods are mysterious and inscrutable, the truly meritorious need not despair of ultimate salvation. The period of suffering is bound to be succeeded by the miracle of final deliverance.

These Mesopotamian counterparts of Job add up to a powerful argument in favor of studying the past. Implicit in them is the conviction that the deserving ruler, although seemingly forgotten by the gods, is bound to be restored to grace. Thus old Sargon, according to the omens, was "one who encountered darkness, yet light emerged for him."[22] The study of the past may show how to emulate the successful king while avoiding the errors of the ill-fated.

Another comforting example was the hero of the Flood. The signal success of Ut(a)napishtim is attributed in the wisdom literature to the teaching
of his father Shuruppak, whom Sumerian and Akkadian sources alike
present as the fountain-head of proverbial wisdom.[23] The interest of Mesopotamians in the Job and Noah themes brings up, in turn, the familiar
passage in Ezek. 14 : 14–23, according to which Noah, Daniel, and Job
were the only mortals to emerge unscathed from universal catastrophes.
To be sure, the Daniel theme as such has not turned up as yet in Mesopotamian sources. But it is independently attested in Ugaritic and there is
the possibility that the Babylonian prototype of this hero may turn out
to have been Adapa. At any rate, since the biblical Daniel is placed in a
Babylonian setting, and since Ezekiel knew his Babylonian culture at first
hand, the Mesopotamian origin of all three of these heroes of Ezekiel should
stand assured beyond all responsible doubt. How each of them had proved
worthy of his exceptional distinction is not made clear. But the popular
explanation, at least, may be contained in the old omen which states that
"if he has abhorred sin, his god will ever walk with him."[24] Thus the
example of the ancient sages who survived extraordinary trials and dis-
asters may help to safeguard against their recurrence. In a capricious
cosmos one cannot hope for more.

CHAPTER II

UGARITIC WRITINGS

by S. E. Loewenstamm

A. The Bible and Canaanite Civilization

THE SPECIAL AFFINITY of the Bible to Canaanite civilization may be deduced from the very fact that Hebrew belongs to the Canaanite languages. Owing, however, to the paucity of information about Canaanite literature, an exhaustive study of the subject has thus far not been possible. The account of Phoenician theology by Philo of Byblos,[1] which is written in Greek and which represents it as containing an admixture of Greek elements, is marked by a considerable degree of distortion inasmuch as Philo denied the existence of gods, following as he did the atheist philosopher Euhemerus' theory that the gods were great men who had been elevated by popular superstition to divine status. Neither have the brief Phoenician inscriptions contributed much to an apprehension of Canaanite civilization. Nor has the realization that the Amarna letters contain Akkadian translations of passages from psalms[2] which resemble those of the Bible greatly affected the evaluation of biblical literature, the approach to which underwent a change only with the discovery of texts written in the Northwestern Semitic language of Ugarit. Passages from these texts for the first time furnished a clear idea of the nature of Canaanite literature in the Late Bronze Age, immediately preceding the period of the Israelite conquest of Canaan.

B. Ugarit: From its Foundation to its Destruction

Together with Hurrian, Akkadian, Sumerian, Hittite, Egyptian, and Cypriot texts, this Ugaritic literature was discovered in the ruins of the tell of the ancient north Syrian city of Ugarit, the present-day Ra's Shamrā, which is near the small port of Mīnat al-Bayḍā', opposite the north-eastern tip of Cyprus. Scholars had first come across the name of this city in the Amarna letters in which it is frequently mentioned. In particular, a letter from Byblos[3] reveals that the city was famous throughout Canaan: "Behold the house of Tyre, there is no house of a governor like it, it is like

the house of Ugarit, very much is that which is found in it." This reference
to the splendor of Ugarit is constantly being confirmed by the Ugarit
excavations begun in 1929 by French archeologists under the direction
of Claude Schaeffer and continued every year except for a temporary
interruption during the Second World War.

These excavations have established that the settlement in Ugarit dates
from the Neolithic period, that is, at the very latest from the beginning
of the 5th millennium. Who its original settlers were cannot be ascertained.
On the other hand, the composition of the inhabitants of the Ugaritic
kingdom during the Late Bronze Age is known from a study of the proper
names in the Ugaritic writings. Leaving aside the names of traders from
Cyprus, Assyria, Babylonia, and Egypt, who lived in this international
commercial center, the inhabitants of the kingdom of Ugarit consisted
of a west Semitic element alongside a Hurrian one, equal to it in numbers
but not in importance, of a small section of Asia Minor origin, as also
of a tiny Indo-Aryan element.[4] The historical events which led to this
composition are not entirely clear. It may, however, be assumed that the
convergence of the three main sections took place not later than the days
of Hammurabi, King of Babylon.

This assumption is based on documents found in Alalakh,[5] the capital of
the land of Mukish which lies to the north of that of Ugarit. In contrast
to the Ugaritic documents, which for the most part belong to the 14th
and 13th centuries B.C.E., the Alalakhian documents were written partly
in the time of Hammurabi and partly in the 15th century. They show
that the composition of Alalakh's population did not change between
these two periods and that already in the days of Hammurabi the same
three sections, known to us from the late Ugaritic letters, existed among
the inhabitants of Alalakh, where however, the west Semitic element
was considerably smaller than the Hurrian one and constituted the
upper class. This points to the antiquity of the Hurrian element also
in Ugarit.

The domination of Ugarit by west Semitic tribes is undoubtedly
connected with the general process of their expansion through Babylonia
and Canaan, a movement which convulsed the Ancient East presumably
in ca. 2000 B.C.E. The founder of the royal house of Ugarit was apparently
King Yaqarum, the son of Niqmadd, a name (found also in the Alalakhian[6]
and in the Mari letters[7]) which clearly attests its west Semitic origin[8],
and which has been preserved in the seal used by the kings of Ugarit
until that country's destruction. The form of the seal shows that it is not
later than the time of Hammurabi,[9] since when, it may be assumed, if

not before that, a single, unbroken dynasty ruled in Ugarit. This continuity lends considerable support to the hypothesis that no significant ethnical changes occurred during the whole of that lengthy period. The Akkadian seal of Yaqarum is, on account of its language and style, the only evidence which directly proves that in the days of Hammurabi Ugarit documents were written in Akkadian. This direct and isolated piece of evidence is, however, further supported by the Alalakhian documents of the same period written in Akkadian, and especially by a great number of Akkadian documents from Ugarit proving that in the Late Bronze Age this language still constituted the medium of international correspondence and prevailed even in legal deeds. Apart from Yaqarum's seal there are extant from the period of Hammurabi a receipt for wool from Alalakh which mentions among the suppliers someone from Ugarit,[10] and in particular a letter from Hammurabi (King of Aleppo?) to Zimri-lim, King of Mari, informing him of the forthcoming visit of the King of Ugarit.[11]

Thus already at that time, Ugarit was incorporated within the broad structure of contemporary international politics. It is therefore not surprising that as early as the beginning of the 2nd millennium B.C.E. the pharaoh Sen-Usert I sent gifts to the temple of Dagan in Ugarit and that later Egyptian kings of the Twelfth Dynasty likewise sent presents to Ugarit. This indicates that a treaty existed between Ugarit and Egypt which, on the one hand, fitted in well with the aspirations of the Egyptian kings of the Twelfth Dynasty to include Canaan within the sphere of their influence and, on the other, safeguarded the freedom of Ugaritic trade on the Mediterranean.[12] Maritime commerce forged strong cultural links between Ugarit and in particular the ancient cultural center of Crete. The abundant merchandise imported from this island and the influence of Cretan art on that of Ugarit[13] are reflected in the Ugaritic myth, which expressly states that Caphtor is the throne of the god Kothar wa-Khasis, the architect and artist of Baal.[14] The prosperity of this civilization was interrupted at the end of the Middle Bronze II Period for a long time which is not represented in archeological finds, so that there is no continuous transition from the Middle to the Late Bronze Period.[15]

It may reasonably be assumed that the events associated with the Hyksos invasion of Egypt caused an upheaval in the life of Ugarit, but the period is obscure, marked as it is by a lack of precise information. In any event, excavations have shown that the city began to recover shortly before the collapse of the Hyksos rule in Egypt. Nor is there any detailed, written information on the history of Ugarit in the 16th and

15th centuries, B.C.E., but it doubtlessly shared the fate of the other small kingdoms in Syria when Egypt began its expansionist policy in Canaan and its conquests reached their zenith in the wars of Thut-mose III during the sixties of the 15th century. At that time, as is attested by 15th century Alalakhian documents, the kingdom of Mukish was a dependency of the Indo-Aryan empire of Mitanni. Although the latter was the adversary of Egypt, the danger posed by the Hittite empire drew the two great powers together. At the beginning of the 14th century, however, the Hittite empire conquered Mitanni and fell heir to its position. From then until the peace treaty between Egypt and the Hittite empire in ca. 1280 B.C.E., Ugarit was in a vulnerable position between these two empires, each of which sought to dominate the small kingdoms in Canaan. The beginning of this period is illuminated by the Amarna letters, and its continuation by the many diplomatic documents found in the archives of Ugarit[16] as also by the numerous gifts of Egyptian kings found in Ugarit,[17] especially a vase which depicts the marriage of an Ugarit king (apparently Niqmadd, a contemporary both of the Hittite King Shuppiluliuma and of Akh-en-Aton) to a pharaoh's daughter.[18] What emerges from these documents is that Ugarit became a Hittite vassal state as early as the beginning of the 14th century, but that it preserved its neutrality and a considerable measure of its independence. Even after Mursilis, the high king of the Hittites (1344–1314 B.C.E.), had made the King of Carchemish a quasi-representative of the Hittite government with regard to Ugarit, relations between Egypt and Ugarit were apparently severed for only a brief period at the beginning of the 13th century. At the time Hittite pressure increased on Ugarit, whose king was compelled to send to Muwatallis, the Hittite king, an auxiliary force which took part in the battles against Ramses II at Kadesh on the Orontes. Ugarit's policy of neutrality and of non-involvement in wars[19] seems to have contributed greatly to the city's prosperity during this period, and even after a large part of it was destroyed by an earthquake in the middle of the 14th century it continued to flourish. Its end however came in the early years of the 12th century when the "Sea Peoples" attacked and completely burnt it.[20]

The final period of Ugarit, which began with its recovery in the 16th century, was the city's golden age. It was then, too, that the royal palace was built; those parts of it which have thus far been uncovered extend over an area of more than 12,000 sq. yards, while the walls of its fortifications are 17½ yards wide.[21] At that time the city's cultural life increasingly freed itself from subservience to Akkadian culture and developed its own alphabetical script in which some Hurrian documents were written, as also a great many in Ugaritic, these including, apart from administrative and legal documents and letters, great epics of which considerable sections have been found.

C. UGARITIC LITERATURE AND THE BIBLE

The cradle and background of this literature lies in northern Canaan. Mount Casius (Jabal al-Aqra'), the abode of Baal-zephon,[22] rises north of the city of Ugarit. In the city of Harnam, which was near Kadesh on the Orontes, lived Danel, the righteous judge and father of the hero of the epic of Aqhat.[23] The southernmost cities alluded to in the epic are Tyre and Sidon;[24] the southernmost mountains, Lebanon and Sirion, are mentioned next to each other in poetic parallelism, as in biblical poetry.[25] This area may also include Lake Huleh, if indeed *šmk*, described as "buffalo filled,"[26] is the Lake of Samko of the Talmud and Semachonitis of Hellenistic literature.

The social background of Ugaritic literature is an absolute monarchy with a well ordered bureaucratic machinery, a monarchy ruling over a people that has lived in its land for untold generations. Although material civilization here reached the pinnacle of prosperity, Ugaritic poetry has preserved an ancient literary gem which testifies to the people's way of life in bygone days: "The gods proceed to their tents, the family of El to their tabernacles."[27] Hence the gods of Ugarit, now honored with magnificent temples, also formerly dwelt in tents and tabernacles. When, however, the Ugaritic epic which enlarges upon the building of Baal's temple was composed, those days belonged to the distant past.

Although Ugaritic syntax is close to that of the Bible, only about half its vocabulary is found in biblical Hebrew. If to this is added the fact that Ugarit was destroyed at the beginning of the period of the Judges, the assumption of a direct influence by Ugaritic literature on that of the Bible appears to be extremely presumptuous and rather questionable. As regards its subject matter, Ugaritic literature differs from biblical not only in its polytheistic elements, but in the complete absence of any national aspect in the composition of its deities, which fitted well with the international character of city life. Formally, Ugaritic literature represents that stage of the epic where it develops from one devoted to the activities of the deity to that in which human actions are of paramount importance. Biblical literature, on the other hand, represents the post-epic stage of artistic prose. These differences cannot, however, obscure the obvious affinity between Ugaritic and biblical literature in point of style and trend of thought, and it must, therefore, be assumed that in southern Canaan a literature developed which, while resembling that of Ugarit, was closer to the language of the Bible, and that it was this literature which had an impact on the Israelites' form of expression and even on their concept of the universe. This assumption is supported by biblical passages which show that the idolatry practiced in Ugarit was likewise cultivated by the Canaanites in Palestine, namely, the worship of the gods, El, Baal, Resheph, and Dagan, and of the goddesses Asherah, Anath, Ashtoreth, and Shamash.

The alphabet furnishes clear evidence of the common background of the biblical and Ugaritic civilizations, notwithstanding the profound differences between them. At first glance the Ugaritic is completely different from the Hebrew-Phoenician alphabet. The former has thirty letters as against twenty-two in Hebrew, and these are in cuneiform writing which bears no resemblance to the ancient Hebrew script. An analysis of the two alphabets shows, however, that the differences are merely various stages of the same cultural development. The history of writing in the Ancient East is rooted in antiquity, when the great cultures spontaneously developed systems of writing that had hundreds of complicated signs, most of which indicated certain concepts (ideograms) as well as phonograms. The educated Canaanites of the 2nd millennium, who found these unwieldy systems ready to hand, set about rationalizing the system of writing, reduced the number of signs to a few dozen, to each of which they gave the value of a consonant, simplified the shapes of these signs, and made the knowledge of writing available to all (cf. Jud. 8:14). This process appears to have taken place in the middle of the 2nd millennium when the inhabitants of Canaan began to free themselves from Akkadian rule and to develop a literature in the vernacular language. This process resulted in three alphabets: a) the Proto-Sinaitic alphabet, whose short documents, found in Sinai, belong to the middle of the 2nd millennium: according to Albright,[28] whose investigations include the latest findings, this alphabet consisted of twenty-seven letters; b) the Ugaritic alphabet, comprising thirty letters, and known from documents of the 14th and 13th centuries B.C.E.; c) the Phoenician-Hebrew alphabet. Historically, these three alphabets are closely connected. Thus some paleographic finds have shown that the forms of the letters of the Proto-Sinaitic are the prototype of those of the Phoenician-Hebrew alphabet.[29] Tablets from Ugarit, on which the letters of the Ugaritic alphabet are engraved in their traditional order, prove that, with the omission of those of its eight letters which have no parallel in the Phoenician-Hebrew

Ordinal number	Ugarit characters	Equivalent Hebrew or Arabic characters	
1		א also vocalic a	a
2		ב	b
3		ג	g
4		ح	ḫ
5		ד	d
6		ה	h
7		ו	w
8		ז	z
9		ח	ḥ
10		ט	ṭ
11		י	y
12		כ	k
13		שׁ also שׂ	š, ś
14		ל	l
15		מ	m

Ordinal number	Ugarit characters	Equivalent Hebrew or Arabic characters	
16		ذ	ḏ
17		נ	n
18		צ Originally ظ	ẓ
19		ס	s
20		ע	e
21		פ	p
22		צ	ṣ
23		ק	q
24		ר	r
25		שׁ Originally ث	ṯ
26		غ	ġ
27		ת	t
28		א also vocalic i	i
29		א also vocalic u	u
30		₂ס	ś

Fig. 1.
Ugarit alphabet.

Fig. 2.
Ancient Ugaritic alphabet written on clay tablet found at Ra's Shamrā (Ugarit) Prof. C. A. Schaeffer, *Orientalia*, 19 (1950), fig. 374.

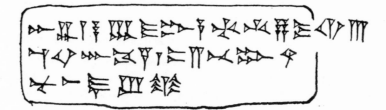

Fig. 3.
Impression of the seal ring of Yakarum son of Niqmadd, King of Ugarit.
J. Nougayrol, *PRU* pl. XVII, fig. 24

alphabet, this order corresponds exactly to that of the latter. Thus they merely represent different stages in the development of the same alphabet.[30]

Stylistic affinity is particularly conspicuous in poetic composition. The parallelism of the hemistich is the dominating principle alike in Ugaritic as in biblical poetry, and while Akkadian literature employs it only occasionally, it is completely alien to the spirit of Greek literature.

Moreover, the two parallel words in the two hemistiches of the verse are common to Ugaritic and biblical poetry, as for example the nouns "house" (*bayit*, Ugar. *bt*) and "yard" (*hazer*, Ugar. *hzr*),[31] the verbs "to fear" (*yare*, Ugar. *yr'*) and "to be afraid" (*shata'*, Ugar. *tt'*),[32] and many others. These parallelisms are at times the subject of textual criticism of the Bible. Finding a difficulty in the verse: "Therefore will I give men (*adam*) for thee, and peoples (*le'ummim*) for thy life" (Isa. 43:4), scholars have suggested emending *adam* to *adamot*. Ugaritic inscriptions however show that the word *adam* is an appropriate parallelism for *le'om*, as in: "Smiting the Westland's peoples (*l'im*), smashing the folk ('*adm*) of the sunrise."[33] This typical verbal parallelism in the two hemistiches of a verse is a particularly telling example of the interrelation of words and roots in the literary style of Canaan which finds expression in all manner of combinations. For example, an Ugaritic poem which addresses praises to the god declares: *hkmt šbt dqnk ltsrk*.[34] At first sight the translation appears to be "Art wise indeed, thy beard's grey hair instructs thee" (cf. Ps. 16:7; 94:12). But this rendering is disproved by even a cursory study of the Bible, in which "hoary head" (*seiva*) occurs in parallelism with "old man" (*zaqen*) (Lev. 19:32) and with "old age" (*ziqna*) (Isa. 46:4); the two roots are also found in the parataxis *ziqna we-seiva* (Ps. 71:18) *zaqanti wa-savti* (I Sam. 12:2), and also simply in proximity *hadar zeqenim seiva* (Prov. 20:29). The biblical passages thus demonstrate the traditional coupling in the literary style of Canaan of these two roots and establish that the Ugaritic text should be translated: "The grey hair of thine old age." For further biblical examples of two synonyms in the construct relation, compare *simhat gili* ("the joy of my happiness" [Ps. 43:4]), *geshem matar* ("the shower of rain" [Job 37:6]), etc. It is worth noting the phenomenon that the Israelite poet was able to adapt to the spirit of his people even the coupling of words connected with obviously pagan phraseology. Of King Keret's son it was said:[35] "He suckles (*ynq*) milk (*hlb*) of Asherah, he sucks (*mss*) the breast (*td*) of the virgin Anath." This expression occurs twice in Isaiah. The prophet announces to Jerusalem: "Thou shalt also suck (*weyanaqt*) the milk (*halav*) of the nations, and shalt suck the breast (*shod*) of kings" (Isa. 60:16).

In another passage he depicts Jerusalem as a mother suckling her children, who are addressed as follows: "That ye may suck, and be satisfied with the breast of her consolations; that ye may drink deeply with delight of the abundance of her glory" (Isa. 66:11). Biblical poetry thus changes the breasts of the goddesses, the source of blessing according to the ancient conception, to those of nations, kings, and Jerusalem, thereby divesting an ancient Canaanite expression of its literal meaning.

A special type of parallelism is that of ascending numbers: "El replies in the seven chambers, inside the eight surroundings [?] of closed rooms."[36] This form occurs also in the Bible: "Then shall we raise against him seven shepherds, and eight princes among men" (Micah 5:4). Moreover the Ugaritic epic has even preserved traces of the form of proverb that has an opening line which mentions in its first hemistich X, in its second X + 1 things, to which a certain principle applies, and which are then enumerated. When Baal is angry during a banquet he quotes from the Ugaritic wisdom literature a proverb which begins: "Two [kinds] of banquets Baal hates, three the rider of the clouds"[37] and he then proceeds to enumerate three kinds of banquets which are hateful to him. This literary form is to be found in the Bible too. Compare, for example, the proverb that begins with the words: "There are six which the Lord hateth, yea, seven which are an abomination unto Him" (Prov. 6:16), and which then continues with an enumeration of the seven abominations. Thus even the particular type of proverb that summarizes the things hateful to the Deity is rooted in Canaanite literary tradition. Furthermore, one group of verses in the Ugaritic epic is distinguished by its special structure, as for example: "Now thine enemy, O Baal, now thine enemy wilt thou smite, now wilt thou cut off thine adversary"[38] (cf. Ps. 54:9; 138:7). This structure, which imparts vitality and dramatic tension to a verse, occurs also in the Bible, as in the sentence: "For, lo, Thine enemies, O Lord, for, lo, Thine enemies shall perish; all the workers of iniquity shall be scattered" (Ps. 92:10). With his fine literary sense, R. Samuel ben Meir (Rashbam) noted the distinctive character of these verses.[39]

This affinity between the Bible and Canaanite literature is not limited to outer form, but finds expression also in inner content. Mention has first and foremost to be made of the emphatic moral demand that the leading figures of the nation concern themselves with the needs of the helpless poor, a demand which recurs throughout the literature of the Ancient East. Thus the Ugaritic writings describe Danel the righteous judge as "judging the cause of the widow, adjudicating the case of the fatherless."[40] When King Keret's son rebels against his father he justifies his action with the complaint: "Thou judgest not the cause of the widow, nor adjudicat'st the case of the wretched."[41] The Bible, as is well known, has fully accepted this moral concept, which occurs in the Pentateuch, is repeated in the Prophets, and reiterated in the Hagiographa. Similarly, the precept of filial respect is clearly alluded to in a legal document. In his will a certain man bequeaths his property to his wife, instructing her to leave it to the son who would honor his mother.[42] The righteous judge Danel, who is childless, asks of the gods a son who will observe the obligations of honoring one's father. Of these he makes a complete list, among them being that the son "takes him [his father] by the hand when he's drunk, carries him when he's sated with wine."[43] This throws new light on the immensity of Ham's iniquity in transgressing this traditional commandment. The motif of the righteous man who is childless and who asks a son of heaven is well known from the biblical narratives, beginning with Abraham. This motif which is explicit in the epic of Aqhat the son of Danel is also implicit in the epic of King Keret, who at the god's command goes forth to war in order to marry Hurriya, who would bear him sons and daughters. During his expedition Keret makes a vow to Asherah that he would give her double Hurriya's weight in silver and three times her weight in gold if she would grant him his request. A similar vow is to be found in talmudic literature (Tosefta, 'Eruv. 3,1).

D. THE UGARITIC PANTHEON

A central position in the Ugaritic concept of the universe is occupied by the pantheon with its chief deity El, the merciful king, whose old age is the source of his wisdom;[44] compare the biblical verse: "Is wisdom with aged men, and understanding in length of days?" (Job 12:12). When the Ugaritic writings bestow great praise on another god (apparently one of the artificer gods) they use the expression, "Thou hast insight like El,"[45] indicating that El is the prototype of the sage. El is the father of the gods and goddesses who are called the generation of gods, the children of El, the children of gods, or the assembly of gods; they are the seventy children of Asherah, the wife of El,[46] and their number is the same as that of the sons of Jacob, Gideon, and Ahab. El is also the "father of man," that is, the father of mankind, and generally *bny bnwt*, the creator of all creatures. No Ugaritic myth regarding the creation of the world is extant, but it is quite clear that El is the creator of all mortals. When Baal intercedes for Danel, who longs for a son, he turns to his father and asks him to bless Danel, "so shall there be a son in his house, a scion in the midst of his palace,"[47] which implies that the birth of the child depends solely on the blessing of El. It is El who appeared to Keret in a dream and told him the manner in which he would acquire a wife and sons. It is therefore not surprising that he is the first of the gods to whom Keret offers sacrifices. A reference to El's manner of creating has been preserved in the story of Keret's illness. Seven times El asked the gods who would cure Keret. Seven times the gods remained silent, whereupon El, declaring that he himself would cure Keret, molded clay from which he created the angel of healing.[48]

One cannot disregard a certain parallelism between the titles attributed to the Ugaritic El and those of God in the Bible. The God of Israel is likewise the prototype of the sage, as can be seen from the wise woman's remark to David: "And my lord is wise, according to the wisdom of an angel of God" (II Sam. 14:20), the expression "angel of God" being here merely a substitute for "God" in order not to compare a mortal to the Almighty. God is also invoked as El, as in the verse: "Heal her now, O God [El], I beseech Thee" (Num. 12:13). He, too, is the sole Creator who in His wisdom forms His creations from clay, He blesses the righteous man who is childless, He is the only healer, and He, too, appears in the midst of sons of gods, although in the Bible these sons of gods are reduced to the status of being merely His servants. The Bible may even have preserved a faint echo of the marriage of God in the rather astounding words of the prophets which liken the Lord to Israel's spouse. However, El in the Ugaritic writings occasionally shows signs of old age and weakness, as when he hesitates to grant the request of Anath his daughter to permit Baal to build his palace. When Anath threatens that his grey hair would flow with blood, El is intimidated and gives in to his daughter.[49] This also shows that El transferred his rule on earth to Baal, and even when Baal died a temporary death El did not resume the reins of government, but handed them over, on Asherah's recommendation, to one of his sons, the tyrannical Ashtar.[50]

In all these aspects El differs fundamentally from the God of the Bible, in which no signs of weakness due to old age are described even if we accept the Septuagint and the Dead Sea Scrolls version that reads in Deut. 32:8: "When the Most High gave to the nations their inheritance, when He separated the children of men, He set the borders of the peoples according to the number of the children of God [El],"[51] (instead of "Israel"). This version then implies that the God of Israel transferred the effective rule of the nations of the world to their guardian angels and reserved for Himself the direct rule of Israel alone. But this idea, unusual in the Bible, in no way alters the image of the God of Israel as a man of war who says of Himself: "I will make Mine arrows drunk with blood, and My sword shall devour flesh" (Deut. 32:42). All these warlike traits, which are foreign to the Ugaritic El, are attributed by the Ugaritic epics to the younger generation of the gods and goddesses, and particularly to the image of Baal. The intrepid warrior is the god Hadd or Hadad, the god of thunder and rain, who is called the rider of the clouds, who peals his thunder in the clouds and flashes his lightning,[52] who showers his rain on earth,[53] and attends to earth's fertility, as can be seen from the sign given for its resurrection, namely, that El would dream that "the heavens fat did rain, the wadies flow with honey. So I knew that alive was Puissant Baal! Existent the Prince, Lord of Earth!"[54]

Enemies, however, arose against the rule of Baal. There was, first, his brother *Zebul Yamm* (Prince of the Sea), also called the Judge of the River, who is the predecessor of the ruler of the sea known from the Jewish legends. *Zebul Yamm* sent his messengers to the assembly of the gods, demanding Baal's surrender. El complies with his demand and even declares: "Thy slave is Baal for ever." But Baal was filled with anger, declared war, and smote Yamm with two clubs supplied to him by Kothar wa-Khasis. The second series of enemies were various monsters. In his battles with these monsters, Baal, it is implied, smote Leviathan the *evil* (*bzh*) serpent and dispatched the tortuous ('*qltn*) serpent, the ruler(?) who has seven heads.[55] The tortuous serpent is also mentioned in the list of Baal's enemies vanquished by Anath, his sister and ally, and along with the serpent there was also the sea-dragon (*tannin*). His third enemy was his brother Mot, the god of death. Baal's contest with Mot was the hardest of all, and at one stage things came to such a pass that Baal agreed to become Mot's slave for ever and to descend — together with his winds, his rains, and his entourage — to Mot's dominion in the depths of the earth, also known as "*bt hptt* of the earth." This picture of Baal's descent to the depths of the earth changes to another which describes how Mot, having swallowed him, boasts: "I made him like a lamb in my mouth; like a kid in my gullet he's crushed." These two pictures are combined when Mot addresses Baal and says: "Thou must come down into the throat of Mot son of El, into the miry gorge of the hero of El."[56]

But Baal's death was not final, for he returned and regained his throne. A similar fate befell Mot, whom Anath in revenging her brother slew, and he, too, returned to life. Most scholars interpret this myth as symbolical of the seasonal changes, Baal dying each year at the end of the rainy season, whereupon Mot is restored to life and rules during the entire summer until he is killed at the beginning of the rainy season, when Baal, rising from the depths of the earth, renews his reign. Thus Baal symbolizes the rainy period and Mot the dry summer.[57] Some scholars have suggested that Mot, like grain, is similarly a fertility symbol,[58] their contention being that the description of Mot's death at the hands of Anath alludes to the fate of grain. But such an analogy is without foundation. The description of Mot's being cleaved with a sword, burnt, ground in a hand-mill, and the remnants scattered in fields where they are eaten by the birds, symbolizes absolute destruction, reminiscent of the destruction of the golden calf (Ex. 32:20).[59] Mot is literally the god of death. He wields the staff of bereavement and widowhood, boasts as he strides through the earth: "Lifebreath, I have taken away among men, lifebreath among earth's masses," and brags: "With both my hands I eat."

The myth of Baal and Mot does not necessarily symbolize the changing seasons of the year. For one thing, Mot does not hold unlimited sway, not even after his victory over Baal, for after the latter's death El appoints Ashtar as his successor. For another, summer is not, as Gordon has pointed out, a dead season but one of ripening fruit.[60] It is rather in the periodic alternations every seven or eight years of plenty and of drought, which are referred to in the Ugaritic epic and to which Cassuto and Gordon[61] have rightly drawn attention, that these scholars have sought the basis of the myth.

E. UGARITIC MOTIFS IN THE BIBLE

While traces of most of these motifs are to be found in biblical poetry, it would be a mistake to look for all of them in the Bible. Israel's poets ascribed to God not only the best of El's attributes, but Baal's distinguished characteristics as well. The God of Israel is also described as He that "rideth upon the clouds" (Ps. 68:4), as thundering from heaven (II Sam. 22:14), as pouring down bounteous rain (Ps. 68:10), as He who supplies the corn, and the wine, and the oil (Hos. 2:10). Moreover, the description of God's might is to a considerable extent influenced by the traditions of Baal's victories, as in the passage which attributes to God victory over three of Baal's foes — the sea, Leviathan, and the sea-monster: "Thou didst break the sea in pieces by Thy strength; Thou didst shatter the heads of the sea-monsters in the waters. Thou didst crush the heads of Leviathan" (Ps. 74:13–14), or in verses that associate the rivers with the sea, the latter symbolizing God's enemies in the Bible, as for example:

"Is it that Thine anger is kindled against the rivers, or Thy wrath against the sea?" (Hab. 3:8). In such and similar language Israel's poets spoke of God's might in ancient times so as to reawaken it in days of national trouble and distress. Hence the Bible describes the future destruction of Israel's wicked enemies in imagery taken from the same sphere, as in the prophecy: "In that day the Lord with His sore and great and strong sword will punish Leviathan the slant serpent, and Leviathan the tortuous serpent; and He will slay the dragon that is in the sea" (Isa. 27:1).[62]

On the other hand, biblical phraseology dissociates itself from the myth of Mot, due to the basic monotheistic concept with its necessary corollary that "the Lord killeth, and maketh alive" (I Sam. 2:6). It is entirely out of the question that the eternal God of Israel should be portrayed as defeated and dying, which explains why the Bible has preserved only a very faint echo of the myth of Baal's struggles with Mot, as for example in the verse which states that on the day of salvation the Lord "will swallow up death for ever" (Isa. 25:8). This does not, however, mean that the Canaanite myth of Mot was obliterated from the memory of the people. The image of the Canaanite Mot in all its terrifying fearfulness appears in such similes as: "He who enlargeth his desire as the nether-world, and is as death, and cannot be satisfied" (Hab. 2:5). The Bible has also retained a trace of the descent to the nether regions in expressions such as: they that go down into the pit, that go down into silence, who are gone down into the nether parts of the earth. Moreover, the picture of Mot descending to the nether parts of the earth, the domain of death, and of death personified as swallowing the dead, tends in the Bible to merge into one, except that here the personification of devouring death has become blurred. Thus we read in the story of Korah: "And the earth opened her mouth, and swallowed them up ... So they, and all that appertained to them, went down alive into the pit" (Num. 16:32–33). While this occurrence was indeed a miracle, it recalls the general notion that it is natural for mortals to descend into the pit, which swallows them up as in the metaphor: "Let us swallow them up alive as the grave, and whole, as those that go down into the pit" (Prov. 1:12). Moreover, even the designation of the pit as "*bt ḥptt* of the earth" has left traces in the Bible, which tells that King Azariah (Uzziah) as leper dwelt in *bet ha-ḥofshit* (II Kings 15:5). As the leper is likened to a dead person (Num. 12:12), so is the house of the lepers compared to the pit. This explains the origin of the strange phrase: "Set apart (*ḥofshi*) among the dead, like the slain that lie in the grave" (Ps. 88:5–6). Perhaps this and the usual meaning of *hofshi* are both hinted at in a reference to the nether-world: "The small and great are there alike; and the servant is free (*hofshi*) from his master" (Job. 3:19).

All the examples that have been given show the extent to which the Bible absorbed the myths of the Canaanite gods. It attributed to the God of Israel the noble traits of the chief Canaanite gods, but not those characteristics of theirs which it considered improper and which do not accord with the concept of the transcendent God, the world's sole Ruler. Baal's struggles with his enemies, his peers, were transformed into the mighty deeds of the One God who punishes the rebellious who symbolize the wicked in general and Israel's enemies in particular. The pantheon of the children of the gods was reduced to the status of the assembly of the ministering angels of the One God. A certain conflict is noticeable as regards the tradition of the god of death, whose main function in the Bible falls to the One God, while at the same time a trace is preserved of the monster which God will devour at the end of days.

CHAPTER III

THE CANAANITE INSCRIPTIONS AND THE STORY OF THE ALPHABET

by S. Yeivin

A. Introductory Survey

DURING THE 17th and 18th centuries material containing inscriptions in the Hebrew-Phoenician script began to accumulate in private and public collections. Early excavations and accidental finds and discoveries throughout the 19th and 20th centuries constantly added inscribed objects and documents of this nature. Though not as sensational and spectacular as the revelations of Egyptian, Mesopotamian, and other Near Eastern civilizations, this material attracted a good deal of attention because of its possible connection with biblical studies.

Already in 1867 the French *Académie des inscriptions et belles-lettres* had decided on the systematic publication, under the title *Corpus Inscriptionum Semiticarum*,[1] of all such Semitic inscriptions written in both the Hebrew-Phoenician and South Arabian alphabets.

Since the study of the material and its preparation for final publication necessarily took a long time, further means had to be devised to make new discoveries available to the scholarly world for immediate study. Thus since 1900 the same *Académie* has issued the *Répertoire d'épigraphie sémitique*,[2] in which it publishes a preliminary account of new epigraphic material as it appears. Of course, new finds and accidental discoveries as well as further studies of previously known epigraphic documents are published and discussed in numerous scholarly journals.[3]

Though a very large quantity of such epigraphic material was already known by the beginning of the present century, chronologically the earliest west Hebrew-Phoenician inscription known at the time was the Phoenician dedications to the Baal Lebanon from Cyprus, dating from the early 8th century B.C.E.[4] Even then it was noted by various scholars that this signary presupposed a long history of development.[5] A find made at Gezer in 1908 did not help much toward solving the problem, since the rather rough shape of the letters in this document, an agricultural calendar, was due not only to the early stage of writing it represented, but also to the unpracticed hand of the writer. Even its date was disputed for a long time, though it was realized that it antedated any inscription known at the time.[6]

B. The Inscriptions of Sinai

In 1904–1905 Petrie discovered in Sinai near and about the Egyptian copper mines at Wadi Maghāra and the adjacent temple of Ṣerābīṭ al-Khādim several objects and stelae (some of the latter originally engraved on the rocks) bearing inscriptions in hitherto unknown characters.[7] This material was not published until 1917 by Gardiner and Peet.[8] In working on the publication of the Egyptian epigraphic material recorded by Petrie in Sinai, Gardiner became interested in these enigmatic inscriptions, and in 1916 published an article,[9] in which he advanced the plausible suggestion that the word *Baalat* appears in alphabetic characters in several of these inscriptions. He proposed to identify this script as the original prototype of the Semitic alphabets, derived, on the acrophonic principle, mainly from the Egyptian pictorial hieroglyphics, and thought that this epoch-making discovery of the alphabetic principle may have been made as early as the end of the Middle Kingdom (the beginning of the 18th century B.C.E.).

Working independently, Sethe tried to prove, in an article published in 1916, that the Semitic alphabet was derived from Egyptian hieroglyphic signs and that its spread in Asia was facilitated by the Hyksos. A year later, when Sethe became acquainted with Gardiner's work, he saw in it a confirmation of his own theory, and assigned the Proto-Sinaitic inscription and the first invention of the alphabet to the earliest Hyksos period (ca. 1750 B.C.E.).[10]

New expeditions to Sinai, organized by the University of Harvard in 1927,[11] by Finnish scholars in 1928,[12] again by the University of Harvard in 1930, and by the Catholic University of Washington in 1935,[13] brought to light some more material in the same early script, all of which was assembled in the Cairo Museum.

Leibovitch and Jean are the only dissenting voices, the former suggesting that this script consists of syllabic signs, in which were recorded the dedications of the Madjoi, Nubian police who served in Sinai in the final stage of the New Kingdom.[14] Otherwise practically all scholars who dealt with this material agreed with Gardiner's original suggestion that the script was an early stage of an alphabetic signary in which some early Semitic idiom was rendered. Grimme went so far as to read into the inscriptions a reference to Moses and Hat-shepsut,[15] but his views have been almost unanimously rejected. Lately, Albright has suggested partial transliterations of some of them. Basing himself on his short campaign of excavations at Abū-Zneima, the ancient port for the Egyptian copper mines, Albright suggested that the Proto-Sinaitic script should be assigned to about 1500 B.C.E. at the earliest.[16] This does not necessarily follow, and is certainly impossible in view of the existing evidence.

In 1889 Petrie discovered at Kāhūn a few objects inscribed with strange signs which seemed similar to the Semitic alphabet.[17] Opinions differed at the time whether these objects belonged to the original settlement founded by Sen-Usert II (1897–1878 B.C.E.) or to the remains of a languishing later settlement of the early Eighteenth Dynasty. The invention of the Proto-Sinaitic alphabet must have preceded the period of these objects, since they exhibit a slightly more advanced stage in the development of the signary in question. On either dating, the Proto-Sinaitic signary is necessarily a good deal earlier than the 15th century B.C.E.

C. FINDS IN ISRAEL

Meanwhile, cognate material was being discovered in Israel. In 1929, a party of visitors to Gezer found on Macalister's dump-heap a small sherd of a Middle Bronze II incense-stand (?), on which had been engraved before firing three sings reminiscent of the Proto-Sinaitic signary, but representing a somewhat advanced stage of development.[18] H. L. Ginsberg proposed to read the signs כלב [19] Soon afterwards the German excavators at Shechem found in an unmistakably Middle Bronze II context a small fragmentary stele, the border and back of which were inscribed with several alphabetic signs, some new, but others exhibiting a certain similarity to the Proto-Sinaitic signary.[20] During the thirties the excavators of Lachish uncovered more fragmentary inscriptions in the same script. One of these, incised on a dagger, belongs to the Middle Bronze II period,[21] while four have been dated to the Late Bronze II times.[22] Another ostracon, inscribed in ink and found under uncertain conditions at Beth-shemesh, dates probably from the early 12th century B.C.E.,[23] while a gold ring, found in a tomb at Megiddo, is to be assigned to the second half of the 13th century.[24] An ostracon uncovered at Tel Ḥasi (Tell al-Ḥāsī) during the excavations in 1890–1893 can now be assigned to the 14th century B.C.E.[25] Two incised graffiti on a bowl and a handle from Beth Eglaim,[26] a fragmentary ostracon of the 13th–12th century B.C.E. found on the surface of Tel Rehob (Tell aṣ-Ṣārim) in the Beth-shean Valley,[27] a single letter incised on a potsherd from Tell Beit Mirsim (12th century B.C.E.),[28] an

Fig. 4
Inscribed sherd found at Beth-shemesh.
Encyclopaedia Biblica I, fig. 386.

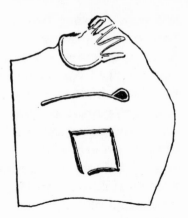

Fig. 5.
Inscribed sherd found at Gezer
Encyclopaedia Biblica I, fig. 383·

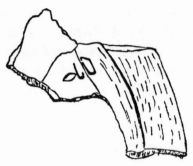

Fig. 7.
Old Canaanite
inscription on gold ring
found at Megiddo.
P. L. O. Guy–R. M. Engberg,
Megiddo Tombs, Chicago, 1938,
pag. 117.

Fig. 6.
Inscribed sherd found at
Tell al-Ḥāsī.
Encyclopaedia Biblica I, pag. 384.

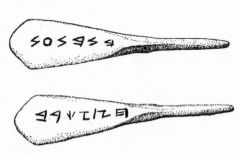

Fig. 8.
Phoenician inscription on obverse
and reverse of bronze arrow-head found in
the Valley of Lebanon.
(At slightly different scales).
Prof. J. T. Milik, *BASOR* 143 (1956), 3.

Fig. 9.
Inscribed sherd found at
Tell aṣ-Ṣārim (Rehob).
Encyclopaedia Biblica I, fig. 385.

ostracon, bearing two late Proto-Sinaitic letters, which comes from the Late Bronze stratum at Hazor,[29] and a small sherd of a jar with several signs, apparently a Canaanite version of Proto-Sinaitic script, recently found at Tell Nagila in a Middle Bronze II–III stratum,[30] complete the list of such finds in Israel.

All these may be divided into two groups.[31] One (Gezer, Shechem, the Lachish dagger, and the Tell Nagila sherd — if it is indeed from the Middle Bronze II–III Period), which shows a more archaic type of signary, belongs to the 18th–16th centuries B.C.E.; the other (all the rest), which exhibits a growing similarity to the early forms of the Hebrew-Phoenician alphabet (except for Lachish 4[32]), belongs to the second phase of the Late Bronze Period and probably continues into the first phase of the Early Iron Period (roughly mid-14th–mid-12th centuries B.C.E.). There is a gap of some 200 years between the two groups, which may be entirely fortuitous. And yet it may, after all, not be accidental. Would it be too daring an hypothesis to connect the use of this signary with the origins of the Hebrew people, the signary having been borrowed (?) by the Patriarchs from its West-Semitic inventors in Sinai, no longer used in Canaan when the Hebrews emigrated to Egypt, and reappearing in Canaan with the first penetration of the Israelites there.[33]

D. Finds in Other Near Eastern Areas

Meanwhile the years 1920–1939 brought sensational epigraphic discoveries in other areas, too, of the Near East. Montet's excavations at Byblos revealed the earliest two Phoenician inscriptions in the tomb of Ahiram, King of Byblos, now definitely assigned to the 11th century B.C.E.[34] Schaeffer's dig at Ugarit (Ra's Shamrā) brought to light an entirely new script in a cuneiform alphabetic signary, promptly deciphered by Virolleaud, Dhorme, and Bauer.[35] Dunand, the successor of Montet at Byblos, published in 1930 a limestone stele inscribed in an unknown hieroglyphic script, and in 1935 announced the discovery of several documents in this entirely new signary.[36] By the time Dunand published all his documents in this script,[37] representing two forms, the one monumental (documents a, g), the other cursive (documents b, c, d, e, f, h, i, j), it became obvious that the number of available signs precludes its being alphabetic. Whether it is a purely syllabic or a mixture of syllabic and ideographic script, it is as yet impossible to say. Nor is it possible to ascertain definitely what language it uses, though the probability of its being a Phoenician dialect is quite strong.[38] In spite of Dhorme's valiant attempt at decipherment,[39] his results are more than doubtful.

M. F. Martin[40] has recently tried to decipher from new infra-red photographs these inscriptions (particularly those on the back of the spatula of Azarbaal) through a careful examination of each individual sign.[41] The results of this attempt are unsatisfactory not only because the translation is meaningless, but also because of the entirely improbable principle used in deciphering the inscriptions: to write half a line from left to right and the other half from right to left is something quite extraordinary even for a scribe bent on devising a new system of writing. The same applies also to the suggestion that some of the signs that "have been read" face one way while others in the very same inscription face the opposite direction. Furthermore the duplication of a sign for emphasis (expressed in Hebrew by the *dagesh forte*) is in itself improbable, and is moreover unknown in any Semitic signary.

A basalt stele from Khirbat Balū'a in Moab contains a few lines in a hitherto unknown and indecipherable script, which distantly resembles some of the Linear A signs from Crete.[42] A bold attempt at deciphering it has been made by W. A. Ward and M. F. Martin,[43] based likewise on a re-examination and a new photograph of the stele. But here, too, the results are disappointing. The attempt to reconstruct Egyptian hieroglyphic signs has failed. First because writing from left to right in an Egyptian inscription, which means reading it in this way, is, where it was not antithetically arranged, rather rare.[44] But the decisive argument against their solution is that, with the exception of two signs, not one of those reconstructed is found in conventional Egyptian hieroglyphics, nor do they resemble any other known signary. The two exceptions (the "water" line, Egyptian N, and the seated figure, which incidentaly is totally unlike the hieroglyphic norm), even assuming their shapes to be correct, bear some resemblance to the known signs in Proto-Canaanite inscriptions. Further, according to Vincent's original transcription, several signs in the stele are similar to those in the Succoth tablets. Finally, there is no logical reason for assuming that an obscure Moabite kinglet of the 13th (or 12th) century B.C.E. should have erected a monumental stele in honor of his gods and to his own glory and have written on it an inscription in Egyptian, a language totally unintelligible to his subjects. Nor can it be assumed that he was compelled to do so by reason of the suzerainty of Egypt, for this was certainly non-existent at that time in this remote land.

In 1964, H. J. Franken, who excavated at Succoth(?) (Tell deir 'Allā), announced the discovery of three clay tablets inscribed in a hitherto unknown signary and dated archeologically to the Late Bronze II Period (end of the 13th or beginning of the 12th century B.C.E.).[45] While some resemble Proto-Canaanite signs that developed from the Proto-Sinaitic ones, most of the signs are similar to those on the Khirbat Balū'a stele.[46] Van den Branden immediately attempted to decipher and translate these inscriptions: according to him their language is an Arabic dialect written in a form of South Arabian alphabetic script. His decipherment appears to be doubtful, especially since he turned the tablets upside down to decipher them.[47]

In any event the similarity between the signary of the Khirbat Balū'a stele and that of the Succoth tablets suggests the existence of another version of a Proto-Canaanite signary of Proto-Sinaitic provenance which was current in Transjordanian countries at the end of the 13th and the beginning of the 12th centuries B.C.E. and from which the South Arabian alphabet developed in the course of time.[48]

E. ALPHABETIC SCRIPT IN THE ANCIENT EAST

The various discoveries in and outside Israel described above, enable us to trace the history of an alphabetic script in the Ancient East.

Some facts stand out quite clearly. First, the fully-developed Hebrew-Phoenician script, containing twenty-two signs, though in archaic forms, goes back (in inscriptions and graffiti)[49] to at least the 11th century B.C.E. Moreover, the Ugaritic cuneiform alphabet proves that some form of an alphabetic script was known at least as early as the end of the 13th century B.C.E., for practically all scholars are agreed that it was an invention of Ugaritic scribes on the model of an existing Hebrew-Phoenician alphabetic signary, and adapted to cuneiform signs in order to enable them to copy their material on clay tablets.[50] An Ugaritic abecedary[51] shows the same order of signs as that of the traditional order of letters in the Hebrew alphabet,[52] with the additional signs (30 in all) inserted in various places. And indeed these insertions prove that they are additions to an existing model, and not the original signary from which superfluous signs were omitted.[53]

Secondly, we can now perceive that during the second and third quarters of the 2nd millennium B.C.E., the West Semites of the western half of the Fertile Crescent were anxiously groping for their own systems to express their speech in writing, in marked contrast to the non-Semitic Hurrians, Hittites, Mitannians, and Elamites, who were content to adopt, and to a certain extent adapt, the widely-known and complicated cuneiform system for writing their own languages.[54]

Finally, we shall attempt a plausible chronological reconstruction of the development of an alphabetical script. Some time during the 19th century B.C.E. the Semites working in the Sinai mines, spurred on by the Egyptian system of writing, invented a rudimentary signary to express their own speech, to dedicate votive offerings to their goddess the Baalat, identified by the Egyptians with their Hat-Hor, or to other gods,[55] or to commemorate their chiefs of gangs (?).[56] This signary, which provided among other things an easy way of establishing ownership or identity, seems to have spread quite quickly among Semitic tribes, so that we find it in both Egypt (Kāhūn) and Canaan.[57] It should be stressed that it was apparently invented and certainly at first employed by the lower strata of society for their personal everyday use, while the upper classes and learned scribes continued to avail themselves of the "cultured" systems of Mesopotamian cuneiform, or — where Egyptian influence was strongest (as at Byblos of the 18th century B.C.E.) — Egyptian hieroglyphs.[58]

The suggestion has recently been made that there may be a connection between the invention of this Proto-Sinaitic signary, or at least its development and spread, and the patriarchal families.[59]

This popular system had, however, one advantage over the other, "civilized," systems of writing — its comparative simplicity due to a very limited number of signs employed. How was this achieved? The peculiar structure of Semitic languages emphasizes the cardinal importance of the consonantal skeleton of words, while the intervening vowels play only a secondary role in differentiating various shades of meaning. Consequently, there was no urgent need of different signs to express combinations of various vowels with one and the same consonantal sound. It followed that one sign could express all the combinations *ba, be, bi, bo, bu*, while all words could be resolved into two, three, or more combinations of such syllables. Thus while the Egyptians, for example, had to use different signs in writing or determining even such homonyms as ꜣ.*t* ("power," and "time"), or '*m* ("to know," and "to swallow"), depending on the pictorial aspect of the ideograms or phonograms employed in the process, the new Semitic script could make use of one combination of three signs to write even such different words as *dᵉvora, dever, dᵉvir, davar,* for their respective meanings became clear from the context. Moreover, the innovators were not bound by traditionally sanctified historic spellings, as were the older scripts.[60]

But this explanation leads us also to a logical conclusion. This Semitic signary, and its final offspring the Hebrew-Phoenician system of writing, is not, properly speaking, an alphabet, but rather a simplified syllabic system in which the number of signs depends on the number of consonantal sounds expressed.[61] The word "expressed" is used here advisedly, for it is still a moot point whether the Hebrew-Phoenician script expresses the whole gamut of consonantal values current at the time of its fixation.[62] It was only slowly and in the course of time that the idea of "alphabeticity," if one may coin such a word, was evolved, and most probably not until the Greeks adopted this signary for their own use around 900 B.C.E.[63] Finding there a number of consonantal signs for which they had no need, they began to employ them as phonetic complements to indicate the missing, but for their purpose essential, vowels. It was probably only then that the entirely theoretical divorce between vowel and consonant was born, and with it the notion of a true alphabet. For properly speaking such a division has no foundation in fact.[64]

Meanwhile, at Byblos, official circles, too, began to look for a system of writing their language. They modeled themselves on the principle of the "cultured" systems of the time, the cuneiform and hieroglyphic, and tried their hand at a syllabic signary.[65] Since none of the documents in question was found *in situ* in an undisturbed archeological stratum, their dating cannot be definitely fixed. Dunand's arguments for an early date in the 3rd millennium B.C.E. are unconvincing.[66] The documents are apparently to be assigned rather to about the middle of the 2nd millennium B.C.E.,[67] in the gap between the earlier and later groups of "Canaanite" ostraca. This dating seems to derive support from a group of similar ostraca found in the tomb of Amen-hotep II in the Valley of the Tombs of the Kings.[68] It had proved apparently too clumsy and difficult, and was therefore quickly abandoned, perhaps not without giving rise to an attempt to devise a so-called alphabetic system from its cursive form, for one stele from Byblos, inscribed with somewhat similar signs, bears an inscription which seems to be decipherable on an alphabetic principle.[69]

Since the mid-14th century the popular alphabetic script, of the Proto-Sinaitic Canaanite variety, seems to have been gaining ground, so that when the Ugaritic scribes looked for a prototype on which to model an adaptation of the cuneiform signary for their documents in their own language, they invented an official alphabetic script and even made an attempt to indicate vowels in certain cases.[70] Its use had spread for a time as far south as the Judean hills, for one document in this script was found at Beth-shemesh, in a Late Bronze layer,[71] while a bronze knife blade inscribed with the same signary was picked up on the surface in eastern Lower Galilee.[72]

It seems very likely that toward the end of the 12th century B.C.E., with the disappearance of the Ugaritic center and its script, the later

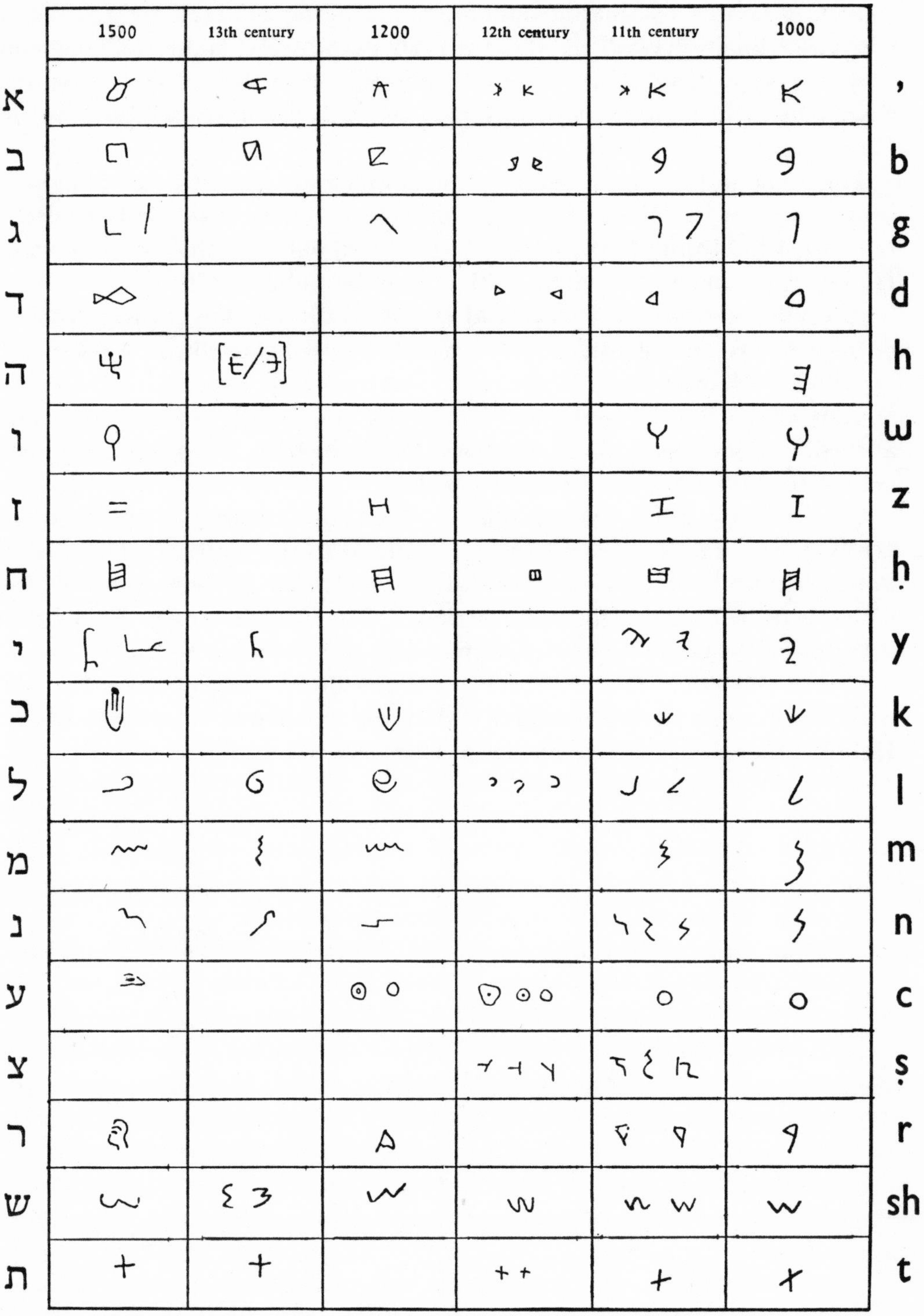

	1500	13th century	1200	12th century	11th century	1000	
א	𐤀	𐤀	𐤀	﹁ ⊀	﹁ ⊀	⊀	'
ב	⊓	𐤁	𐤁	﹁ ⊌	9	9	b
ג	∟ /		⌃		﹁ ﹁	﹁	g
ד	⬦			▷ ◁	◁	◁	d
ה	4	[ᴇ/ᴣ]				∃	h
ו	⸕				Y	Y	w
ז	=		⊢		⊥	I	z
ח	⊟		⊟	▫	⊟	⊟	ḥ
י	⸀ ⸆	⸀			﹁ ﹁	⸽	y
כ	⸙		⋃		⌄	⌄	k
ל	⸑	6	℮	⸀ ⸀ ⸀	⸑ ⸍	⸌	l
מ	⸿	⸿	⸿		⸿	⸿	m
נ	⸝	⸝	⸝		⸌ ⸿ ⸒	⸒	n
ע	⸗		⊙ ○	⬭ ⊙ ○	○	○	c
צ				⸣ ⸌ ⸵	⸣ ⸿ ⸽	⸵	ṣ
ר	⸘		ᴀ		⸵ ⸷	⸷	r
ש	⸡	⸿ ⸽	⸡	⸡	⸡ ⸡	⸡	sh
ת	+	+		+ +	+	⨯	t

Fig. 10.
Development of the Canaanite alphabet in the period 1,500–1,000 B.C.E.
F. M. Cross Jr. in *Western Galilee and the coast of Galilee*, Jerusalem, 1950, 19.

variety of the Proto-Sinaitic signary, much better adapted to writing on papyrus,[73] finally crystallized into the early shape of the Hebrew-Phoenician script. In view of what has been said above,[74] it seems probable that this development took place in early Israel, but was promptly adopted by the Phoenicians.[75]

The relative paucity of material both in Israel as well as in Phoenicia proper and in its Hittite-Aramean hinterland makes it not only difficult, but rather hazardous to trace fully documented paleographic developments. However, a somewhat general outline may be indicated.[76]

After the Proto-Sinaitic material discussed above, our earliest Israelite documents are the recently acquired bronze arrow-heads, three of which are inscribed with the possessive phrase: "The arrow of 'Evedleva'ot," i.e. the servant of the lioness (goddess). They were purchased from a dealer and allegedly found near al-Khadr, west of Bethlehem. Typologically they belong to the 12th–11th centuries B.C.E.[77]

Of a slightly later date (probably the 11th century) is an inscribed arrow-head (in a private collection), acquired in the Valley of Lebanon.[78] Paleographically it agrees well with the Azarbaal spatula from Byblos, which is to be dated to the same period.[79] The next document from Israel is the so-called Gezer Calendar, apparently of Solomonic times.[80]

It is at this point that we reach the limits of our subject here. For it is with the history of the monarchy that the further development of the Hebrew-Phoenician alphabetic script is associated.

CHAPTER IV

THE BIBLE AND ITS HISTORICAL SOURCES

by J. Liver

A. The Nature and Evaluation of the Sources

AN ACCOUNT OF Israel's history during the period covered by this
volume, that is from the days of the Patriarchs to the beginning of
the Monarchy, is given in the Bible from Gen. 11 to I Sam. 10. Not only
is such an account to be found nowhere else, but epigraphical and historical
material containing actual information on the history of Israel in biblical
times, which is in any event sparse, is particularly scant for this period.

It is not, however, as an historical source that the biblical account of
Israel's history is to be defined but rather as an historical description
presented from the over-all viewpoint of Israel's place in human history,
from a defined religious outlook, and based on a moral judgment of men and
their actions. It is precisely these aspects, which characterize historical
writing worthy of the name, that raise an array of problems for the modern
historian who sets out to give an account of the history of Israel from his own
approach and with criteria that differ from those of the ancient narrator.

The early period of Israel's history — that preceding the Settlement and
the Settlement itself — is associated with problems of the transmission and
compilation of the biblical narrative which, in its extant form, was composed after these historical events had taken place and for which the ancient
author relied on such sources as were available and as suited his purpose.
This involves the question of the nature of these sources. Were they contemporaneous with the events related? Did they originate in written
accounts or in an oral tradition? Were they a factual account or merely
legends and folklore? There is the further question of how far the biblical
narrative reflects the way of life and social regime of the times to which it
refers and how far the author imposed the pattern of his own society on
earlier periods. And finally, to what extent did he have a reliable tradition
about the order and development of events? To what extent is the picture
of the past which he presents based on a schematic concept? The fundamental issue in establishing the main outlines of the history of the period is to
find a method that would not only permit the historical significance of the

existing sources to be evaluated but that would also determine how they may assist, either alone or in conjunction with external sources, in elucidating the problem of Israel's beginnings and in describing Israel's history in ancient times. Moreover, the standpoint adopted on the historical nature of the traditions of the Pentateuch and the Book of Joshua has a significant bearing on the entire biblical period, and particularly on an apprehension of the development of Israel's religion, cult, and social institutions.

In appraising the written sources relating to the beginnings of Israelite history it is impossible to employ the method (usual for adequately documented periods) that determines whether a particular source is to be accepted or wholly rejected. Since no ancient authoritative material, such as chronicles, is extant on important and decisive events in early Israelite history, it is more important to make full use of all available sources, including popular accounts and stories containing legendary elements.

In evaluating these sources in the Bible scholars differ completely. Some view the existing traditions as authentic historical information, on the basis of which the / have written a detailed history of Israel, including even events in the lives of the Patriarchs. Others again deny any value or historical significance to all or most of these traditions, regardin them, insofar as they embody actual historical or social conditions, as an anachronistic projection of national feelings and of internal conflicts characteristic not of the earlier traditions themselves, but of the later period when these traditions crystallized and were formulated. Opposed to these two extreme approaches is the middle view which regards the biblical traditions not as historical evidence in the full sense of the word, but as having generally an historical basis and as preserving memories of actual events and situations. Essential for an historical account of the early Israelite period is an elucidation of how these traditions developed and the extent to which they represent a factual narrative. Scholars have, in their investigation of these data contained in the biblical account, arrived at different, occasionally even diametrically opposed, conclusions, so that they hold divergent views on almost every issue, as well as in reconstructing the subject as a whole.

It is impossible, without blurring the distinctive features of this or that work, to group into a number of well-defined systems (as demanded by the limited scope of the present discussion) the various studies written on the beginnings of Israelite history and the different scholars' appraisals of the biblical sources. But though these appraisals may vary from one scholar to another, with each giving a different interpretation of Israel's history, they may, at least basically, share a common approach.

B. Different Theories in Evaluating the Historical Sources in the Bible

The evaluation of the Bible as the basis of Israel's history has been profoundly influenced by the Documentary theory associated with the name of J. Wellhausen.

This theory combines a literary and critical analysis of the sources with a comprehensive outlook that views the Pentateuch as a compilation and redaction of literary sources made over a lengthy period, and Israelite history as an organic unit governed by certain laws of evolution.[1]

Crystallizing by stages in the 19th century,[2] the fundamental hypotheses of this school are based on distinction of double or parallel narratives, on collections of laws that are contradictory in detail and spirit, on characteristic linguistic usages, and so on. Its main assumptions are these: First, the Pentateuch contains independent literary documents which underwent a prolonged and repeated process of redaction but yet to some extent retained their original form. Secondly, these documents, containing the account of the nation's history from its beginnings until the Conquest or even thereafter, constitute parallel compilations of the same events. Thirdly, the various documents are distinguished from one another by a distinctive social and religious outlook, narrative style, and terms and expressions. Fourthly, the various documents comprise both a narrative section and legal passages whose connection can be determined. And fifthly, each of the different documents, whose relation to one another is one of gradual development, represents a stage in the evolution of religious thought and historical outlook.

The basic tenet of this theory is its view on the emergence of monotheism and the evolution of the worship of God in Israel. Its fundamental assumption is that the centralization of the cult and of divine worship took place in the days of Josiah, and only after he had introduced the religious and cultic reform described in the Book of Kings (II Kings 22–23) did the outlook which led to that reform find expression in the Book of Deuteronomy. There is the further assumption that the monotheism — discernible in all the documents of the pentateuchal books — is not early, but was due to the activities and influence of the prophets, there having been before that a popular monolatry in Israel, that is, the worship of one God which did not, however, deny the existence of other gods. And since the early literary documents of the Pentateuch were also subject to prophetic influence, they are much later than the events they describe and reveal an adjustment to a later religious outlook which distorted the character and significance of these passages.

In its main outlines Wellhausen's hypothesis distinguishes four principal sources, themselves composed of different documents. The oldest of these dates from about the 9th century B.C.E. and the latest from the beginning of the Second Temple period. The earliest source is the Jahvistic (J), the second, slightly later one, the Elohistic document (E).[3] They were composed — the former in Judah, the latter in Israel — in the 9th and 8th centuries B.C.E., at about which time they were fused into a composite work JE by a redactor who combined passages from the former with some from the latter. Next in point of time is the Deuteronomic work (D) which, although based on the narratives in JE, has a more advanced religious outlook, being the first to demand the centralization of worship. Hence it originated in or close to the days of Josiah. The latest source is the Priestly Document (P), composed in priestly circles in the days of the Babylonian exile and at the beginning of the Second Temple period. Emphasizing worship and ceremonial, it unified and left its imprint on the Pentateuch as a whole.

The Wellhausen school, which dates all the early biblical sources centuries after the events they describe, maintains that they give a distorted picture of ancient times, and hence it ascribes to them very little historical value. This approach has led to extreme skepticism in reconstructing the initial period of Israelite history. Many adherents of this school, while theoretically agreeing that the late sources preserve ancient material, nevertheless refrained in practice from making use of the pentateuchal traditions relating to the early periods, regarding them as projecting the beliefs and views of the times in which, according to them, the different sources were composed. Because of their preconceived theories they failed to utilize the rich extra-biblical material to determine to what extent these traditions reflect a background that goes back to ancient times. Whereas there was sparse external evidence available in the days of Wellhausen, these scholars did not greatly change their views even when it became clear from the abundant material of the Ancient East that many pentateuchal narratives, particularly those in the Book of Genesis, are supported by the cultural heritage and social background of the Ancient East, and even from periods preceding the crystallization of the Israelite nation.

For the school of Documentary theory the antiquity and the historical basis of this or that individual tradition are not crucial. While the more modern biblical criticism founded on this theory tends to regard some of the material embodied in the sources, including P, as early, most general works on Israelite history have nevertheless retained the fundamental Wellhausen view of gradual development, and especially of the evolution, in the Israelite religion, of the monotheistic idea. They assume, moreover, that their historical schema provides a means of determining the trustworthiness of traditions. It is not enough to fix the antiquity of a narrative and the probability of a source. What has also to be decided is the extent to which that tradition fits into a specific over-all picture of Israelite history.

This approach, which holds with the trend of historicism in the philosophy of history, is fraught with many dangers. It is true that no historical schema can be formulated without assuming a certain degree of evolution, and that a scientific investigation can renounce neither a philological and literary examination of the sources nor rational criteria. But their extreme historicism has exaggerated both the emphasis on the evolutionary principle and its schemata. They have therefore been obliged to fit all social phenomena and institutional developments into a certain schema, without regard to the chronology of the data or the relative importance of the different traditions. If a phenomenon seemed, according to the predetermined schema, in advance of its time, it was assigned to a later date on the basis of "internal evidence"; if it appeared primitive it was attributed to an earlier period. Finally adopting a subjective historical approach, this school multiplied schemata which differ greatly from one another and some of which are arbitrary and quite fantastic.

As regards the basic assumptions of the Wellhausen school two important interrelated subjects have to be distinguished. The one is the question of the compilation and redaction of the Pentateuch and the interpretation of its conflicting traditions; the other concerns the conclusions regarding the history of the people of Israel. As to the former, the existence in the Pentateuch of different literary units produced at various periods and from divergent approaches, has to be considered a fact, being proved in relation to the legal passages and to a lesser extent in relation to the narrative sections. The books of the Pentateuch probably underwent a process of redaction in keeping with the concepts of later times, and this expressed itself in the choice and presentation of the traditions. It is however not at all clear that the legal and narrative passages have, as assumed by the Wellhausen school, a common source, nor that the various narrative sections belong to several principal sources that consisted of comprehensive compilations, nor that a later redactor put the various sections together from these compilations. It is, in particular, very doubtful whether there was a gradual, evolutionary affinity between the different units (insofar as these existed). On various sides[4] objections have been raised against the historical assumptions on which this school is based, against the view that the centralization of worship is peculiar to the Book of Deuteronomy, and against connecting this book or a major part of it with the religious reform instituted by Josiah. Even scholars who accept the other basic hypotheses of the Documentary school no longer regard these assumptions as axiomatic for dating the different documents.

All these considerations cast grave doubts on the Wellhausen theory as a philological and historical criterion for judging the authenticity and antiquity of the various traditions, especially since it, too, does not reject the principle that an early factual kernel may assume a late literary form, and that, on the other hand, an ancient story may be basically legendary. Other criteria have therefore to be sought to elucidate the historical significance of the Scriptures.

An independent approach is adopted by Y. Kaufmann in evaluating the sources relating to Israel's early history, although he, too, affirms the Documentary criticism of the Pentateuch. But while Kaufmann theoretically accepts, albeit in a moderate form, the Documentary theory and also a connection between the Book of Deuteronomy and Josiah's reform, he repudiates several principles of the Wellhausen school.[5] He regards the Priestly Document as much earlier than the Book of Deuteronomy,[6] and not as having originated during the days of the Second Temple; in particular, he denies the view that the pentateuchal literature was written under the influence of the prophetic writings, and rejects the view about the evolutionary development of the Israelite faith, which he considers a unique revealed religion whose distinctive monotheism preceded the Conquest. In the biblical narrative dealing with the beginnings of Israel's history Kaufmann distinguishes, alongside sources that include parallel accounts, cross-sectional strata — the patriarchal stratum contained in the Book of Genesis and in the early part of the Book of Exodus, and the tribal stratum that extends from the rest of the Book of Exodus to the beginning of the Book of Judges. Each of these strata has its characteristic features which differentiate it as a separate entity. These basic assumptions led Kaufmann to consider the principal narratives dealing with the history of the period as historical evidence, and although they occur in legendary form in the Pentateuch and in the early chapters of the Book of Joshua, this is not to be regarded as indicating their artificial adaptation to a later theological schema. They are rather to be viewed as traditions that have genuine historical roots. The stories about the Patriarchs reflect their alien status in Canaan. The Exodus was a single, unique circumstance, the Conquest of Canaan a uniform, all-embracing conquest, in which all the Israelite tribes participated under a single leader in fulfil-ment of an ancient promise that they would inherit the land. Nor did the children of Israel maintain close contact with the Canaanites, but destroyed them. Passages that do not fit in with the historical conditions of the period of the Conquest and the Settlement, such as the lists relating to the division of the land in Josh. 13–19, are regarded by Kaufmann as comprising a realistic as also an ideal element rooted in an ancient promise. Hence he confirms the historical authenticity of the biblical account of Israel's begin-nings alike in its principal details and its general structure. This he does by the use of a distinctly critical approach in a literary analysis of the Scriptures and by a complete rejection of critical criteria applied to the development of ancient Israelite social institutions and to the crystallization of the Israelite faith.

This approach presents many difficulties in explaining historical con-ditions, especially those aspects of the Conquest that are supported by factual data derived from archeological finds. It is also doubtful whether the different strata in the Pentateuch and in the Former Prophets, which Kaufmann takes as evidence of the antiquity of the traditions, can be regarded as proof of their historicity. For he himself in principle assumes the use of various sources in the compilation and redaction of the Penta-teuch, and it is therefore possible that this dissimilarity in the strata was the work of the redactor who, in combining these sources, gave each stratum its characteristic features.

The elucidation of the historical significance of various passages, partic-ularly those dealing with the early period of Israelite history, the knowledge of which is chiefly derived from accounts that bear the imprint of folk traditions, is greatly facilitated by a method which investigates the literary forms and categories in the Bible, the manner in which these developed, and their place in the life of the people and in the social structure. Associated with the name of Hermann Gunkel,[7] this method is based on the division of the text into the smallest possible literary units in order to determine the social conditions under which they crystallized, their primary function in the social pattern, and how they evolved from their original forms until they were set down in writing. The aim of this investigation was not primarily historical, but rather, by using literary criteria, a concern with literature as such. But it is precisely by means of literary criteria that the antiquity of the narrative element in the Pentateuch has been demonstrated. Not only were traditions describing the early history of the nation probably developed and transmitted orally in the form of poems and stories, but the narrative cycles were also shaped in this way. Gunkel and his followers emphasized the emergence of the biblical traditions from the folk tale under the influence of mythological and etiological motifs and of cultic ceremonies and sites. But in this way they diminished the value of these traditions as an historical source for the early history of Israel. For according to this school the folk tale by its very nature clothes historical memories in a legendary garb which tends to blur the chronological and local circumstances of the events described, so that any historical kernel that may be embodied in the tale is submerged beneath the legend.

Although the adherents of form criticism and research into the history of tradition accept the basic assumptions of the Wellhausen school, they nevertheless deviated from these assumptions. They did so by asserting an affinity between the biblical narratives and the folk traditions which crystallized orally at an early period in Israelite history, long before the formation, according to the Wellhausen theory, of the sources. Indeed it is this affinity which is the determining factor in the historical evaluation of the traditions. The weak point of this school lies in its excessive emphasis on the cultic, etiological, and legendary aspects of the narratives, and hence in the scant value of these as a source for Israelite history, according to these scholars.

The investigation of literary forms and categories and of their place in the way of life is of considerable importance also for the study of biblical law and ritual, and of the many lists in the Bible. In this field A. Alt broke new ground[8] by combining the methods used by the school of Gunkel with the sociological approach influenced by Max Weber. He also sought to understand the world of the Bible against its geographical background. Using stylistic and formal criteria in his study of biblical law Alt compared it to ancient Mesopotamian law, but sought to explain the unique character of some of the biblical laws in relation to the nomadic or semi-nomadic society of ancient Israel. His study of the geographical and territorial lists, which aimed at tracing the events and history of the Settlement in different regions of the country, is likewise based on the formal criteria of their structure in relation to archeological and historical data, with special reference to the geographical conditions of the country. The investigation of these sources and no less of the family genealogies, and other ethnographical data in the Bible, are of considerable help in a study of Israelite history, and unless these sources are related to their appropriate period and background and the fullest use is made of them, it is impossible to give a comprehensive account of Israel in biblical times.

Several scholars have attempted to combine the Documentary theory with form criticism and research into the history of tradition in a comprehensive theory. This has however yielded no definite criteria for elucidating the historical significance of the biblical traditions concerning Israel's early history. For scholars are divided on the question of the cycles of traditions and their relation to general concepts. This approach, to be found in the work of M. Noth,[9] a pupil of Alt, has produced a twofold criterion as regards the traditions: on the one side, an examination of the development of the oral traditions and stories by emphasizing the etiological and local aspects in explaining the growth of numerous traditions, thereby denying their historical value; and on the other, an examination of the narrative cycles on the assumption that they crystallized within the context of a comprehensive outlook and hence changed their local folk color; they were then repeatedly redacted and combined in the course of subsequent generations, as maintained by the school of Documentary theory. Noth erects a complicated system of principal subjects in the Pentateuch, which are, in the order of their formation, the Exodus, the entry into the Promised Land, the promises to the Patriarchs, the wandering in the wilderness, and the revelation at Mount Sinai. Noth maintains that round these subjects narrative cycles were woven, each independent of and unrelated to any other cycle. It was only at a later stage that they were combined. To the body of traditions in the Pentateuch and the Book of Joshua he denies, save to this or that tradition, any contemporary historical significance. For the beginnings of Israelite history one can, according to his theory, rely neither on the way of life reflected in the patriarchal accounts nor on archeological evidence, nor does he attribute much value to the biblical traditions. He can therefore lay claim to no data on pre-Settlement Israelite history, nor does he regard the accounts of the Settlement as authentic. And since, according to his theory, he considers even the kernel of the traditions of Israel's early history as unhistorical, he is compelled, when explaining their emergence, to adopt an arbitrary and complicated theory sustained by dogmatic assumptions.

A radically different approach, likewise based on research in literary forms and in oral traditions, is represented by the Scandinavian school of Uppsala, which is associated with the name of I. Engnell.[10] According to this school, the bulk of the biblical material was transmitted orally over a lengthy period, and even after some of it had already been committed to writing the process of oral transmission continued. In this way the traditions and cycles of traditions crystallized during many generations, with each generation adding to these traditions according to its own outlook. The place of documents in Wellhausen's theory is here taken by circles of transmitters of tradition. This process of the crystallization of the traditions continued, according to Engnell, until after the Return from Babylon, when, from material that had received its particular character at various times, and from a fusion of written texts and oral traditions, the Pentateuch and the Former Prophets were written down in two comprehensive compilations, the one extending from the Book of Genesis to that of Numbers, the other from that of Deuteronomy to the end of the Book of Kings. At a somewhat later stage these were combined into the Pentateuch and the Former Prophets, more or less in their present form.

This school stresses the importance of cultic elements and general conceptions in the shaping of the traditions, and contends that a lengthy and complicated process of oral transmission separates the written text from the actual events. Hence the Scriptures are not documents that express a uniform outlook but a fusion of layers of traditions, each one grafted on to the next so that they defy separation. Similarly, in neither their classification nor their development can the basic forms of the traditions be ascertained, nor the historical events that found expression in the biblical accounts in question.

The basic assumptions of the Scandinavian school are arbitrary, if only because the evidence on writing in the Ancient East and in Israel does not fit in with the theory that Israel's historical traditions and early poetry were for centuries transmitted orally. This school is, moreover, unable to describe the factual historical development which should be a basic factor in elucidating the traditions. For according to the Scandinavian school there exist only traditions that have changed their character. It is, then, impossible to give an account of the early period of Israelite history or to comprehend the process of the crystallization of the traditions except on the basis of entirely subjective conjectures. Nor is this theory able to explain the formation of the Bible or to help in arriving at an understanding of the historical significance of the Scriptures.

Attempts at evaluating the biblical sources by applying critical criteria and by endeavoring to find the factual historical kernel of these traditions have been made by several scholars, among them Kittel and Albright.[11] The common feature in the approach of these two, who are separated from each other by a generation, is their repudiation of exaggerated historicism and their widest possible use of external data, in particular the results of archeological and historical investigations, as well as the literature relating to the Ancient East. Both Kittel and Albright accept the principles of Wellhausen's literary analysis but reject the extreme evolutionary approach to the Israelite religion, as also its historical conclusions. To the kernel of the biblical accounts of Israel's beginnings both ascribe real historical significance, looking upon them as early traditions based on an ancient Israelite epic and rooted in contemporary events. Moses and Joshua they regard as central historical figures, the sojourn of the children of Israel in Egypt as an historic reality, but they nevertheless adopt a critical attitude to the traditions in the Pentateuch and in Joshua by classifying and distinguishing between the embellishment and the historical kernel, and by comparing the traditions with one another and with epigraphic and archeological data. Accordingly, the account of history that emerges does not necessarily agree with that in the Bible.

These two scholars naturally differ both in their general outlook and in details, and in this respect Albright is further from the Wellhausen school than Kittel. In contrast to the extreme criticism which maintains that there are conflicting biblical traditions on Israel's beginnings, Albright holds that their kernel is identical in the parallel accounts, which differ chiefly, and then not to any great extent, in particulars. For only where different versions were current did the Scriptures quote parallel accounts, which thus reflect the maximum and not the mean differences between the traditions. But where there were identical traditions, the Bible gave only one version. Hence the difference in the contents of the early traditions is much less than assumed by scholars who emphasize the contradictions between the sources. As for the passages ascribed to the Priestly Document, the literary formation of which Albright, agreeing with the school of Wellhausen, regards as late, these, too, are valuable material for the beginnings of Israelite history. They contain cultic, genealogical, and other data rooted in ancient sources to which those later writers had access. According to their language, they embody several early documents. Hence Albright gives little support to the Documentary theory, nor has he much use for its methods either in its view of historical literary development or in its assessment of the authenticity of the Scriptures. In its evaluation of the historical significance of the biblical sources Albright's view reflects a synthesis of literary and historical criteria supported by comparative material from the Ancient East and by archeological data from Palestine and the neighboring lands.

C. The Criteria for Evaluating the Biblical Material as an Historical Source for the Beginning of Israel's History

The question therefore arises what are the available biblical sources for writing Israel's pre-monarchical history and what is the suitable method

of examining them. Owing to the lack of assured criteria reference is again
made here to several general assumptions previously mentioned, namely
the combination of critical criteria and the acceptance as historical of the
kernel of the traditions. For no contemporaneous chronicles are extant but
only traditions. Nor are there any external data bearing directly on these
traditions. And though the criticism of literary forms may help in com-
prehending the development of the traditions, it is of no assistance in
deciding the question of the historicity or non-historicity of a particular
tradition.

Accordingly, a certain belief in the authenticity of the kernel of the
traditions is an essential factor in writing Israel's pre-monarchical history.
Reliance on the Scriptures coupled with a measure of criticism is infinitely
preferable to sweeping theories that lack factual support, or to classifying
the sources on the basis of their agreement with general theories. The
historian can and should be greatly assisted by the indirect information
contained alike in the Bible, in archeological data, and in the sources of
the Ancient East. To go much beyond this is inadvisable, although pro-
nouncements, even subjective ones, cannot be entirely precluded.

But first there must be elucidated a) the extent of the historicity of the
biblical traditions relating to this period; and b) the extent to which the
traditions, insofar as they are unhistorical, either reflect the earlier generation's concept of the events or are the creations of later times, this applying
also to the laws, the cultic texts, and the genealogical and geographical
lists attributed to this period. And here there arise several general questions:
a) What date is to be assigned to the extant texts, and since when is there
evidence, if only indirect, for the existence of the biblical text more or less
in its preserved form? b) When were the comprehensive compilations, that
is, the Pentateuch, the Books of Joshua, Judges, and Samuel, composed?
c) What are the written sources incorporated in these compilations?
d) When were formed the various traditions that lie at the basis of the
biblical account of Israel's beginnings, to what extent do they contain
historical evidence, and what were the processes of transmission until
these traditions were embodied in the extant sources? Although no
definite answers can be given to these questions, the sources cannot be
evaluated unless a position is taken on them.

The extant biblical text is based on manuscripts written long after the
canon was fixed. Among the Dead Sea Scrolls parts of the Bible were found
dating from the 2nd century B.C.E. to the 2nd century C.E., but only
excerpts of the Pentateuch and of the historical books have so far been
published. A Greek translation of the Pentateuch and the Prophets is extant

from the days of the Ptolemies, but complete manuscripts of it date only from the 4th century C.E. onwards. Much earlier papyrus fragments of a Greek version of the Bible have also been found. The differences between the Hebrew text and the Greek renderings are minor and in the main do not alter the meaning of the text, but they show that the Greek translation is based on a Hebrew version which, if not completely identical with, is very close to, the Masoretic text, as attested by the Dead Sea Scrolls. The variants in the published scrolls do not indicate any essential deviation from the biblical text, most of these being confined to the writing with or without *matres lectionis*. Such differences also exist between later manuscripts and the several systems of the Masoretes. There are however fragments which agree with or reflect a version close to that of the Septuagint. A comparison of the Septuagint with the Hebrew text testifies to a text which is prior to the Greek renderings and which existed after the process of compilation and redaction had been completed.

It cannot be definitely said when the Pentateuch and the Books of Joshua, Judges, and Samuel were composed. Many scholars contend that the Pentateuch assumed its final form not earlier than the Return, and the Book of Joshua at about the same time, while the Books of Judges and Samuel are substantially early and not far removed from the events they describe. There is however the insistent question what are the written sources that are embodied in the Pentateuch and in the Book of Joshua or that were accessible to their compilers. During recent times the view prevalent among scholars has, with slight or significant modifications, been that of the Wellhausen school according to which these books of the Bible consist of passages that were put together from several comprehensive compilations composed and set down in writing at various times between the division of the kingdom and the Return. As noted above, the criteria of the Wellhausen school do not provide a basis for writing a history of Israel. Nor are other criteria sufficiently elaborated for fixing the date when the different passages were composed. Nonetheless it may be said that the Pentateuch and the Book of Joshua contain late passages, although perhaps not as late as the Wellhausen hypothesis would have it. In any event, most of them were written after the Settlement. Not only were the non-narrative passages, that is, laws, cultic directives, various lists, and speeches, set down in writing later than the time of the Settlement but they are based on the social structure of a people living on its own land. Hence the various passages in the Pentateuch and the Book of Joshua, whether written in the days of the earlier kings or many generations afterwards, are considerably later than the events described in them. In point of historical memory there is no essential difference whether the period separating the events and the date when they were committed to writing is two or five centuries. Migrations and movements of population, modifications in the social structure and in the concept and beliefs — all these tend to destroy the continuity of the historical memory. A few generations of upheavals and changes can more effectively efface from memory the true picture of the past than many generations of settled, undisturbed life. Hence one of the decisive questions is not the date of the sources of these books, but rather since when was it customary in Israel to write history. For from the time when past events were first written down some records must have survived and have been available to later writers. No less important are the questions how there arose traditions that bear obvious indications of being folk tales, and what were the processes of transmission until they were committed to writing as an historical record of Israel's beginnings.

D. The Growth of Historiography in Israel

The creation of historical literature in Israel, as among other nations, is the result of a lengthy development sustained by the cultural tradition and social structure of the nation. Historical writing is characterized by connecting individual events into an organic sequence, by separating mythological and legendary elements from a story interwoven with actual, realistic features, and at later stages of development by utilizing and combining different traditions, and by a comprehensive historical outlook. This development usually proceeds by stages, in each of which the description of events assumes a characteristic literary form, being in the early stages couched in the form of epic poems and songs of praise, followed by the epos which combines a series of events into one unit, while in the later stages a rational distinction is made between legend and reality. The beginnings of historical writing are also to be found in prose stories depicting heroic exploits and episodes in the lives of the ancestors of the tribe or nation, in the genealogies of these ancestors, in brief chronicles, and so on. The development of historiography differs from one society or nation to another, nor does it in every instance conform to predetermined patterns, the historical outlook being shaped by the social structure and by the level of civilization. The historiosophic approach of the Bible is conditioned by the belief in Israel's uniqueness, and accordingly from the very outset its history constitutes the realization of God's word. Nor can external influences be disregarded, particularly that which rich cultures with a

Mari, aerial view of the excavated palace area.   Prof. A. Parrot, Paris.

Hammath, view of the town and mound.   National Museum, Copenhagen.

Ugarit, aerial view of the excavations. Prof. C. A. Schaeffer, Paris.

Minat-al-Baydā, aerial view. Prof. C. A. Schaeffer, Paris.

Qaṭna, view of the area defended by an earth rampart.

Byblos, aerial view (looking west).

Megiddo, aerial view of the excavations.
Oriental Institute, University of Chicago.

Tell Beth-shean (seen from the south).
The University Museum, Philadelphia.

Shechem, general view of the tell
and the village of Balāta.
Prof. G. E. Wright.

Hazor, the fosse and earth rampart on the southern side of the mound.
Prof. Y. Yadin, Jerusalem.

Tell Jericho, aerial view (seen from the south).
Prof. K. M. Kenyon, London.

Tell Lachish (looking south).
Biyalik Institute, Jerusalem.

Jericho, Middle Bronze Period plastered earth rampart.

Prof. K. M. Kenyon, London.

Jericho, Middle Bronze Period
stone glacis.
Prof. J. Garstang.

Tell al-Jarisheh, brick revetment of Middle Bronze Period glacis.
Archaeology Institute, Hebrew University, Jerusalem.

Gezer, remains of a stone-built tower
in the Middle Bronze Period wall.
W. G. Dever, Hebrew Union College,
Jerusalem.

Shechem, view of the Middle Bronze Period east gate.
Prof. G. E. Wright.

Hazor, Middle Bronze Ia Period casemate wall by the north gate.
Prof. Y. Yadin, Jerusalem.

Megiddo, Middle Bronze II Period wall (stratum XII).
Oriental Institute, University of Chicago.

Har Yeruḥam, remains of Middle Bronze I Period private house.   Dr. M. Kochavi, Tel Aviv.

Jericho, view of a street from the
Middle Bronze Period.
Prof. K. M. Kenyon, London.

Nahariya, general view of the Middle Bronze Period temple (looking west).
Dr. M. Dothan, Department of Antiquities, Jerusalem.

Nahariya, the "high place" in the courtyard of the Middle Bronze Period temple (looking north).
Dr. M. Dothan, Department of Antiquities, Jerusalem.

Megiddo, view of temple dating from the end of the Middle Bronze Period.
Oriental Institute, University of Chicago.

Hazor — lower town, temple from the Late Bronze Period (stratum IX).
Prof. Y. Yadin, Jerusalem.

Lachish, the Late Bronze Period "Fosse Temple."

Rabbath-Ammon, remains of temple from the Late Bronze Period.
Prof. J. B. Henessy, British School of Archeology, Jerusalem.

lengthy tradition of writing exercises on young nations, such as the influence which the Canaanite culture had on the settling Israelite tribes. Even though the stages in the growth of Israel's historical literature cannot be precisely fixed, there are sources in the Bible that testify to a development in historiography from short epic poems to a comprehensive compilation written according to a plan and containing an historical evaluation of events and of their circumstances.

An example of historical literature, which presents a clear picture of events through a relevant description of the same and an explanation of their causes and development, is to be found in the Books of Samuel and Kings, in the historical account of the kingdom of David and Solomon and of subsequent times. The historiographers of that period used various sources, such as royal and Temple chronicles, the stories of prophets, folk tales, and official and administrative lists, all of which they incorporated into a homogeneous compilation. Later chapters however contain cycles of popular historical accounts that have a notable legendary element, such as the stories in the Book of Kings about Elijah and Elisha. The continuation of popular literature under the monarchy does not, however, contradict the fact that from the days of David and Solomon an historical literature and an indisputable tradition of historical writing existed in Israel. From that time, too, there dates the cultivation in Israel of historical traditions embodying the final crystallization of the account of Israel's beginnings as presented in the early books of the Bible. But insofar as these traditions and stories about the Patriarchs, about the wandering in the wilderness, and about the Conquest provide evidence of a social and historical background, they for the most part reflect the pre-monarchical period.

The traditions and patterns of Israelite historiography began to take shape from the outset of Israel's existence as a nation. It is impossible to trace the development of the traditions in pre-Settlement times, although several poetical passages in the Pentateuch undoubtedly date from that period. The historical statements in the ancient poems and in the folk tales doubtless originated, and in the main assumed definite form, in an oral tradition. From the days of the Settlement and perhaps even earlier, the art of writing was known in Israel, as is clear both from the fact that alphabetic writing was used in Canaan, and from the evidence about writing in the Bible itself. At first there was apparently only a limited degree of literary writing in Israel, writing being used chiefly for practical purposes, while early traditions, poetry, stories, cultic practices, and perhaps also the tribal legal traditions took their form through oral transmission until they were committed to writing.

Since it is characteristic of oral traditions[12] to be transmitted from father to son in the family or tribe, this tended in the course of time to emphasize their local aspect. Nonetheless, factors operated in Israel which helped to preserve the patriarchal, and to mold and foster a general national, tradition. These traditions were cherished and spread by itinerant Levites well-versed in song and cult, as also by the priests of the high places and central shrines to which the people came on pilgrimage to appear before God at appointed seasons and festival days. Both these groups, while teaching the divine law, recounted Israel's ancient traditions, the exploits of the Conquest, and the battles against Israel's foes. But in telling of the events of the past their purpose was not to set forth history for its own sake but rather to teach and to instruct. The religious and moral lesson was their chief concern, not historical accuracy. This didactic character of the oral traditions was responsible in many instances for their formulation and preservation in poetic form, the better to imprint them on the minds of the people. In preserving the continuity of their common tradition, the central cultic sites of the tribal league in Canaan played a highly significant role. In cultic centers such as Hebron, Beth-el, and Shechem stories grew up about what had happened to the Patriarchs in these places, about their stay there, and about how God had revealed Himself to them. At the same time cultic practices were fostered, and the legal tradition preserved. There, too, a start was undoubtedly made in historical writing, characterized as it was from its beginnings by the religious conception of Israel's history as the fulfilment of God's word.

These general remarks do not answer the questions how and to what extent a written source can be differentiated from an oral one, nor the degree of historicity in the oral traditions, nor how a tradition with an historical kernel is to be distinguished from a folk tale. Between the different elements there is no clear line of demarcation, although it may be assumed that poems, as well as narratives bearing the stamp of a folk tale, are mostly based on an oral tradition. With regard to the trustworthy transmission of unwritten traditions, literary prose must be distinguished from poetry and cultic formulae, since these latter, recited in fixed literary forms, were more easily repeated and transmitted than prose, their definite stylistic patterns safeguarding them from changes in their contents. But even here no hard and fast rules can be laid down, since the first phase in the formation of the traditions, before they assumed definite shape, was mainly in prose recounted in different versions. Only later were they set out as poetry in fixed patterns and formulae which thereafter did not change much. It is therefore possible that extant prose traditions were committed to writing at this primary stage. In other instances however the prose versions of early traditions represent a secondary adaptation, later than the poetical forms.

E. Folk Tales and Historical Traditions

A large part of the Pentateuch and the Books of Joshua, Judges, and Samuel consists of consecutive narratives which, in a continuous historical account within a pragmatic framework, include speeches put in the mouths of bygone figures, poems and laws, lists and cultic directives, and so on. While the narratives may be distinguished from these latter and even from the pragmatic framework, there are no formal criteria for differentiating the historically based narratives from those founded solely on a folk tale or a legend. In general, the fundamentally historical narratives also reveal a significant addition of folk, legendary or even mythological elements. It is doubtful whether, at the time when these stories took shape in the nation's tradition, any distinction was made between their narrative embellishment and their historical kernel. Once the distinctly folk and legendary motifs have been isolated, the main difference between history and poetry in these stories lies in the probability of the narration. But whether historical or not, the stories are early. In them Israel is depicted as an association of tribes and families, as a nation conscious of a common destiny and with its tribes and families bound by close genealogical, religious, and cultic ties. These stories are not the invention of later generations, but are rooted in a society and regime which existed in Israel from the days of the Settlement and the Judges to the beginning of the Monarchy, having emerged during the formation of the oral tradition. Besides being historical traditions, they are also an invaluable source of information on the social and cultural pattern of the period.

In an historical assessment of the sources that are based on an oral tradition the main problem is, as previously remarked, to distinguish between an early tradition which has an historical basis and a story founded on myth, legend, and folk imagination. A notable feature of the folk tale in the Bible is the etiological character of many of these stories,[13] that is, assigning a cause to explain some arresting circumstance. So, for example, in connection with the history of the Patriarchs there is the comment on the name of the city of Zoar (Gen. 19:20–22) and the transformation of Lot's wife into a pillar of salt (verse 26), on the digging of the wells by Isaac and the name of Beer-sheba (Gen. 26:33), on the revelation of God to Jacob and the names of Beth-el (Gen. 28:19) and Penuel (Gen. 32:31).

In the account of the wandering of the Israelites in the wilderness there are the etiological stories about the names of Marah (Ex. 15:23), Massah (Ex. 17:7), and Taberah (Num. 11:3). In the narrative of the Conquest there are etiological elements in the account of the capture of the city of Ai and the heap of stones raised there (Josh. 8:29), as also in the story about the Gibeonites and the way in which they were made hewers of wood and drawers of water for the altar of the Lord (Josh. 9:27). In the period of the judges there is the etiological account of the jawbone of an ass with which Samson smote the Philistines, which is associated with a place called Ramath-lehi ("the hill of the jawbone") (Jud. 15:17). There is the story of Eli's grandson being named Ichabod ("no-glory") after Israel's defeat by the Philistines in the battle of Eben-ezer (I Sam. 4:21). There are also etiological elements in the stories about David (II Sam. 5:20). In most of these instances the etiological interpretation does not reflect the historical facts. A significant proportion of the etiological stories, especially those containing mythological elements or attempts at ethnographical explanations, as in the Book of Genesis, are undoubtedly not grounded in historical events. Some scholars tend however to deny all historical value even to those stories of the Conquest and the Settlement which have a clear etiological element.[14] In this they have really gone too far. Etiological explanations served as a mnemotechnic and didactic aid. When past events were recounted, it was natural to point to the site where they had occurred, especially if some landmark there or an ancient relic was conspicuous or well-known among the people, and to associate the name with what had taken place there. Occasionally an event was actually responsible for the name given. Etiological stories without any historical basis probably arose due to the use of etiology as an aid to the memory. For the notion that a place-name or landmark had an etiological explanation would never have occurred to people had they not been accustomed to hear similar explanations in other instances. In principle it cannot be determined whether a certain etiological story is founded on a reliable historical tradition or whether it is an invention for the purposes of the story. In contrast however to the etiological stories about the Patriarchs, it must be remembered with regard to the traditions of the Conquest and the Settlement that writing was already then practiced in Israel and a start had at that time apparently also been made with historical writing. The existence of written documents, including probably chronicles, restrained the imagination of narrators and prevented imperceptible changes from being introduced in the course of time in this basic historical data. The narrators who aimed at teaching their listeners the word of God were able to weave etiological motifs into their stories, especially those current among the people, and to invest their heroes with an aura of the miraculous. But it should not be assumed that they consciously deviated from the fundamental historical facts. Nor should it be assumed that at a time when there was a continuity of tradition and when writing was practiced, the central historical events should so have been forgotten that the narrators' account of them no longer had any basis in reality.

F. Historical Poetry in Ancient Israel

There is no historical Israelite epic extant. There are only fragments of the creation epos depicting the beginning of the world and the struggles of creation, which were embodied in prophecy and in the late wisdom literature.[15] Nor is there any evidence of an Israelite epic that told of the beginnings of the nation's history, in particular the Exodus and the Conquest, subjects especially suitable for an extensive historical epos. It is however almost certain that a national-historical epic existed in Israel.[16] The Bible mentions two works which dealt with the battles of the Israelites during the years of wandering, of the Conquest, and of the Settlement up to the beginning of the monarchy. These are "the book of the Wars of the Lord" (Num. 21:14) and "the book of Jashar" (Josh. 10:13; II Sam. 1:18). From the former, two verses, written in poetical language, are quoted in the Book of Numbers (Num. 21:14–15), and deal with the wars of the children of Israel in Transjordan and the capture of the Arnon region. From the latter there are two quotations:[17] the first records Joshua's entreaty during the battle in the Valley of Aijalon: "Sun, stand thou still upon Gibeon..." (Josh. 10:12–13), while the second, which follows the introduction to David's lament over Saul and Jonathan, is contained in the parenthetic clause: "and said — To teach the sons of Judah the bow. Behold, it is written in the book of Jashar" (II Sam. 1:18). The lament deals chiefly with the military valor of Saul and Jonathan and concludes with the words: "How are the mighty fallen, and the weapons of war perished!" (verse 27). It is impossible to conclude from these passages whether they are fragments from extensive epics or are from collections of brief war poems and ballads. This applies in particular to the book of Jashar which contained David's lament over Saul and Jonathan. This lament is not an epic, although one like it may have been part of a lengthy epic. The book of Jashar was apparently a collection of individual poems, of which David's lament formed one of the last passages and which were intended to encourage those going into battle. The book of the Wars of the Lord is, as its name implies, Israel's war epos from the days of Moses onwards. It appears to have included, besides Num. 21:14–15, other poetical passages in the Pentateuch, in particular those in Num. 21, namely, the Song of the Well and the subsequent enumeration of the stages of the wanderings of the Israelites (verses 17–20), the poem deriding Sihon (verses 27–30), and the early parts of the Song at the Red Sea (Ex. 15) which declares: "The Lord is a man of war, the Lord is His name" (verse 3) in an allusion to the title of the epic, "the book of the Wars of the Lord." This work may also have been the source of the verse: "The hand upon the throne of the Lord: the Lord will have war with Amalek from generation to generation" (Ex. 17:16), as well as of the Song of the Ark recited before the Ark in time of war: "Rise up, O Lord, and let Thine enemies be scattered . . ." (Num. 10:35–36).

The poem of victory over Sihon in Num. 21, which was apparently included in the book of the Wars of the Lord, is by the ancient poets (verse 27), whose distinctive theme was political-historical and connected with wars and other important events in Israel's national or tribal life. Such poems also included derision of an enemy and praise of a hero, and doubtless, as in the book of Jashar, also the songs recited before the men going into battle, and elegies over heroes killed in war. The Song of Deborah (Jud. 5) resembles this type, being a song of victory that gives an epic account of the battle and refers to the part played in it by the various tribes, praises the heroes who fought in the name of the Lord and derides the enemy. To the poems of this sort belong also the parables of Balaam (Num. 23–24) who, according to an ancient tradition rooted in a belief in the magical power of blessings and curses, was invited to curse Israel when they sought to enter Canaan from the east. The parables consist chiefly of an historical-political poem dealing with the might and power of the tribes of Israel, and of statements about Israel's neighbors put into the mouth of this ancient figure in the form of a blessing and a curse. Doubtful though it is whether, in their final form, Balaam's extant parables are pre-monarchical, it is certain that this type of poetry is early. The Bible similarly contains blessings of and promises to Israel and their tribes, ascribed to the Patriarchs. There is, in particular, the blessing of Jacob (Gen. 49), as well as that of Moses (Deut. 33). Both give a brief description of the status and specific character of the various tribes in their respective territories in Canaan. These poetical blessings apparently assumed their definitive form on festivals and days of appointed season when the tribes gathered together at the central shrines where men well-versed in song recited their parables and put into the mouths of the Patriarchs prophetic statements about, and blessings of, Israel and the tribes. Dealing as these poems did with actual political events, their formulas were in the main fixed, but were nevertheless liable to change according to prevailing circumstances. It is with the patterns of life in the days of the judges that the tradition of the tribal blessings is associated. Those in Gen. 49 and Deut. 33 were mainly recited at the time of the Settlement, but in their present form they also contain elements originating from the early period of the monarchy.

To the national-historical poetry of the days of the judges and the beginning of the monarchy belong several psalms, such as Ps. 83 and apparently also the enigmatic Ps. 68, the former of which is a national lament calling on God to deliver Israel from the menace presented by their enemies, Edom, the Ishmaelites, Moab, and the Hagrites, while the latter deals with the victory of the tribes over their foes. Other psalms, too, belong to this period.[18]

Besides these historical psalms, the Book of Psalms contains others which treat of the earliest days of Israel's existence, such as Pss. 78, 105, and 106, with their historical and religious approach to the beginnings of Israel's history, and their reference to God's lovingkindness towards His people and the people's ingratitude. In their present form these psalms are not pre-monarchical. Ps. 106 is apparently even later, dating from about exilic times. Their poetical traditions are, however, in the main early, as is their schema regarding the beginnings of Israel's history. Of Pss. 105 and 106, the former is a hymn of thanksgiving to God for His lovingkindness towards Israel, and the latter a poem of rebuke for the sins of the nation which repeatedly rebelled against the word of the Lord, who nonetheless continued to show mercy to them. These two psalms mention the principal events in Israel's history up to the Conquest, with no reference to the monarchy or the building of the Temple. The historical schema of these psalms is accordingly pre-monarchical, having apparently originated in the days of the judges at shrines where the ancient national epics were recited at festivals and appointed seasons. They may even be based on the hymns and psalms of the divine worship that took place at these shrines. Ps. 78 which, in its general lines, is based on a very similar schema to that of Ps. 106, reflects an historical outlook dating from the beginning of the monarchy, its historical schema culminating in David's selection as king and in the erection of the Temple. Another prominent motif is God's rejection of Ephraim and His choice of the tribe of Judah. These psalms, then, are important evidence for the historical and religious outlook of the period.[19]

G. THE LISTS IN THE BIBLE

The biblical books dealing with the pre-monarchical period contain lists of various kinds: genealogical schemata, tribal and family genealogies, enumerations of the borders of the tribal territories and towns, lists of the levitical and priestly cities as also of the stages of the Israelites' journey in the wilderness, and so on. These lists differ radically from those of the monarchical period, the latter, even the earliest among them, such as those of David's mighty men and officials (for example, II Sam. 8:16–18; I Chron. 27:25–34) or of Solomon's officers (I Kings 4:7 ff.), having been drawn up for administrative purposes and having originated in the royal archives. By contrast, some of those dealing with the pre-monarchical period are based on memories and oral traditions, whereas others are schematic. Most of the lists of the towns in Josh. 13–19 do not apparently reflect the actual situation at the time of the Settlement or even of the judges, nor are they based on contemporary traditions. Yet they cannot be regarded as a late compilation by the priestly circles, as maintained by followers of the Wellhausen school. It was probably in Israel's pattern of life and social regime that the various lists originated at this or another period. Some are even early. As with the evaluation of other historical sources in the Bible, corroborative evidence, not always available, is necessary for determining the precise nature and the date of the compilation of this or that list. But where this can be done, an historical source of the utmost importance is obtained.

The numerous genealogical lists in the Bible may be subdivided, on the one hand, into schematic genealogies which, found mainly in the Book of Genesis, are a projection of historical, ethnographical, and even mythological traditions, and, on the other, into tribal genealogies and genealogies of clans, these occurring chiefly in the Book of Numbers and in the early chapters of the Book of Chronicles.[20]

In general the genealogical schemata in the Book of Genesis reflect territorial and ethnic ties among tribes and nations during a specific period of time. The ethnographical and political data in these lists are indicative of the date of their compilation. In its final version the extensive and detailed ethnographical schema of the table of the nations, which embodies comparatively early traditions dating from the time of Egypt's sovereignty over Canaan, is undoubtedly not earlier than the division of the kingdom. Some scholars however assign it to a much later period. Also late is the list of the tribes comprising the sons of Ishmael (Gen. 25:13–16). Other lists, such as that of the sons of Nahor (Gen. 22:20 ff.), point to an early historical situation.

Generally, the various schemata of the Israelite tribes and their family lists are, in their final form, not later than the beginning of the monarchy, and reflect, in the status of the tribes and the relations of the families, an early period, that is, from the days of the Settlement until those of David. They are principally based on oral traditions, and one list may combine traditions that originated at different times. The list in the tribal census in Num. 26 of families according to their tribes dates from the beginning of the monarchy and is apparently connected with the census taken by David. To his day, it seems, is also to be assigned the main formation of the genealogies in I Chron. 1–9, even though they do not constitute one unit but are, by their nature, a combination of different types of list, some very late. There is considerable schematization also in the tribal genealogies which contain, in the form of schematic genealogies, memories of the tribes' settlement and of their respective ties. From a close study of these lists and a comparison of their details much information can be obtained about the tribes and families, the process of their settlement, their ties with one another and with the local population.

The geographical lists in Josh. 13–21 include enumerations of the borders of, and of the towns in, the tribal territories, as also of the priestly and levitical cities. The lists of the borders are based on early traditions dating from the days of the Settlement and of the judges and are therefore a source of prime importance for the history of the tribal settlement.[21] It is otherwise with the lists of the towns. These reflect the conditions neither of the period of the settlement nor of the judges, and are probably not based on contemporary traditions. They are essentially detailed lists originally compiled in writing for administrative purposes at a time when Israel had a central administration and registers of towns and provinces. It is improbable that they are very late lists unrelated to actual conditions, as was widely held by the school of Documentary theory. Similarly, the view that the lists in the Book of Joshua are early, unrealistic, and utopian is wholly unfounded.[22] Their detailed but nevertheless incomplete character, the inclusion of some towns of secondary significance, and the omission of others with an important historical past stamp them as authentic. Nonetheless, their primary function was not that described in the Book of Joshua, since they were originally compiled for administrative purposes apparently at various times during the monarchy, based as they are on the monarchical regime and society.[23] It was, it seems, only at a final stage in the redaction of the Book of Joshua that they were incorporated to other earlier lists.

Of little value for the pre-monarchical period, they are extremely important for the history of the monarchy.

The list in Num. 33[24] of the stages of the Israelites' journey in the wilderness has special significance for the traditions of early Israelite history. Its author apparently sought to present a comprehensive picture of the Israelites' journeyings from Egypt to the plains of Moab. For this purpose he used, apart from the traditions of the wanderings embodied in the pentateuchal narrative itself (verses 3–17), also other sources (verses 18 ff.), on the basis of which he enumerated the stages of wandering in the wilderness, most of which would otherwise have been unknown. He apparently also relied on ancient poetical sources which mentioned stages such as those in Num. 21:19–20. It is impossible to decide when this list, as at present extant, was drawn up and redacted. Its form is based on ancient poetical traditions, among them undoubtedly also such as these, which consist mainly of an enumeration of places and stages. Poetical traditions of this type may originally have been used as a mnemotechnic aid in telling of the events connected with the migrations and stages in those particular places. Since these lists were poetic in form they were remembered even when the stories associated with some of the stages had been forgotten.

H. The Collections of Laws

Most of Israelite law in biblical times is embodied in the Books of Exodus, Leviticus, Numbers, and Deuteronomy, and is linked with the story of the Exodus, the revelation at Mount Sinai, and the wandering in the wilderness. The laws are among the most important acts of God in the wilderness and combine with the historical narrative, eminently theological in character. Civil and criminal laws intermingle with speeches, ethical admonitions, and cultic regulations. These laws occur either in small units within the narrative or in larger ones that give the appearance of being collections of laws. They are however not systematic legal compilations but rather collections that combine religious precepts with legal matters.

The following are the principal collections of laws in the Pentateuch: 1) Ex. 21–23. Called by scholars the Book of the Covenant, it comprises various civil and religious laws. 2) The entire Book of Leviticus. Scholars refer to the latter part of this book, which forms a distinct section, as the Book of Holiness. The remainder of the Book of Leviticus, the laws in the Book of Numbers, and parts of the cultic regulations in the Book of Exodus bear a certain resemblance to one another in linguistic usages and in the spirit of the laws. They may be regarded either as a single collection or as smaller collections of laws which developed against a common background. These have been designated the Priestly Code. 3) The laws in Deut. 14–26.

The extent to which biblical law may be used in depicting the history of pre-monarchical times depends on when these laws were conceived, whether they were actually practiced, and when they were assembled in collections. Another significant question is the chronological and local connection between the various legal collections, all of which, occurring in the Pentateuch as obligatory, exhibit some duplication and repetition, as well as some diversity and difference in legal and cultic injunctions.[25]

Although said to have been revealed by God to Moses at Mount Sinai, these laws are in the main, those, not of a nomadic, but of an agricultural society, living on its land and marked by settled cities and landed property. This is so as regards everyday law. The cultic regulations, too, suit a shrine or shrines with a ramified hierarchy. Hence biblical law, as it came to us in the Pentateuch, did not precede the Settlement. But neither does the civil and criminal law nor the cultic regulations in the pentateuchal legal collections chime in with the monarchy, which is mentioned in only a few isolated passages in the Book of Deuteronomy (Deut. 17:14 ff.). The background of these laws as a whole is a farming community, with a comparatively primitive economy and still maintaining a tribal and family regime. Hence these laws, at least those governing everyday life, clearly reflect pre-monarchical times, and although some laws were probably reinterpreted later, they mostly suited Israelite society during the early stages of its settlement.

For determining the date of the cultic regulations and the religious laws no such criterion of everyday life can be used. However, those to whom these regulations applied and who observed them were neither the king nor priests appointed by the king but the congregation of Israel. In the pentateuchal laws the king is not mentioned as taking part in the observance of the cult nor did he have any standing as far as the cult was concerned. This is in contrast to the situation that obtained during the monarchy when the king was intimately associated with the sanctuary, and determined and directed divine worship in Israel. That the religious laws and cultic regulations are pre-monarchical is a conclusion bound up with a general outlook on the development of the Israelite religion and its cultic institutions. Due to the many contradictions in the legal collections, particularly in regard to cultic regulations, to the different status of the priests and the

Levites, to the divergent injunctions concerning the observance of the festivals, and so on, it is difficult to assume that all these laws are pre-monarchical. While they may be the cultic regulations of several early shrines, the more widely accepted view that the various legal collections represent a lengthy development of cultic regulations in Israel cannot be entirely rejected. Their date and that of the religious injunctions included in the legal collections and the question of the final formation of these collections are bound up with the view adopted on the development of the cultic institutions and regulations in Israel. Nor can a consideration of the date of the laws and the interrelation between the various legal collections be separated from a consideration of the actual question of their formation itself.

I. THE PRAGMATIC FRAMEWORK

In their extant form the Pentateuch and the Former Prophets present an account of Israel's history from the days of the Patriarchs until the destruction of the kingdom of Judah, and chiefly comprise individual stories and laws, lists and poetical passages. Each of these constitutes an independent entity. They were made into a comprehensive compilation by the pragmatic framework which consists of introductory, connecting, and concluding remarks interposed between the separate chapters, and of incidental comments which occur either in the narrative chapters or as reasons for the laws. To this pragmatic framework belong also statements put into the mouths of venerated figures of the past, such as the Patriarchs, Moses, and Joshua, as well as those made in the name of the Lord. These utterances, which have a religio-political content, express the author's view, this having been customary in ancient historical literature when authors ascribed to renowned persons what they thought the latter would have said under the circumstances depicted in the story. The pragmatic framework of the Pentateuch and the Books of Joshua, Judges, which treat of the pre-monarchical period, expresses a religio-historical conception identical in its general lines in the various books. God had assigned Canaan to the Patriarchs, Abraham, Isaac, and Jacob, and had chosen Israel, had brought them out of Egypt and given them the land of Canaan for an inheritance, and this despite the people's backslidings and repeated rebelliousness against His word. The misfortunes and afflictions which befell the Israelites were a punishment for their sins, and the nations left in Canaan, which the Israelites were unable to drive out, remained to test whether Israel would observe God's commandments or turn aside after strange gods.

Historically, the question that arises is when were the introductory statements and speeches composed and when did the view which they express come into being. While this question is important for an account of the historical development that took place, it has greater significance for a comprehension of the religio-historical outlook of those times. By its nature the pragmatic framework is an essential part of these books or of their comprehensive units, and the question of the date of its compilation is, therefore, also that of the date of these comprehensive units. As previously noted, opinions differ on this question, which is bound up with the entire problem of the redaction and compilation of the Pentateuch and of the development of religious beliefs in Israel. An analysis of the stories and traditions shows, however, that the chief elements of the pragmatic framework — the promise to the Patriarchs that their descendants would inherit the land of Canaan, the choice of the nation, their disobedience of God's commandments, the divine punishment and forgiveness, and the special relation between the people and the one God — are interwoven into the individual stories, so that this conception cannot be separated from the essence of the stories and traditions. The cycles of the stories, and even part of the actual stories themselves, probably crystallized in the way in which they did only in order to give an answer to these questions and to explain why the Israelites had not inherited the whole country, despite God's lovingkindness towards His people, and why they were being subjected to the pressure of the nations round about. These questions are relevant to the political conditions in the days of the judges.[26] Nor can it be assumed that they arose at a later period under David and Solomon or subsequently, under the Kingdom of Israel or of Judah. For whereas in the pentateuchal literature the period of wandering in the wilderness is one of sinning and rebelliousness against God, in later prophetic literature it is the ideal period of perfect faith in God and of His lovingkindness towards His people.

The religio-historical conception which found expression in the pragmatic framework of the Pentateuch and the Books of Joshua, Judges had in the main presumably taken shape in the pre-monarchical period. This conception left its imprint on the historical thought of later generations too. Nevertheless, some speeches and connecting and concluding remarks in these books embody later viewpoints. For example, in Gen. 17:6–8, 16; 35:11–12, alongside God's promises to the Patriarchs that a mighty nation would descend from them and that the land of Canaan would be given to their descendants as an inheritance, there is also the promise that kings would come forth from them. Here is reflected the idea of kingship and sovereignty that clearly belongs to the monarchical period. This applies also to poetical passages as, for example, in Isaac's blessing of Jacob and Esau (Gen. 27:28–29, 39–41) that Jacob would be lord over his brethren and Esau would serve him. The background to this is the monarchy, probably under David and Solomon. On the other hand, the admonitions at the end of the Book of Leviticus (Chap. 26) and of the Book of Deuteronomy (Chap. 28), with their threat of the total destruction of the land and the exile of the people among the nations, are in their extant form much later, although they undoubtedly contain earlier elements too. Even if it is argued that they are pre-exilic, they were nevertheless composed only at a time when actual danger threatened. And although the pragmatic framework of the Pentateuch and the Books of Joshua, Judges contain elements that are later, and even very much later, than the time when the stories were formulated, the essence of the historical conception in these books is associated with the period when the stories and traditions about the beginnings of Israel's history took shape, which is the period of the Settlement and of the Judges.

CHAPTER V

THE CHRONOLOGY OF THE ANCIENT NEAR EAST IN THE SECOND MILLENNIUM B.C.E.

by H. Tadmor

INTRODUCTION

THE CHRONOLOGICAL FRAMEWORK of the Ancient Near East in the 2nd millennium B.C.E. extends over two main periods, between which the 16th and 15th centuries form the line of demarcation. The 16th century saw both the end of the Hyksos period in Egypt (of which few records are extant), and the beginning of the Eighteenth Dynasty (for which sources are numerous). Similarly, the 15th century witnessed the close of the undocumented "dark age" which had descended on Mesopotamia after the Kassite conquest of Babylon, towards the middle of the second millennium. The central problem of the former period is the dating of the First Babylonian Dynasty; that of the latter period is the coordination of the chronological data on the kings of Assyria, Babylon, Egypt and Hatti, data which combine to form a single, overall pattern, the mainstay of which are historical synchronisms between the rulers of these countries.

A. THE DATE OF THE FIRST BABYLONIAN DYNASTY

1. HISTORY AND METHODS OF RESEARCH

The chronological research at the end of the last century centered around the dating of the First Babylonian Dynasty,whose 6th king was Hammurabi. This question is decisive since the dates of the kings of Sumer and Akkad, of the various dynasties of the several Mesopotamian cities, and the dating of the early archeological strata are all based on dates of the First Babylonian Dynasty. The date proposed for Hammurabi was in constant modification, for new historical material was constantly coming to light. Thus, a contemporary scholar has suggested 1806 B.C.E. for the founding of the First Dynasty, as against 2506 or 2425 put forward by a number of scholars at the end of the last century.

As to the present century, up to the end of the thirties the beginning of the

First Dynasty was usually assigned to the 22nd, 21st or 20th century B.C.E. Research at that time was based mainly on the following factors: data in the Babylonian king-lists on the regnal years of the Babylonian dynasties; chronological data in the inscriptions of Babylonian kings concerning their predecessors; Assyro-Babylonian synchronisms based on Babylonian chronicles; and (in a few chronological systems) on chronological data of Berosus.

After 1912, most systems took into account the probable dates based on "astronomical" observations of Venus in the days of Ammizaduqa (10th king of the First Dynasty); in the course of time these latter even became a chronological cornerstone. These observations had been drawn up by the royal astronomers in the 8th year of Ammizaduqa's reign and record Venus' disappearance before sunrise and its reappearance after sunset. Since this planet reappears on the same day of the month every 275 years (less 8 days), as well as every 56 or 64 years (less 28 or 32 days), the dates of these observations can be assigned to several years — with a difference of 275, 56 or 64 years between them. Therefore, such astronomical data offer mere alternatives between which a scholar must decide on the basis of independent historical criteria. A further difficulty is the fact that there are only late copies extant of the original tables on which the observations were recorded. Assuming that ancient "astronomers" erred or that later copyists corrupted the original, the data can be used only after suitable corrections have been brought to the text.[1]

The discovery of the Mari documents and their preliminary publication (in 1937) made it known that Shamshi-Adad I, King of Assyria, was a contemporary of Hammurabi. Since Shamshi-Adad I reigned in the 19th century, scholars were compelled to adjust the date of Hammurabi accordingly, lowering their original figures by some 100-200 years.[2] Only then was the true significance of an economic text from Sippar, published long ago, fully appreciated.[3] This document is dated to Hammurabi's 10th year and the witnesses swore by both his life and that of Shamshi-Adad; hence the latter was still alive in the Babylonian king's 10th year. Thus, a minimal synchronism, previously not sufficiently paid attention to, was established between these rulers. In the meantime, several documents were published, clearly demonstrating that Shamshi-Adad was for several years Hammurabi's contemporary.

The historical and chronological re-evaluation, which relied largely upon conclusions drawn from several excavations carried out in the thirties in the Khābūr region and in Syria (see section 9, below), resulted in the adoption of new chronological systems for the beginning of the 2nd millennium.

In 1940, Albright, Sidney Smith and Ungnad simultaneously published studies suggesting, each on the basis of his system, that Hammurabi was to be dated to the beginning of the 18th century (see note 5, below). The latter two suggested an exact date — 1792 B.C.E., i.e. the lower astronomical alternative of the Venus observations.

The publication in 1942 of the Assyrian king-list discovered ten years previously, in the excavations at Khorsabad (see note 7, below), brought further suggestions for the date of Hammurabi. Albright changed his views by accepting the chronological data in the king-list, and took a lower astronomical alternative than the Venus observations in the days of Ammizaduqa, thus assigning Shamshi-Adad to ca. 1750 and Hammurabi to 1728 — which is 64 years later than suggested by Smith and Ungnad. Cornelius arrived at the same conclusions, though for different reasons. A different position was taken by Böhl and Weidner, who accepted the data of the Khorsabad king-list at face value; they proposed to date Hammurabi to the end of the 18th and the beginning of the 17th century, thus freeing themselves of dependence upon the Venus observations. Neither does Landsberger's penetrating study published in 1954 use these observations in arriving at his far-reaching suggestions on Hammurabi's date: ca. 1900 B.C.E.

There are other astronomical data which could lead, in the views of their various proponents, to the adoption of one or the other of the systems for establishing the date of Hammurabi: the lunar eclipse in the month of Tammuz which portended the downfall of the last king of the Gutians; another in the month of Sivan in the days of one of the kings of the Third Dynasty of Ur; yet another in the month of Adar which presaged the downfall of Ibbi-Sin, the last king of Ur III.[4] But these cannot contribute substantially toward the solution of the problems at hand, for most of them would fit almost any of the prevailing chronological systems, and thus each system could, in fact, select from the numerous alternatives of complete or partial lunar eclipses any particular date that would suit it.

The various systems put forward since 1940 for establishing the date of Hammurabi and of the First Babylonian Dynasty can be summarized in five basic suggestions:[5]

    a) Landsberger: First Dynasty — ca. 2000–1700 B.C.E. (Hammurabi — ca. 1900–1850).

    b) Thureau-Dangin; Goetze: the "higher chronology," First Dynasty — 1950–1651 B.C.E. (Hammurabi — 1848–1806).

    c) Smith; Ungnad: the "middle chronology," First Dynasty — 1894–1595 B.C.E. (Hammurabi — 1792–1750).

d) Albright; Cornelius: the "lower chronology," First Dynasty — 1830–1531 B.C.E. (Hammurabi — 1728–1686).

e) Böhl; Weidner: First Dynasty — 1800–1507 B.C.E. (Hammurabi — 1704–1662).

2. The Chronological Value of the Assyrian King-list

Any enquiry into the date of Hammurabi of Babylon and his contemporary Shamshi-Adad I of Assyria must rest to a great extent on the Assyrian king-list. However, a complete Assyrian king-list was discovered only in 1932/33 in the excavations at Khorsabad (Dūr-Sharrukin). Before this, scholars had merely a very fragmentary copy of the king-list from the city of Ashur (and named after its editor as "the Nassouhi king-list"), as well as several small, odd fragments from Ashur.[6] A detailed study and a partial transliteration of the Khorsabad king-list were published by A. Poebel in 1942–1943, but the full publication came only in 1954, by I. J. Gelb.[7] A further copy of the Assyrian king-list, from a private American collection (known as the "*SDAS* list") was published together with it. All these lists are copies of one canonical Assyrian king-list compiled at the beginning of the 10th century B.C.E. or perhaps even earlier. This list enumerates the Assyrian kings from the earliest period known to its compiler, and is divided into four parts. Three parts deal with 32 kings whose regnal years are not stated, while the main, fourth part, begins with Erishu(m) son of Ilushuma, the 33rd king who reigned at the beginning of the 2nd millennium B.C.E. The copy from Khorsabad ends with Ashur-nirari V (no. 107), Tiglath-pileser III's predecessor, who died in 746, while *SDAS* ends with Sargon II (721–705).

Before proceeding to discuss the chronological details of the Assyrian king-list, we must first consider the sources and editorial procedures of the ancient compilers.

In Assyria the regnal years were reckoned according to the so-called eponyms (*limmu*) by whose names the years were known. To facilitate administration, lists of eponyms were drawn up for the life of each king. In the course of time, however, there was apparently felt a need to summarize the *limmu*-lists of several kings. Since it was an established usage, at least from the 11th century on, for a king to assume the office of a *limmu* in the first year (and at a later period, in the second year) of his reign, the number of years between the eponymous years of the successive kings should indicate ideally the length of their reigns.[8] This method does not differ basically from that of counting according to the "name of the year," a system employed in the Sumerian cities by the kings of Akkad,

Isin, Larsa and, later, in Babylon during the First Dynasty. According to this latter method, each regnal year was named after a specific event; already in a king's lifetime the years were arranged and, after his death, they were summarized and recorded as "regnal years" in the king-lists. Similarly, in Assyria, in the extant lists of eponyms — from the 11th century onward — the summaries of the eponyms between the *limmu*-year of a king and that of his successor indicate, in fact, the length of reign.

The method of chronological reckoning based on the number of eponyms presupposes a stable government in the capital and continuity of tradition. It may, however, be assumed that in times of crisis, when government was slack, or deficient, the continuity of the chronological tradition was also affected, resulting in chronological gaps.

Another important source from which the compilers of the Assyrian king-list gathered material were the historical chronicles.[9] Though so far the earliest extant fragments of these chronicles are from the 14th century B.C.E.,[10] there are sufficient grounds to assume that they were kept already in the time of Shamshi-Adad I, and that the compiler of the Assyrian king-list excerpted his data from them on the exact date (i.e. the name of the *limmu*-year) for the accession of Shamshi-Adad I: "Shamshi-Adad son of Ila-kabkabi went to Karduniash [= Babylon] at the time of Naram-Sin. In the eponymy of Ibnī-Adad, Shamshi-Adad came up from Karduniash, Ekallāte he seized and three years in Ekallāte he resided. In the eponymy of Ātamar-Ishtar, Shamshi-Adad came up from Ekallāte, Erishu son of Naram-Sin he deposed from the throne, the throne he seized and 33 years he reigned."[11]

These chronicles also gave the compilers of the Assyrian king-list their information on both the usurpers and the legitimate kings who reigned in times of political turbulence and who had never served as eponyms. In one case the chronicles even record the reign of one month only, for a king named Ashur-shaduni (no. 64).[12]

The events related in the chronicles were dated according to the respective eponyms.[13] It seems that at the end of the reign of each Assyrian king the chronicler would state its exact duration, as well as that of the reign of the Babylonian contemporary.[14] In addition, it should be noted that not only the compilers of the king-lists but also those who composed the chronologically arranged historical inscriptions of several Assyrian kings (namely Enlil-nirari and his brother Arik-den-ili — 14th century, and Tiglath-pileser I and his son Ashur-bel-kala — 11th century) drew their information, sometimes verbatim, from the chronicles.[15]

Returning to the chronological data of the Assyrian king-list, if it were certain that not a single name had been omitted, the Assyrian king-list could well be the mainstay of Assyrian chronology from Shamshi-Adad I to the latest Assyrian kings. But there are difficulties arising from the source itself. In all the extant copies, the regnal years of two 15th century kings, Ashur-rabi and Ashur-nadin-ahhe (nos. 65–66), are broken off, while the reigns of eight other rulers are indicated by the obscure sentence "*ṭuppišu šarrūta ipuš*": "he ruled in accordance with his *ṭuppu*." Effective chronological use of this source is dependent on the explanation of the latter term and on the restoration of the defective portion. Various suggestions have been made to restore the missing years of kings nos. 65–66. These range from less than one to as much as 40 years, and include an intermediate suggestion of 22 years which assumed an average of 11 years for each Assyrian king in the period under discussion.

The meaning of the obscure expression *ṭuppišu šarrūta ipuš* is a much more difficult matter; as part of a complete sentence, it denotes the regnal years of two 12th century rulers (nos. 84–85) and six earlier ones, all of them usurpers (nos. 42–47) and successors of Ishme-Dagan the son of Shamshi-Adad I. This expression, which usually occurs in various combinations in administrative documents, most probably refers to a brief span of time, the precise duration of which was unknown to the ancient compiler.[16]

While rulers nos. 84–85 apparently reigned for an extremely short period, their reigns therefore having been included in that of their predecessor Ashurdan I (no. 83 [see B 2, below]), the length of the six usurpers' rule cannot be ascertained. In any event, it is quite impossible to assume (as Poebel does) that the accession and deposition of all these kings took place within a year. The upheavals following the death of Ishme-Dagan, the son of Shamshi-Adad I, apparently lasted many years. And indeed, it is not surprising that the main chronological gap in the Assyrian king-list is in the period of Ishme-Dagan's successors. A fragment of a king-list from Ashur (KAV 14) enumerates three names after that of Ishme-Dagan: Mut-Ashkur the son of Ishme-Dagan; Rimusha his son; and Asinu, apparently the son of Rimusha — all of whom are entirely missing from the canonical king-list. (To complicate matters, this fragmentary list,[17] in turn, omits the names of twelve other rulers included in the Khorsabad and parallel versions.) Another ruler omitted from the king-list is Puzur-Sin,[18] who deposed Asinu, the last descendant of Ishme-Dagan.

Hence, the chronology of the Assyrian kings might be established from the 15th century onward, while the dating of the rulers before this period depends on the restoration of the broken-off regnal years of kings nos. 65–66, and on estimating the gap in the historical tradition under the successors of Shamshi-Adad I.

To use mathematical terms, if the regnal years of the two kings Ashur-rabi and Ashur-nadin-ahhe are represented by x; the length of the six preceding kings' rule (referred to as *ṭuppišu*) by y; and the gap in the historical tradition for the period after Ishme-Dagan by z; then the date of the latter's father, Shamshi-Adad I, is 1726 (= the sum of the successive regnal years in the king-list) $+ x + y + z$. On the assumption that Hammurabi ascended the throne in Shamshi-Adad's 23rd year, and that he reigned 11 years during the latter's lifetime, Hammurabi should be dated to $1726 + x + y + z - 23$.

The length of x should seemingly be put at about 40 years, at least.[19] This estimate of the gap is based on the fact that the kings of the two generations before and the two generations after Ashur-rabi and Ashur-nadin-ahhe reigned for a comparatively short time. The length of y and z total possibly several dozen years, for the upheavals after the days of Ishme-Dagan I apparently continued for some time, during which ten kings ruled, in either one or several centers. According to the middle and higher chronologies, $y + z$ totals 50 and 110 years, respectively. A gap of 110 years, however, appears to be too long a period, although not impossible. The assumption of a 50-year gap seems preferable at present.

We now turn to the other sources which can shed light on the date of Shamshi-Adad I and Hammurabi. These consist mainly of chronological data from the inscriptions of Assyrian and Babylonian kings on their predecessors, as well as Babylonian king-lists.

3. STATEMENTS OF "TIME-SPANS" BY ASSYRIAN KINGS ON THEIR PREDECESSORS

These data, contained in royal Assyrian building inscriptions commemorating the renovation of temples, give the time that had elapsed since the erection or repair of the sanctuary by an earlier Assyrian king. Several such chronological statements have been found.

a) The statement of Shalmaneser I (1273–1244), the earliest of this type, is associated with the repair, at the beginning of his reign, of the temple of Ashur.[20] This inscription states that 159 years had passed between the repair of the temple by Erishu(m), King of Assyria, and that by Shamshi-Adad I, and another 580 years since then (i.e. its repair by Shalmaneser I). It does not state whether Shamshi-Adad's reign (33 years) is included in the 580 years, but if so, then, according to this tradition, he ascended the throne in 1853 and ruled until 1820. The former date is, however, somewhat too low for the proponents of the higher chronology, which would date Shamshi-Adad's last year to 1837 (= Hammurabi's 11th year [see 7 b, below, and note 37]); on the other hand, it is too high for the adherents to the middle chronology. If Shamshi-Adad's 33 years are not included in the 580 years, then he should be dated to 1820 (i.e. 1273 + 580−33), which is very close to the date assigned to him in the middle chronology: 1815 B.C.E.

b) The statement of Tukulti-Ninurta I (1243–1207), the son of Shalmaneser I. He states in his building inscriptions that 720 years intervened between himself and Ilushuma the father of Erishu(m) I.[21] Ilushuma's reign is thus to be assigned to 1963. This does not agree with Shalmaneser's data, according to which Erishu(m) the son of Ilushuma reigned 159 + 580 years before him, that is, in 2012. These 720 years have apparently to be taken as a round figure, the product of 12 × 60, and hence as a round and simplified cycle of years — and not to be used in any chronological calculations.

c) The statement of Tiglath-pileser I (1115–1077). In the first edition of his annals (= the Ashur Prism), dating from his 6th regnal year, it is stated that the temple of Anu and Adad, built by Shamshi-Adad I, had fallen into decay in the course of 641 years.[22] Ashurdan I (1179–1134) started its restoration but did not finish; 60 years later Tiglath-pileser again began repairs — at the very beginning of his reign. By his 6th year the task was accomplished.

Now, if the 641 years are considered as an exact number referring to the period between Shamshi-Adad's accession and that of Ashurdan I, and the 60 years as a round figure — to be emended to 64 (= the span of time between Ashurdan and Tiglath-pileser according to the Assyrian king-list) — then, the date arrived at for Shamshi-Adad will be 1820 (= 1115 + 641 + 64). Surprisingly enough, the year 1820 is exactly that arrived at on the basis of the evidence of Shalmaneser I (see 3 a, above). This coincidence, if not merely fortuitous, may indicate that there was, in the Middle Assyrian Period, a fixed tradition concerning the date of Shamshi-Adad I.[23]

On the other hand, it should be remembered that the proponents of the lower chronology consider the 641 years as referring to the period between Shamshi-Adad's accession and Tiglath-pileser's 6th year (= 1109, when the Anu-Adad temple was completed). The 60 years between Ashurdan I and Tiglath-pileser are included — for the sake of that calculation — in the 641 years, and the date arrived at for Shamshi-Adad I would then be 1750.

d) According to the statement of Esarhaddon (680–669), which is more detailed than the earlier ones, 126 years separated the renovation of the temple of Ashur (in the city of Ashur) by Erishu(m) I from that by Shamshi-Adad, a further 434 years had elapsed until its restoration under Shalmaneser I, and another 580 years (or 586 in a parallel version) until it was restored by Esarhaddon.[24]

The first part of this chronological statement involves no difficulty, as it is quite apparent that the 126 years between Shamshi-Adad and Erishu(m) do not include the former's 33 regnal years, which are, however, included in Shalmaneser's statement on the same interval of time (159 years). The difficulty lies in the latter part of Esarhaddon's statement, concerning the length of time between Shamshi-Adad and Shalmaneser I: 434 years, which represent too short a period even for the proponents of the lower chronology. Even if one accepts the assumption that 434 is a mistake for 494, it is far from clear how Esarhaddon's scribes arrived at this calculation and what their source for it was.[25]

4. THE CHRONOLOGICAL SIGNIFICANCE OF THE BABYLONIAN KING-LISTS

A Babylonian king-list enumerating the regnal years of the kings of Babylonia, starting with the First Dynasty, is extant only in a late, fragmentary copy from the Persian Period, known as the "Babylonian King-list A". The Babylonian king-list is incomplete but can be partially restored on the basis of two other king-lists: list B, which gives the names of the kings of the First and Second Dynasties, and list C, published by Poebel in 1955, which preserves the names of the kings of the Fourth Dynasty (= the Second Dynasty of Isin).[26] According to King-list A, the Second Dynasty (called the "Dynasty of the Sea-Land") ruled for 368 years and the Third (the Kassite) Dynasty for 576 years and 9 months. It is generally agreed that the kings of the Second Dynasty, who reigned on the shores of the Persian Gulf ("the Sea-Land") rather than in the city of Babylon, were in part contemporaneous with the last kings of the First Dynasty (from Samsuiluna's 8th year) and in part with the early Kassite rulers (until the time of Agum III). Therefore, the 368 regnal years of the Second Dynasty — which figure is generally regarded as exaggerated — are of no value to the present chronological discussion. More problematic are the 576 regnal years of the 36 kings of the Kassite Dynasty who gained control of the city of Babylon after the First Dynasty. This number of years, often

TABLE I

BABYLONIA ca. 1900–1600 B.C.E.

King no.	First Dynasty			Third (Kassite) Dynasty	Second (Sea-Land) Dynasty	Eshnunna
1	Sumuabum	(14 years)	: 1894			
2	Sumulael	(36 years)	: 1880			
3	Sabium	(14 years)	: 1844			
4	Apil-Sin	(19 years)	: 1830			
5	Sin-muballit	(20 years)	: 1812			Dadusha
6	Hammurabi	(43 years)	: 1792			Ibalpiel ca. 1785
7	Samsuiluna	(38 years)	: 1749	1 Gandash	1 Ili-man	Şilli-Sin
8	Abi-eshuh	(28 years)	: 1711	2 Agum I	(or Ilima-	
9	Ammiditana	(37 years)	: 1683		ilum) 1742	
10	Ammizaduqa	(21 years)	: 1646			
11	Samsuditana	(31 years)	: 1625		6 Gulkishar 1590	
				9 Agum II 1590		

TABLE II

ASSYRIA AND MARI ca. 1900–1700 B.C.E.

Assyria		Mari	
Erishu(m) I	ca. 1940		
Ikunum			
Sargon I			
Puzur-Ashur			
Naram-Sin		Yaggid-lim	
Erishu(m) II		Yahdun-lim	
Shamshi-Adad	(33 years) : 1813		
Ishme-Dagan	(40 years) : 1780	Yasmah-Adad (Son of Shamshi-Adad of Assyria)	
Mut-Ashkur		Zimri-lim	ca. 1795
Rimusha	1740–1690	(Son of Yahdun-lim)	
Asinu			
Puzur-Sin			
Adasi	ca. 1690		
Belu-bani	(10 years)		

considered to be the product of round, artificial figures, was written in the following manner: $9 \times 60 + 36$ years and 9 months. Its peculiar character was emphasised especially since it was preceded by another "typological" number: 36 kings (actually, in the extant copy of King-list A, the names of only 22 kings are partially or fully preserved. The others are restored from the synchronistic king-list from Ashur and from chronicles.) Since no data have been preserved on the regnal years of each of the Kassite kings, it is impossible to establish the reliability of the total of 576 years. Some scholars have, indeed, suggested that 60 years (one *šušu*) be deducted from 576 years on the assumption that the compiler of the king-list erred and wrote 9 *šušu* + 36 years instead of 8 *šušu* + 36 years, the mistake stemming from the harmonious numbers 9 and 36, which recur in the summary of the dynasty.[27] A closer perusal of the number of generations of the Kassite kings, and their contemporaries, shows that the dynasty's 36 kings apparently represent about 22 generations; at an average of 25 years per generation, the period covered by the dynasty would be approximately 550 years. For the time being, there is no real proof requiring that the total of 576 years be reduced. The average of 16 regnal years for each Kassite king, which derived from this very tradition, though also somewhat high, is not impossible.[28]

5. The Kassite Dynasty

The date of the Kassite invasion of Babylonia, and of the founding of the Third Dynasty, is a decisive factor in the quest for the date of Hammurabi. Though the dating of the beginning of the Kassite Dynasty is still a matter of discussion, its end can be dated with a high degree of certainty: it came to a close in 1159 B.C.E. (see Table I and Table VI). If, indeed, the total of 576 years as given in King-list A is followed, then Gandash, the first Kassite king, would have come to the throne in 1735 B.C.E. ($=1159+576$), and on the assumption that he immediately followed Samsuditana, the last ruler of the First Dynasty, Hammurabi is to be dated to 1933 — and this is too high even for the highest chronological system.

A basic and so far unsolved problem is whether Gandash began his rule in the city of Babylon or somewhere else in Babylonia, with the possibility that the early Kassite rulers reigned concurrently with the First Dynasty. Indirect support for the beginning of the "Kassite era" in 1735 B.C.E. (which is the 15th year of Samsuiluna according to the middle chronology) might be seen in the fact that in Samsuiluna's 8th year the Babylonians for the first time in their history encountered the Kassite hordes. Details of this war are unknown, but the Babylonians apparently suffered a setback; this most probably, led to the revolt of the south and the establishment of the "Second ["Sea-Land"] Dynasty" in lower Mesopotamia. The enigma here is, where did the Kassites settle after their invasion of Babylonia (other invasions occurred later, at the start of the reign of Abi-eshuh, the son of Samsuiluna). It is generally assumed that they settled somewhere along the middle Euphrates, their kings ruling from there. Indeed, this supposition finds support in documents found at Terqa (Tell 'Ashara), the capital of the kingdom of Hana on the middle Euphrates,[29] which mention various local rulers of Hana, including Yaggid-lim, Yahdun-lim and Zimri-lim, kings of Mari (see below, 7a), as well as Ishar-lim, Hammurapih and Kashtiliash (the latter — a typical Kassite name — is either homonymous or simply identical with one of the early Kassite dynasts).

The final question is that of the beginning of the actual Kassite rule in Babylon proper. According to the middle chronology, this occurred in the 6th generation of the Kassite kings, in the time of Agum II, a younger contemporary of Samsuditana, the last king of the First Dynasty, at the end of the 16th century. Samsuditana's death and the end of the First Dynasty fit in with events described in the Hittite and Babylonian traditions, according to which the Hittite king Mursilis set out against Babylon (see 8 a, below), plundered the city and seized the statue of Marduk, taking it as booty. This predatory raid, which marks the end of the First Babylonian Dynasty, as well as the end of the "Old Babylonian Period", paved the way for the Kassite domination; indeed, it has been suggested that the Kassites were allied to the Hittites (since the latter had to cross the region of the River Khābūr and the Land of Hana in order to reach Babylon). A possible reference to some sort of relations between the Kassite king and the Hittites is found in an inscription of Agum II (extant only in a late copy) stating that Agum restores to Babylon "from the distant Land of Ḥani" (apparently a late and corrupt name for the Land of the Hittites) the statues of Marduk and his consort.[30] Indeed, according to a Babylonian epic text (also in a late copy), Marduk dwelt 24 years[31] in the land of the Hittites.[31] Hence, Agum II seems, in fact, to be the first Kassite king to have reigned in the city of Babylon after the fall of the First Babylonian Dynasty.[32]

6. STATEMENTS OF TIME-SPANS BY BABYLONIAN KINGS ON THEIR PREDECESSORS

Like their Assyrian counterparts, the Babylonian kings occasionally mentioned in their building inscriptions the time which had elapsed between their early predecessors and themselves. Such statements do not, however, give precise chronological evidence, and are therefore of less value than similar Assyrian data; nor can any chronological system be built on them. The earliest among the statements was found on a boundary stone from the 4th year of Enlil-nadin-apli of the Fourth Babylonian Dynasty (see Table VII), stating that 696 years elapsed between him and Gulkishar, a Babylonian king of the Second Dynasty and a contemporary of Samsuditana, the last king of the First Dynasty.[33] Hence, the First Babylonian Dynasty came to a close about 1800, and accordingly Hammurabi reigned in ca. 2000 B.C.E. Obviously "696 years" must not be taken literally, but rather as a rounded figure: 700 years (= 696 years + the 4 first regnal years of Enlil-nadin-apli). It is possible that the 700 years were calculated and rounded off on the basis of the data in the Babylonian king-list, on the assumption that the Kassite Dynasty was not contemporaneous with, but succeeded the Second Dynasty.

Also chronologically valueless are the statements in the inscriptions of Nabonidus (555–539 B.C.E.) that Hammurabi preceded by 700 years Burnaburiash the 14th century Kassite king, i.e., that he reigned in the 21st century. This tradition on the part of Nabonidus was arrived at by adding up the totals of the successive Babylonian dynasties. Accordingly, 1500 years intervened between Nabonidus and Rim-Sin King of Larsa (an older contemporary of Hammurabi), and 3200 years between Nabonidus and Naram-Sin of Akkad (23rd century B.C.E.).[34]

7. THE KINGS OF MARI, ESHNUNNA AND YAMHAD

Detailed data from the time of Hammurabi are found in the records of kings of Mari (on the upper Euphrates), of Eshnunna (Tell Asmar on the Diyālā River, north of Babylon) and of Yamhad (the capital of which was Aleppo in North Syria). Most of this material dates from the time of Zimri-lim, who regained the throne of Mari from Ishme-Dagan, the son of Shamshi-Adad I.

a) *Mari*. The Mari Letters mention Yahdun-lim, Zimri-lim's father and a contemporary of Shamshi-Adad of Assyria, who reached the shores of the Mediterranean in his campaigns, and Yaggid-lim, his grandfather, who had made a treaty with Ila-kabkabi, Shamshi-Adad's father.[35] These documents show that Zimri-lim ascended to the throne shortly after the death of Shamshi-Adad, having deposed Yasmah-Adad, the son of Shamshi-Adad and ruler of Mari. Zimri-lim's reign appears to have ended upon the conquest of Mari in Hammurabi's 32nd year, at which time its fortifications were destroyed. Names are known for 32 years in Zimri-lim's reign, among them 6 (at least) being alternative year-names, so that Zimri-lim appears to have reigned only 26 years.[36] There is no way, however, in which these can be made to fit the period between the liberation of Mari from Assyrian rule after Hammurabi's 11th year (which was also the year of Shamshi-Adad's death) and his 32nd year. If, indeed, Zimri-lim is assigned a reign of 26 years, one of the following assumptions must be made: (1) that in the early part of his reign (from Hammurabi's 6th year), Zimri-lim ruled and had date-formulae of his own somewhere outside Mari; (2) that for several years, he continued to reign in Mari after its conquest by Hammurabi — though probably not in his royal palace — and was autonomous enough to employ his own date-formulae. In the present state of our knowledge, there is no clear-cut solution for this chronological "riddle".[37]

b) *Eshnunna*. The kings of Eshnunna, contemporaries of Shamshi-Adad and Hammurabi (namely, Dadusha, Ibalpiel his son, and Ṣilli-Sin), are known from the Mari Letters, and from documents from Eshnunna itself, from Ishchali and from nearby Tell Harmal. The list of "year names" of the kings of Eshnunna, discovered at Tell Harmal,[38] mentions several events in the days of Dadusha and Ibalpiel which would fit into the history of Assyria and Babylonia, and thus serve as synchronizing factors. These are Shamshi-Adad's death in the 5th year of Ibalpiel's reign, and the defeat of the armies of Assyria in his 10th year. On the assumption that Shamshi-Adad died in Hammurabi's 11th year, one year after the date of the "Oath of Sippar" (see note 3), Shamshi-Adad's dynastic rule in Mari would have ended 5 years later; that is, in Hammurabi's 16th year. This would, then, be the latest possible date for Zimri-lim's return to Mari (see above, a, end).[39]

c) *Yamhad* (*Ḥalab/Aleppo*). The Mari Letters mention the names of Yarim-lim and a certain Hammurabi, kings of Yamhad, contemporaries of Zimri-lim and Hammurabi of Babylon. However, several homonymous kings of Yamhad are mentioned in tablets of the Old Babylonian Period from stratum VII at Alalakh (Tell Atchana), in the region of Aleppo and subject to it.[40] Tablets from the same archives frequently mention the rulers of Alalakh: Yarim-lim, a Yamhadite prince, who established the local dynasty of kings at Alalakh, his son Ammitaqum who reigned for about 40–50 years, and the latter's sons Irkabtum and Hammurabi.[41] As against the three generations of rulers at Alalakh, the contemporary kings of Aleppo — Abba-El, Yarim-lim II, Niqmepa, Irkabtum and Yarim-lim III — represent five (or at least four) generations. Although there is as yet no general agreement on the precise genealogical relationship within each dynasty — since some of the kings and rulers at Aleppo and Alalakh bore identical names — it is nevertheless clear that the kings of Yamhad and the rulers of Alalakh (stratum VII) were not contemporaries of the great kings of the Mari Age, but rather of the kings of the later dynasty of Babylon, from Samsuiluna onwards (one generation before the sack of Babylon by Mursilis I).[42] Thus, the time elapsed between the end of Alalakh VII and the end of the First Dynasty of Babylon cannot have been very long. Evidence for such a dating was found in a Hittite historical composition describing the wars of Hattusilis I in Syria, which mentions Zukrashi, the general of the king of Aleppo (see below, 8). This "general" was apparently identical with the Zukrashi who bears the same military rank and is mentioned in the Alalakh Tablets from the time of Ammitaqum of Alalakh and Yarim-lim III of Aleppo.[43]

Other fragmentary Hittite tablets, possibly belonging to the same composition,[44] refer to a war of Hattusilis I against Yarim-lim (III), Hammurapi II his son — kings of Aleppo — and a certain [Ir]-kabtum, whose association with the others is not clear. Most probably this war, or at least this phase of it, took place after the destruction of Alalakh.[45] These synchronisms between the Hittite king and the rulers of Aleppo fit in well with the middle chronology. Accordingly, the end of Alalakh VII would be assigned to the last quarter of the 17th century, i.e. to the days of Hattusilis I, who destroyed Alalakh in the generation before the conquest of Babylon by his grandson, Mursilis I.

8. The Evidence from Hittite Chronology

As pointed out in the preceding section, the dating of the First Dynasty of Babylon is closely connected with the date assigned to a particular major event in early Hittite history (hereforth "event *a*"): the invasion, conquest and plunder of Babylon by Mursilis I, toward the end of Samsuditana's reign (the last king of the First Dynasty of Babylon).[46] With the death of Telepinus, a late successor of Mursilis (see Table VIII below), began the so-called "Middle Hittite Kingdom", which lasted till the accession of Shuppiluliuma — the founder of the empire (ca. 1385; see below, B 3 b). This period — in essence a "dark age" — is sparsely documented, and the

TABLE III

YAMHAD (ḤALAB/ALEPPO), ALALAKH AND HATTI ca. 1800–1600 B. C. E.

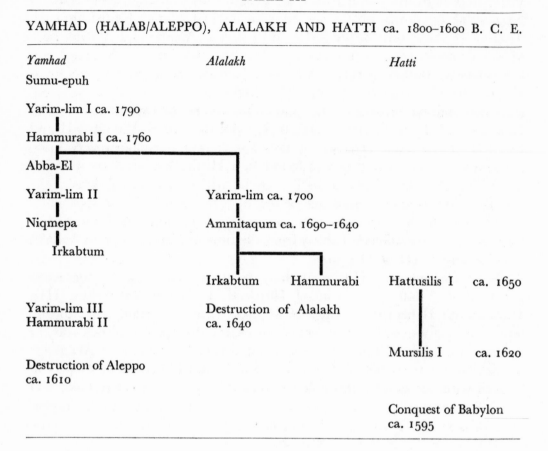

Yamhad	*Alalakh*	*Hatti*
Sumu-epuh		
Yarim-lim I ca. 1790		
Hammurabi I ca. 1760		
Abba-El		
Yarim-lim II	Yarim-lim ca. 1700	
Niqmepa	Ammitaqum ca. 1690–1640	
Irkabtum		
	Irkabtum Hammurabi	Hattusilis I ca. 1650
Yarim-lim III	Destruction of Alalakh	
Hammurabi II	ca. 1640	
		Mursilis I ca. 1620
Destruction of Aleppo		
ca. 1610		
		Conquest of Babylon
		ca. 1595

main source for relative chronology are the so-called "sacrificial or offering lists": documents for cultic use, mostly fragmentary, listing the offering of sacrifices and libations to the statues of deceased kings, queens and other members of the royal house.[47]

A single event of chronological significance within that period ("event *b*") is the capture and destruction of Aleppo by Tudhaliya ("II"), a few generations before Shuppiluliuma, founder of the Hittite empire (see below, B 3 a). It is widely accepted that event *b* took place some years after the conclusion of the Syrian expeditions of Thut-mose III and Amen-hotep II (i.e. after Amen-hotep's 9th year) and a considerable time after the death of Saushshatar, King of Mitanni (see B 3 b, below). In terms of Egyptian chronology, this can be dated to approximately 1430 (± 10 years) (for the higher alternative for Thut-mose III, see below, B 1 b). The problem then, is what was the length of time (in terms of generations of kings and queens known from the offering lists) between events *a* and *b*. Goetze, who was the first scholar to introduce the Hittite evidence as a decisive factor in determining the date of Hammurabi — suggested that there were nine or ten kings between events *a* and *b*, representing, together with their respective consorts, at least five or possibly seven generations.[48] Following Goetze, and taking 25 years as an average generation, it would seem that about 175 years separated the two events. If, indeed, *b* is dated to 1430 ± 10, then *a* (= the conquest of Babylon by Mursilis I) should be dated to approximately 1605 ± 10 — which is very close to 1595, its date according to the "middle chronology."[49]

9. ARCHEOLOGICAL AND HISTORICAL DATA

a) Archeological data from the excavations at Chagar Bazar and Tell Brak (in the district of the Khābūr River in Mesopotamia) have shed some light on the period of Hammurabi. Stratum I at Chagar Bazar comprises four building-periods, many additions and repairs, representing no less than 300 years. Since the end of this stratum was dated by the appearance of "Nuzi ware" to the first half of the 15th century, M.E.L. Mallowan considered it to have begun at the latest in 1750, and perhaps even earlier. Since tablets from the time of Shamshi-Adad I were found in the early phases of this stratum, the excavational results tally with the middle chronology.[50]

b) It has been suggested[51] that additional support for the middle chronology is likely to be forthcoming from the date of the cylinder seals found in stratum VII at Alalakh, and which fit in mainly in the 18th century.[52]

c) An Old Babylonian cylinder seal, found in Tholos B at Platanos in Mesara, Crete, has been the focal point in the chronological controversy, and it was for a time thought that this evidence weighed in favor of the middle chronology. However, no firm conclusions can apparently be drawn from this find, since there is no agreement on the date of the Minoan pottery from the same tomb.[53]

d) Similarly, no precise chronological conclusions can be drawn from the discovery of four Mesopotamian cylinder seals from the end of the 3rd and the beginning of the 2nd millennium, which were found at Tod in Egypt, in a treasure dating from the time of Amen-em-het I. This discovery fits in with the middle (and according to Albright also with the lower) chronology, while Landsberger adduced proof from it for the higher chronology.[54]

e) Certain difficulty in assigning the date of Hammurabi to 1792–1750 arises from the realm of international relations in the Ancient East: Babylonian documents, especially the Mari Letters from the time of Hammurabi, make no mention of Egypt — despite the fact than in those days, at the end of the Twelfth and the beginning of the Thirteenth Dynasties, Egypt was still a very influential political and economic power. This absence of Egypt in the Mari Letters is all the more surprising since they do mention several cities in the west and south-west, such as Ugarit, Byblos, Hazor and even distant Crete.[55] This fact, then — which actually lends itself to several explanations — cannot serve as a main argument for the lower chronology, which would place the Mari Age in the days of Egypt's decline, that is, at the end of the Thirteenth Dynasty and the beginning of Hyksos rule. The question of the nature of Egyptian rule in Canaan and Syria during the Twelfth and Thirteenth Dynasties has not yet found a satisfactory definition.[56]

To sum up: There are as yet no data which could be considered as decisive proof in favor of any of the current chronological systems for the Old Babylonian Period; however, on the basis of the present evidence, the middle chronology appears to be somewhat preferable, assigning Hammurabi, as it does, to 1792–1750 (and Shamshi-Adad I to 1813–1781), and the end of the First Dynasty of Babylon to 1595. But it is not impossible that additional discoveries concerning the duration of the Kassite Dynasty and the beginning of the Kassite rule in Babylon, or the duration of the "Middle Hittite Kingdom," may introduce changes in the accepted dates.

10. The Chronology of the Twelfth Dynasty of Egypt

Egyptian chronology is not reconstructed solely on the basis of king-lists on the pattern of Assyrian and Babylonian chronology. The Turin Papyrus — the most complete of the lists which enumerate the dynasties of the Egyptian kings, from the Old Kingdom to the New — is so fragmentary as to be of little use.[57] The number of a king's regnal years is often fixed according to the highest number of years contained in the existing documents from his reign. The complete list of Egyptian kings in the works of Manetho, excerpts of which have been preserved by Josephus, or transmitted indirectly by early Christian chronographers, especially Africanus and Eusebius, presents numerous difficulties, for in the course of transmission many names have become unrecognizably corrupted, the sequence of kings distorted and the data of the regnal years confused.[58] The necessity of relying on Manetho is due to the fact that for certain periods in Egyptian history there are no other extant chronological data.

It is for this reason that various astronomical data from the Twelfth, Eighteenth and Nineteenth Dynasties are of great significance; these deal with the exact time of the appearance of the new moon and the heliacal rising of Sothis (Sirius) — a phenomenon which played an important role in the origin and structure of the Egyptian civil calendar. The special character of this calendar, and its dependence on astronomical factors, enable a calculation of the time of the various observations, thus aiding to establish the chronology of the periods under discussion.

The chronology of the Twelfth Dynasty is fixed with the aid of astronomical data contained in the al-Lāhūn Papyrus; this records a heliacal rising of Sothis on the 16th day of the 8th month in the 7th year of an Egyptian king whose name is not mentioned in the source, but who can safely be identified with Sen-Usert III. The date according to a recent calculation of R. Parker is 1870 ± 6, and in conjunction with some lunar dates (i.e. observations of the appearances of the new moon, dating from the same dynasty) it is fixed more precisely to the year 1872. The Turin Papyrus has recorded information on the duration of this dynasty: 213 years, which should be emended to 223 years. Consequently, the Twelfth Dynasty is dated by Parker to 1991–1786 B.C.E. (and see Table IV).[59]

According to the Turin Papyrus, the following, Thirteenth Dynasty comprised more than 50 kings. Of these, approximately the last 25 were contemporary with the Asiatic princes who were ruling in the Egyptian Delta after 1720/10 B.C.E. One of the kings of the Thirteenth Dynasty, Nefer-hotep I (ca. 1740–1730) still held hegemony of Byblos in the days of '*ntn* (Entin), prince of Byblos, who is identified by Albright with Yantin-hammu of Byblos, mentioned in the Mari Letters.[60]

11. THE HYKSOS

The so-called "400 Year Stele" from the days of Ramses II, discovered at Tanis in 1863, and rediscovered in 1932 by P. Montet, records a celebration commemorating the 400th anniversary of the introduction of the cult of the god Seth (Sutekh), the chief deity of the Hyksos, in the city of Avaris.[61] This has generally been taken as chronological evidence for the commencement of Hyksos rule in the Delta. The exact date of the celebration is not specified, though most probably it took place during the later years of Hor-em-heb, the last king of the Eighteenth Dynasty (ca. 1325/20, according to the "higher" dates for the Eighteenth Dynasty; see C 1, below). Hence the establishment of the cult of Seth in Avaris, and with it the commencement of Hyksos rule in the Delta, can be dated to about 1725–1720 B.C.E. However, it may reasonably be argued that the figure 400 is rounded and possibly exaggerated, and should not be regarded as chronological evidence in reckoning the beginning of Hyksos rule in Egypt, for which other, indirect data do exist.

According to some direct and indirect evidence, Ka-mose, the last prince of the Seventeenth Dynasty, fought against Apophis, one of the last kings of the Hyksos Dynasty (Manetho's "Fifteenth Dynasty") and Ah-mose, Ka-mose's successor, captured Avaris, in approximately the 10th year of his reign.[62] If the latter event is dated to ca. 1560 (see C 1, below), then the beginning of the "Fifteenth Dynasty" would date to ca. 1670, on the basis of data in the Turin Papyrus, which assigns 108 regnal years to this dynasty.[63] The founder of the dynasty appears to have been Salitis, of whom Manetho relates that he ruled in Memphis in the days of Tutimaios (probably Dudi-mose, one of the last kings of the Thirteenth Dynasty). Khyan, one of the most famous Hyksos kings, belonged to the Fifteenth Dynasty; according to monuments dating from his reign, he ruled over the whole of Egypt, even to the south of Thebes.

The Hyksos rulers whom Manetho designates as the "Sixteenth" Dynasty were actually local rulers contemporaneous with the kings of the Fifteenth Dynasty and possibly their vassals. Data on these rulers are scant, and even their sequence and number are not clear. Samuqen and Anat-her, known only from scarabs bearing their names, were apparently among the early rulers of this "dynasty."

At the beginning of the 16th century, the local princes of Thebes

TABLE IV

EGYPT ca. 2000—1500 B.C.E.

Twelfth Dynasty

(According to R. A. Parker)

Amen-em-het I	1991–1962
Sen-Usert I	1971–1928
Amen-em-het	1929–1895
Sen-Usert II	1897–1879
Sen-Usert III	1878–1843
Amen-em-het III	1842–1797
Amen-em-het IV	1798–1790
Sebek-nefrure	1789–1786

Thirteenth Dynasty

Sehetibre	ca. 1770
Sobk-hotep	ca. 1750
Nefer-hotep	ca. 1740–1730
Dudi-mose	ca. 1675

Seventeenth Dynasty

Ka-mose	ca. 1585

Hyksos Kings

"Fifteenth Dynasty"		*"Sixteenth Dynasty"*
Salitis	ca. 1675	Anat-her
Khyan	ca. 1650	Samuqen
Apophis I	ca. 1620–ca. 1580	

End of Hyksos rule in Egypt   ca. 1560

(= Seventeenth Dynasty), felt strong enough to start driving the Hyksos out of Upper Egypt. Ka-mose, the last king of this dynasty, embarked upon a campaign against the Hyksos which continued for a number of years and culminated in the capture of Avaris by his successor Ah-mose I, the founder of the Eighteenth Dynasty (see B 1 a, below).

B. THE CHRONOLOGIES OF THE 16TH–11TH CENTURIES IN EGYPT, MESOPOTAMIA, ANATOLIA AND SYRIA

1. EGYPT

a) *General*. The chronology of the Eighteenth and Nineteenth Dynasties has previously been determined solely on the grounds of Egyptian data: astronomical evidence and regnal years. In the absence of king-lists for this period, the regnal years are either estimates based on the highest known dates in contemporary documents, or the figures given by Manetho (see above, A 10), which are frequently so corrupt as to be almost useless.[64] The numerous synchronisms between Mesopotamia, Hatti and Egypt in the 15th–13th centuries are also of little use, since Mesopotamian dates themselves are much disputed. It is chiefly due to M.B. Rowton's studies, after the publication of the Assyrian king-list in 1942–43, that the Egyptian chronology of the Eighteenth and Nineteenth Dynasties can be checked and re-evaluated by means of Mesopotamian synchronisms.[65] Since the astronomical data merely suggest possibilities, but offer only one decisive solution, and since the regnal years of several kings are unknown, the Mesopotamian synchronisms (as well as the Hittite) are indeed a major factor in determining Egyptian chronology.

b) *The Eighteenth Dynasty*. The chronology of the Eighteenth Dynasty depends to a large extent on astronomical evidence: the observations of the heliacal rising of the star Sothis (Sirius) in the 9th year of Amen-hotep I (the second king of the dynasty), preserved on the reverse of the Ebers Medical Papyrus. The main problem, however, is that the site of these observations is unknown. L. Borchardt assumed that the Sothic observations in ancient Egypt were made at Heliopolis near Memphis, and thus, with the assistance of Neugebauer, conducted similar observations in 1926/27, fixing the 9th year of Amen-hotep I within the range of 1544–1537 B.C.E.[66] If, however, the Sothic observations were conducted at Thebes, the royal residence during the early years of the Eighteenth Dynasty, then the date must be lowered in accordance with the lower angle of vision (*arcus visionis*), thus falling within the range of 1525–1517 B.C.E.[67] Below are two alternative sets of dates for the early kings of the Eighteenth Dynasty:

King and Regnal Year[68]	Higher System (=Memphitic Sothic dates)	Lower System (=Theban Sothic dates)
(Amen-hotep I's 9th year)	(1537*)	(1518**)
Ah-mose (Manetho: 25 years 4 months)	1570–1547	1552–1527
Amen-hotep I (20 years + 7 months)	1546–1526	1527–1506
Thut-mose I } Thut-mose II }	1525–1504	1506–1490

*According to Hayes (see note 66).   **According to Hornung (see note 67).

Another crucial problem in the chronology of the Eighteenth Dynasty is the date of Thut-mose III, for which there are certain astronomical data: (1) the appearance of the new moon on the 21st day of the 1st month of the 2nd season in the Egyptian civil year. (In 1942 Faulkner suggested that the figure was miscopied and corrected it to the 20th day.[69]); (2) the appearance of the new moon on the 30th day of the 2nd month of the 2nd season; (3) a Sothic date on the 28th day of the 3rd month of the 3rd season in an unknown year of this king.

With the aid of (3), and the two lunar dates, the accession of Thut-mose III to the throne has been fixed — according to Borchardt's calculations, subject to emendations by Edgerton (see note 66, above) — to one of the following dates: (a) May 7, 1515; (b) May 4, 1504; (c) May 1, 1490 B.C.E. The first alternative is too high, since it does not leave enough time for the reigns of Thut-mose I and II (see note 68 above), and goes against the synchronisms between Akh-en-Aton and Ashur-uballit of Assyria (who ascended the throne in 1365; see below, Table VI). The second alternative, though rejected by Parker on astronomical grounds — since it does not fit the second lunar date[70] — appears to be somewhat preferable on historical grounds. The third alternative, that of 1490, was originally preferred by Borchardt and is again widely accepted by scholars, especially those who prefer the lower (Theban) Sothic dates for Amen-hotep I (see note 67).

The chronology of the period between the death of Thut-mose III (= 1450 or 1436) and) that of Hor-em-heb,[71] the end of the Eighteenth Dynasty, is marked by the problem of coregencies. So far, no documents with double dates have been found for the Eighteenth Dynasty, similar to those found for the Twelfth. Hence, the question has arisen whether the periods of coregency — even where proven to have existed — should be taken into account in calculating the chronology here. Below are the possible cases of coregencies of chronological significance:

1. Thut-mose III and Amen-hotep II; a coregency of a minimum of 4 months and a maximum of 4 years has been assumed by various scholars.[72] It would seem, however, that this coregency lasted for somewhat over two years, and that Amen-hotep's regnal years should be reckoned from its inception.

2. Amen-hotep II and Thut-mose IV; a coregency of about two years is assumed by Aldred.[73]

3. Amen-hotep III and Amen-hotep IV (Akh-en-Aton); see below.

4. Akh-en-Aton and Smenkh-ka-Re; the three regnal years of Smenkh-ka-Re were possibly contemporaneous with the three last years of Akh-en-Aton, his father-in-law, but the evidence on this point is not conclusive and some scholars reckon his reign independently.[74]

The most debated of all the coregencies is that of Amen-hotep III and his son, Amen-hotep IV (Akh-en-Aton). Since the excavations at Tell el-Amarna, Akh-en-Aton's capital, and since the discovery of the tomb of Tut-ankh-Amon, a view has crystallized that Amen-hotep III continued to live and rule as king several years into the reign of his son, Amen-hotep IV. The length of the coregency, however, is also debated. A length of 8/9 years has been suggested, though another theory, of 11/12 years, seems to fit the evidence better. In any event, scholars studying the Amarna period are still sharply divided over the matter of the very existence of this coregency.[75]

The evidence adduced for such a coregency is taken from the monuments of the period, which depict Amen-hotep III alongside his son in a manner which can be interpreted as indicating that the father was still alive at the time; other monuments display the cartouches of both kings side-by-side. Prosopographic factors and other indirect evidence from several documents of this period lend weight to this view.

A decisive place in this controversy is held by the Amarna Letters written in Akkadian, most of which date from the reign of Akh-en-Aton. According to the coregency theory, the bulk of this correspondence between Akh-en-Aton and the kings of Mitanni, Hatti, Babylon and Assyria as well as the numerous petty kings in Canaan, should be attributed to a relatively short period, between the 8/9th or the 11/12th year of Akh-en-Aton and his 17th (and last recorded) year.[76] This, on the present evidence, does not seem likely. Some scholars, however, such as Kitchen, have interpreted the pertinent historical synchronisms between the Amarna Letters and the Hittite archives — in accordance with the theory of coregency.[77] The matter is as yet far from being settled, and only a new and thorough investigation into the Amarna correspondence, and new prosopographic and archeological evidence, might shed some light on it, bringing some more definite solution to this extremely complex issue.

The last problem reflecting on the chronology of the Eighteenth Dynasty is the length of the reign of Hor-em-heb, its last king. The highest year attested for him is his 8th year. A "regnal year 27" in a graffito found in the temple of Ay at Thebes has been interpreted as referring either to Hor-em-heb, or to some sort of era beginning with Amen-hotep III's death, or even to Ramses II.[78] Further evidence is provided by the so-called "Mes" date: in a juridical document known as the "Mes Inscription," from the days of Ramses II, mention is made of the 59th year of the reign of Hor-em-heb.[79] The only way to retain this date is to assume, as has been done, that the scribe reckoned the years of Hor-em-heb's reign from the death of Amen-hotep III, as if claiming that Hor-em-heb was the latter's chosen successor.[80]

There is no way of knowing the number of years Hor-em-heb lived after "the year 59". Since he was middle-aged at the time of his accession, it may be assumed that this year was very close to the end of his reign, that is, his last or penultimate year. Accordingly, Hor-em-heb reigned ca. 27 years, i.e. 59 — 34 (the latter figure being the sum of the regnal years of Akh-en-Aton, Smenkh-ka-Re, Tut-ankh-Amon and Ay ($17 + 3 + 10 + 4$ years respectively). Recently, the validity of the "Mes" date has been challenged by J.R. Harris, who suggests a maximum of 12 years for the reign of Hor-em-heb, with a possibility of a minimal reign of 8 years.[81] If Harris' proposal be accepted, the only chronological data linking the death of Amen-hotep III with the accession of Ramses I would have to be abandoned.

Finally, the evidence of historical synchronisms in the Amarna period: It is quite evident that only the "lower chronology" of Thut-mose III admits a coregency of Akh-en-Aton with his father. According to the "higher chronology," the coregency should have begun in 1390 (= Amen-hotep III's 27th year, i.e. a coregency of 12 years) or 1386 (= Amen-hotep III's 31st year, i.e. a coregency of 8 years), and Akh-en-Aton's last year (= his 17th) would have been 1374 or 1370. Both dates contradict the well-known synchronisms between Akh-en-Aton and Ashur-uballit I of Assyria (1364–1329), attested by Amarna Letter no. 15. The synchronism between Akh-en-Aton and Burnaburiash II of Babylon (1380–1342) —

well-attested by several Amarna Letters — fits the higher as well as the lower dates for Thut-mose III.

Of special importance is the synchronism between Burnaburiash and a king of Egypt, believed to be Tut-ankh-Amon (Amarna Letter no. 9). The chronological significance of it is that it agrees only with system II below, that is, the "lower chronology" and no coregency. However, the very identification of the Egyptian king in question (named Niphururia) with Tut-ankh-Amon, though philologically proven, is rather doubtful on historical grounds, more so since there are no other known letters in the Amarna archives addressed to "Niphururia."[82]

To sum up: We have presented above the major issues involved in the dating of the Eighteenth Dynasty. The complex nature of the internal Egyptian evidence, on the one hand, and the paucity of external synchronisms, on the other hand, preclude for the time being a clear-cut chronological solution. And, indeed, no single chronological system for the Eighteenth Dynasty kings has been agreed upon by Egyptologists. Table V gives three alternative, current, systems for this period.

c) *The Nineteenth and Twentieth Dynasties.* The chronology of the Nineteenth Dynasty depends upon the astronomical evidence of the dates of the new moon in Ramses II's 57th regnal year, according to which he ascended the throne either in 1304, 1290 or 1279 B.C.E.[83] The last date is inacceptable since it can neither be coordinated with the dates of the Eighteenth Dynasty nor be fitted into the known Mesopotamian synchronisms. Opinion is divided between the two former alternatives 1304 and 1290, for the accession of Ramses — and 1237 or 1223, for his 67th and last recorded regnal year. Those who follow the "higher" dates for the Eighteenth Dynasty prefer the first, while the adherents to the "lower" dates tend — though not necessarily — toward the second date.[84]

Unfortunately, it is still impossible to establish decisively which of the two dates fits better with the well-documented, historical synchronisms between Egypt, Mesopotamia and Anatolia, from the reign of Ramses II. Of special significance is the chronological evidence inferred from an Akkadian letter of Hattusilis III, King of Hatti, to Kadashman-Enlil II of Babylon. Two mutually opposing inferences have been drawn from the historical circumstances posed by this document:[85] (a) Either Kadashman-Enlil ascended the throne a few years *before* the signing of the treaty between Egypt and Hatti, which event took place in Ramses II's 21st regnal year (1284 ["higher"] or 1270 ["lower"]); since Kadashman-Enlil began to reign in about 1280 B.C.E., the 21st year of Ramses II must be placed sometime after that date, that is, in according with the lower alternative.[86]

TABLE V

EGYPT ca. 1600–1000 B.C.E.

Eighteenth Dynasty	According to Hayes	According to Hornung	According to Aldred
Ah-mose	* 1570–1546	1552–1527	
Amen-hotep I	1546–1526	1527–1506	
Thut-mose I	1525–ca. 1512	1506–1494	
Thut-mose II	ca. 1512–1504	1494–1490	
Thut-mose III	1504–1450	1490–1436	1490–1436
Amen-hotep II	1450–1428	C 1438–1412	C 1444–1412
Thut-mose IV	1425–1417	1412–1402	C 1414–1405
Amen-hotep III	1417–1379	1402–1364	1405–1367
Akh-en-Aton	1379–1362	1364–1347	C 1378–1362
Smenkh-ka-Re	C 1364–1361	C 1351–1348	C 1366–1363
Tut-ankh-Amon	1361–1352	1347–1338	C 1362–1349
Ay	1352–1348	1338–1334	C 1355–1349
Hor-em-heb	1348–1320	1334–1306	1349–1319

Nineteenth Dynasty

Ramses I	ca. 1317
Seti I	ca. 1316
Ramses II	ca. 1304
Mer-ne-Ptah	ca. 1237
Amenmeses ⎫	
Seti II ⎬	ca. 1228–1208
Mer-ne-Ptah-Siptah ⎭	

Twentieth Dynasty

Set-nakht	1207–1206
Ramses III	1206–1175
Ramses XI	1117–1092
Heri-hor	1110–1094

Legend :
C = Coregency

Twenty-First Dynasty	1092–943

* According to new astronomical data brought by J. G. Reed in *JNES* 29 (1970) 1–11, Ah-mose was already reigning in 1579, i.e. at least 9 years earlier than the date suggested by Hayes. Reed's date for Thut-mose III is 1490.

(b) Or Kadashman-Enlil ascended the throne a few years *after* the signing of the treaty. The accession of Ramses II must, then, have preceded that of Kadashman-Enlil by at least 21 years. Hence, the higher alternative for Ramses II is the only one which would fit the circumstances of this synchronism.[87]

Additional synchronisms between Egypt and Western Asia have been provided by an Akkadian letter of Hattusilis III to a king of Assyria, thought to be either Adad-nirari I or his son, Shalmaneser I,[88] and by a Hittite letter of Hattusilis III to Tukulti-Ninurta of Assyria.[89] It has been inferred from these two letters that the accession of Shalmaneser I (ca. 1273) preceded the treaty between Egypt and Hatti in Ramses' 21st year — this in agreement with the lower dates for Ramses.[90] A more detailed analysis, however, proves that the chronological inferences drawn from these and related documents cannot be treated as totally exclusive to any of the proposed chronological schemes. Only fresh data can provide a solution of the complex synchronistic evidence for this period, and offer a satisfactory chronological result.

Additional evidence for the chronology of the Nineteenth Dynasty is found in the so-called "era of Menophres." According to the tradition of Theon of Alexandria, a new era which he called "that according to Menophres" (τὰ ἀπὸ Μενοφρέως) commenced 1605 Egyptian years (= 1604 Julian years) before 284 C.E., the beginning of the "era of Diocletian." Hence, the "era according to Menophres" began in 1320 B.C.E. No pharaoh by the name of Menophres is mentioned in Manetho, and it has been suggested that this name is a corrupt abbreviation of either Seti I's full name or that of Ramses I.[91]

It is generally held that the "era according to Menophres" began with the start of a Sothic cycle in Egypt, i.e. the cycle inaugurated by the heliacal rising of Sothis on the day of the New Year in the Egyptian civil calendar.[92] The last pre-Christian Sothic cycle, which is known to have ended in 139 C.E., began — according to modern calculations — in one of the years between 1321 and 1318, or 1320 and 1317, or — according to another method of calculation — between 1314 and 1311.[93] If Theon's tradition implies that "Menophres" was Ramses I or Seti I, then the first year of either of these two kings should be assigned to one of the above-mentioned dates. As Ramses I reigned about 12 years and 4 months, and Seti about 13–14 years (see below),[94] it follows that only the higher alternative for Ramses II (i.e. 1304–1237) could fit the "era of Menophres."

Though it is possible to establish the exact date of Ramses II (by preferring the higher alternative), the chronology of the beginning and the end of the Nineteenth Dynasty remains uncertain. The date of its beginning depends upon the unknown quantity x, representing the length of time Seti ruled after his 11th known year. If x is 2 years, Seti's accession took place in 1316 and that of Ramses I and the death of Hor-em-heb in 1317, that is, slightly over 60 years after the death of Amen-hotep III, as required by the minimum reckoning of Hor-em-heb's reign, according to the "Mes" date; and see above.

The chronology of the Nineteenth Dynasty from Mer-ne-Ptah on, and that of the Twentieth and Twenty-First Dynasties, are determined by the data of regnal years found in royal inscriptions and in contemporary documents. The highest date for Mer-ne-Ptah's reign according to his inscriptions is the year 8; it is very possible that he died in that or the following year, so that already his 7th year saw the first preparations for the king's funeral ceremonies.[95] It is, therefore, difficult to accept Manetho's statement, quoted by Josephus, that Mer-ne-Ptah ruled 19 years; he seems to have reigned 9 years at the most (1237–1228 B.C.E.).

The last kings of the Nineteenth Dynasty, Amenmeses, Seti II and Mer-ne-Ptah-Siptah (proven to be identical with Ramses-Siptah) — including the reign of Queen Tewesret — reigned for 5, 6, 8/9 years, respectively.[96] A total of 20 years for the reign of these kings is a reasonable estimate. It follows then that the Nineteenth Dynasty ended in ca. 1208 B.C.E. The gap assumed to have intervened between the Nineteenth and Twentieth Dynasties and which, according to some scholars, lasted between 5 and 20 years, simply did not exist.[97] The two year reign of Set-nakht — founder of the Twentieth Dynasty — should then be placed in 1208/7–1206. Set-nakht's successor, Ramses III — the most famous king of the Twentieth Dynasty — ruled, then, from 1206 to 1175;[98] his 8th regnal year — the year of the great war between Egypt and the Sea-Peoples — thus fell in 1199. From contemporary documents it can be deduced that the minimal total of regnal years for the Twentieth Dynasty is about 105.[99] Manetho's total of 135 years — according to Africanus (but 178 according to Eusebius) — appears, on the present evidence, to be too high. A total of 115 years for this dynasty has been postulated by Peet and Černý.[100] If the higher figure is accepted, the dynasty will be dated to 1207–1092. The eight successors of Ramses III, from Ramses IV to Ramses XI, would then be dated to 1175–1092. Ramses XI, the last king of the dynasty, who according to the monuments reigned 27 years, would then be dated to 1119–1092. Accordingly, the seven year "reign" of the high priest Heri-hor — who ruled independently in Thebes during the years 19–25 of Ramses XI's reign and introduced his own era, the "Era of Repeated Births" (mentioned also in the account of Wen-Amon's journey to Byblos) — would be dated to 1110–1094 (with a margin of error of ± 5 years at least).[101]

Information on the kings of the Twenty-First Dynasty is scanter even than on the previous dynasty. The order of the kings, the length of their reigns and the total figure for the entire dynasty depend — almost solely — upon the testimony of Manetho as preserved by Africanus and Eusebius. According to the most recent studies, the total rule of the six (or possibly seven) kings of the Twenty-First Dynasty lasted 151 years (according to Černý), 142 years (according to Gardiner) or 149 years (according to Young),[102] whereas Manetho's (Eusebius') total is 130 years. If, indeed, the total of 149 years is adopted, the death of Psusennes II — its last king — and the accession of Shishak I, the founder of the Twenty-Second Dynasty, would be dated to 943 B.C.E. (again with a margin of error of approximately ± 5 years).

2. ASSYRIAN-BABYLONIAN CHRONOLOGY IN THE 14TH–11TH CENTURIES

a) *Assyria.* For the period under discussion, Assyrian chronology serves as the cornerstone of the absolute chronology for Babylonia, Syria and Anatolia. The Assyrian chronological data are founded on a consecutive king-list (see A2, above) and, from the end of the 11th century, on the lists of eponyms (*limmu*). A solar eclipse in the month of Sivan, in the eponym year of Pur-Sagalē (= the tenth regnal year of Ashurdan III, in the mid-8th century) has long been identified as the eclipse of June 15, 763 B.C.E.[103] This astronomical date is the starting-point in the absolute chronology of Assyria.

There are several slight discrepancies (of one year only) between the various recensions of the Assyrian king-list.[104] Moreover, there is a difference of 10 years with regard to Ninurta-apil-Ekur (no. 82 in the king-list), who lived in the 12th century and reigned 13 years according to the "Nassouhi king-list" from Ashur, but only 3 years according to the list from Khorsabad and the parallel list *SDAS*. A detailed examination of the Assyrian-Babylonian synchronisms in the 14th–12th centuries has, however, shown that the version of 13 years is to be preferred.[105] As for the chronological designation "he reigned for *ṭuppišu*" (see A2, above) in connection with Ninurta-tukulti-Ashur and Muttakil-Nusku, his brother (nos. 84 and 85 in the Assyrian king-list), designating a period of time unknown to the compiler of the king-list — it may be assumed from contemporary documents (showing that Muttakil-Nusku ruled at least 12 months)[106] and from Babylonian synchronisms, that the two brothers reigned no more than 2–3 years, and apparently did not manage to hold a *limmu* office. Their regnal years were, in this case, included within the *"limmu* period" of their father, Ashurdan. On this assumption, the 46 regnal years of Ashurdan are considered to have included the brief rule of his sons. (For the list of the Assyrian kings and their dates, see below, Table VI.)

b) *Babylonia.* The chronology of the Babylonian kings in the 14th–11th centuries is dependent upon the Assyrian chronology and is fixed by both the data contained in the Babylonian king-list and by the numerous synchronisms with Assyria, preserved in the Assyrian and Babylonian chronicles, in the annals of the Assyrian kings and in contemporary treaties and letters.[107]

The Babylonian king-list for this period (= King-list A; cf. note 26) is only partially preserved. In some cases the number of the regnal years is broken off or hardly legible; still, it is almost the only source for the chronology of the 15 last kings of the Kassite Dynasty (from Kurigalzu II on). The data on the 11 kings of the Fourth Dynasty (= the "Second Dynasty of Isin") are preserved in a contemporary document — "King-list C" — published by Poebel in 1958.[108]

Any attempt to determine the dates of the kings of Babylon in the 14th–11th centuries must face the following problems:

(i) The names of the kings from the first half of the 14th century and their respective numbers of regnal years are not preserved in King-list A. However, the dates on economic documents, especially those from Nippur, show that Burnaburiash II — Akh-en-Aton's contemporary — reigned at least 27 years and possibly 28; and Kurigalzu II, his son, apparently for 25 years.[109] The confusion and disorder in Babylonia just prior to Kurigalzu's accession (= the brief reigns of Karahardash [or Karakindash] and Nazi-bugash) lasted apparently about 2 years, at the most.[110]

(ii) There is a discrepancy in the case of Kudur-Enlil II (king no. 26 in the Kassite Dynasty); according to King-list A he reigned 6 years, while his highest recorded year in a contemporary economic document (from Nippur) is his 9th.[111]

(iii) Another discrepancy is in the case of Shagarakti-Shuriash, the 27th Kassite king; according to King-list A, he reigned 13 years, but the existence of his 18th year, which appears on an unpublished economic tablet in the Hilprecht collection at Jena, has recently been reported.[112] However, the version of King-list A (13 years) has to be accepted for the time. The latest year for this king so far known from economic documents is his 12th, and it is very probable that he died in his 13th regnal year.[113]

(iv) A possible case of a chronological lacuna: a Babylonian chronicle ("Chronicle Pinches") records that Tukulti-Ninurta of Assyria, after de-

TABLE VI

ASSYRIA ca. 14th–10th CENTURIES B.C.E.

Ashur-uballit	(36 years) : 1364
Enlil-nirari	(10 years) : 1328
Arik-den-ili	(12 years) : 1318
Adad-nirari I	(33 years) : 1306
Shalmaneser I	(30 years) : 1273
Tukulti-Ninurta I	(37 years) : 1243
Ashur-nadin-apli	(3 years) : 1206
Ashur-nirari	(6 years) : 1203
Enlil-kudur-uṣur	(6 years) : 1197
Ninurta-apil-Ekur	(13 years) : 1192
Ashurdan I ⎱ Ninurta-tukulti-Ashur ⎰	(46 years) : 1179
Muttakil-Nusku	reigned *ṭuppišu*
Ashur-resh-ishi I	(18 years) : 1133
Tiglath-pileser I	(39 years) : 1115
Ashared-apil-Ekur	(2 years) : 1076
Ashur-bel-kala	(18 years) : 1074
Eriba-Adad II	(2 years) : 1056
Shamshi-Adad IV	(4 years) : 1054
Ashur-naṣir-apli	(19 years) : 1050
Shalmaneser II	(12 years) : 1031
Ashur-nirari IV	(6 years) : 1019
Ashur-rabi	(41 years) : 1013
Ashur-resh-ishi II	(5 years) : 972
Tiglath-pileser II	(33 years) : 967
Ashurdan II	(23 years) : 934
Adad-nirari II	(21 years) : 911

The dates refer to each king's first complete year; accession took place a year earlier. The margin of error is ± 2 or 3 years, at most.

feating Kashtiliash III (Kassite king no. 28), ruled over Babylonia for 7 years. The number 7 here might well be a round figure, and these years are not recorded in the Babylonian king-list, probably constituting a gap in the tradition of Babylonian chronology.[114]

(v) Two further lacunae are also possible: the first, a brief Elamite interregnum during the conquest of Babylon by the Elamite king Kidin-hutrash, probably after the reign of Adad-shuma-iddina (Kassite king no. 31);[115] and the second, an Elamite domination of Babylonia for some years after the end of the Kassite Dynasty.[116] Though these two Elamite interregna might have lasted several years, they were possibly included in the regnal years of the Babylonian kings who reigned after Adad-shuma-uṣur (Kassite king no. 32) and Marduk-kabit-ahheshu, the founder of the Fourth Dynasty. The close fabric of the Assyrian-Babylonian synchronisms in the 14th–11th centuries does not admit three interregna in Babylon but rather only one — that after the defeat of Kashtiliash by Tukulti-Ninurta I.

There is no astronomically fixed date in Babylonian chronology for the 14th–11th centuries B.C.E.[117] For many years it has been accepted that a fixed point could be furnished by the deaths of the Assyrian king Enlil-kudur-uṣur and the Babylonian king Adad-shuma-uṣur in the battle described in the Assyrian Synchronistic History (referred to as "the battle").[118] However, a correct interpretation of this text[119] has eliminated this fixed point, thus leaving open the question of an absolute date as a starting-point for the Babylonian chronology in this period. The tight network of the Assyrian-Babylonian synchronisms in the 14th–11th centuries has led scholars to suggest several other fixed points for the Babylonian chronology, especially from the reigns of Tiglath-pileser I, Ashared-apil-Ekur and Ashur-bel-kala of Assyria and their contemporaries, kings of Babylonia. Rowton[120] has suggested equating the two year reign of Ashared-apil-Ekur (1076–1075) with the 5th and 6th years of Marduk-shapik-zeri of Babylonia, resulting in 1080–1068 for the reign of the latter (with a margin of error of ± 5 years).

Another synchronism, however, might be used as the starting-point for the Babylonian chronology in this period: the military campaign of Ashur-bel-kala of Assyria against Babylon in his 5th year, described in the "Broken Obelisk,"[121] which most probably took place in conjunction with the removal of Marduk-shapik-zeri from the Babylonian throne and the accession of Adad-apla-iddina. According to this suggestion,[122] 1070 would be the year of Adad-apla-iddina's accession and his first regnal year, 1069. This might, then, be used as the starting-point for the absolute chronology of the Babylonian kings from Burnaburiash II until the end of the Fourth

TABLE VII

BABYLONIA ca. 1400–1000 B.C.E.

King *The Third (Kassite) Dynasty*
no.

20	Burnaburiash II	(28 years)	: 1380
21	Karahardash or Karakindash;		
	Nazibugash	(ca. 2 years)	: 1352
22	Kurigalzu II	(25 years)	: 1350
23	Nazi-Maruttash	(26 years)	: 1325
24	Kadashman-Turgu	(18 years)	: 1299
25	Kadashman-Enlil II	(15 years)	: 1281
26	Kudur-Enlil	(9 years)	: 1266
27	Shagarakti-Shuriash	(13 years)	: 1257
28	Kashtiliash III	(8 years)	: 1244
	(Interregnum in the days of		
	Tukulti-Ninurta)	[7 years]	: 1236
29	Enlil-nadin-shumi ⎫		
30	Kadashman-harbe ⎭	(ca. 3 years)	: 1229
31	Adad-shuma-iddina	(6 years)	: 1226
32	Adad-shuma-uṣur	(30 years)	: 1220
33	Melishihu (Melishipak)	(15 years)	: 1190
34	Marduk-apla-iddina	(13 years)	: 1175
35	Zababa-shuma-iddina	(1 year)	: 1162
36	Enlil-nadin-ahhe	(3 years)	: 1161
	End of Dynasty		1159

The Fourth Dynasty (= The Second Dynasty of Isin)

1	Marduk-kabit-ahheshu	(18 years)	: 1158
2	Itti-Marduk-balatu	(8 years)	: 1140
3	Ninurta-nadin-shumi	(6 years)	: 1132
4	Nebuchadnezzar I	(22 years)	: 1126
5	Enlil-nadin-apli	(4 years)	: 1104
6	Marduk-nadin-ahhe	(18 years)	: 1100
7	Marduk-shapik-zeri	(13 years)	: 1082
8	Adad-apla-iddina	(22 years)	: 1069
9	Marduk-ahhe-eriba	(1 year)	: 1047
10	Marduk-zeri-[. . . .]	(12 years)	: 1046
11	Nabu-shuma-libur	(8 years)	: 1034

The dates indicate the first complete year of each king; accession took place a year earlier.

Dynasty (Table VII, above), with a margin of error of ± 2 years, for it is quite possible that Adad-apla-iddina's accession took place as early as the 4th or as late as the 6th year of Ashur-bel-kala.[123]

3. ANATOLIA AND SYRIA IN THE 15TH–12TH CENTURIES

The considerable evidence on the historical connections among Mesopotamia, Syria and Egypt from the end of the 15th century till the decline of the great powers of the Ancient East at the end of the 13th century creates a sound though not absolute chronological, synchronistic network between the kings of Hatti, Mitanni, Kizzuwadna, Alalakh, Ugarit, Amurru, Carchemish and other Syro-Palestinian states, and the kings of Egypt, Assyria and Babylonia.

a) *Hatti*. As there is no evidence on the length of the reigns of most of the Hittite kings,[124] their estimated dates are arrived at through synchronisms with the contemporary kings of Egypt. The only date which could be fixed absolutely is the 10th year of Mursilis II. The annals of that king mention an ominous portent connected with the sun — most probably a solar eclipse.[125] Forrer has identified it with the eclipse of March 13, 1335 B.C.E.[126] Hence, the first regnal year of Mursilis was 1344. Shuppiluliuma, his father, who apparently reigned some 40 years (see note 124), would have ascended the throne in ca. 1385, or possibly a few years earlier. This date fits in with the historical evidence according to which Shuppiluliuma was a contemporary of Amen-hotep III and Akhen-Aton. Shuppiluliuma died a few years after the death of an Egyptian king called Nibhururiyaš in the Hittite sources. This was probably Tut-ankh-Amon (= Nb-ḫpr.w-rʿ),[127] who died in 1303/2 or 1338 (see above, B 1 b, Table V).

Tudhaliya, often called the "II", one of Shuppiluliuma's predecessors (possibly his great-grandfather) — the king who conquered Aleppo and briefly re-established Hittite supremacy in North Syria — should be dated to about 1440, the time of Amen-hotep II (see A 8, above) thus preceding Shuppiluliuma's accession by some 60 years.[128]

Telepinus, the very last king of the so-called "Old Hittite Kingdom," who concluded a treaty with Ishputahshu of Kizzuwadna,[129] must be placed at about 1500 B.C.E., that is, before the period of Mitannian supremacy in Syria and in Kizzuwadna under Saushshatar (see below, b).

If Mursilis II ascended the throne in 1344 and reigned about 30 years (see above, note 124), then the accession of Muwatallis his son took place in ca. 1314. In Ramses II's 5th year — 1300 according to the higher dating of the Nineteenth Dynasty — Muwatallis fought against Egypt in

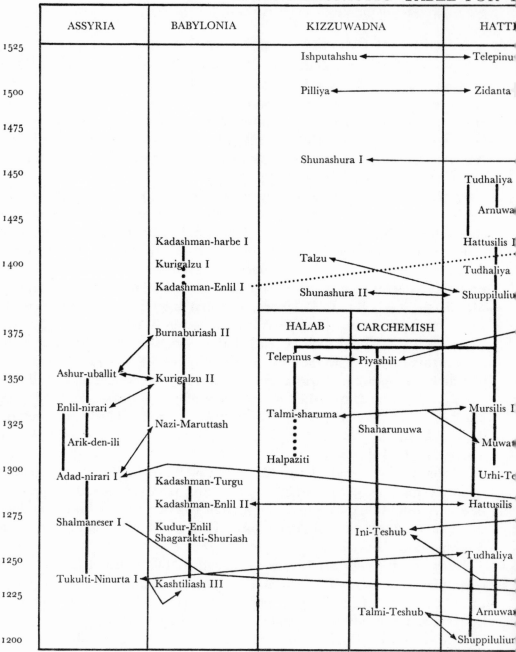

	ASSYRIA	BABYLONIA	KIZZUWADNA	HATT
1525			Ishputahshu ← → Telepinu	
1500			Pilliya ← → Zidanta	
1475				
1450			Shunashura I ←	Tudhaliya
1425				Arnuwa
1400		Kadashman-harbe I	Talzu ←	Hattusilis I
		Kurigalzu I		Tudhaliya
		Kadashman-Enlil I ⋯	Shunashura II ← → Shuppiluliu	
1375		Burnaburiash II	HALAB | CARCHEMISH	
	Ashur-uballit		Telepinus ← Piyashili	
1350		Kurigalzu II		
	Enlil-nirari			Mursilis I
1325	Arik-den-ili	Nazi-Maruttash	Talmi-sharuma ← Shaharunuwa	Muwa
1300	Adad-nirari I	Kadashman-Turgu	Halpaziti	Urhi-Te
1275	Shalmaneser I	Kadashman-Enlil II ←	Ini-Teshub ←	Hattusilis
		Kudur-Enlil Shagarakti-Shuriash		Tudhaliya
1250	Tukulti-Ninurta I	Kashtiliash III		
1225			Talmi-Teshub ←	Arnuwa
1200				Shuppiluliu

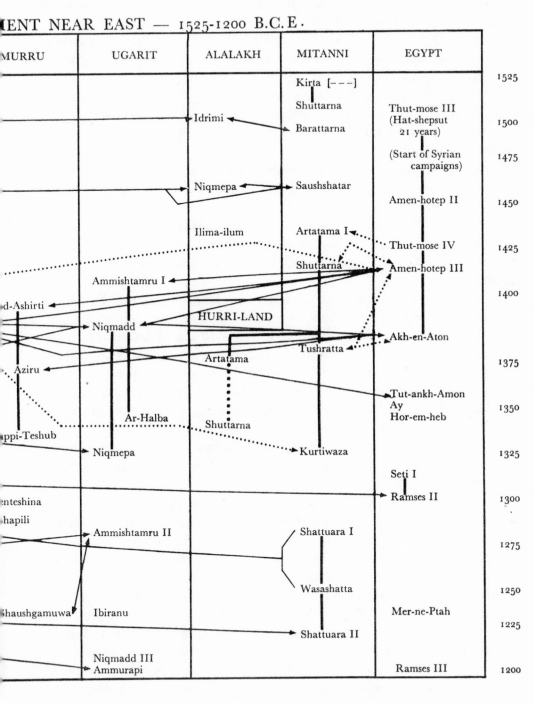

MURRU	UGARIT	ALALAKH	MITANNI	EGYPT	
			Kirta [– – –]		1525
			Shuttarna	Thut-mose III	
		Idrimi	Barattarna	(Hat-shepsut 21 years)	1500
				(Start of Syrian campaigns)	1475
		Niqmepa	Saushshatar		
				Amen-hotep II	1450
		Ilima-ilum	Artatama I	Thut-mose IV	1425
			Shuttarna	Amen-hotep III	
	Ammishtamru I				1400
d-Ashirti		HURRI-LAND			
	Niqmadd			Akh-en-Aton	
		Artatama	Tushratta		1375
Aziru					
				Tut-ankh-Amon Ay Hor-em-heb	1350
	Ar-Halba	Shuttarna			
ppi-Teshub					
	Niqmepa		Kurtiwaza		1325
				Seti I	
				Ramses II	1300
nteshina					
hapili					
	Ammishtamru II		Shattuara I		1275
			Wasashatta		1250
haushgamuwa	Ibiranu			Mer-ne-Ptah	1225
			Shattuara II		
	Niqmadd III Ammurapi			Ramses III	1200

LEGEND:

———— Attested synchronism

········ Marriage ties

▬▬▬ Filiation

•••• Probable filiation

the battle of Kadesh and died, it seems, a short time after. He was succeeded by his son, Urhi-Teshub, who reigned 7 years (see note 124, above). Hattusilis III — Urhi-Teshub's uncle — ascended the throne about Ramses' 15th year (that is, ca. 1290 B.C.E. in the higher dating for Ramses II), and was thus a contemporary of Adad-nirari I and Shalmaneser I, kings of Assyria, and of Kadashman-Turgu and Kadashman-Enlil, kings of Babylon. Further, his son Tudhaliya IV ascended the throne in the days of Shalmaneser I and was also a contemporary of Shalmaneser's son, Tukulti-Ninurta I.[130]

Tudhaliya IV appears to have had a long reign; he was succeeded by his sons Arnuwanda III and Shuppiluliuma II.[131] The length of their reigns is unknown, though it is estimated that that of the latter ended close to 1200. Whether he was the last king of Hatti, or whether another king succeeded him on the eve of that kingdom's destruction by the Sea-Peoples (i.e. before the 8th year of Ramses III; see above, B 1 c), is also unknown.

b) *Mitanni and Alalakh.* The tablets from Alalakh stratum IV mention the following kings: Idrimi, Niqmepa his son, and Ilima-ilum the son of Niqmepa. The name of an earlier king, Abba-El son of Sharra-El, appears on a seal used in the days of Niqmepa.[132] Idrimi, Niqmepa's father, is undoubtedly identical with Idrimi the son of Ilima-ilum, King of Mukish, known from his inscribed statue from Alalakh.[133] Idrimi's inscription also mentions his lord, Barattarna "the mighty king, king of the Hurri warriors,"[134] while two tablets from Alalakh IV prove the subordination of Niqmepa to Saushshatar, the great king of Mitanni. The same two Alalakh tablets bear an earlier (dynastic) seal with the name of another king: "Shuttarna son of Kirta king of Mitanni".[135]

The historical data as a whole suggest that in the days of Barattarna and, especially, in those of Saushshatar, the kings of Mitanni extended their sway over North Syria and perhaps even over Kizzuwanda in southern Anatolia. The date of Mitannian hegemony under Saushshatar is debated; it could be assigned to one of the following periods: (i) before the Syrian expeditions of Thut-mose III, who conquered the entire Alalakh region and fought against the king of Naharina (= Mitanni) in his 33rd regnal year, that is, 1458 or 1472 B.C.E.; (ii) during the decline of Egyptian rule in Syria, in the later years of Amen-hotep II, that is, after approximately 1440 B.C.E. The second alternative is the more difficult to accept, as it is unlikely that the sudden Hittite expansion in northern Syria, and the conquest of Aleppo, took place in the days of Saushshatar.

Mitannian hegemony in North Syria under Barattarna and Saushshatar should, then, be dated to the last years of the 16th century and the beginning of the 15th century.[136] It follows that both Idrimi of Alalakh and his overlord Barattarna of Mitanni should be dated to approximately 1525–1500, and that Niqmepa and his overlord Saushshatar to approximately 1500–1475. Barattarna's predecessor in Mitanni — Shuttarna the son of Kirta — would then be placed at about 1550–1525. If Shuttarna was the first king of Mitanni, it would appear that the establishment of Mitanni as a kingdom within the "Ḥurri-lands" is to be dated very close to the end of the Hyksos Dynasty in Egypt (ca. 1560, according to the higher dates for the Eighteenth Dynasty), and it is not impossible that there was some connection between the two major historical events.

The later Mitannian kings, from Artatama I (the father-in-law of Thutmose IV) and Tushratta (the contemporary of Amen-hotep III and of Shuppiluliuma) down to Shattuara II (the contemporary of Shalmaneser I and the last king of Mitanni), are known from the Amarna Letters, from the political treaties, the archives of Boghazköy and from the historical inscriptions of the Assyrian kings[137] (see Table VIII)

c) *Amurru, Ugarit and Carchemish.* The Amarna Letters, the political treaties of the Hittite kings from the archives at Boghazköy (Hattusa) and especially the Akkadian (as well as Ugaritic) political documents found in recent years at Ugarit, make it possible to reconstruct a synchronistic, relative chronology for those kings, princes and rulers of the major Syrian states during the 14th–13th centuries who are mentioned in these texts. The approximate dating of the Syrian kings is dependent in part upon the synchronisms with Egypt, in part upon those with the Hittite kings and in part on internal synchronistic evidence.[138] A tentative synchronistic table of these kings is offered in Table VIII.

Judging from the pace of chronological research in the last decades, it is doubtless that future work and additional discoveries will reduce the gaps and increase the accuracy of dating in the chronology of the second millennium B.C.E. The present chapter has not touched directly upon the Hebrews — or the Aramaeans — who were still in their formative stages in the later part of the second millennium. It is only in the first millennium, with the rise of their kingdoms, that we are able to reconstruct the chronological scheme using the biblical evidence and especially the absolute synchronisms with Assyria, Babylonia and Egypt. But this is beyond the range of the present discussion.[139]

CHAPTER VI

THE NORTHWEST SEMITIC LANGUAGES

by H. L. Ginsberg

A. The Northwest Sub-Family Defined

THIS SUB-FAMILY of Semitic languages is marked off from its fellows particularly by two isoglosses:

(1) Proto-Semitic *w* is represented in initial positions for the most part by *y*. Thus to *warada* "he approached (a place), came (to water)" in Arabic, corresponds *yārad* "he came, or went, down" in Hebrew. (Non-initial *w*, however, remains unaffected: Arab. *'awrada* "he caused to come, brought [cattle] to water" is paralleled by Heb. *hōrīd* [< *haw*-] "he brought down," and Arab. *mawrid* "road leading to water, watering-trough" by Heb. *mōrād* [< *maw*-] "descent".)

(2) In Proto-Northwest Semitic, nouns whose singular was formed on the pattern *q.tl*(*at*) expanded the singular theme by the insertion of an *a* (or other vowel) between the *ṭ* and the *l* before plural endings; e.g. the plural of Hebrew *'ebed* (< *'abd*) "male slave" is *'ḫādīm* (< *'abadīm*), that of *šipḥā* "female slave" is *špāḥōt* (< *šipaḥōt*).

Within the Northwest Semitic sub-family, we distinguish a Canaanite and an Aramaic stock. These we subdivide provisionally as follows:

(a) Canaanite
i) Phoenic (Ugaritic, Phoenician [Byblian and Common] and Punic; probably also Philistine or Ashdodite).
ii) Hebraic (Hebrew and Moabite; probably also Ammonite and Edomite).

(b) Aramaic
i) Common (several distinct ancient and modern languages and dialects).
ii) Samalian.

Cuneiformists speak of a third Northwest Semitic stock, namely Amorite, on the basis of West Semitic proper names and other linguistic features occurring in Akkadian records found in Mesopotamia (e.g. at Babylon and Mari) in the first half of the 2nd millennium B.C.E. But the data hardly suffice for determining whether the language in question is distinct from Canaanite or Aramaic, let alone for gaining a more intimate knowledge of it.

B. The Emergence of the Canaanite Languages

1. General

The earliest considerable monuments of Northwest Semitic speech that have been recovered date from the second half of the 2nd millennium B.C.E. and represent the Canaanite stock. Among the *distinguishing features* which mark off this group as a whole from Aramaic, may be named the following:

(a) *Lexical Features*, i) The word for "to go" is the simple conjugation of the root *hlk*, which exists in other Semitic languages, in the perfect tense and in its kin (the participle and the infinitive absolute); but it has a secondary root *ylk*, which is peculiar to Canaanite, in the imperfect and in its kin (the imperative and the infinitive construct), and some of the derived conjugations (the Gt conjugation in Ugaritic, the hiphil in Hebrew) are likewise formed from this secondary root.

ii) The Canaanite words for "roof" (Ugaritic *gg*, Hebrew *gaḡ*) and "table" (Ugar. *ṭlḥn*, Heb. *šulḥān*), "window" (Ugar. *ḥln*, Heb. *ḥallōn*), "old" (of things: Ugar. *yṯn*, Heb. *yāšān*), "old age" (Ugar. *dqn*, Heb. *zóqen*) and "to drive out" (*grš*) are confined to the Canaanite languages.

(b) *Morphological Features of the Verb*. i) In the imperfect, the preformative of the third person plural feminine is *t-*, in contrast to the *y-* (East Aramaic *l/n*) of other languages; e.g. "they (f.) will stand" is *tāqómnā* in Hebrew but *yaqumna* in Arabic, *yqūmān* (Syriac *nqūmān*) in Aramaic. In Ugaritic and in the Tell el-Amarna tablets, *t-* is often the preformative of even the *masculine* third person plural.

ii) In the hollow verbs, the places of the D and tD (piel and hithpael) conjugations are often taken by the polel (pōlẹl < *pawlil) and hithpolel (hiṭpōlẹl < *hitpawlil) in Hebrew and by analogous formations (vocalization problematic) in Ugaritic and, no doubt, the other Canaanite languages (for which examples are lacking). Thus the biblical Hebrew has no piel or pual from the root *kwn*, but it has a polel *kōnẹn*, and it similarly has a polel and a hithpolel from *rwm*; while Ugaritic has from these roots a *knn* "to establish" and a *rmm* "to exalt." (In Hebrew some geminate verbs are vocalized in the same way — e.g. *hiṯmōḏēḏ* instead of *hiṯmaddēḏ* — but we cannot tell from the spelling whether Ugaritic and Phoenician have anything analogous.)

iii) In Hebrew, and probably in all the Canaanite languages, the active participle is simply the stem of the imperfect inflected as a noun in the following cases: a) in all the hollow verbs, e.g., *qām*, (Ugar. *qm* "one who rises up against"), *mēṯ*, *bōš*, *ṭōḇ* (Ugar. *ṯb*); b) in most stative verbs, e.g. *ḥāpēṣ*, *zāqēn*, *yāḵōl*, *qal*, *dal* (Ugar. *dl*); c) in the N conjugation, e.g. *niḵbāḏ* (Ugar. *nkbd*).

iv) Characteristic, too, of Canaanite, though perhaps originally not absent from Aramaic (see presently) is the vocalization of the preformatives of the imperfect in the simple conjugation. They take *a* if the following syllable has *u* or *i*, but *i* if the following syllable has *a*. In Hebrew, attenuation (of *a* to *i* under certain circumstances) and other secondary developments have blurred the original picture considerably. Even here, however, *yāšīr* and *yāšūḇ*, for example, still contrast with *yēḇōš* (< *yibās*), *yēmar* and *yēqal* with *yāḡōl* and *yāmōḏ* (< *yagull, yamudd*), and *yaḥrōš* "he will plow" with *yeḥraš* "he will become deaf"; while in Ugaritic the law is in full force, as is certain thanks to the script's indication of the vowel quality with aleph. Thus with *u* and *i* imperfects, we have in Ugaritic *amlk, amt, anḫ-n, abky, aqbr-n, ašt*; but with *a* imperfects, *ibqʿ, iqḥ, iqra* and *imḫṣ*. Even some of the Tell el-Amarna letters, which are Akkadian in intention, occasionally observe this rule because their authors are Canaanites who have not mastered Akkadian perfectly. However, there is, further, direct testimony to the former observance of this rule by some Arabs, and it cannot be proved that it was not originally observed in Aramaic (the antithesis between *neḷap̄* [< *niʾlap*] and *neḵoḷ* [< *naʾkul*] in Syriac suggests that it was).

v) Finally, Hebrew, Phoenician, and apparently a Canaanite gloss in a Tell el-Amarna letter (*ḫi-iḫ-bi-e* = *heḫbīʾ* "he hid" [?]) share the peculiarity of attenuating the *a* of the first syllable in the perfect of the derived conjugations to *i* unless it is followed by *w* (Heb. *hišlīḵ* but *hōrīḏ*, piʿel but pōḷeḷ [< *pawlil*; see B, b, ii, above]).

2. THE PHOENIC GROUP

Within the Canaanite stock, it is the Phoenic group that emerges first. The oldest written records of Phoenic speech date from the third quarter of the 2nd millennium B.C.E. and comprise a) the Ugaritic writings and

b) the Canaanisms and Canaanite glosses in the Akkadian letters of Syro-Palestinian origin from Tell el-Amarna. The marks which distinguish all the languages of this branch from the Hebraic include:

(a) *Lexicographical Features. Mnm* (vocalization uncertain) is a pronoun similar in sense and usage to Hebrew *m'ūmā* "anything." The verb "to give" is *ytn*, as against Hebrew and Aramaic *ntn*, Akkadian *ndn*. "To be" is *kwn* (as in Arabic, in contrast to Hebrew *hyy/hwy*, Aramaic *hwy*). *Pa'm* (Ugaritic *pa'n-*), *ḥarūṣ* (Ugaritic with the original ḫ) and *qart* are here the regular (in Hebrew only rare and/or poetic) words for "foot," "gold," and "city" respectively. Further, *'alp* is the regular word for "ox," whereas in Hebrew it is both rare and confined to the plural.

(b) *Syntactical Feature.* Whereas the Hebraic group has both a perfect and an imperfect consecutive, and an infinitive absolute consecutive to boot, the Phoenic languages certainly possess only the former (and in the case of Ugaritic, even that only inferentially, since poetic texts and short letters and lists afford no scope for the use of the perfect consecutive) and something quite peculiar in lieu of the latter: either the infinitive absolute or a third person (singular?) perfect which does not change with the person (or number?) of the subject.

To the well-known examples of the perfect consecutive in the Punic Sacrificial Tariffs of Carthage and Marseilles (*wkn, wn'nš*) is to be added *wysgrnm* (Eshmunezer inscription, line 9).[1] It is not, as is taken for granted, a simple imperfect but a consecutive perfect; Phoen. *wa-yisgirū-nēm* (not -*yas-*!) being equivalent to Heb. *w-hisgīrū-m*. The proof is that in a clause subordinate to the one in which *wysgrnm* occurs even a simple future without "and" is also, though illogically, expressed by the perfect. For the passage in question reads thus: *wysgrnm h'lnm hqdšm 't mmlk(t) 'dr 'š mšl bnm* "and may the holy gods deliver them into the hands of a mighty prince who shall rule over them."

As for the Phoenician substitute for the imperfect consecutive, the only example of it known before 1947 was *Kilamuwa*, lines 7–8: *w'dr 'ly mlk dnnm wškr 'nk 'ly 'yt 'šr* "the king of the Danunites being too powerful for me, I hired the king of Assyria against him."[2] Here neither *w'dr* nor *wškr* can be any sort of imperfect, and the latter is obviously not inflected for the first person. The most obvious thing to do used to be to take at least *wškr* as an infinitive absolute consecutive, and maybe *w'dr* too. However, in the Karatepe inscriptions we find similarly employed, with *'nk*, forms which differ from every Hebrew infinitive absolute in taking pronominal suffixes (*yrdm 'nk yšbm 'nk* "I uprooted them, I resettled them"),[3] and from the Hebrew infinitive as a narrative tense in not being preceded by "and." Accordingly, Friedrich's view that they are third person singular perfects (*yrdm* = Heb. *hōriḏām*, *yšbm* = *hōšīḇām*) cannot be ruled out. (The syntax will then be somewhat analogous to the use of the singular of the verb before plural subjects in Arabic.)

3 THE INDIVIDUAL CANAANITE LANGUAGES IN THE 2ND MILLENNIUM B.C.E.

(a) *Ugaritic.* The extant copies of the Ugaritic writings, all found at Ugarit near the northern end of the Syrian coast, date from ca. 1370 to ca. 1200 B.C.E.; and since the content of many of them is literary, its composition may antedate the tablets considerably.

Ugaritic differs from the other Northwest Semitic languages known to us in that it forms the causative conjugation with the preformative *š* instead of *h* (Hebrew and early Aramaic), ' (later Aramaic), or *y* (Phoenician). Unlike the other Canaanite languages it retains nearly all the original Semitic consonants. Thus *ḥ* is (except in a very few short texts which may stem from Phoenicians) always distinguished graphically from *ḫ*, *ġ* from ', and *ṯ* from *ṣ*. Other phonemes probably remained distinct always but were only occasionally distinguished from similar ones in writing. Thus the Proto-Semitic *ḏ* is usually represented by the same sign as Proto-Semitic *d*, but in certain words — and by some scribes apparently in all words — by a special sign; while Proto-Semitic *ḍ*, normally represented by the sign *ṣ*, is in one document represented by the sign *ṭ*. Only Proto-Semitic *š* and *ś* seem to be consistently represented by a single symbol and hence, no doubt, by a single phoneme. Other archaisms of Ugaritic are the retention of the Gt conjugation of the verb, of all the moods of classical Arabic, and of the cases of the noun and its cognates (adjective and participle), as also the absence of an article. Again, not only the noun, but also the adjective, the verb, and — probably — the pronoun and the pronominal suffixes, regularly distinguish dual from plural. The shift of *ā* to *ō*, which is characteristic of Tell el-Amarna Canaanite as well as of Phoenician and Hebrew, has probably not taken place in Ugaritic, since original *ā* is represented by the sign *a*, not *u*. Ugaritic is also characterized by a generous use of the adverbial ending *-am* and of an emphatic enclitic *-m(a?)*, vocative participles *y* (=*yā*) and *l*, and lexical peculiarities such as *rgm* "to speak" (Heb.-Phoen. *dbr*), *g* "voice," and by the modification of original *šamš* "sun" to *šapš* (partial assimilation of the *m* to the following *š*).

By singular good fortune, the recovered Ugaritic monuments include large portions of an unsuspected epic, and especially religio-epic, literature which not only acquaints us with the mythology of the Canaanites but raises interesting questions by a number of striking parallels in style, motif, and diction, with Greek epic poetry.

(b) *The Tell el-Amarna Tablets.* Though the language of the great majority of these documents, which date from the 14th century B.C.E., is Akkadian in intention, a number of them exhibit verbal forms which follow Canaanite rather than Akkadian paradigms or represent compromises between the two, and some contain actual Canaanite glosses to Akkadian words. They show that in Palestine and Phoenicia, unlike Ugarit, the shift of *ā* to *ō* has already taken place. Like the Ugarit texts, they frequently employ *t-* instead of *y-* as the prefix of the third person plural *masculine.*

(c) *Hebrew, Phoenician, Moabite.* Toward the end of the 2nd millennium B.C.E. the most important of the Canaanite languages, Hebrew, makes its appearance in literature. That the Song of Deborah (Jud. 5) dates from around 1100 B.C.E. has always been admitted by scholars, and in recent years there has been a growing inclination among them to date various other biblical documents (e.g. parts of Joshua, Judges, I Samuel) before 1000 B.C.E. From around 1000 B.C.E. dates the oldest connected Phoenician text, the inscription on the sarcophagus of King Ahiram of Byblos. The single Moabite inscription that has survived (if one disregards one or two name engravings on seals), that of King Mesha, dates from the third quarter of the 9th century. Between its limited length and the ambiguity of the spelling, it leaves many doubts about the structure of the Moabite language.

4. Evolution of the Canaanite Languages down to 1000 B.C.E.

By this time, the case endings and the short vowels at the end of verbal forms have disappeared almost entirely from both Hebrew and Phoenician. However, Phoenician proper — as against Punic — always retained the *-i* of the genitive at least before pronominal suffixes (proof will be given below). With the dropping of the case endings, the stress in nominal formations came to rest on the last syllable; and where the syllable did not end in a double consonant (as in *'abd,* for example) its vowel was lengthened. (This did not apply where the syllable in question lost the stress, as when the whole word became proclitic because it was in the construct state or when an ending which took the stress was added.)

In the verb, the feminine singular ending -*at* became -*a* in both Hebrew and Phoenician; but in the noun (in the widest sense) the -*t* of the feminine ending was dropped (except in the construct state and with added endings) only in Hebrew. Perhaps the genitive case was retained in Phoenician in the absolute state as well as before pronominal suffixes. In that case, the reason why it retained the feminine singular -*t* in the noun though not in the verb is obvious: it is because in the noun the -*t* was not always final even in the absolute state.

The shift of *ā* to *ō* has already been mentioned. Further, Phoenician regularly shifts *aw* (*au*) to *ō* and *ay* (*ai*) to *ē*, and the other Canaanite languages do so in varying measure. In Phoenician, the number of consonants has, by 1000 B.C.E., been reduced to twenty-two. It would seem that this occurred as early as the 14th century. In Ugaritic ABCs, the twenty-two characters which have counterparts in the Phoenician alphabet are arranged in the same sequence as in the Phoenician alphabet, with the extra ones fitted in here and there; and mention has already been made of the fact that some writers in Ugarit failed to distinguish between two consonants that correspond to a single Phoenician consonant, and that these writers may very well have been Phoenicians (3, a, above). Hebrew, on the other hand, though it had only twenty-two signs because it borrowed the Phoenician alphabet, employed at least the sign *š* for two distinct phonemes (*š* and *ś*), and there are also indications that in early times *ḥ* continued distinct from *h* and *ġ* from ʻ in pronunciation.

By 1000 B.C.E., all the Canaanite languages have a definite article: it is *ha*- followed by gemination of the following consonant.

C. Diffusion and History of the Canaanite Languages

1. The Phoenic Group

(a) *Phoenician*. Whereas Ugaritic, as we have seen (B, 3, a, above), is known to have been in use only in a limited area and for a limited period, Phoenician spans a vast area of diffusion and at least a millennium and a half of duration.

Within Phoenician, we distinguish the Byblian dialect from Common Phoenician; and within Common Phoenician, Phoenician proper from Punic. As far as can be made out from the limited material, Byblian differed from Common Phoenician mainly in having more archaic pronominal suffixes of the third person. They are: m.s. older (Ahiram) -*h*, later -*w;* f.s. -*h* pl. -*hm*. In Common Phoenician, on the other hand, the situation is more complicated, and roughly parallels that which obtains in Hebrew. In the latter there are (mainly) two sets of third person suffixes: 1) m.s. -*ō*, f.s. -*āh*, pl. -*ām;* 2) m.s. -*hū*, f.s. -*hā*, pl. -*hēm*. Similarly, in Common Phoenician we have (mainly): 1) m.s. and f.s. -*o* and -*a* respectively (neither expressed in the consonantal orthography), pl. -*m;* 2) m.s. and f.s. -*yu* and -*ya* respectively (both spelled -*y*), pl. -*nm* (probably pronounced -*nēm*). Generally speaking, in both languages the first set of suffixes is employed with consonantal themes,[4] and the second set is commoner in Phoenician than in Hebrew for two reasons: a) Hebrew, inconsistently, uses -*m* instead of -*hēm* with the perfect afformatives -*tī*, -*ū*, and -*nū* though they end in vowels. Thus the Hebrew for "and they will deliver them" is (imperfect: *yasgīrūm*, or) (perfect consecutive) *w-hisgīrū-m*, but the Phoenician is (imperfect: *yasgirūn-ōm*), or *wa-yisgirū-nēm;* the Hebrew for "we added them" is *ysap̄nū-m*, but the Phoenician *yasapnū-nēm*. (But note Phoen. *lm* "to them," as against Heb. *lāhēm*, with *lāmō* only a poetic variant.) b) Because Phoenician proper (as against Punic) always retained the genitive ending -*i*, and every noun which is governed by a preposition — including '*t* even when it has the function of an accusative particle — or by another noun in the construct state is in the genitive case, the Phoenician theme will often end, in -*i* where the corresponding Hebrew theme ends in a consonant. This will explain why "of his being king," which is *lmolkō* in Hebrew, is not *lmlk* but *lmlky* (i.e. *la-moloki-yu*) in Phoenician; and similarly why "that he may give" — Hebrew *ltittō* ("for his giving") — is *ltty* (*la-titti-yu*), "that he may be" *lkny*, "that they may be" *lknnm*, "that they may dwell" *lšbtnm*, "to destroy them" *lqstnm*, "to its (the sun's) setting-place" '*d mb'y;* "in their heart" *blbnm*, or — after a noun in the construct state — *mškb nḥtnm* "their resting place," and with '*t:* '*t 'mnm* "their mother" (object of the verb).

In Common Phoenician (the situation in Byblian Phoenician is unknown), the preformative of the causative conjugation is not *hi-* but *yi-*. (The *h* was dropped, and since the early Semites had difficulty in beginning a word with a vowel, *yi-* was substituted for *i-*.)

The old negative particle *lā* (Ugar., Arab., Aram., Akkad., Heb. *lō*) is unattested in Phoenician. The regular word is *bal* (rare in Hebrew).

Instead of the Heb.-Ugar.-Moab. '*ēn* "there is not," Phoen. uses ' *y*. In conditional, or quasi-conditional, relative clauses the verb is negated by the compound of the foregoing two: '*bl* or '*ybl*. — As of the old case system, Phoenician probably conserved not a little of the old mood system.

Common Phoenician was spoken in Phoenicia (apart from Byblos and its vicinity) and, by the side of Cypriote, on Cyprus. Phoenician inscriptions however have been found not only in these countries but all over the East Mediterranean world (including Greece, Mesopotamia, and Egypt), bearing witness to the presence of Phoenician sailors, travelers, colonists, or metics. The longest inscriptions, royal ones dating from the 9th to the 8th centuries, have been recovered from Zenjirli and Karatepe respectively, in southern Asia Minor. Yet here Phoenician may have been employed almost exclusively as a written language having, very few native speakers; for each of these localities employs, in addition, the language which historical geography would have led us to expect to find as its vernacular at the date in question. (On Zenjirli, see E, below.) In the East Mediterranean world, Phoenician epigraphy, and probably Phoenician speech, come to an end in the 1st century B.C.E. Classical authors attest the existence of a Phoenician literature, but it has perished.

(b) *Punic.* In the world of the Western Mediterranean, where the Phoenicians established extensive colonies, particularly in and about Carthage in North Africa (i.e. in Algeria, Tunisia, and Libya), an offshoot of (Common) Phoenician, of which the earliest specimen may date from the 8th century, continued to be written until at least late in the 2nd century C.E. and to be spoken until the 6th. Early Punic hardly differs from Phoenician proper except in expressing the suffixes -*o* and -*a* graphically (by means of '). After the fall of Carthage in 147 B.C.E., however, popular spellings often betray a loss of the distinctive Semitic sounds under Berber influence and employ analytical substitutes for the construct state construction probably from the same cause. Further, the genitive ending -*i* may have disappeared or have been in process of disappearing, to judge by *lmbmlktm* "together with their working" (Leptis, 5:2),[5] where we should have expected **lmbmlktnm.*

Apart from a few sentences in Latin script, Punic, like Phoenician proper, is known almost exclusively from inscriptions, for Punic literature, like Phoenician literature, has perished.

(c) *Philistine or Ashdodite — Probably a Phoenic Dialect.* The closest 'neighbors of the Philistines, the Israelites, report that the national deity of the former was the old Semitic god Dagon (Jud. 16:23; I Sam. 5:1–5) and tacitly assume that Philistine speech did not differ greatly from Israelite (Jud. 14–16; I Sam. 14:9–10, 12; etc.). The alien thing about the Philistines is their being uncircumcised (I Sam. 17:26; II Sam. 1:20), not their language. In effect, by the 8th century the Philistine kings and their officials bear good Semitic names, as is testified both by the annals of Assyrian kings and by the seal — executed in the Phoenician-Old Hebrew alphabet — of

'Abd'il'ib son of Shab'at, servant of Mittit ben Ṣidqa. (The king is perhaps identical with the Mitinti whom Sennacherib mentions as the king of Ashdod in 701. His father's name happens to be identical with that of the man who was king of Ashkelon at that time.) Evidently the non-Canaanite Sea People which settled in southwestern Palestine in the 12th century B.C.E. constituted only a thin upper stratum upon a Canaanite base, to which it assimilated culturally. In the 5th century B.C.E. the speech of the (Persian) province of Ashdod still differs from that of Judah, just as do those of the provinces of Ammon and Moab (Neh. 13:23–24); which evidently means that all of these districts still spoke their several ancestral Canaanite languages, and not Aramaic. That Moabite belonged to the Hebraic branch is known from the Moabite inscription (the Mesha stele), and presumably Ammonite was closely related to it. Ashdodite, on the other hand, being descended from the old pre-Israelite speech of Canaan, was in all probability a Phoenic idiom.

2 The Hebraic Group

The simplest mark by which this group may be distinguished both from the other Canaanite one and from the rest of the Semitic languages is the common verb '*ś'h* "to do, to make." More profound is the imperfect consecutive tense (on the construction which takes its place in Phoenician, see B, 2, b, above). Moabite, the only Hebraic language besides Hebrew of which we have specimens of connected sentences, shares both these criteria with Hebrew. On the other hand, it diverges from Hebrew by retaining the Gt conjugation (*w'lthm* = Heb. *wā'illāhem*) and — even more surprisingly — by forming its plural masculine and its dual by adding -*n* (-*īn* and -*ēn* respectively) as against Hebrew -*īm* and -*aim*. It further does not drop the *t* of the feminine ending -*at*, as in *bmt* (= Heb. *bāmā;* see B, 4, above). For historical reasons it is to be assumed that Ammonite was very similar to Moabite, while Edomite may have resembled Hebrew even more closely.

The most important, however, not only of the Hebraic but of all the Canaanite languages is Hebrew. It was a living speech from about the 13th century B.C.E. to the 2nd century C.E. inclusive, and its literature has never ceased to be studied and even added to. An attempt to revive it as a vernacular in Jewish Palestine, begun late in the 19th century C.E., has resulted in a new idiom, with a rich press and a flourishing literature, which is the official language of the State of Israel.

Hebrew as a living language, which alone can be treated here, passed through two main periods of unequal length:

i) The Biblical, or pre-Roman Period, ca. 1225 B.C.E. to 63 B.C.E.

ii) The Roman Period, 63 B.C.E. to ca. 200 C.E.

The Biblical Period in turn falls into two subdivisions:

a) The Golden Age, ca. 1225 B.C.E. to ca. 500 B.C.E.

b) The Silver Age, ca. 500 B.C.E. to 63 B.C.E.

Hebrew is the language of a people named Israel which acquired a distinctive character — and perhaps only came into being — in the 13th century B.C.E. in the inhospitable land between the Isthmus of Suez and Palestine, and around 1200 B.C.E. conquered and settled in the greater part of Palestine. What has survived of its literary production during the Biblical Period constitutes the greater part of the Hebrew Bible (a small portion of the "Hebrew" Bible being not Hebrew but Aramaic). Since the dating of much of the Bible is controversial, it is best to state which is the earliest document about whose dating there is a general agreement, without prejudice to others being even earlier. It is, then, recognized on all hands that the Song of Deborah (Jud. 5) cannot date from later than the first half of the 11th century, and the latest great author of the Golden Age is Deutero-Isaiah (Isa. 34–35, 40–66), who was active between 550 and 500 B.C.E. The latest product of the Silver Age is apparently the Book of Esther (ca. 100 B.C.E. ?). True, even supposing the foreign word 'appiryōn (Cant. 3:9) is not of Greek origin, the linguistic character of Canticles is pronouncedly later than that of Esther; but that is probably because the latter consciously archaizes. — The literary monuments of biblical Hebrew are supplemented by a small corpus of inscriptions, seal engravings, and ostraca.

Of course, it must not be imagined that the language underwent a violent change upon the establishment of Roman suzerainty over Judea by Pompey in the year 63 B.C.E. The first eight *mishnayot* in Mishnah Avot, chapter 1, contain sayings by scholars of the 2nd and early 1st centuries B.C.E. (The saying in the first *mishna* is attributed to the men of the Great Assembly, whose date is uncertain but may well be earlier than the 2nd century B.C.E.) Yet the language of these sayings is indistinguishable from that of the bulk of the rabbinic Hebrew literature of the Roman Age. On the other hand, the Hebrew sectarian literature of the 1st centuries B.C.E. and C.E. which was recovered in the nineteen-forties and fifties from the caves around Khirbat Qumran tries to imitate biblical Hebrew. However, it is different from, and recognizably later than, biblical Hebrew; and since the line has to be drawn somewhere, the politically critical year 63 B.C.E. is a convenient point.

An obvious barrier to an exact knowledge of biblical Hebrew is the

Late Bronze Period stele dedicated
to the god Mekal,
found at Beth-shean.
The University Museum, Philadelphia.

Hazor, Late Bronze Period shrine and stelae.
Prof. Y. Yadin, Jerusalem.

Nahariya, figures found
in the Middle Bronze Period temple.
Dr. M. Dothan, Department of Antiquities, Jerusalem.

Megiddo, gilt bronze statuette of deity,
Late Bronze Period (stratum VII B).
Oriental Institute, University of Chicago.

The goddess Anath, bronze figurine from
Nahariya, Middle Bronze Period.
Dr. M. Dothan, Department of Antiquities, Jerusalem.

Warring deity, statuette from Megiddo,
Late Bronze Period.
Department of Antiquities, Jerusalem.

The goddes Hat-hor, 14th century B.C.E. bust
found at Beth-shean.
Department of Antiquities, Jerusalem.

The god Baal holding lightning in his left hand, and wielding a mace with his right hand. Stone tablet from Ugarit, Late Bronze Period.
Prof. C. A. Schaeffer, Paris.

The goddess Anath,
ivory tablet from Ugarit.
Prof. C. A. Schaeffer, Paris.

Statue of a seated god from Hazor,
Late Bronze Period.
Prof. Y. Yadin, Jerusalem.

Statue of a goddess from Tell Zippor,
Late Bronze Period.
Dr. A. Biran, Department of Antiquities, Jerusalem.

Clay tablets bearing the image of a fertility goddess, Late Bronze Period.
Dr. A. Biran, Department of Antiquities, Jerusalem.

Clay tablets bearing the image of a fertility goddess,
Middle and Late Bronze Period respectively.
Department of Antiquities, Jerusalem.

Towerlike incense burner from Beth-shean, 12th century B.C.E.
The University Museum, Philadelphia.

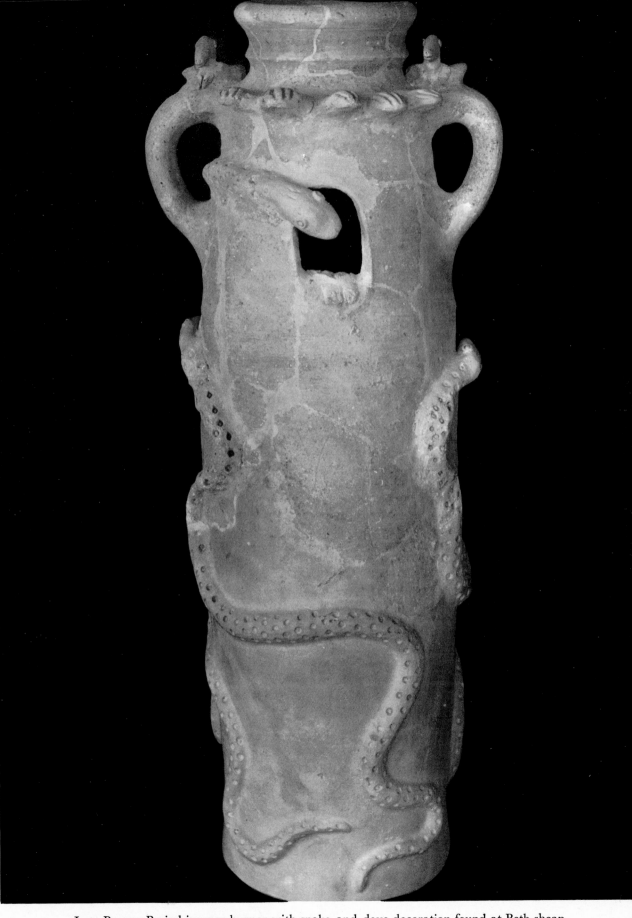

Late Bronze Period incense burner with snake and dove decoration found at Beth-shean.
Department of Antiquities, Jerusalem.

Late Bronze Period cultic stand,
from Beth-shean.
Department of Antiquities, Jerusalem.

Late Bronze Period cultic stand,
from Megiddo.
Department of Antiquities, Jerusalem.

Late Bronze Period cultic mask
from Hazor.
Prof. Y. Yadin, Jerusalem.

Late Bronze Period stone altar from Hazor.
Prof. Y. Yadin, Jerusalem.

Stele of Ramses II found at Beth-shean.
The University Museum, Philadelphia.

Stele of Seti I found at Beth-shean.
The University Museum, Philadelphia.

The Mer-ne-ptah stele, from Thebes, on which the name of Israel is mentioned for the first time. At the bottom the name "Israel" in the abbreviated form as it appears on the stele.

Department of Antiquities, Jerusalem.

Ramses II's "400 year stele," found at Avaris (Zoan).

Statue of Ramses III found at
Beth-shean.
Department of Antiquities, Jerusalem.

Late Bronze Period stele bearing the image of a warrior,
found at Shikhan in Transjordan.
Louvre, Paris.

Late Bronze Period basalt plate found at Beth-shean, on which are carved
in low relief a lion fighting a dog.
Louvre, Paris.

End of 13th century B.C.E. stele in the Egyptian style found at
K. Balu'ah, Transjordan.

fact that it is written in a script which, for the most part, expresses only the consonants, the vowels and diacritical marks having been supplied not even in its last period as a living language but centuries after it had ceased to be one. This pointing obviously reflects a *phonology* which is more anachronistic the older the text it is applied to. More serious however is the fact that the consonantal skeleton permits to a considerable extent of being read in accordance with an anachronistic *morphology*.

Bearing this in mind we may say that the Hebrew of the Golden Age was more archaic than Phoenician not only in retaining the -*hēm* which the Phoenician changed to -*nēm* but also in retaining not only the pual and the hophal but also the passive qal conjugation in full vigor. It is only because the passive qal was completely supplanted by the corresponding (original) reflexive niphal as early as the Silver Age of biblical Hebrew, and because consequently any later reader who came across the graph *ygnb*, for example, in a context which showed that its sense was passive naturally read it as a niphal form, that our masoretic vocalization interprets it as *yiggānēḇ* (Ex. 22:11), though the graph *wgnb* which occurs with likewise passive signification only five verses before (Ex. 22:6) shows that the author expressed the idea of "to be stolen" by means of the passive qal, not the niphal, of *gnb*. It has already been pointed out (B, 1, b, above) that the biblical Hebrew tense system is different from and probably more original than, the Phoenician.

On the other hand, Hebrew is less archaic than Phoenician in its complete abandonment of the case endings and in the loss of the Gt conjugation in all but one or two petrified survivals from weak verbs, where it resembles other conjugations of strong verbs (*hištīn* — from a verb *šyn*, but to the native speech instinct the hiphil of a root *štn*; and *hēṭel* — actually perhaps "hiphtael" of *hll*).

The modal modifications of the imperfect (jussive and cohortative) and imperative (cohortative) and their uses cannot be described here in detail. But it may be mentioned that modifications are frequently maintained with pronominal suffixes of the third person singular where the unsuffixed forms do not show them. Thus the *un*suffixed forms of the jussive singular are identical with those of the indicative in the sound verb; but (in prose) "let him watch it" (*yišmréhū*, jussive) is distinguished from "he will watch it" (*yišmrénnū*, indicative). In the case of the cohortative, on the other hand, it is just the verbs tertiae *w/y* that do not distinguish it from the indicative; but again the distinction reappears when a third person singular suffix is added: *naʿśḛhā* (cohortative) "let us do it." The imperfect consecutive is based upon the jussive.

Like Phoenician, Hebrew expresses (momentary) prohibition by means of *'al.* However, it expresses ordinary negation not — except, rarely, in poetry — by means of *bal* but by means of *lō*, and it expresses "there is not" and negates nominal sentences not by means of *'y* (see C, 1, a, above) but of *'ēn.* A permanent or solemn command can be expressed by means of the infinitive absolute, a permanent prohibition by means of *lō* with the imperfect indicative. For further refinements, see D, below.

In the Silver Age, Hebrew dropped the passive qal and the use of the infinitive absolute as an imperative. Other changes: 1) *Še-* gains ground at the expense of *'šer* (see Ecclesiastes and Canticles; Esther consciously archaized). 2) Because most of western Asia was under Persian rule from 538 to 333 B.C.E., a number of Persian words were borrowed; e.g. *pat̲še̲ḡen, partmīm, pardēs, karmīl.* 3) These Persian words did not come to Hebrew directly but through the medium of Aramaic. For Aramaic was the language of administration in the western provinces of the Persian empire, where it was the spoken language of a constantly growing proportion of the population. Other, non-Persian words borrowed by Hebrew from Aramaic during the Silver Age are *šarḇīt̲, ṭinnēp̲, 'illū* (for Golden Age *lū*). — More profound is the imitation of Aramaic language patterns. Because in late Aramaic *d(ī)* performs the functions not only of old Hebrew *'šer* and *še-* but also of old Hebrew *kī* — *'šer* and *še-* usurp the functions of *kī* in later Hebrew; in the Bible, most clearly in Canticles: 1) *'Al tir'ū́nī še-'nī šharḥoret̲, šeš-šzāp̲át̲nī haš-šā́meš* "Heed not *that* I am swarthy, *that* the sun has gazed upon me" (Cant. 1:6). 2) *pit̲ḥī lī . . . šerōšī nimlā ṭāl* "Let me in . . . *for* my head is drenched with dew" (Cant. 5:2). Similarly Aramaic *dī-lmā* serves as a model for *šal-lāmā* "lest" (Cant. 1:7). An even profounder imitation of Aramaic is the construction *miṭṭāt̲ō šelli-Šlōmō* (Cant 3:7), literally "his bed, Solomon's" as a periphrasis of *miṭṭat̲ Šlōmō* "Solomon's bed."

[Perhaps an Aramaic word is sometimes borrowed by way of *incorrect* translation. Thus the Aramaic *hēk̲dēn* "how, then" is possibly composed of *hēk̲* (Heb. *'ēk̲*) and *dēn* (Heb. *ze̲*) "this," and a correct literal rendering of it into Hebrew would be **'ēk̲ze̲.* But popularly *hēk̲dēn* was analyzed as *hē* (Heb. *'ē*) "which" and *k̲dēn* (Heb. *kāk̲ā*) "so"; hence the translation-loan *'ēk̲āk̲ā* (Cant. 5:3 [twice]; Esth. 8:6).]

But the two books just cited, Canticles and Esther, prove that Hebrew was still capable of producing both beautiful poetry and excellent prose in the Silver Age. To be sure, much of the Silver Age material sounds either generally poor (the Hebrew of Daniel) or unaccountably awkward in spots (that of Ecclesiastes), or partly the one and partly the other

(Chronicles), but in such cases it is open to the suspicion of being not original Hebrew but translated from the Aramaic original. That Ecclesiastes and the Hebrew parts of Daniel are translated from Aramaic has been demonstrated; the claim that it is also true of sections of Chronicles requires further study. The remarkable Book of Job can definitely be dated in the Silver Age.

Much — perhaps most, but certainly not all — of the change which the language underwent in the Roman Age can be traced to the influence of Aramaic. Not only was the Jewish diaspora Aramaic-speaking where it was not Greek-speaking, but the same was true of the greater part of Palestinian Jewry. (Hebrew seems to have survived longest in popular use in western Judea.) It was, then, under Aramaic influence that the following features were eliminated except in elevated style: the infinitive absolute, the cohortative, the consecutive tenses, the infinitive construct with subjective recta, the passive qal conjugation (ousted by the niphal, as already in not a few cases in biblical Hebrew) apart from the participle (see immediately). Largely under Aramaic influence, too, a precise new system of tenses was developed, in which the appropriate part of the auxiliary verb *hāyā* plus the participle of the main verb was obligatory for expressing the imperfect (i.e. durative or iterative) aspect of the infinitive, imperative past, and non-indicative future (for the future indicative, the participle alone is sufficient). The periphrastic construction found in Cant. 3:7 (see above) becomes very frequent. An inner Hebrew development, on the other hand, is the substitution of *niṯ* for *hiṯ* in the perfect of the tD conjugation, which thus evolved from a hithpael into a nithpael. The cause is the analogy of the niphal, which like the hithpael, begins with *hi-* in the imperative and in the infinitive, but with *ni-* in the perfect. So too, the loss of the feminine imperfect plural can hardly be due to Aramaic influence, since the only Aramaic dialect which shares it is Nabatean.

Among the demonstratives, *zō* almost completely supersedes *zōṯ* in the feminine singular (already in Ecclesiastes), and *'ēllū* takes the place of *'ēlle*; and when demonstratives are employed attributively the article is commonly omitted both from them and from the words they qualify. The biblical Hebrew demonstrative *hallāz(e)* is represented by *hallā* and forms a plural *hallēllū*. If a noun is qualified by an adjective, the latter alone takes the definite article. The accusative particle *'ṯ* with pronominal suffixes also serves a as demonstrative. The biblical word for "now" *'attā* has mostly been replaced by a new formation *'aḵšāw* (< *'aḏ kšehū?*). There are numerous new conjugations: *hō'īl w-* "since, inasmuch as," and a number of compounds of *še-* (*kiwwān še-* "when, as soon as, once," *bišbīl še-* "just because, in order that," *kšem še-* "as, even as," *kdérek še-* "in the manner that").

Many additional words are borrowed from the Aramaic: e.g. *nistakkel* "to look," *pēreš* "to become separated, or to explain," *taba'* "to solicit, or demand," *thūm* "limit."

An interesting phenomenon of this period is the large number of Greek words that are borrowed by Hebrew as by other languages of Near Eastern countries under Roman rule. The process of hellenization which began when Alexander conquered the Orient was neither reversed nor halted when the Orient came under Roman rule but on the contrary advanced further. More natives acquired some knowledge of Greek or became entirely Greek-speaking, and this applies to Palestine no less than to other countries and to Jews no less than to other peoples. The language of Roman administration in the Orient was not Latin but Greek. Well-known Greek and Graecized Latin words borrowed by the Hebrew in this period are *traqlīn* τρικλίνιον, *sanhedrī(n)* συνέδρι(ν) (vulgar forms of συνέδριον), *ligyōn* λεγεών, *hedyōt* ἰδιώτης, *parṣōp* πρόσωπον. At least one Greek sound was adopted in the process. Since Hebrew, in which the letter *pe* was either a spirant (like English *f*, but bilabial) or else an aspirated *p* (as in English *pool*, only more so), the Hebrew language had no sound sufficiently close to that of the Greek π, which is completely devoid of breathing like the French *p* in *poule*; and consequently Greek words containing the letter π were borrowed together with the peculiarly Greek sound. (That explains why neighboring consonants frequently became emphatic in the loanword, like the sibilant in *parṣōp*.)

This Hebrew, perceptibly removed from its biblical ancestor and known as mishnaic, or talmudic, Hebrew, is both concise and picturesque, and has left behind a vast literature in the shape of the Mishnah, the Tosefta, the *Baraitot* in the two Talmuds, and the Hebrew parts of a vast midrashic literature. Just when it lost its popular base entirely and became exclusively a learned tongue is not known — perhaps around 200 C.E. (Hebrew documents from the time of Bar Kokhba's revolt [132–135 C.E.], discovered in the nineteen-fifties and early nineteen-sixties, confirm that it was still alive then.) However, scholars in the 3rd and 4th centuries C.E. still handle it on occasion with skill.

D. THE CHARACTER OF THE CANAANITE LANGUAGES

1. Originally common to all Northwest Semitic languages, and always retained by the Canaanite ones, was a beautiful suppleness of the sentence.

In prose, that which has the strongest psychological stress must, except in certain cases, come first. In the Hebrew original of the following translated verses, the expressions with the psychological stress, here italicized, stand at the head of their clauses.

(a) I heard *the sound of you* walking in the garden, and I was afraid, because I am *naked* . . . Who told you you were *naked*? Did you eat *from the tree from which I had forbidden you to eat*? (Gen. 3:10–11.)

(b) Why did you not tell me that she was *your wife*? Why did you say, She is *my sister*? (Gen. 12:18–19.)

(c) Similarly, the italicized portion comes first in the original of the Phoenician inscription of Yeḥawmilk, line 9: (For) he is *a righteous king*.[6] And correspondingly in Ugaritic (I AB:12–19): I am *your slave*.

2. The normal position of the verb is at the beginning of the clause anyway. Consequently, when *the verb* has to be stressed the infinitive absolute is added to it in biblical Hebrew:

(a) We have indeed been treated by him like *foreign women*; for he has sold us, and has also *consumed* (*wayyōḵal gam 'āḵōl*) the money he got for us (Gen. 31:15).

(b) And if you did go (*hālōḵ haláḵtā*), because you longed so (*niḵsōp̄ niḵsáp̄tā*) for your father's house, why did you steal my gods? (Gen. 31:30.)

(c) And in Phoenician (the Tabnit inscription): And if you do expose me (*ptḥ tptḥ 'lty*) and do disturb me (*wrgz trgzn*).[7] Similarly in Ugaritic (II AB 4–5: 34–35): Is it that you are *hungry* (*rġb rġbt*) . . . or that you are *thirsty* (*ġmu ġmit*)?

3. Further, unlike Ugaritic, both the Phoenic and the Hebraic group possess the valuable aid to lucidity of a definite article (*ha-*, with gemination of the following consonant).

4. Further, Hebrew and Phoenician have each a complicated but very charming play of tenses. A good example of the latter is: *hannōšḵīm bšinnēhem wqār'ū šālōm wa'šer lō yitten 'al pīhēm wqiddšū 'ālāw milḥāmā* "who declare peace when they get something to chew, but launch a war upon him who omits to put food into their mouths." (Micah 3:5).[8] Biblical Hebrew also has graceful uses of the infinitive construct: *b-ḇō-ī* "in my coming" (= when I was coming). The other Canaanite languages probably had this facility too, though the only analogous usage attested is the Phoenician infinitive with the preposition *l* and a subjective pronominal suffix; e.g. *l-kn-y* "for its being" (= that it may be). The richness of the Canaanite languages, especially the Hebraic ones, in nuances expressed by means of verbal forms and word order makes them splendid media not only for lyric and prophetic rhapsody but also for

narrative prose, whether legend (Genesis) or history (Samuel). But their unmodified primitive Semitic dearth of subordinating conjunctions, limited capacity for constructing complex sentences, lack of facility in forming adjectives, and almost complete inability to form compound words, make them poor vehicles for scientific and philosophical thought. And as a matter of fact, it was not until nearly a millennium after Hebrew had ceased to be a living language that it came to be employed in either original or translated works of scientific or philosophical thought. (The book of Ecclesiastes is "philosophical" only in a popular sense.)

E. The Emergence of the Aramaic Sub-Family of Languages

It was indicated above (A, 2, b) that the primary cleavage within this sub-family is between Common and Samalian Aramaic. The latter occupies within Aramaic a position analogous to that held by Ugaritic within the Phoenic branch of Canaanite. It is only known to have been used over a short period and in a limited area, namely, in the 9th and 8th centuries and in and near Zenjirli, in southern Anatolia, in what was then the kingdom called *Y'dy* (vocalization unknown) in Samalian and *Sam'al* in Common Aramaic. Common Aramaic, on the other hand, is still spoken in some widely scattered speech islands of various sizes in western Asia. The oldest specimen of it is probably the phrase *yḡar šāhḏūṯā* "cairn of witness" (Gen. 31:47; 10th century B.C.E.). There follow a short votive inscription of Barhadad, probably one of the two 9th century Aramean kings Ben-hadad of I Kings 15:18 ff. and II Kings 8:7 ff. (unless they are one and the same individual), and an ivory plaque in which is incised the legend *lmr'n ḥz'l* "of our lord Hazael," presumably the Hazael who, as related in II Kings 8:7 ff., succeeded the second Ben-hadad (or the first, if the above passages in Kings refer to the same person). At Sefire (Sujin), in northern Syria, a long treaty between the Aramean state of Arpad and an unknown other state Katikka was engraved in stone, in Common Aramaic, around the middle of the 8th century.

Meanwhile Samalian Aramaic had also been employed graphically. The earliest text in this language is a short one, of the second half of the 9th century B.C.E., engraved on a gold object which was dedicated to his god Rakabel by Kilamuwa, king of *Y'dy*, who is better known for his much longer epigraphic account of his *res gestae* in the Phoenician language. The corpus of Samalian texts comprises further two longer inscriptions, known as the Hadad and Panamu inscriptions, of the 8th century.

Since the Panamu inscription is a memorial to King Panamu, who died in 732 B.C.E., set up by his son King Birrakab, it was presumably executed early in the latter's reign. Now, several other epigraphs of this monarch are extant, and they are all composed in Common Aramaic. It would therefore seem that at some time in the third quarter of the 8th century B.C.E. the local vernacular, Samalian, was (as a "provincial" dialect) superseded, for purposes of royal epigraphs, by Common Aramaic. Possibly Kilamuwa's above-mentioned Samalian votive inscription similarly postdated his Phoenician stele, and likewise bears witness to a language policy: Kilamuwa would then have begun by employing the old cultural language of the region, Phoenician, and then have substituted the native Samalian speech as the official language in the second half of the 9th century B.C.E.

The shibboleths of Aramaic are:

1) The dropping of the initial *'a* of the numeral 1 (Proto-Aramaic **ḥad* (m.), **ḥadah* (f.), instead of **'aḥad*, **'aḥadah*.

2) The shift of Proto-Semitic *ḏ* first to a phoneme which resembled *q* and was therefore represented by the same sign as *q* in the alphabet which the Arameans borrowed from the Phoenicians but which later, unlike genuine *q*, was shifted to '.

3) The relative particle *ḏī* (whose vowel, to be sure, was mostly dropped in later times) as against, for example, Hebrew *zū* and Ethiopic *za*.

4) The vowel scheme *a-i* in all tenses of the derived active conjugations (as against *i* in the first syllable of the perfect in Hebrew and Phoenician), and specifically *ī* in the second syllable of the third person masc. perfect of such conjugations if the final radical is *y*.[9]

5) The assimilation of the initial *y* of the roots *yd'* and *yṯb* to the following consonant: a) in the imperfect of the simple conjugation (**yidda'*, **yiṯṯib*), b) in the infinitive of the simple conjugation (**l[a]midda'*, **l[a]miṯṯab*, and c) in the substantives *madda'* and *maṯṯab* in Common and Samalian Aramaic respectively. The latter is spelled *mšb*, which cannot be read **moṯab*, because *aw* is no. contracted to *ō* and is always written *plene* in these inscriptions.[10]

6) The generalization of the nominative construct of the words for "father," "brother," and "father-in-law," namely, *'abū-*, *'aḥū-*, and *ḥamū* for all cases of the construct state except before the suffix of the first person singular (paralleled in modern colloquial Arabic, where *'abūy* etc. is said even in the latter case).

7) The characteristic common words **bir* "son," **māri'* "lord," **qušṯ* "truth (fullness)" (in Hadad, lines 26, 32,[11] with *t* as in Syriac; other dialects have *ṭ*), **mawmāt* "oath" (*ibid.* line 26), **ba'aṯar* "after," **qudām*

"before" (also Arabic), *p-m* (with a varying short vowel) "mouth" (also Arab. *fam*).

While all these features are not equally distinctive, some of them are extremely so, and their sum total is impressively so; for which reason Samalian, which shares them with Common Aramaic, *is* recognizably *a branch of Aramaic*.[12]

But it also possesses features which seem very strange to those who first make its acquaintance with some knowledge of Common Aramaic, and it lacks the most characteristic feature of Common Aramaic: the emphatic state of the noun and the near-nouns (the adjective and the participle). This state is mostly formed by adding -*ā* to the base; thus the absolute of *ḡbar* "a man" (stem *gabr-*) is *gabrā*, and that of *ṭāḇ* "good" (m.s.) is *ṭāḇā*. In Old Common Aramaic, and in western dialects even in Roman and Byzantine times, the emphatic state is truly emphatic. Here *gabrā* means "the man" as distinct from "a man," and *ṭāḇā* "the good one" (m.) as distinct from "a good one" or just "good." In some of the later languages, however, lhe emphatic state became the normal one, and the use of the absolute state was greatly restricted. But of that more later. What matters here is that in Samalian, on the contrary, the emphatic state is completely wanting.

No less strange from the point of view of Common Aramaic, is the formation of the plural. The masculine plural ending distinguishes a nominative and an oblique case, like Old Akkadian and Arabic, and is identical with the Old Akkadian masculine ending: nominative -*ū*, oblique -*ī*. The feminine plural ending is spelled -*t*, and comparative Semitics leaves no reasonable doubt but that the *t* was preceded by *ā*. What is speculative is whether this ending too distinguishes a nominative and an oblique case in the Akkadian-Arabic manner: nominative -*ātu*, oblique -*āti*. What makes it doubtful is the evidence for the disappearance of final short vowels in the singular: the feminine singular ending -*at* could not have become -*h* (whether pronounced -*ā* or -*ah*) if the *t* had been followed by a vowel. Among the strange *lexical* features of this particular brand of Aramaic may be mentioned **'anāki* (as against Common Aramaic **'anā*) "I" and *gm* (Heb. *gam*) "moreover."

The rest of the Aramaic-speaking world, *so far as we know*, employed only varieties of Common Aramaic. When this world came into being is not known exactly, but it is in no case later than the last century of the 2nd millennium B.C.E. Around 1100 B.C.E. the Assyrian King Tiglath-pileser I repeatedly drove back Aramean invaders who had crossed over from the right to the left bank of the Middle Euphrates. Then, at the tail end of the millennium, we find the Israelite king Saul warring with the king of the Aramean state of Zobah in Syria (I Sam. 14:47), while David, at the very beginning of the 1st millennium B.C.E., became embroiled with a whole series of Aramean states west of the Euphrates (II Sam. 10:6 ff.). In effect the Arameans subsequently to Tiglath-pileser I established a series of states all over the lands of the Middle and Lower Euphrates and Tigris. In the 9th century those east of the Euphrates, and in the 8th century those to the west, were absorbed by Assyria; but their language, instead of giving way to that of the conquerors (Akkadian), gained ground at the expense of the latter even before the fall of the Assyrian and neo-Babylonian empires (612 and 539 B.C.E. respectively), and eventually supplanted it entirely. It was the language of international communication which Judean diplomats had to know by the end of the 8th century (II Kings 18:26; Isa. 36:11), and in which at the end of the 7th century a West Asiatic princeling — perhaps of Ashkelon — addresses an appeal to the king of Egypt to save, in the latter's own interest, this loyal vassal from "the army of the king of Babylon." (The analogy of Akkadian as the language of the Tell el-Amarna tablets, in which loyal — or purportedly loyal — vassals beseech the pharaoh of their day to save their kingdoms in his own interest from annexation by anti-Egyptian neighbors, will occur to many.) When the neo-Babylonian empire was succeeded by the Persian (539 B.C.E.), Aramaic was made its principal language of administration, a circumstance which contributed to its still further advance at the expense of the other Semitic languages of the Fertile Crescent: Akkadian, Hebrew, Phoenician, and less important dialects.

After the fall of the Achaemenian empire, Greek offered Aramaic serious competition in Graeco-Roman Syria and Palestine. Nevertheless, the latter remained the language of a majority of the population of the Fertile Crescent — and was even adopted as their written language by the Arabic-speaking Nabateans — until the Arab conquest of that region in the 7th century C.E. This date will therefore be made the lower limit of our historical sketch, though Aramaic dialects continue to be spoken by small and widely scattered groups to this day.

F. The Internal History of Aramaic

In the earliest Common Aramaic, all the Proto-Semitic consonants remain distinct. (This also applies to Samalian Aramaic.) Also, the old passive conjugations (differing from the corresponding active ones only in vocalization) are still vigorously alive (though the reflexive naturally has to be substituted in the infinitive), and the jussive is distinguished in some forms from the indicative and can be negated only by *'al*, as in Canaanite. On the other hand, both of the original reflexives of the simple conjugation, the nG (corresponding to Hebrew niphal) and the Gt, are missing, and instead there is, on the analogy of the reflexive of the intensive conjugation (the tD, hithpaal or ethpaal), a tG conjugation (hithpeel or ethpeel). Analogously, a t-modification of the *haphel*, or causative, conjugation is developed in the shape of the *ettaphal*, though it seems at first to have been confined to the prefixed forms of the verb and to have been employed only in a passive signification (cf. Ezra 4:21; Dan. 2:5). Unlike Samalian, Common Aramaic lost all trace of the case endings completely in earliest times, and with them the final *-t* of both the singular and the plural feminine ending of the absolute state. (The feminine ending of the singular absolute, written *-h*, was perhaps at first pronounced *-ah*, and only later *-ā*.) In the plural, however, a substitute for the final *-t* arose in the shape of *-n*, which was probably borrowed from the *-n* of the corresponding masculine ending *-īn*.

The well-known Aramaic shift of the dental spirants (*d̠*, *t̠*, *t̠,*) to stops (*d*, *t*, *t̠*) took place in the 7th century B.C.E. Probably at the same time, the *q*-like sound (perhaps *g*) — by which, as stated above, Proto-Semitic *d̠* was represented in the Proto-Aramaic — was shifted to *ġ* (written '). (*Q* continued to be written occasionally in such cases long after the shift, and similarly *z* for original *d̠* long after it had been shifted to *d̠*.) *Ġ* and *ḫ*, however, seem to have remained distinct from ' and *ḥ* until Roman times. (See below, on the cuneiform Aramaic incantation from Uruk.)

In Hellenistic times, the initial *hit-* of the perfect, imperative, and infinitive of the reflexive conjugations was reduced to (')*it-* on the analogy of the imperfect and the participle. The syncope of the *h* of the causative conjugation (haphel) in the latter tenses was completed in Roman times, but the analogous reduction of the initial *ha-* to (')*a-*, though carried out consistently elsewhere, has left a few exceptions in Mandean. In Roman times, the original passives are completely replaced (outside the participle) by the *t-* conjugations discussed above. The process started in Persian times, when the original passives began to be avoided in the imperfect (cf. *yittśām*, Ezra 4:21; contrast *śīm* [perfect], Ezra 4:19) and even in the participle if the sense is fientive (cf. *mit̠qat̠(t̠)lin*, Dan. 2:13; contrast *qṭīl* [perfect], Dan. 5:30). The final *-m* of many suffixes and afformatives becomes *-n*. Accented *i* before *r* becomes *a*. It is in the Roman Age, too, that the characteristic Aramaic vowel reduction takes place

THE NORTHWEST SEMITIC LANGUAGES

As a rule, every other short vowel in open, pretonic syllables is reduced to zero; and the reduction begins not, as in Hebrew, two places back from the tone but immediately before the tone. The positional alteration of occlusive (*dagesh*) and fricative (*raphe*) pronunciations of the letters *bgdkft* (also attested for Hebrew by the Masorah) arose some time before the 5th century C.E., but how long before is not known.

Down to the end of the Persian Period, only slight dialectical variations can be observed among the records of (Common) Aramaic that have come down to us; unless the incantation tablet from Uruk (Erech) in southern Babylonia (composed in Aramaic and written in neo-Babylonian cuneiform) should chance to be pre-Hellenistic. This text offers examples of East Aramaic features which emerge into full view in the Roman Age, and even of the specifically Babylonian Aramaic ones. Most notable among these eastern traits is the plural masculine emphatic ending *-ē* (for non-Eastern *-ayyā*). There is however also a syntactic construction which is peculiar to Mandaic, the Aramaic of southern Babylonia. A connection with Babylonian Aramaic generally may be detected in the pronominal suffix for "his" with plural masculine nouns: it is *-aihi*, which is closer to the later Babylonian *-ēh* (indistinguishable from the suffix with singulars and feminine plurals) than is the non-Babylonian *-auhi*. Finally, a striking feature of this short text is the repeated use of the absolute state of the noun where the emphatic would be expected. One suspects that we have here hypercorrect forms, due to a striving for "correctness" in a *milieu* which was notorious for the opposite "error"; for in East Aramaic, as is well known, the emphatic state is the normal state of the noun, the absolute being restricted to certain special cases. (Generally speaking East Aramaic employs the absolute state where Akkadian employs the caseless form; except before a following rectum, where Aramaic employs instead the construct state.) The scribe seems to distinguish *ġ* from ', expressing the former by *ḥ* and leaving the latter unexpressed.

It is however only from Roman and later times that abundant material in clearly East Aramaic and West Aramaic dialects is available; West Aramaic being on the whole closer to the old standard Aramaic than East Aramaic, though by no means lacking in innovations. Most of the more profound innovations in East Aramaic are due to the influence of Akkadian, and must therefore go back to the time when the latter was still a living language (down to the 3rd century B.C.E.?). Of those mentioned in the preceding paragraph, the plural ending *-ē* and the roles of the statuses — cf. the end of the preceding paragraph — are to be accounted for in this way. Others are probably the disappearance of most of the pronominal suffixes with -in(n)- (innāk ,— innēh, etc.) (in the case of the third person plural, however, the element -inn has spread even to the independent pronouns), and the substitution of the jussive with l (later partly changed to n) for the third person of the indicative imperfect (at first only in positive sentences); though the manner in which Akkadian influence could have produced these changes is somewhat complicated.

The East Aramaic languages of Roman and Byzantine times are: Syriac, the language of a vast and important Christian literature; Jewish Babylonian, the language of the Babylonian Talmud and of a voluminous post-talmudic (gaonic) literature; Mandaic, the language of a gnostic sect which arose in southern Babylonia in the last three centuries before the Arab conquest and which still survives in Iraq and in the Persian city of Ahwaz (where it has even preserved its Aramaic speech), and of that sect's literature. The West Aramaic dialects include Galilean (the Palestinian Talmud and Midrashim, the ancient Palestinian Jewish Targums[13] of which Kahle published some Genizah fragments and which survive in fragments in the Fragment Targum and in altered form in Pseudo-Jonathan); Samaritan; and Christian Palestinian (the latter being preserved, apart from inscriptions, only in translations from the Greek).

It is customary to include under West Aramaic much else that is Jewish and also Palmyrene and Nabatean. But in fact the Nabateans attempted, with progressively diminishing success, to write the old standard Aramaic while actually speaking Arabic; the Palmyrenes, from all indications, did the same while actually speaking an idiom very similar to Syriac; while older Jewish writings like the book of Daniel and M⁰gillat Ta'anit, as well as Jewish deed-forms, are similarly couched not in any spoken dialect but in something approaching old standard Aramaic. Also a quasi-standard Aramaic, though much modified by transmission in a Babylonian Jewish milieu, is the language of Targum Onqelos (to the Pentateuch) and of the Targum to the Prophets.

Syriac, Galilean, and Christian Palestinian borrow an immense number of words from the Greek, sometimes along with some of their Greek inflections. The Persian influence in Jewish Babylonian (and in Mandaic) remained much less profound, at least until the 7th century C.E., which we have adopted as the lower limit of our historical survey.

PART TWO: THE HEBREWS AND THE PATRIARCHS

CHAPTER VII

WARFARE IN THE SECOND MILLENNIUM B.C.E.

by Y. Yadin

A. Introduction

THERE ARE TWO BASIC FACTS that have to be kept in mind when setting out to discuss the subject of warfare at any period and in any country, but especially in the Palestine of the second millenium B.C.E.:

1. It is impossible to understand the nature of the various elements employed in warfare, such as fortifications, weapons, army organization or tactics, except through their close interconnection. This is particularly true of the period we are dealing with here, when the invention of new and powerful weapons called for urgent counter-measures in defensive weapons, fortifications and warfare methods.

For example, the extensive use of a powerful bow with great penetrative force resulted in the invention of the coat of mail, which in turn may have brought about changes in the form of such basic weapons, as the axes. Covering the body with heavy armor plate may, in turn, have caused a diminution of the large and awkward shield, since its main function was reduced to guarding the face and those parts of the body left vulnerable even when it was armor-clad. As a matter of fact, the development of every element in the art of warfare can be traced to its origins only in the light of the general development of warfare methods. In considering the latter we shall try to discuss that problem also.

2. Since war is necessarily a two-sided process and in ancient times it was usually waged by the inhabitants of neighboring countries, the interaction of the material cultures of the two sides was most strikingly expressed in warfare; this applies in particular to countries that had long been at war with each other, or to allies in need of each other's help. For example, the battering-ram of one country affected immediately the character of fortifications in neighboring countries where the performance of these weapons was evident.[1] Similarly when certain weapons such as the curved sword appeared in one country they were quickly adopted by others, whether friends or enemies.

At the same time, interestingly enough, some nations continued in their own traditional ways and were in no hurry to adopt other countries' innovations in warfare. A considerable time could therefore elapse between the appearance of a certain weapon in one country and its acceptance by the army of another country.

The two above mentioned factors: the interdependence of the various elements in the art of warfare and the relationship between the introduction of a new weapon in one country and the reaction to it in another country, determine our approach to the study of the art of warfare in the biblic lands in the second millennium B.C.E. On the one hand, we have to analyse each element separately, and on the other, to consider reciprocal interactions of the methods of warfare in the various countries that fall within our scope.

As a result of the archeological discoveries of the last deeade we are able to understand better than in the past the ways of second millennium warfare. The epigraphic material from Mari[2] and Ugarit[3] is of first-rate importance in this respect. Together with the material from Tell el-Amarna,[4] Anatolia[5] and the Egyptian documents,[6] these finds clarify a number of previously obscure details in the numerous reliefs and frescoes, mainly from Egypt, which formerly represented our chief source of information. The letters from Mari are especially valuable, since they deal with a period from which we possess hardly any sources dealing with matters of warfare. By bringing to light mighty fortifications and weapons, archeological discoveries have enabled us to perfect our knowledge of many phenomena left unexplained by the reliefs and literary sources. Our discussion will accordingly be based not only on a comparison of the art of warfare in different countries, but on written, carved and painted documents and on actual archeological finds.

B. Weapons

The second millennium represents the most important period in the history of the art of warfare in the Near East since the main weapons and methods of fortification came into extensive military use at that time, and did not change radically until gunpowder was invented. In the second millennium we witness, for the first time, the general use of the composite bow, the "sickle" sword, the coat of mail, the battering-ram, and the horse-drawn war chariot. Furthermore, other weapons extensively used even in later periods such as the battle-axe, the spear and the sling, were improved and adapted to the revolutionary methods of warfare resulting from the main inventions of the second millennium.

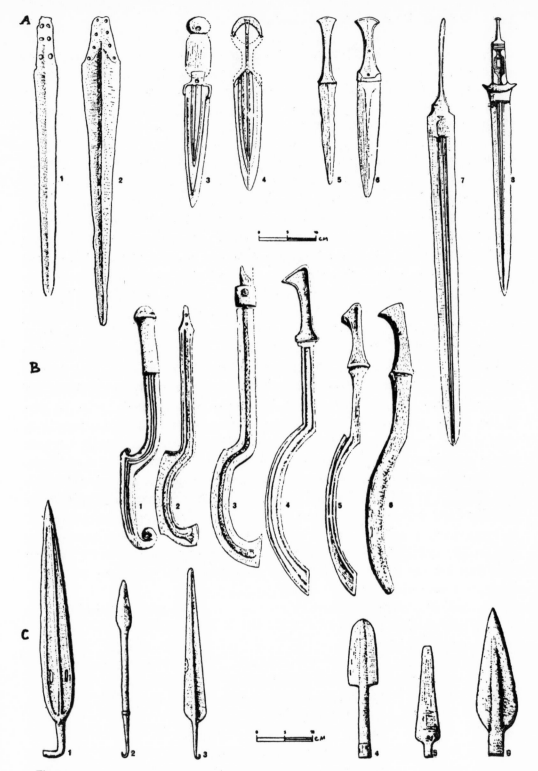

Fig. 11.
Weapons from the Middle and Late Bronze Periods:
A: straight swords; B: sickle swords; C: spear and javelin heads.
Drawing by "Carta", Jerusalem.

1. *The Composite Bow.* The warrior's desire to strike his adversary from a distance was the main factor in the invention and development of the bow.[7] Maximal range and effective penetration of the arrow were achieved by drawing the bow string as far as possible and suddenly releasing it. Until the invention of the composite bow the penetrative force of the arrow was improved either by increasing the size of the bow and using hard resilient timber, or by changing its shape to a double-curved bow, the object being to bring the string as close as possible to the warrior's gripping point i.e., the double-curved bow ᗡ. But the composite bow excelled these expedients. It was not made of wood only but also sinews, tendons, thin plates of horn, and glue which aglomerated them all into a unitary mass.[8] The warrior was provided with a weapon of enormous range and penetrative power which nevertheless did not impede his movements or mobility since it was much smaller than the usual bows. When not strung, composite bows tended to bend outward, but when the string was taut they assumed a triangular or double concave shape. It is therefore easy to distinguish on the reliefs whether the bow under consideration is composite, plain or reinforced (timber wound with thread). The double curved bow can also be composite, but is not necessarily so. Though the composite bow was already used — at least in Mesopotamia — at the end of the third millennium,[9] the armies of Canaan and Egypt adopted it only in the first half of the second millennium, when it finally became one of the most efficient weapons of that period. Not every king could have that bow manufactured in his own country because it was very expensive and difficult to make. This fact is evidenced by the many documents especially from Tell Amarna, where the Canaanite kings request the pharaoh to send them a number (generally small) of bows, and in particular by the unique document from Ugarit where Aqhat promises Anath various materials for the manufacture of the composite bow[10] and its arrows — reeds of a special quality.[11]

'adr *t*(?) qbm d-Lbnn	'adr. gdm. br'umm
'adr — qrnt b y'lm	mtnm b'qbt. *t*r
'adr. b ġl'el. qnm.	tn lk*t*r. w Hss
Yb'l qšt lk	ḥṣ't lybmt l'emm.

Let me vow *t*qbm [birch tree?] from Lebanon
    Let me vow tendons from wild bulls
Let me vow horns from wild goats
    Sinews from the hocks of bulls.
Let me vow reeds from the March of El
    Give them to Kothar-and-Khasis

That he make a bow for thee
arrows for the Progenitress of the Peoples.

The bow was the main weapon of the chariotry. On account of their great mobility and the considerable range of their bows they became the most feared units in warfare. The bow was also the principal weapon of the infantry, whose main task was to fight in open battle or to cover assaults of walls (see below). We learn it not only from the stelae and the Egyptian military equipment in the Tell Amarna letters,[12] but also from Nuzi and Ugarit documents specifying infantry equipment. We learn that a considerable proportion of the archer units were also equipped with slings,[13] and that their quivers contained twenty-five to thirty arrows.[14] The composite bow-equipped warriors were able to shoot quickly and efficiently as many as twenty-five arrows which, by penetrating armor at long range, undoubtedly decided the outcome of many a battle, as written documents and other monuments confirm.

2. *The "sickle" sword*. The extensive use of chariots necessitated the use of short range weapons. The spear was good, but not convenient at a gallop; the same applies to the straight, comparatively short sword that was in use during the second millennium until the introduction of the longsword by the Sea Peoples, in the second half of that millennium. This appears to be the reason for the extensive use of the curved sword (or the "sickle" sword, as it is erroneously called) from the beginning of the second millennium until its place was taken by the straight longsword at the end of the same millennium.[15] The curved sword, with its long hilt and curved, sickle shaped blade (its sharp edge is on the *convex* side and not on the concave side as with the sickle), was clearly a striking weapon (similar to the axe). It could be used not only in infantry battles but also from a moving chariot. This weapon, the beginnings of which we find as early as the Third Dynasty of Ur, or even earlier, was widely used during the second millenium in the entire Near East – from Syria, Anatolia and Palestine down to Egypt – where it was adopted by the Egyptian army at the time of the New Kingdom, possibly together with the chariot. In the first half of the second millennium the different types of this sword have a long hilt and a short blade. In fact, they represent a direct development of the anchor or crescent-shaped axe so widespread at the end of the third millennium (see below). The need for an improved axe, suitable for cleaving or piercing helmets and coats of mail and for purposes of battle engineering, caused the blade to be narrowed, the broad-bladed axes to disappear, and their replacement by the above-mentioned sickle sword. Towards the second half of the same millennium the hilt grew

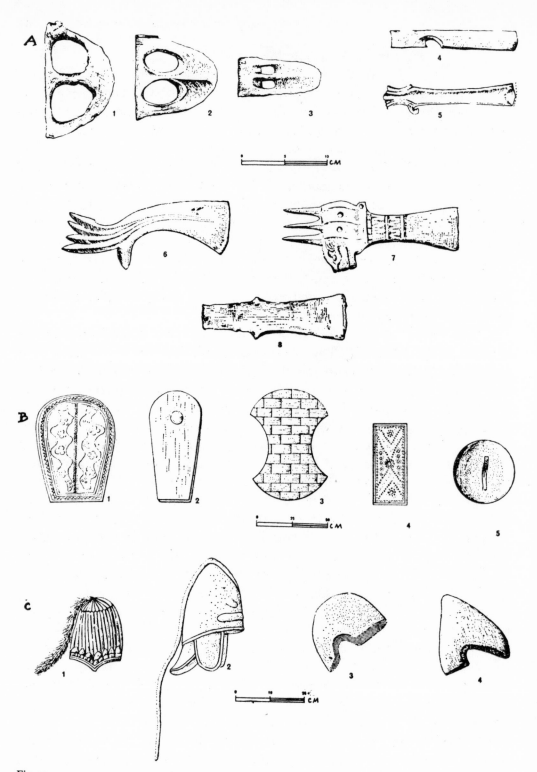

Fig. 12.
Weapons from the Middle and Late Bronze Periods:
A: axe heads; B: various types of shields; C: various types of helms.
Drawing by "Carta", Jerusalem.

shorter and the blade longer. All similarity with the anchor-shaped axe vanished and the curved sword began its independent existence. In its turn the curved sword was gradually straightened and gave way at last to the straight longsword, the purpose of which was to cut and stab at the same time. The expression "to hit with the edge of the sword" common in the Bible, particularly in descriptions of battles of the second millennium, doubtlessly refers to swords of the sickle type,[16] which were called *Khpsh* in Egypt.

3. *The Coat of Mail.* The use of the composite bow and chariot, which prevented the warrior from holding a shield in his hand, resulted in the invention of the coat of mail. This also came to be used by the infantry as protection against the deep penetrating arrows shot from the composite bows.

Even though the earliest examples found in excavations, on paintings and in reliefs date from the middle of the second millennium,[17] i.e. from the beginning of the Late Bronze Period, one may assume that the coat of mail came into use much earlier, since the examples found clearly represent an advanced stage of the coat of mail, which scarcely changed during the following periods. We have to remember that we possess almost no pictorial representations from the second phase of the Middle Bronze II Period. The scales — whose top was usually rounded — were linked by threads that passed through very fine perforations at the sides of the scale, while similar perforations enabled them to be sewn and fastened to a leather or cloth lining. We learn from documents that over 1,000 scales went sometimes into the making of this type of coat of mail,[18] and that horses, too, were protected by coats of mail already in this period.[19] The existence of the coat of mail brought about the improvement of the weapons of attack; it was necessary, for example, to reinforce arrowheads by making them thicker (especially along their middle) so as to penetrate a coat of mail. Similarly, it appears that beginning with the Middle Bronze II the axe gradually changed into a piercing weapon with an elongated blade and a narrow edge.

4. *The Axe.* The axe is one of the commonest weapons in the second millennium, being extremely efficient both in hand-to-hand fighting and in various engineering tasks during battles. The basic difference between the axes of the second millennium and those of the third millennium is that all the axes of the second millennium are made to pierce and penetrate (with long blade and narrow edge), while those of the third millennium are mainly cutting axes, with a short blade and a long edge (anchor or crescent-shaped axes, etc.).[20] Apparently this change also followed the introduction of the coat of mail and the helmet: we note that in contrast

to all the axes used in the third millennium, in Egypt as well as in Syria and Palestine, the Sumerian axes were precisely piercing axes,[21] for – as appears from the Sumerian monuments of the First Dynasty in Ur – the Sumerian army already wore a kind of body armor and improved helmets.[22] From the beginning of the second millennium axes continued to a certain extent the tradition of the long-edged anchor shaped axes, except that it is even more obvious they were used for piercing. To this type must be attributed the "eye-axe" and the "duckbill-axe" that were dominant at the beginning of the Middle Bronze Period.[23] In the course of time perfect piercing axes came into use and continued so until the end of Middle Bronze III.[24] From the second half of the second millenium we witness the extensive use of piercing axes provided with a lug and without shaft hole,[25] that were common in the one or the other form throughout the whole of the Near East. Egyptian reliefs of the New Kingdom clearly show that the axe was the weapon *par excellence* of the infantry next to the curved cutting-sword, which in fact (as was mentioned above) took the place of the ancient cutting-axe.

5. *The Battering-Ram.* There is no doubt that the two most revolutionary weapons introduced in the 2nd millennium were the battering-ram, a powerful weapon in siege warfare, and the chariot, which dominated the open battlefield. These two weapons decided the fate of many a campaign. For unknown reasons the Egyptians did not use the battering-ram (see below) and it therefore does not appear on the reliefs of the New Kingdom. We possess no siege warfare reliefs from the Middle and Late Bronze from other Near-Eastern countries, so that it was generally believed until recently that the ram was not used before the beginning of the first millennium. We have now learnt from the Mari Letters that already in the eighteenth century an improved battering-ram existed, in Syria at least.[26] This ram, called (wood) *Yāshibu*, enabled attackers to overcome fortified cities in a matter of a few days. According to Ishme-Dagan he was able to conquer a certain town with the aid of the ram in no more than a week. Another letter tells of the conquest of a fortified city in one day.[27]

From an important Hittite document describing the siege of Urshu we learn of the existence of a battering-ram, its structure, and how it was used. The entire passage is worth quoting:[28]

> "They broke the battering-ram. The king waxed wroth and his face was grim: They constantly bring me evil tidings. Make a battering-ram in the Hurrian manner and let it be brought into place. Make a 'mountain' and it [also] be set in its place. Hew a great

Fig. 13.
Primitive pole-like battering-ram.
The warriors actioning it are protected by a mobile shelter.
Wall relief at Benī Ḥasan, 20th century B.C.E.
Prof. P. E. Newberry, *Beni Hasan* 2, London, 1893, pl. XV.

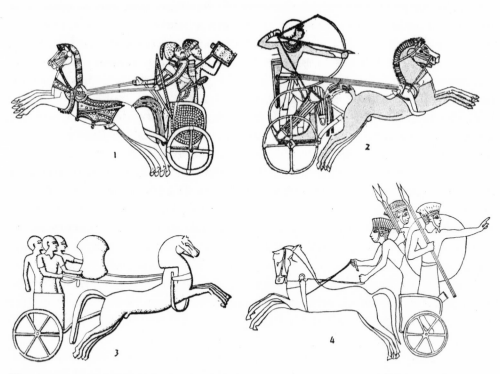

Fig. 14.
War chariots of the Middle Bronze Period;
1 – Canaanite chariot; 2 – Egyptian chariot; 3 – Hittite chariot; 4 – Philistine chariot
Drawing by "Carta", Jerusalem.

battering-ram from the mountains of Hazzu and let it be brought into place. Begin to heap up earth."

The "mountain of earth" is, of course, a ramp which had to be heaped up near the wall and above the moat (see below) to enable the battering-ram to pound the wall. The appearance of beaten earth and stone glacis, which became an integral part of second millennium fortifications through-out the Near East (Anatolia and particularly in Syria and Palestine), must evidently be attributed to the invention of the battering-ram; for the main purpose of the glacis was to protect the lower part of the wall and the city mound against direct battering (see below).

6. *The Chariot.* The horse-drawn chariot, which was used in battle everywhere, is undoubtedly the most remarkable phenomenon in the development of the art of warfare. The light chariot represented a fast mobile firing-base for the composite bow, and also solved the main tactical problem of all generations, namely – "the problem of fire and movement." The first appearance of the horse-drawn chariot is shrouded in mist; we do not know what transpired at the end of the third and the beginning of the second millennium. Lack of monuments prevents us from following the disappearance from the battlefield of the cumbersome chariot, drawn by wild asses, which was common in Sumer in the middle of the third millennium and its replacement by the light horse-drawn chariot in the first half of the second millennium.[29] The many wall paintings of Egypt from the beginning of the second millennium do not depict the chariot, but it does not follow that it was not yet widely used or that it was not used at all in battle. The absence of pictorial representations in general, and of battle scenes in special, in the entire Near East during the 18th and 17th centuries, makes it very difficult to determine when the chariot actually came into use on the battlefield. The Mari Letters enable us to establish with certainty that in the second half of the 18th century horse-drawn chariots were already used though, at least in the neighborhood of Mari, not as yet extensively.[30] Since the chariot was brought to Egypt from Canaan (as its Egyptian name proves), and because in its first appear-ance on Egyptian monuments and on Kassite cylinder seals from the 16th century in Mesopotamia[31] it is already highly developed, we can conclude with certainty that in Middle Bronze II the chariot was widely used and that its shape had already reached a high degree of perfection. The axle of all Middle and Late Bronze chariots was placed nearer to their back end, which in contrast to the Sumerian chariots, increased their mobility, especially when turning. This was technically possible because the chariot

was very light; its body, which at times was open at the sides, consisted of a wooden frame covered with leather. Even though the axle was moved toward the back end of the chariot, this change did not make it very difficult for the horses. The number of horses harnessed to the chariot was always two; however, from the written documents we can deduce that the full complement (including the outrigger) was three, (similar to what we see at a later period on the Ashur-nasir-pal reliefs).[32]

The chariot is manned by two people: the charioteer who holds the reins and a warrior armed with a composite bow (the Egyptian monuments, which describe the battle of Kadesh show that the Hittite chariots carried three warriors). On the sides of the chariot were fixed quivers for arrows and a special container for the bow. The Egyptian chariots – especially from the beginning of the Nineteenth Dynasty – carried sometimes quivers for the hurling javelins of the "weaver's beam" type (the "loop javelin"), which were, no doubt, brought there by Aegean mercenaries.[33] With the Mesopotamian chariots, on the other hand, (according to the cylinder seals)[34] the long spear is almost always kept at the back of the chariot. This was customary in Assyria and in the Neo-Hittite Kingdoms in the first millennium.

The construction of chariot wheels differed in Mesopotamia, Canaan or Egypt. While the wheels of the Kassite chariots had six spokes,[35] the "Canaanite chariots"[36] and after them the Egyptian chariots – in the first half of the Eighteenth Dynasty – had only four spokes, a fact that suggests their comparative lightness. This lightness is evidenced also in Egyptian wall paintings, which depict gift-bearing Canaanites carrying a chariot on their shoulders. From the end of the 15th century we see six or more spokes[37] appearing on the wheels of the Egyptian chariot. It can be assumed that at the end of the Bronze Period the six spokes already formed part of the chariot wheels in Canaan too (a re-borrowing from Egypt, as can be deduced from the chariot reliefs on the Megiddo Ivories).[38]

The chariot was of an extremely intricate design, both as regards the structure of its different parts which enabled it to move quickly forward and sideways, and as regards the different kinds of timber and metal required for its manufacture.[39] Each part was built from a different kind of timber, according to its function. Detailed lists of dozens of parts are contained in the ḪAR.RA-ḫubullu dictionaries,[40] as well as in later documents from Ugarit (see below) from Taanach,[41] from Tell Amarna, the Papyrus Anastasi I, etc. In addition to the names of the parts, the documents inform us of the places where the timber and other materials originated, since they were mentioned in the correspondence between rulers who built the chariots (particularly in Egypt) and those in whose countries the required trees grew. Some of the Ugarit documents recently published give the names of chariot parts and of the harness, the material of which it was made, and so forth. These and similar documents as well as Egyptian wall paintings, inform us of the existence of well equipped workshops at the royal residences, where chariots were manufactured and repaired. This was where "the artificers of chariots" as they are called in the Ugarit documents, worked headed by "the chief artificers."

Here is one of the most typical of the documents:[42]

ṯmn mrkbt dt	Eight chariots which
'rb. bt. mlk	entered the King's Palace.
yd'apnthn	with their wheels
yd hzhn	with their 'arrows'
yd trhm	with their harness[43]
w — l. tt mrkbtm	And two chariots
lnn utpt	have no quivers
w. *tlt* smdm.w.ḥrṣ	and three axles [?] and three pairs
apnt.db.rb.hršm	of wheels where given to the Chief-artificer [for repairs?].

C. The Army

1. *Combat Units.* Even before the discoveries at Mari we possessed extensive information about the organization of the Egyptian army, and in Palestine during the Tell Amarna period; now the Mari Letters have brought to light significant details about army organization in the Middle Bronze. These letters enable us to understand not only some of the problems connected with fighting methods and army organisation but also the structure of army units and the strength of the expeditionary forces.[44]

Though the territorial units sometimes numbered as many as 10,000 men (i.e. a myriad), they were generally smaller though always divided decimally. The large units consisted of smaller units: of battalions of a thousand men. The letters also mention units of 3,000 soldiers[45] (amongst them a unit of 2,000 Habiru)[46] and even units of 1,000, 500, one half of a thousand, of 600 and even 100. In special operations, and particularly in foray expeditions, the Mari Letters[47] mention units of 300 men, a suitable force for this kind of operation.[48]

While the basic unit, as it seems right to assume, consisted of ten soldiers,[49] we also hear of units of 50 men — no doubt platoons. There is some ground for assuming that the armies of the Egyptians, Hittites, and

Canaanites (at least from the middle of the second millennium onwards) also fought in comparatively large units. Thus we learn from Egyptian documents that the army of the Hittites and their allies in the battle of Kadesh numbered 16–17,000 warriors, including the chariotry; there must have been three times 2,500, which is 7,500, and another 9,000 infantry.[50] We estimate the Egyptian army at 20,000 men, or four brigades, each of approximately 5,000 combatants.[51] According to a very important piece of information in the Papyrus Anastasi I, the Egyptian unit consisted of 5,000 men and was frequently composed in this period (Ramses II) of mercenaries from the conquered nations.[52] Thus Rib-Addi asks Pharaoh to send him a battalion of 5,000 men and 50 chariots to save Byblos.[53] We also possess numbers of the units of the chariot corps in battles from the middle of the second millennium onwards.

In the battle of Kadesh the Hittites, as we said, had 2,500 chariots (3,500 according to E. Meyer);[54] on the other hand, in the battle of Megiddo some two hundred years earlier, Thut-mose III, according to his account, took in booty 929 chariots.[55] Also Amen-hotep II when mentioning booty specifies a number close to this — 820 chariots which represented, of course, the spoils taken from several cities.[56]

Such numbers, however, (2,500 in one army) could exist only in the large armies; the kings of individual towns in Canaan possessed far fewer troops, as we know from the Amarna Letters. The latter generally mention units of 50 chariots,[57] 30 chariots,[58] occasionally 10 chariots,[59] even of 5 chariots.[60] Similarly, in documents from Anatolia there appear 100 chariots,[61] 30 chariots[62] — we read of units under the command of *Rab-Hamsha* (chief of fifty)[63] with whom one may compare the chief of fifty in the Egyptian army.[64] These numbers lead to the conclusion that the tactical combat unit consisted of 50 chariots which were divided into 5 basic units of 10 chariots each. The basic units could also form units of 30 chariots, namely 3×10. In Egypt we also know of chariot units consisting of 25 chariots.[65] In expeditionary forces larger than these, units of "fifty" and units of "thirty" were attached to larger units, but the decimal basis (in all its multiplications) was preserved. The extensive training required for operating the chariots, the very considerable expense required for their manufacture, and the training of the horses as well as the absolute military superiority of the chariot force, led to the force being composed mainly of members of the nobility, which were known by the name of Maryannu.[66] It is a particularly interesting fact that the chariotry was the only mobile force among all the Mediterranean armies during the Middle and Late Bronze, since cavalry battalions (though not individual horsemen)[67] appeared in the armies only at the end of the second millennium and at the beginning of the first millennium.

2. *Logistics and Administration.* Operations in large formations and over long distances like those mentioned in the Mari Letters and in the Egyptian documents could not be carried out without thorough and comprehensive arrangements for mobilization, supply and counting of booty. The documents from Mari, Nuzi and Ugarit referring to payments note exactly the names of the soldiers, the service personnel and the payments made to them, types of weapons, details of their distribution among the soldiers and the quality of the arms kept in the royal depots. A high level of administration and storekeeping emerges.[68] We find an instructive example in a passage from the Papyrus Anastasi I mentioned above: the Egyptian writer poses the problem of provisions, which affected the expeditionary force:[69]

> "There is brought thee a peace offering before thee: bread, cattle and wine. The number of men is too great for thee, whereas the provisions are too small for them . . . Thou receivest them, placed in the camp. The troops are ready and prepared. Make them quickly into portions, that of each man at his hand."

This document shows that the army did not carry with it all the supply and equipment required. An important part of these was prepared by the vassal countries and delivered at different places to the expeditionary forces. Similarly, we learn from Thut-mose III's battle at Megiddo that a large part of the fodder for the animals and rations for the troops consisted of crops from the country,[70] and this is also evident from the letters of the Canaanite kings discovered at Tell el-Amarna. The authors of the letters inform the pharaoh that they have prepared the requirements of his army according to what the military scribes had written them.[71] These scribes were obliged to acquire expert knowledge of the topographical conditions in various countries and of the roads that led there. They used to be sent in advance of the expeditionary force to the different countries in order to prepare the supplies, etc. The Egyptian wall reliefs which describe the battle of Kadesh enable us to follow clearly the excellent supply arrangements made for the expeditionary force. Special ox-drawn carts transported naturally only the most important equipment which was the responsibility of a special corps.[72] Water supply was one of the most serious problems. In addition to the large water stations along the main routes, which the Egyptian kings prepared,[73] the soldiers were also equipped with special water flasks. These arrangements did not suffice in every instance – at least with some nations — and we learn from some of the documents that for lack of water a whole army was forced to cancel its campaign.

The letter of Rib-Addi tells us about such a case:[74]

> "Further: The King of [Mi]ta[n]a has marched as far as Ṣumura, and desired to go as far as Gubba, but there was no water for him to drink, and so he has returned to [h]is land."

Compare this with what the Bible tells us about Jehoram King of Israel, and Jehoshaphat King of Judah who fought against Moab and nearly lost their troops in the wilderness for lack of water (II Kings 3:9). The preparation of equipment on the battlefield and before the battle was also carried out according to specific instructions. An interesting order of this type is preserved for us in the descriptions of the siege of Megiddo, in the war of Thut-mose III.[75]

> "Prepare ye." Make your weapons ready, since one will engage in combat with that wretched enemy in the morning...."

This command should be compared with Josh. 1:10 ff. "Then Joshua commanded the officers of the people, saying: Pass through the midst of the camp, and command the people saying: Prepare you victuals: for within three days ye are to pass over this Jordan...." From Ugarit we hear also about the preparation of provisions before a battle.[76] From many documents and also from the Egyptian wall reliefs we know of a special service responsible for guarding, counting and distributing the plunder. The Mari Letters mention frequently special guards-units appointed to watch over the booty.[77] A very interesting document[78] specifies the laws governing the distribution of spoils among the king, the officers and the soldiers.[79]

Conscription was naturally the main concern of the armies throughout the Near East, since in addition to the units of the permanent army it was frequently necessary to recruit from among the people additional troops, for garrison and other duties. On this subject too, the invaluable Mari Letters provide a great deal of information about conscription undertaken from time to time in various towns and lands, for the purpose of a military expedition.[80] There is evidence that in Egypt there existed a kind of quota for such conscription, namely: "One to a hundred".[81] The Ugarit documents confirm the existence of detailed lists of soldiers according to town and military aptitude (infantry, chariotry, etc.).[82] Particularly instructive are the Egyptian documents where the lists of various military officials show how important were the tasks of military scribes in the organization of the military units, their conscription, and book-keeping.[83] They were mainly attached to military units, at times in considerable numbers. (In one document we read of twenty scribes attached to a single expedition). We also know of chief scribes of a camp. They used to work at the general headquarters and were also sent to combat units to supervise the military administration, particularly the accounts. By virtue of their office they were also in charge of the battle diary and the war records.

An official of a different kind was in charge of the conscripts. He was responsible not merely for the allocation of the militia units and their attachment to the garrisons for training, but also for public works that the army had to carry out.

Another high officer, an "administrative officer," who did not take part in the actual fighting, was responsible for the troop movements, equipment and supplies. Other officers were in charge of the arsenals and the works.

3. *Engineering and Transport.* The documents at our disposal enable us not only to follow the character of the administrative services, but also the existence of high level combat services, such as engineering and military transport, medical services, communications and reporting. There existed, no doubt, special engineers to supervise the erection of siege ramps, etc. Already in the Mari period we hear of special methods for the transport of siege equipment by boat or transport carts.[84] This piece of transport engineering precedes by at least two hundred years another engineering operation which was considered — until the publication of the Mari documents — one of the most daring innovations of Thut-mose III.[85] The Barkal stele describes his expedition beyond the Euphrates: "When my majesty crossed over to the marshes of Asia, I had many ships of cedar built on the mountains of God's land near the Lady of Byblos. They were placed on carts, with cattle drawing [them]. They journeyed in [front of] my majesty, in order to cross that great river which lies between this foreign country and Naharin."[86]

4. *Medical Services.* We do not possess much information concerning the existence of organized medical services. However from the reports in the Mari Letters it transpires that such a service did exist. The army commanders frequently announced that the troops are well, there are no dead nor sick.[87]

Another document from Egypt indirectly proves the care of wounded. One of the reliefs of Ramses II describing his battles with the Nubians shows: "Two negroes leading away a wounded comrade to his family."[88]

5. *Communications.* The problem of communication during battle — how to transmit brief operational orders, give warning calls or pass information from place to place — has since time immemorial constituted one of the

most difficult and vital problems of fighting units. Even if we had no detailed information on this subject we would assume that armies organized in large units and as highly developed as those of the second millennium, would have had permanent arrangements in the vital communications matter. We have, in fact, information that enables us to follow several of these systems of communication.

The earliest and most interesting information in our possession comes from Mari. It shows a highly developed system of signalling by beacons and torches according to an agreed code. The system was based on the number of torches used.[89]

The transmission of certain information by means of "fire signals" was widely used, as we learn from the following letter:

"When I [Masum] had made ready the city of Himush over against him, and he saw that the land was hastening to [my] aid, he raised a fire signal, and all the cities of the land of Ursum on the other side acknowledged it".[90]

There were also pre-arranged signals for quickly coming to the rescue of the attacked, as we learn from another letter.[91] Sometimes the fire signal was a double one.[92] The use of fire as an agreed signal is mentioned in the Bible in connection with the conquest of Ai (Josh. 8:8, 19–21) and in the battle of the Benjamites (Jud. 20:40); and likewise in the Lachish Letters.[93] Communications and signalling arrangements for the fighting units in action were also transmitted by trumpet calls as we know from the Egyptian monuments of the Late Bronze,[94] by special signals such as lifting up the hands (Joshua in the battle of Ai: "And they run as soon as he had stretched out his hand," Josh. 8:19) or with special instruments. A widely-used method of communications was, of course, the sending of messengers, horsemen. Though, at that time, as we have said, cavalry was not as yet in use, the sending of runners and mounted messengers for the speedy transmission of information was already common at the time of Mari.[95]

We find a good example during the battle of Kadesh. When the position of Ramses II grew serious, he dispatched a mounted runner to summon the second unit. Below the rider engraved on the reliefs, we read:

> "The scout of the army of Pharaoh, going to hasten the division of Ptah saying: 'March on'."[96]

Frequently, the messages were, of course, transmitted by runners on foot, and the following letter by Rib-Addi is instructive: "The messenger of the King of Acco is more heeded than [my] messenger, because a horse was given to him."[97]

6. *Intelligence and Reporting*. The safety of long campaigns, the operation of large forces under various geographical conditions and pretty good means

of communication — all of which distinguish second millennium warfare —
necessitated the existence of developed intelligence systems able to supply
the rulers not merely with general information before the operation
(strategic intelligence), but also with current information during the course
of the battle (tactical intelligence). Different documents — be they from
Mari, from Egyptian sources or the Bible — all prove the most efficient
operation of various intelligence factors. To obtain information they employed special spies to mislead the enemy with "simulated spies," and by
continuous communication between subordinates and officers they obtained
a flow of continuous information as regards the enemy's force and intentions.
It is interesting that already during the Mari period fighting reconnaissances
were conducted into enemy territory in order to capture living sources of
information, "informers" ("men of tongue" as they are called in the
letters), so as to "interrogate" them for the purpose of obtaining important
intelligence concerning the enemy camp.   Thus, Ibalpiel writes to
Hammurabi his master:

"Now let a light armed force (*sabum qallatum*) go to raid the enemy
column and capture informers (*awīlē ša lišanim*)".[98]

"Informers" are also mentioned in other letters written for military
intelligence.[99] From a considerable number of such letters we learn that
lower commands and army commanders dispatched rapid and detailed
reports to their superiors about all the enemy's military activities.

King Zimri-lim received a detailed report from one of his commanders
in which the sender stresses that the information was based on hearsay and
not first hand. The report specifies the movements of a certain tribe:
informing that they have reached a certain river, but have not crossed
it yet. For the time being they are not arrayed in battle order.[100] In a
similar manner information is supplied about the movements of the *Banu-
Yamina* indicating the direction in which they are moving.[101] Occasionally
the king receives information from a subordinate who has been sent to
investigate a certain matter. The subordinate hastens to inform him about
the matter. ("Yesterday I left Mari . . . and I hasten to write"). If the
particulars are not known precisely, the man will investigate them and
immediately inform the king.[102] The reports frequently give the enemy's
numbers, his intentions and the date of the event; the following version
is fairly common; "In the month of X in the sixth day . . . 6,000 soldiers
of Y arrived at Z. It is said that their intention is to occupy city so and
so . . ."[103]

The descriptions of the battle of Kadesh, as they are preserved in the
Egyptian sources, also tell how both sides used all kind of stratagems to

obtain information, and to deceive the enemy. However, the events of the battle show that both sides failed in several instances in the course of the battle. In the beginning the Egyptians did not know of the enemy concentrations at Kadesh and Pharaoh fell into a trap. Later on, when the Hittites attacked the Egyptian vanguard they did not know that Pharaoh kept another force at the rear, and they were thus hemmed in between the vanguard and the rear force.[104] The extortion of information from prisoners was, of course, carried out in the usual manner. Below a drawing where we see how captured spies are beaten, is written simply:

"They [the Egyptians] are beating them [the spies] to make them tell where the wretched chief of Kheta is."[105]

The questions the spies were asked enable us to follow the method of investigation, which endeavored to trace all details relating to the enemy. They were asked:

(a) "Of what nationalities is the enemy camp composed?
(b) Which forces are represented (chariotry, infantry)?
(c) How are they armed?
(d) What are their numbers?
(e) Their exact emplacement and state of readiness."[106]

The strategic intelligence service, naturally, strove to obtain extensive information. The most perfect example in our possession is contained in the instructions that Moses gave the spies:

(i) And see the land, what it is.
(ii) And the people that dwelleth therein, whether they are strong or weak, whether they are few or many.
(iii) And what the land is that they dwell in, whether it is good or bad.
(iv) And what cities they are that they dwell in, whether in camps, or in strongholds.
(v) And what the land is, whether it is fat or lean; whether there is wood therein, or not (Num. 13:18 ff).

We also read of the sending out of spies for obtaining tactical intelligence in preparation for Joshua's campaign against both Jericho (Josh. 2) and Ai (Josh. 7:2–3).

D. OPEN BATTLE

1. *The March and the Halt.* Though most of the monuments and descriptions of campaigns deal with battles for the conquest of fortified cities (see below), we possess some documents from which we are able to draw a number of

general conclusion, about the order of marches and in open battles. The setting in motion of large camps, the number of whose soldiers, as we saw above, reached 10,000 sometimes, obviously required army marching drill and fighting in orderly battle formation, compact and under command control. Already from Egyptian models of the Middle Kingdom in Egypt[107] we can see the troops marching in columns, ten soldiers to each rank. Even if we were to assume that those models do not precisely represent the number of soldiers in each rank, they clearly prove the custom of compact and orderly marching. The marching of a body of troops into battle is described poetically yet realistically enough in a Ugaritic document, which appears to be typical of the entire period of the second millennium. In the legend of Keret we read the description of the preparations for a battle and the conscription of the army:[108]

"They march in thousands *serried*,
and in myriads *massed*.
After two, two march;
after three, all of them."

The formations of an army on the march and on the way to battle are represented in an extremely realistic manner which confirms what has been said above concerning the descriptions of the battle of Kadesh.

These reliefs show that the "unit of the young men" (the Canaanite auxiliary force which fought on the side of Ramses) moved in a phalanx of ten frontal ranks, each section of ten soldiers being formed in a column. The Hittite army stationed near Kadesh is represented in a similar formation; this force is not yet engaged in the battle, and its phalanx is constructed in a marching formation i.e. in columns, each rank consisting of ten soldiers who were disposed in a frontal rank. It does not seem difficult to conclude from these descriptions how the army changed from marching formation to fighting formation. It can moreover, be presented in the following schematic form:

	Battle		March
Frontal ranks	. . . .	. . . .	March
ten rows	. . . .	. . . .	in columns
deep	. . . .	. . . .	ten men
	. . . .	. . . .	wide
	. . . .	. . . .	↑
	. . . .	. . . .	
	. . . .	. . . .	
	. . . .	. . . .	

———————→

Organizing the actual march, which at times had to cover hundreds of miles at speed, was a pretty difficult problem, especially if we remember that the armies of those days consisted of chariotry and infantry. Calculations of the time table in the war of Kadesh show that the Egyptian army succeeded in covering a distance of some 650 km in thirty days, that is to say, some 20 km a day on an average, which is a suitable average for a mixed force of vehicles and infantry.[109]

There is no doubt that the second millennium army commanders were expert in protecting the marching army, though the two most famous battle descriptions that have survived, of the battle of Megiddo and of the battle of Kadesh, show that pharaohs "sinned" by neglecting these principles. When a large army consisting of several secondary units is on a march, basic principle requires that the different units advance one after the other separated by suitable tactical distances, and that each unit move in formation and spaced in such a way as to enable it to go over instantaneously from marching formation to defence or attack formation. When Thut-mose III decided to march through the Megiddo pass, he did so against the advice of his commanders, who said:

> "What is like to go [on] this [road] which
> becomes [so] narrow? It is [reported] that the foe
> is there, waiting on [the outside while they are]
> becoming [more] numerous. Will not horse [have to]
> go after [horse, and the army] and the people similarly?
> Will the vanguard of us be fighting while the [rear
> guard] is waiting here in Aruna, unable to fight?"[110]

In the battle of Kadesh, on the other hand, the main defeat of Ramses II was due to the fact that four of his units — though moving in suitable formation — kept too large spaces between one unit and the next, so that no tactical communication could be kept between them.

We find an echo of the formation of these marches in the descriptions of how the Israelites marched in the wilderness. They occasionally mention the marching order of the units (the standards), the vanguard and the rear party.

The terrain sometimes made it impossible to ride in chariots; in which case they were either carried or had to be abandoned.[111]

In many instances the army was forced to march at night, and security arrangements obviously applied with equal stringency to this type of march. In a Hittite document King Mursilis points out that large armies cannot camp inside fortified towns: for one thing, their area is too small (see below) and for another, the army is usually in enemy country.[112] Suitable arrangements and a great deal of training are therefore required to encamp an army in the open field. These arrangements have to ensure comfortable camping conditions for the army, and at the same time protection from a surprise attack.

The two earliest camp descriptions preserved — the written description of the battle of Megiddo (see below, the battle for the town) and the reliefs of the battle of Kadesh — make possible a good reconstruction of the camping arrangements. When Thut-mose III's army reached the neighborhood of Megiddo it was decided to set up camp.

> "Then a camp was pitched there for his majesty.... Resting in the enclosure of life, prosperity, and health. Providing for the officials. Issuing rations to the retinue. Posting the sentries of the army. Saying to them: "Be steadfast, be steadfast! Be vigilant, be vigilant!"[113]

The Egyptian camp, with the army camping in it, is illustrated to perfection on the Egyptian wall reliefs that represent the battle of Kadesh. The camp was set up in the shape of a rectangle and was protected on the four sides by rows of round topped shields which were placed one next to the other. At the sides of the camp were several openings which led to the two main roads that divided the camp into a number of quarters. In one quarter were pitched the tents of the king and his ministers, while on the rest of the area camped the armed forces, the carts and the beasts of burden. A camp of this type — with all its well conceived arrangements — could be struck or pitched at great speed. The descriptions of Israelite tribes on the march and particularly the descriptions of the camping arrangements in their general, as well as in detail, are strongly reminiscent of the camping arrangements of the Egyptian army mentioned above.

2. *Combat.* We do not possess sufficient sources to follow the principles applied by the infantry when fighting an open battle, though in a general manner one may assume that several of the accepted principles of combat such as maintenance of aim,[114] offensive spirit, surprise, concentration of power, security arrangements, maximum mobility, coordination of the different forces,[115] etc., were already known by then and put into practice.

On the other hand, the descriptions of chariot battles emphasize (Thut-mose IV,[116] Tut-ankh-Amon,[117] Seti I,[118] and especially the battle of Kadesh where the chariots played a decisive part) that in the tumult of the beginning battle the chariotry commanders had excellent control over their force, and were able to operate it at speed, unit by unit, according to the progress of the battle. The events of the battle of Kadesh enable us to follow the tactical methods employed in operating the chariot units.

(a) The chariot charge for the purpose of penetrating and disrupting the enemy formations.

(b) The encircling of the enemy units by the four flanks, as is written below one of the reliefs:

> "He found surrounding him 2,500 horse in four formations on his every side".[119]

A piece of interesting information preserved in the descriptions of the battle of Kadesh tells that the chariots were drawn by stallions. The King of Kadesh therefore tried to disrupt the Egyptian chariotry formations by having a mare run in front of them and exciting the horses. The narrator tells how he succeeded in catching and killing the mare, thus thwarting the enemy's design.[120]

Large armies, particularly those including cavalry, abstained as far as possible from night marches.[121] Some armies of the smaller nations or the nomadic tribes naturally chose night fighting to gain an advantage over the larger army by surprise and the neutralization of the chariot forces. In a Babylonian document from the middle of the second millennium we learn the exact details of a night attack that took place in the third watch.[122] We already mentioned the security arrangements Mursilis made to prevent a night attack. The commanders of large armies naturally expressed their contempt and anger at hostile night attacks, as we know from Mursilis' words in that document:

> "They did not dare to attack me in daylight, and preferred to fall on me during the night. In the night we will attack him".[123]

Similar to the above forays and those of the *Banu Yamina* which are mentioned in the Mari Letters, was the system of fighting in open battles employed by the Israelite tribes under Joshua's leadership. In fact, they were in the nature of surprise attacks on the enemy camps (Josh. 11:7)

The ambush was likewise an important weapon of the nomadic tribes in their war against regular armies. We hear of an ambush in one of the Taanach Letters of the 15th century.

> "and thou dost remember that I was ambushed in Gurra"[124]

Another document — Papyrus Anastasi I — describes typical ambushes in Canaan.[125]

The Israelite tribes also used the method of ambush. This will be discussed further on when we come to the conquest of fortified cities. A special type of fighting, widespread in early times, was the battle between chosen warriors with the agreement of both sides, the result of their fight deciding the result of the campaign.[126] To sum up, we see that in principle, warfare in the second millennium already bore all the tactical characteristics of the following generations.

E. The Fight for the City and Methods of Defence

1. *The Defence of the City.* Open battles between armies of great kingdoms on the one hand, and the forays of nomadic tribes on the other, despite their influence on political decisions in certain periods, represented but a small part of military operations in the second millennium as well as before and after. The main problem actually centered round the defence and conquest of the town. Disregarding several secondary factors, we might say that two basic criteria determined the site and plan of the Canaanite town: strategic-tactical factors and the water supply. Canaanite towns were founded solely in places that met these requirements, though as a matter of fact the security factor usually necessitated the siting of cities on top of hills, while water sources were generally found at the foot of hills. This difficulty was felt in Canaan and other Near Eastern countries.

Other security considerations besides the elementary tactical and defence factors, brought about — particularly at a time when a central authority (internal or external) existed — the establishment of towns in places of a country-wide or even general Near Eastern scale strategic importance, such as the security of main routes or important passes. The need of cities destined to serve also as supply bases, arsenals, encampments for big armies on the march, supplied an additional consideration which influenced the siting of cities and their distance from each other. Since the combination of tactical factors and water supply was possible only in certain places — and these conditions did not really change throughout history — we witness the persistence of cities in the same places; a town was destroyed and another was built on its ruins, the same thing happening again and again. In the second millennium this process brought about a considerable rise of the level at which the towns were built. They were located above the natural level of the hill on which the early cities had been built, and the building area of the tell had diminished as against the original area of the hill. As a result of this last factor and the limited yield of the natural water supply in the vicinity of the town, the area of the Canaanite town did not generally exceed several acres[127] — apart from exceptional cases, such as Hazor (and likewise several towns in Syria and Anatolia); hence even its population was small. Assuming that the number of inhabitants to every built-up 1000 square yds. was approximately sixty souls,[128] we have to conclude that the maximum number of inhabitants of the Canaanite cities in the country was roughly as follows: Tell Abu Huwām 500, Beth-shean 2,000, Dothan 2,500, Megiddo 4,600, Shechem 3,000, Tell al-Far'ah (northern) 1500, Gezer 4,000, Lachish 4,000, Tell Beit Mirsim 2,500, Jerusalem 3,000, Beth-shemesh 1,800, Tell al-'Ajjūl 6,000, as against these, Hazor with its cca. 180 acre area was able to accommodate several tens of thousands of inhabitants.

These facts are of great importance for defence purposes, since it cannot be assumed that the number of warriors at a time of emergency, in any of the above mentioned cities (if we consider the ages from 18—50), represented more than 25% of the entire population, namely, on an average about 500 warriors for the small towns, about 1,000 men for the large town, and several thousands for a town of the Hazor type. To the above numbers we must add, of course, a certain percentage of warriors from the "daughter cities," that is, from the rural settlements which participated in the defence, being situated within the area of government of the royal city. To enable the besieged to withstand a numerically superior enemy the towns planners were obliged to ensure fortifications and superior defence arrangements, out of proportion to the relatively poor standard of the other buildings of the town. These defence arrangements consisted of three elements: the walls, the royal palace and the water supply during the siege. The towns of the first half of the second millennium, which were erected on the majority of the country's tells by new nations, and after a considerable period of cessation of settlement at the beginning of this millennium, followed the planning of the earlier cities, since they depended on the same objective factors: security and water. Apart from these, the new inhabitants faced completely new military problems which greatly influenced the fortification planning of the new cities, since in some places the limited tell area could not contain all the inhabitants, with their cattle and vehicles. Furthermore, they had to take into consideration the chariots and battle-rams that had developed into military factors of the first degree and a decisive force in the open field, as well as in the battle for cities. In answer to the first problem there appeared cities of the type of Hazor, Qaṭna, Carchemish, etc.,[129] which were characterized by their large dimensions and their division into two separate sections for defence arrangements. The early tell areas which were adjacent to the water supply and had both natural and artificial defences (the walls of the early cities which protected the mountain slopes) became the residence of the king, his ministers and the military nobility, while next to it arose a new city which accommodated thousands of other inhabitants. The planning of the upper city was determined by the outlines of the tell on which it was built. For increased protection it was frequently divided into several quarters, the inner section containing the king's fortress and palace. Each quarter was protected separately so that each section of the town could be defended independently. These characteristic features stand out in most of the large towns of this type, such as Boghazköy in Anatolia, Carchemish or Hazor. The excavations at Hazor have revealed that, in the Middle Bronze Period, the upper city was surrounded by at least two walls, one of which protected the entire upper city, and the second one, which enclosed the highest level, protected the king's palace.

In planning the lower town, the area of which was several times larger than the upper town (in Hazor, for example, it covered 180 acres, i.e., about eight times the area of the upper town), there was no need to consider the restrictions of the tell area; its position at the bottom of the upper town afforded it protection at least on one side. Since at times it extended over an area adjacent to the tell, it was necessary to put up huge fortifications distinguished by the two basic requirements: height and thickness — conditions which nature supplied to the upper city.

The plan of these new towns was at times rectangular (Qaṭna, Hazor) and basically resembled the structure of the tribal and military camps usual at that time. The large area of these towns permitted the accommodation of a great number of inhabitants and many chariots and horses — a self-evident conclusion, though not yet proved by excavations. The Hittite cities were also divided into quarters which were apparently capable of defending themselves independently.

Among the most characteristic town fortifications at the beginning of the second quarter of the second millennium, are the large beaten-earth glacis which protected the tell slopes. These glacis usually consisted of several layers of beaten earth, brick, clay, and the like, which were alternated in such a manner that they look like layered sandwiches, in section. These glacis did not represent an alternative to a wall (which was built on top of them); their function was to widen the bottom of the walls and to cover the slopes of the artificial tell which were loose and vulnerable. It seems that this method of fortification derived from the necessity of defence against the battering-rams which — as we saw above — came into use just at that period.[130] With the improvement of battering-rams in the second quarter of the second millennium, the glacis of beaten earth disappeared to be replaced by stone glacis — wide at the base, narrow and rounded at the top. Glacis of this type were used particularly to protect

Fig 15.
Megiddo, reconstruction of the city gate,
Middle Bronze IIa Period (stratum XIII).
G. Loud, *Megiddo II*, Chicago,1948, fig. 8.
Drawing by "Carta", Jerusalem.

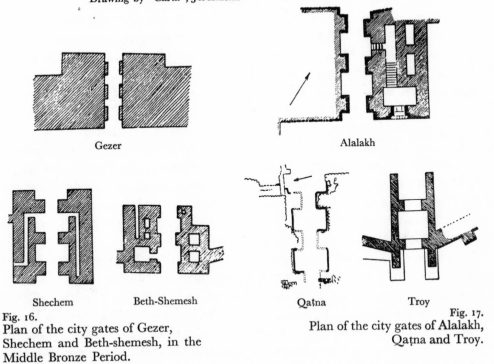

Gezer

Alalakh

Shechem   Beth-Shemesh

Qatna

Troy

Fig. 16.
Plan of the city gates of Gezer,
Shechem and Beth-shemesh, in the
Middle Bronze Period.

Fig. 17.
Plan of the city gates of Alalakh,
Qatna and Troy.

Y. Yadin, "The art of warfare in the lands of the Bible" Ramat Gan, 1963, 99.

the front and lower parts of the tell slopes or for the defence of towns built on relatively low tells — such as Jericho and Shechem — which could be easily damaged by the action of the battering-rams; while it was sufficient for the high parts of the town to have thick, straight brick or stone walls.

The defence of the lower towns (Hazor, Carchemish and also Qaṭna) presented a problem of its own. In the absence of natural slopes, it was necessary to erect large, thick mounds of earth (these too were usually sandwich built), to resist the pounding of the battering-rams and at the same time serve as a solid foundation for the brick walls — and at a slightly later period — even for huge stone walls (parts of which were built on the casemate system).[131] This period also saw an interesting and important oevelopment in city gates. The gate — which is a man-made, vulnerable spot in every fortification — was reinforced and improved, and the relatively simple structure lacking depth and protected only by towers began to be replaced by a large type of fortified gatehouse. This gate consisted of a roofed passage the ceiling of which was supported by six large piers – three on each side. The piers supported the second storey and narrowed down the gateway to the width of a single chariot, but without reducing the width of the gate (which had to provide room for the manoeuvering of shields). It is possible that the gate had more than one double wing door, that is to say: a double wing door on the outside and another on the inside. On the right and left sides of the passage were built as usual, two huge towers with two small rooms each (Mari, Alalakh, Hazor, etc.). The gate of lower Hazor was also fortified by a very strong supporting wall built of basalt. This wall permitted the erection of a rampart parallel to the tell glacis on which the entrance-way was built. In this manner the entrance was placed at an angle of ninety degrees, as against the way to the gate; this arrangement making it difficult for the enemy to burst through.

Another typical element in the fortification of the town — in the first half of the second millennium — is the large moat dug at the bottom of the glacis. It appears that its main purpose was also to afford protection from the battering-rams as well as from the siege-towers (*dimtū*), on which were stationed archers covering the rams with their volleys of arrows. By means of the moat the planners succeeded in keeping these weapons away from the wall and beyond their effective range.

Though most of the cities of Palestine were destroyed in the 16th and at the beginning of the 15th century by the kings of the Eighteenth Dynasty following the expulsion of the Hyksos, they were rebuilt within a short time. Their rebuilding does not, however, reveal far-reaching changes in methods of fortification or other defence arrangements. In many places the fortifications of the former period were repaired or their remains reconstructed and renovated without displaying great changes. The six pier gates continued to exist; but in some instances they, as well as a part of their walls, were built of larger, basalt ashlar. The stone glacis moreover, were stronger than before, and the extensive use of casemate walls greatly strengthened the city's fortifications, particularly against battering-rams. This structural element, which originated in Anatolia, began to spread at that time, until in the Early Bronze Period it had become an integral part of the fortifications in the Near East and constitued an efficient protection from the battering-ram. It solved the problem of protecting the city's lower slopes and at the same time reinforced the walls and prevented their collapse even in the case the ram succeeded in boring a hole or breaching the wall at some point. In addition to the remains of fortifications discovered in excavations, we also possess many Egyptian wall reliefs from this period, which permit us to reconstruct in our minds not only the plans of the fortifications, but even their appearance. The walls were topped with improved battlements which enabled the defenders to use their weapons effectively, and projecting from the towers, balconies were added. All these improvements prevented the attacker from drawing near to the vulnerable spot of a besieged city without danger to himself, since vertical fire covered all the "dead areas" of the wall. The king's fortress, which stood inside the fortified city, constituted a very powerful internal line of defence — a fact strongly emphasized in the abovementioned reliefs. The Canaanite town is represented on the reliefs as standing on its tell, with a large moat protecting it round about, the city gate with its two towers projects a good deal, and the second element, which is represented in a schematic form – perhaps the inner wall of the fortress – stands out above the city wall. Thus the fortress looks like a town surrounded by a double wall.[132]

With strong fortifications, the Canaanite towns of the Late Bronze Period were hard nuts to crack. In order to capture a town the attackers were in need of new methods, with which we shall deal below.

2. *The Conquest of Towns.* In theory, it was possible to conquer a fortified town in the period under discussion — in actual fact in every period — in one of the following five ways, or by combining two or three or even all of then:

(a) To penetrate the town from above the wall;
(b) To penetrate the town by way of the wall or the gates;
(c) To penetrate the town from beneath the wall;
(d) To subdue the town through siege;
(e) To overpower the town by a stratagem.

Fig. 18.
The siege of Ashkelon in the
days of Ramses II,
as represented in a relief in
the temple of Karnak.
W. Wreszinski, *Atlas zur
Altaegyptischen Kulturgeschichte* 2,
Leipzig, 1937, pl. 58.

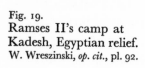

Fig. 19.
Ramses II's camp at
Kadesh, Egyptian relief.
W. Wreszinski, *op. cit.*, pl. 92.

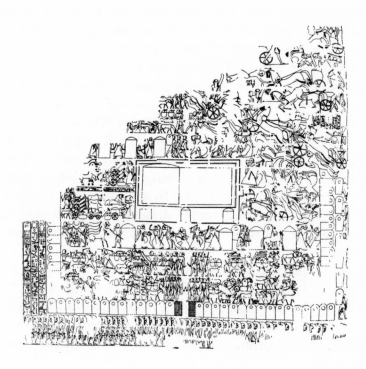

(a) *Penetration of the walls from above.* The first method appears simple from the technical point of view, but it compels the attackers to use long and swaying ladders and to have effective covering-forces. Such attacks on Canaanite towns are shown only in Egyptian reliefs, mainly from the Nineteenth Dynasty. A relief from Deshasheh in Egypt, which clearly illustrates such an attack carried out already during the Early Kingdom (i.e. in the third millennium), proves that this method of warfare was customary throughout the whole of the second millennium. The reliefs show that the attacking force leaned long ladders against the actual walls. Infantry men — particularly those armed with swords or other weapons used for hand-to-hand fighting (spears) — carried out the assault on the city and climbed the ladders. Shields fastened with loops to the shoulders of the climbers protected their backs, one hand grasped the sword while the free hand held unto the rungs of the ladder. This daring operation was carried out under cover of strong units of bowmen, operating in groups. They stood at the flank and covered the climbers with continuous "fire." Their arrows prevented the defenders of the town from bending over the battlements and frustrating the enemy's action.

(b) *Penetration of the walls or the gates.* It was effective too, and was generally carried out in combination with the first method. Battering-rams were the decisive weapon in this operation, and as we saw above they were widely used in the first half, and at the beginning of the second half of the millennium we are discussing. These battering-rams were mainly employed against tower corners and city gates. This operation also required effective covering "fire." As usual, the bowmen shot from special wooden siege towers (*dimtū*). The problem was how to bring the rams up, close enough for their range to be effective (4—5 meters). The solution was to heap up large ramps of earth and create means of crossing the moat and the required gradient on the glacis. It is surprising that none of the Egyptian reliefs of the New Kingdom show battering-rams, in spite of the fact that on some of the drawings from the Middle Kingdom (Benī-ḥasan) it is possible to discern very primitive battering-rams.[133] It may be that this weapon, which was widely used in Syria and Anatolia — it was, in fact, invented by the Hurrians — was not accepted by the conservative Egyptian army which was trained in different methods of break-through. Another explanation, alluded to above, could be that the strengthening of fortifications in the Late Bronze Period, which was directed mainly against the battering-ram, had reached such a high standard that the type of battering-ram common at that time was no longer effective against the walls and the large stone glacis' in Canaan. In place of the rams the

Egyptian reliefs show couples of soldiers infiltrating to the outer side of the gate and holding in their hands axes with which to smash the hinges and bolts of the doors; they are protected by the shields they carry on their backs, and by bowmen shooting from the flank.

(c) *Penetration from beneath the walls*. — Attempts to undermine the foundations of the wall by digging under it and making tunnels in order to gain entrance into a town are familiar from first millennium reliefs, and remains of tunnels of this type were discovered in excavations of second millennium fortifications.[134] Hence, according to a logical conclusion this form of penetration did not require much technical knowledge and one may be permitted to assume that the method was already known in the second millennium.

(d) *The siege*. — The strength of the fortifications and the difficulty of storming them in the ways pointed out above turned the fortified cities of Canaan into fortresses the capture of which required a lengthy siege. The siege, which at first sight appears to be the easiest method of attack, requires the keeping of a large force in a passive state, involving the interruption of its expedition of conquest. A siege forces an army to encamp in the open field, sometimes for a long time, thus aggravating the supply problem. Arrangements for a water supply during a time of siege and food stores enabled a besieged town to hold out for a long time, as we learn from two Egyptian documents. One of these relates that the siege of Sharuhen, at the time of Ah-mose, lasted three years — the longest siege known from those times.[135] During the famous expedition of Thutmose III, Megiddo fell after a seven months' siege.[136] The documents from this expedition supply detailed particulars of the siege arrangements. The Egyptians surrounded the town with a siege-wall intended to prevent the besieged population from fleeing the city, and to enable the besiegers to fend off surprise attacks.[137]

The cutting down of trees for the needs of the siege is strongly emphasized in the Egyptian reliefs,[138] and we find an echo of it in the Pentateuch: "When thou shalt besiege a city a long time, in making war against it to take it, thou shalt not destroy the trees thereof by wielding an axe against them, for thou mayest eat of them, but thou shalt not cut them down; for is the tree of the field man, that it should be besieged of thee? Only the trees of which thou knowest that they are not trees for food, them thou mayest destroy and cut down, that thou mayest build bulwarks against the city that maketh war with thee, until it fall." (Dt. 20:19—20).

(e) *Stratagems*. — From what has been said so far it is clear that warfare against a city was very hard to wage. It is therefore not surprising that parallel to all the other methods of fighting, the attacker tried to penetrate the town by cunning. Despite the strength of the fortifications there existed vulnerable spots in the defences of a town. The fortifications were generally directed to the outside; and if the enemy succeeded in getting inside, outwards directed defence arrangements lost their value. The stratagem employed in the conquest of Ai, as described in Joshua 8, was intended to draw the town's army outside the walls and to enable the ambushers to enter the town while its defenders were away. Another success of cunning was the conquest of Beth-el (Jud. 1:24 ff.) due to the discovery of the 'entrance into the city'[139] which permitted the penetration into town. The very existence of legends concerning the conquest of cities by stratagems testifies to a core of truth. Apart from the conquest of Troy, the most famous of such legends bearing on our period is the story of how the Egyptians conquered Jaffa by cunning at the time of Thut-mose III. Two hundred soldiers were smuggled into the town in baskets which were supposed to contain gifts. The baskets were carried by five hundred soldiers.[140]

All five methods together or each one of them separately enabled in many cases the besieger to break into fortified cities. Decisive evidence proving the fact that the strongest fortified cities were destroyed many times over has been discovered during archeological excavations. This fact confirms what has long been known of the factors of victory in battle, in last analysis neither fortifications nor weapons decide the issue, but the spirit of the warrior.

CHAPTER VIII

THE PATRIARCHS AND THEIR SOCIAL BACKGROUND

by E. A. Speiser

A. Revision of Views on the Subject

FEW PORTIONS of the Bible, if any, have received as much support and illumination from archeological discoveries as the patriarchal narratives in Genesis. Not many decades ago these passages were the favorite targets of attack on the part of higher criticism. Yet today these same passages are recognized by and large as an authentic reflection of the practices and customs of the age in which they are set. Even their historical content, a minor feature from the start,[1] has gained in credibility by virtue of the demonstrated soundness of the accompanying detail.

This drastic change in the critical appraisal of the patriarchal account is directly traceable to the steady flow of pertinent information from various centers of Greater Mesopotamia. Since the Bible itself places the original home of the Patriarchs in the Valley of the Two Rivers, it is to that region that one must look for independent confirmation from extra-biblical sources. A generation ago the required criteria were inadequate or lacking altogether. Recently, however, a number of sites have been furnishing a steadily increasing flow of relevant material, thus pointing up afresh the fallacy of the argument from silence on which the earlier critics had based their negative evaluation.[2] By the same token it would seem to be in order to sound a warning to the positivists as well. Not all of the available information has as yet been fully digested. Each new campaign yields additional material and raises further problems.[3] In these circumstances it would be a needless hazard to go beyond the limits of the evidence at hand. It is sufficient to emphasize that the results so far have borne out the essential reliability of the background that the Bible has sketched. Hence there are good reasons for assuming that many of the remaining obscurities will be cleared up in time.

B. Western Semites in Central Mesopotamia

All objective reviews of the patriarchal account have to start out with the fact that the Bible places the Patriarchs in Haran, a center on the

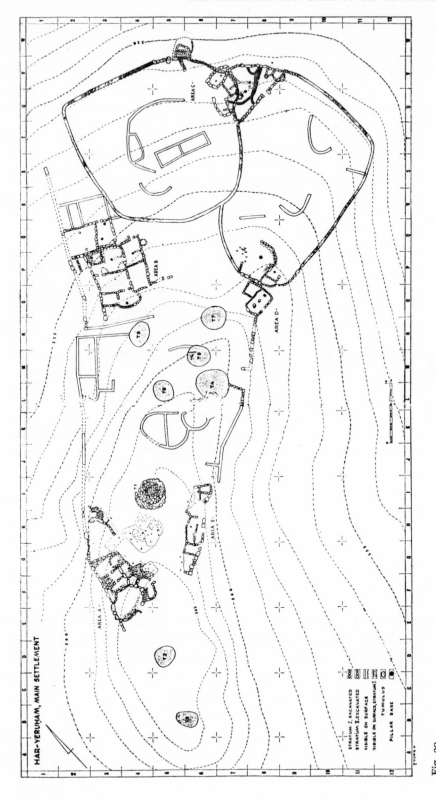

Fig. 20.
Har Yeruḥam, plan of the main settlement in the Middle Bronze I Period.
Dr. M. Kochavi, Tel Aviv.

Balikh River in the Middle Euphrates Valley. Whichever way one may appraise the anterior mention of Ur of the Chaldees,[4] Haran was their actual home beyond all doubt. It is from there that Abraham was bidden

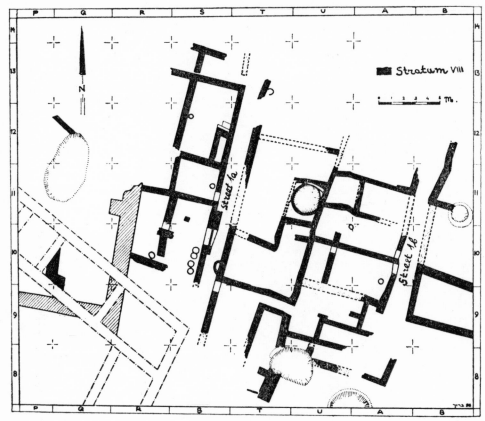

Fig. 21.
Tell Nagila, plan of the streets and buildings in the
Middle Bronze II Period (stratum VIII).
Mrs. Ruth Amiran, Jerusalem.

to set out in search of a more congenial land; and it is to that same district that Isaac and Jacob must look for acceptable mates. It follows accordingly that we too must look to Haran for direct evidence on patriarchal origins. This is the principal reason why the necessary data were so long in making their appearance. Until recently Mesopotamian archeology was preoccupied with the classical sites of Babylonia and Assyria. Our interest in the peripheral areas is a late development, Haran and its vicinity lying within the peripheries. By now however we are in a position to utilize some of the returns from such centers as Mari, Alalakh, Ugarit, Sultantepe, and Nuzi. All of these are, for one reason or another, actual or potential sources of information on the patriarchal age and society. For the present, two of these sources stand out above the others. One is Mari, because of the light which its archives have shed on the historical and social conditions in the West Semitic world in general. The other is Nuzi, in that its records afford the best sidelight available so far on the mixed Hurro-Semitic society which was dominant in the Middle Euphrates area at the time of the Patriarchs. The following pages will therefore deal largely, and necessarily in a summary fashion, with the pertinent evidence from Mari and Nuzi.[5]

C. The Mari Archives

The Mari archives date from the time of Hammurabi and are thus roughly contemporary with the period to which the age of Abraham has to be assigned. The published material bears prominently on Assyria and Babylonia; but it is also keenly aware of Mari's neighbors to the west and northwest where the population was predominantly West Semitic with a substantial admixture of Hurrian elements. In the Valley of the Balikh in particular, which to some extent at least coincided politically with the land of Idamaras, the population included loosely defined groups bearing the collective designations of Benjaminites and Ben-Semalites. The first of these cannot be separated, onomastically if not in other respects, from the biblical Benjamin. Interestingly enough, the Mari official employed in dealing with these groups, a certain Mashum,[6] bears the title of *ṭupšar Amurrim* either in the sense of "Secretary of Amurru Affairs" or simply as "Amurru scribe." In either case, it is obvious that the Benjaminites and Ben-Semalites were regarded as part of the Amurrū or West Semitic population. The presumption is justified, moreover, that the language they spoke was likewise Amurrite, which is why it was necessary to have a *ṭupšar Amurrim* to attend to them.

An important city in the Balikh district was Nahor, identical onomastically with the personal name borne by both Abraham's grandfather and his brother. It is significant, therefore, that we have from the Nahor district a letter which has more than one point of contact with patriarchal passages in the Bible.[7] In the matter of a peace pact affecting two local states reference is made to solemn ceremonies which bear a close resemblance to the one described in the Gen. 15 : 9. The ceremonial slaughter of a young ass is indicated by the West Semitic phrase *hayāram qaṭālum,* which is followed by *ḥayāram mār atānim* (in the acc.), a precise parallel to '*iro . . . bᵉni atono* ("his foal . . . his ass's colt") in Gen. 49 : 11 (cf. also Zech. 9 : 9).

Perhaps most significant of all is the fact that we have from a governor of Nahor, by the name of Itūr-Asdu, a letter which gives us one of the fullest accounts known thus far of the antecedents of prophecy as a political and social instrument.[8] The institution of prophecy in general as an independent force committed neither to the throne nor the altar is known to us prior to biblical times from no other source but Mari. Since the entire material on this subject thus far comprises no more than six documents, it is highly noteworthy that Nahor should be the source of one of these texts. The fact that the practice is now established specifically for a city intimately associated with patriarchal origins, and that it applies in this instance to revelations manifested in dreams, is striking and unexpected proof that the similar experiences reported in the Bible in connection with the Patriarchs need not be viewed by any means as mere inventions on the part of later writers. They were based in all likelihood on a dependable tradition which can now be traced back to the very time and place from which Abraham himself stemmed.

In passing, attention may be called to a letter from Qaṭna, in the heart of the West Semitic area, as furnishing an instructive parallel, in tone and in phraseology, to Abraham's negotiations with Ephron for the cave of Machpelah (Gen. 23).[9] In both instances we find the same elaborate pretense of generosity followed by extravagant demands. The least that we can now say about the Machpelah episode is that its atmosphere is obviously authentic.

D. The Nuzi Documents

No evidence, however, bearing on patriarchal origins compares in importance with the testimony of the Nuzi records. This may seem surprising at first glance. The Nuzi material dates from the 15th–14th centuries B.C.E., and is thus at least three hundred years too late for the age of Abraham. Furthermore, ancient Nuzi was situated in the region of Arrapkha, modern Kirkuk, a long way from the center of patriarchal activities in Mesopotamia. Yet these deviations in time and space prove to be immaterial on further probing. We know from the Alalakh documents that the Hurrians were dominant in that area not only in the 15th but also in the 18th century.[10] Moreover, in Nuzi times the whole Arrapkha region was a province of the Mitannian kingdom, subject to much the same social, linguistic, ethnic, and juridical conditions as those that prevailed in Haran.

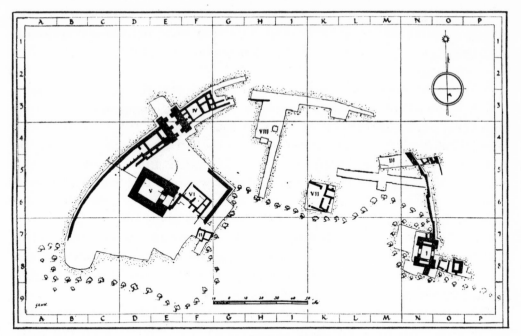

Fig. 22.
Shechem, plan of the city in the Middle Bronze II Period.
Prof. G. E. Wright.

Fig. 23.
Beth-shemesh, plan of the city in the Middle Bronze II Period.
E. Grant, *Ain Shems Excavations.*

By extension, 15th century Nuzi can tell us much about 18th century Haran. Lack of direct evidence from Haran is due solely to the accidents of archeological discovery, and this deficiency may well be overcome in the near future.

It has been made abundantly clear in recent years that Hurrian culture was in many essentials an apt student of Southern Mesopotamia.[11] There is however a significant residue of Hurrian usages and customs which cannot be paralleled in the lands of Sumer and Akkad and must therefore be ascribed to native Hurrian sources. It is such independent Hurrian material that turns out to be especially instructive in relation to the patriarchal background. Many of the details recorded in Genesis could not hitherto be linked directly to South Mesopotamian sources. They now receive striking illumination from records of Hurrian communities. Since the Haran region was predominantly Hurrian in the days of Abraham and the centuries that followed, the missing parts of a long-standing puzzle are at last beginning to fall into place.

The Nuzi parallels shed welcome light on precisely those portions of the patriarchal narratives which hitherto eluded the efforts of countless interpreters, from ancient times down to our own days. In each instance tradition proves to have transmitted its facts correctly even though their exact import may have been lost following the migration of the principals from Central Mesopotamia. There is space here only for a handful of illustrations, which have to be stated summarily instead of being adequately developed. Thus Abraham's efforts to pass Sarah off as his sister (Gen. 12:10 ff.; 20:1 ff.) reflect the Hurrian practice whereby wifehood and sistership could be equated under certain conditions, with the significantly added feature that a "sister" enjoyed in such circumstances a greater degree of socio-juridical protection.[12] The Sarah-Hagar episode (Gen. 16) is now illuminated by Nuzi marriage contracts which stipulate that a childless wife shall herself select a concubine for her husband;[13] the Code of Hammurabi had limited the provision to certain classes of priestesses. For the transfer of the birthright from Esau to Jacob (Gen. 27) there is now a considerable amount of illustrative material from Nuzi which places the whole incident in a new societal light; even the introductory phrases turn out to have a recognized legal bearing.[14] The most revealing single instance of Hurrian cultural features as reflected in the Bible is the appropriation of Laban's teraphim by Rachel (Gen. 31:19 ff.). Innumerable guesses had been made in an attempt to account for this strange act. None had come close to the mark because the necessary data about Hurrian family laws had been lacking. Documents from Arrapkha and Nuzi, however, have shown that under certain specified conditions family property could pass to a daughter's husband, provided that the son-in-law had received the testator's household gods as a token that the atypical transfer of property had been authorized.[15]

E. THE PATRIARCHAL NARRATIVES IN THE LIGHT OF THE NEW EVIDENCE

The foregoing illustrations from Mari and Nuzi — which could readily be multiplied and expanded — give a new perspective to the patriarchal account as a whole. The setting of the Mesopotamian portion of the narratives has proved to be correct down to some of the minutest details. What is more, it is becoming increasingly apparent that the narrators

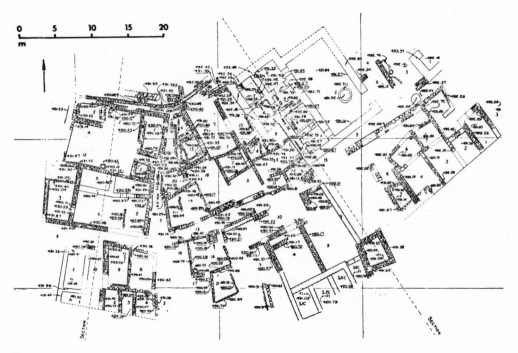

Fig. 24.
Tell Beit Mirsim, plan of the town in the Middle Bronze II Age.
Prof. W. F. Albright.

themselves were often unaware of the underlying significance of the episodes which they were faithfully preserving for posterity. They were no longer clear, for example, of the real meaning of the wife-sister incidents, the transfer of the birthright, or the removal of the household gods — writing as they were hundreds of years after the event and hundreds of miles for the most part from the original locale. The details they set down have been corroborated independently. But the interpretation which is implicit here and there is inevitably out of focus.

The facts just outlined entail two conclusions whose importance goes considerably beyond the question of the patriarchal account alone. First, the narratives involved could not have been invented by any stretch of imagination, not only because the details are authentic but, more particularly, because the narrators themselves did not always know what those details signified. Conscious archaisms presuppose a knowledge of the older stage. In this instance the necessary links had been lost. Secondly, it follows that the narrators, in setting down bits of information whose basic import had been lost, would do so only because tradition had preserved such details with reverent care. Evidently, therefore, the subject matter had acquired a spiritual bearing long before it was committed to writing. To be sure, the heroes of the account have not been directly established as historical figures. On circumstantial evidence, however, their essential historicity can no longer be open to serious doubt.

Lastly, recent researches tend to support the patriarchal account in still another respect. The overall problems and achievements of the composite civilization of Mesopotamia can now be seen in relatively clear focus. In the matter of societal progress, and more especially in law and government, Mesopotamia stands out as a pioneer whose leadership was embraced and followed by many of the neighboring cultures. With regard to religious progress, however, the Mesopotamian achievement was hampered by a concept of the universe in which the gods were capricious and insecure, with the result that the cosmos lacked a viable ethical basis.[16] Abraham was commanded to leave Mesopotamia for the land of Canaan in search of higher religious values. God's covenant with the Patriarchs was destined to become one of the keynotes of the history of Israel. The overriding importance of that covenant, and of the religious quest which it signified, accords perfectly with the demonstrated weakness of the religious solution that was arrived at in Mesopotamia. The stated reason for Abraham's departure corresponds with the now established conditions in his original homeland. The account itself may well have been idealized. Yet it is clearly not out of line with the known facts. Indeed, had tradition failed to transmit to us anything at all about the Patriarchs, we should have to reconstruct much the same social and historical background as is reflected in the Book of Genesis. It was the Patriarchs who gave biblical tradition its very start. And for its part, that tradition was to remain faithful ever since not only to the memory but to the highest ideals of its founders.

CHAPTER IX

CANAAN IN THE PATRIARCHAL AGE

by B. Mazar

A. INTRODUCTORY REMARKS

THE 24TH CENTURY B.C.E. witnesses far-reaching changes in Canaan and the neighboring countries, resulting in the decline of the rich and highly developed civilization of the Early Bronze Period. Archeological excavations reveal a deterioration and destruction of the fortified urban centers and a concurrent decline in material culture. Destruction of the Early Bronze culture brought in its wake an economic collapse, which was not to be remedied for many generations. This seems to have been accompanied by a lengthy process involving the destruction of the settled population over extensive areas and by decisive changes in the ethnic and social composition of the country's inhabitants. Egyptian sources tell of military campaigns by the Sixth Dynasty kings to Canaan for the purpose of suppressing the ';mw. From this period onwards this is the name by which the Egyptians call all the tribes who left their mark on the population of Canaan.[1] Weni, the military commander of Pepi I (second half of the 24th century) mentions in his inscription that he participated in five land and sea campaigns against the ';mw and even tells of his active participation in the destruction of fortified towns and the slaughter of their inhabitants, in the uprooting of orchards and vineyards and in the taking of many prisoners and much booty to Egypt.[2] A relief discovered in the tomb of Anta at Deshasheh provides remarkable evidence for this period,[3] portraying as it does the siege and conquest of a fortress. From the defective inscription accompanying the relief it is possible to discern the name of at least one city, apparently the Semitic name "Nd'l." It is not inconceivable that there could have existed some connection between Egyptian and contemporaneous events in the west of the Fertile Crescent, which constituted a very real threat to Egypt. Already Lugalzaggisi, King of Uruk, who succeeded in uniting the city-states in Sumer (second half of the 24th century), boasts of imposing his dominion on all the countries as far as the "Upper Sea" viz. the Mediterranean. Sargon, Lugalzaggisi's conqueror and the founder of the great Semitic kingdom in Mesopotamia, the kingdom of Akkad (end of the 24th and beginning of the 23rd centuries B.C.E.), also reached the shores of the Mediterranean in the course of his far-ranging campaigns, and one of his successors, Naram-Sin, was to follow in his footsteps. These expeditions undoubtedly caused considerable agitation in all parts of Syria and Canaan.[4] Thus in the 24th century Syria and Canaan entered the political orbit of the large empires in the land of the Nile and in the countries of the Euphrates and the Tigris, and they suffered seriously from the predatory raids and destruction perpetrated by the armies of Egypt and Akkad. This state of affairs was followed by other events which definitely had considerable influence on the fate of Canaan during that period. They are already alluded to in documents from the end of Sargon of Akkad's dynasty.

B. AMURRŪ EXPANSION

This period witnessed the beginning of the enormous expansion of the Amurrū, tribes from the land of Amurru (the Sumerian equivalent is Mar-tu), that is to say from the provinces west of the Euphrates. Shar-kalisharri, one of the last kings of the Akkadian dynasty (ca 2200 B.C.) was forced to engage them in a fierce battle near Basar in the central Euphrates region.[5] The Sumerian and Akkadian sources portray the Amurrū as outsiders and foreigners "who do not know any crops" and do not live in houses.[6]

There seems to be some causal link between the first invasions of the Amurrū tribes into the border territory of the Akkadian empire on the one hand, and the weakening of the political regime in the Land of the Nile at the end of the Old Kingdom (end of the 23rd century) on the other, and between events in Syria and Canaan in the later centuries of the third millennium. The results of archeological research in Canaan indicate that in this period the nomads and semi-nomads determined the character of the population and its material culture, and that their transition to a life of permanent settlement was a very slow and complicated process. The special character of the remains from the 23rd century to 2000 B.C.E. found in Canaan (Middle Bronze Period I[7]) point to a primitive population as regards material culture and standard of living. This is clearly demonstrated by the poor and unwalled settlements, the makeshift building and inferior pottery technique. Further light is shed on the Amurrū settlement by the many shaft graves and tumuli, mostly of individuals, more and more of which are coming to light in various regions and which are at times quite unconnected with permanent dwelling places. Various pottery types such as the caliciform or goblet-shaped jars which were found mainly in the context of graves, weapons made of copper, witnessing a highly developed metal industry and other miscellaneous objects, indicate north-western Mesopotamia and northern Syria as the main cultura source which influenced and inspired the Amurrū.[8] Yet these indications serve more to explain the source of the culture which had nourished the newcomers in their countries of origin before their migration to Canaan than to point to active cultural connections.

Archeological research does, however, throw light on the process of the Amurrū establishment and expansion during the Middle Bronze I in those parts of the country which had been but sparsely or not at all inhabited, including large areas of Transjordan and the Negev as far as the desert fringe. This wave of settlement and the establishment of unwalled settlements was, doubtlessly, encouraged by the continuous movement of nomads and semi-nomads and the land hunger of the surplus population in the purely agricultural and pastoral areas. It is remarkable that the later stages of this period, that is, in the 22nd–21st centuries, a close network of settlements was established in the Negev and in the surrounding areas as proved by the hundreds of archeological sites, remains of settlements and burial grounds.[9] As far as we know the inhabitants of these areas employed themselves in temporary farming, grazing and various other kinds of work. A striking illustration of this development was found in the only settlement so far excavated, the site of Har Jeruḥam: where the two strata of occupation from the Middle Bronze I discovered display different characters. While the early settlement, which was surrounded by a stone fence against which leaned the dwellings and workshops, was a permanent settlement of farmers and shepherds, the later one belonged to semi-nomads, shepherds and coppersmiths who dwelt in tents and used sheep pens.[10]

The poor settlements of Transjordan and the Negev were destroyed at the end of the Middle Bronze I. The ensuing gap in permanent occupation and the conversion of these areas to a domain of nomadic tribes was caused by a fresh wave of newcomers which left its mark on other parts of the country also. Canaan entered a new phase of her history, Middle Bronze II, which continued until the 16th century B.C.E. The chronologically parallel periods in Egypt are the Middle Kingdom and the Second Intermediate Period respectively.

C. Effects of Amurrū Expansion

From the cuneiform archives we know of the tremendous movement of West Semitic tribes at the end of the third and the beginning of the second millennium B.C.E. Akkadian sources call these tribes by the traditional

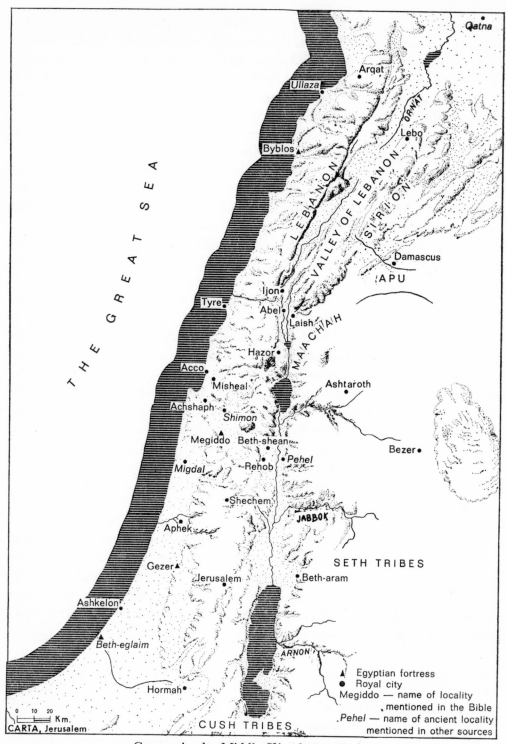

Canaan in the Middle Kingdom period

inclusive name "Amurrū." The pressure on the western border of Sumer and Akkad grew increasingly strong towards the end of the Third Dynasty of Ur. Shu-Sin was actually forced to build a defensive wall in the region north of Sumer to prevent their invading his kingdom, and his son Ibbi-Sin, the last of the kings of Ur, engaged in fierce battles with them.[11] The tremendous assault of the Amurrū from the west on the Euphrates and Tigris Valleys played a decisive role in the destruction of the kingdom of Sumer and Akkad. Mesopotamia was flooded by a multitude of new-comers who spoke various West Semitic dialects. The way of life and the cultural and spiritual traditions which they brought with them differed radically from the concept of monarchy and the accomplished civilizations of Sumer and Akkad. Yet in the course of the time many of these wandering tribes settled in the countries of the Euphrates and the Tigris, lived among the Sumerian-Akkadian population, acquired the achievements of its culture and adopted Akkadian as the spoken and written language. They founded a number of strong kingdoms, one of which, the Early Babylonian Kingdom, reached its zenith at the time of its great King Hammurabi. A great deal of information concerning the West Semites in Mesopotamia and in the area west of the Euphrates, both those who had already managed to settle down and strike roots in the Akkadian culture, though still linked to their origin and genealogy, as well as those who continued to live a nomadic or semi-nomadic life, is to be found in the cuneiform written sources from the time of the Third Dynasty of Ur.

D. Testimonies about Amurrū Culture in Canaan

The large quantity of Akkadian documents from the royal archives in Mari on the Middle Euphrates, which date from the 18th century B.C.E.[12] is particularly rich in data. This stratum of population can be distinguished in the case of the Mari documents and many other documents from the first third of the second millennium by means of the personal names of members of the ruling class. These names are closely related to the personal names which were common in Syria and Canaan during the same period, as transpires in particular from the Egyptian sources of the Middle Kingdom. They are also related to the names known from the stories about the Patriarchs which are found in abundance in the biblical sources.[13] The same applies to the names of tribes and various ethnic units (the tribes of Hana, Banu Yamina, etc.); to the names and appelations of their gods (Dagan, Hadad, Baal, Abu, Akhu, Shumu and 'Ammu); various terms, especially those that derive from their patriarchal social regime, from their nomadic way of life, such as *ummatum* (nation), *gayum* (tribe) or *khibrum* (clan); and to terms which illustrate the form of their settlement, viz. *nawum* (encampment), *khaṣarum* (enclosed encampment). It is also worth noting that the Mari Letters mention the Valley of Balikh with its concentrations of Haran and the city of Nahor, as one of the important centers of the nomadic and semi-nomadic West Semitic tribes, which brings to mind the Israelite tradition of the early dwelling places of the Patriarchs and their connection with the children of Nahor. Moreover, the genealogical table of the sons of Nahor (Gen. 22:20–24) probably reflects a certain historical reality in that it accounts for the expansion of the nomadic West Semitic tribes from their centers in the areas of Haran, Nahor and the Middle Euphrates as far as southern Syria and northern Transjordan.[14] The Mari Letters and the documents from Alalakh in northern Syria, not only tell us about the strong political and economic connections between the Amorite kingdoms in Mesopotamia and the kingdoms of Syria and especially Yamhad (in northern Syria) and Qaṭanum (in central Syria) but also about a common origin and perhaps even about common traditions from ancient times.[15] We can see from a letter addressed to Zimri-lim King of Mari, by one of his governors, just how many kings bore West Semitic names at that period: "There is no king who is all-poweful on his own. Ten or fifteen kings may march behind Hammurabi; likewise after Rim-Sin of Larsa; similarly after Ibalpiel of Eshnunna; similarly, too, after Amutpiel of Qaṭanum. Perhaps twenty kings march behind Yarim-lim of Yamhad."[16] This document, by the way, reveals something of the politically divided state of Mesopotamia and Syria before Hammurabi, King of Babylon, succeeded in establishing his vast empire which included a large part of Mesopotamia.

Into this historical context can be filled also the evidence of the military expeditions to the Mediterranean coast of the Amorite kings Yahdun-lim of Mari and Shamshi-Adad of Assyria who preceded Zimri-lim. The purpose of those expeditions was to impose their suzerainty on these politically and economically important areas, but it would seem that these campaigns did not lead to proper conquests.[17]

These connections doubtlessly greatly furthered the spread of the Akkadian language and culture in the western Fertile Crescent, and not without cause did cuneiform-written Akkadian become the lingua franca of trade and diplomacy in the ancient world. The West Semitic tribes also controlled the main trade routes from Mesopotamia to Syria, to the Mediterranean coast and to Canaan; it was they who took an active part in the caravan trade and who used the donkey as a beast of burden. They controlled the main routes which led from large centers such as Babylon, Sippar, Mari and Haran to Aleppo and to Qaṭanum in Syria,[18] and from there different routes branched off to the coast and to Canaan, while the desert tracks were also of great importance. On the desert routes between the countries of the Euphrates and Canaan (this desert is the *Land of Kedem*, and is mentioned by this name already in the Egyptian Si-nuhe story dating from the beginning of the second millennium B.C.E.) nomadic tribes, tent-dwellers and shepherds, and trade caravans travelled to and from Palmyra, through which caravans passed on their way from the banks of the Euphrates to Qaṭanum or to Damascus (Apum in the Akkadian and Egyptian documents), and was already then an important station on this route which crossed the heart of the desert. From Damascus the route continued along the Transjordanian Heights. This section was known as the "king's highway" (Num. 20:17), from which various routes branched off, the most important of them turning to the Arabah and the Negev and continued via Kadesh-barnea to Egypt. Like the Akkadian documents, Egyptian documents and inscriptions from the beginning of the Twelfth Dynasty (20th century, B.C.E.) such as those found at Serābit al-Khādim in Sinai, mention donkey caravans, which were led by Asiatics and which moved between Egypt and the countries further east.[19] Of striking interest is a fresco from ca. 1900 B.C.E., discovered in the tomb of Khnum-hotep at Benī Ḥasan, which shows a group of people leading donkeys. They are travelling down to Egypt with their merchandise and their tools which include copper articles and even a lyre for entertainment purposes. The inscription which accompanies the portrayal of the caravan explains that these are Asiatics bringing a kind of antimony from the land of Shutu. Their leader is Abshar who is given the title "Ruler of a Foreign Country." The Upper and Lower lands of Shutu are also mentioned in the Execration Texts (see below); the Shutu are known from Akkadian sources as a large group of nomadic and semi-nomadic tribes living on the edge of the Fertile Crescent and in the Syrian desert; and the parallel of Moab – "the sons of Seth" in Balaam's prophecy (Num. 24:17) may hint that their main place of settlement was in those areas which were later seized by the Moabites, including the plains of Moab and southern Gilead – a region which was famous for its perfumes and cosmetics (Gen. 37:25; Jer. 8:22).[20] Egyptian sources from the time of the Middle Kingdom also mention the national and territorial unit "Kushu" in the border districts of the country. Most probably these were groups of shepherd tribes in the Negev and in the neighboring border districts who preceded the Midianites in these areas; an allusion to them might be found in the parallel of the tents of Cushan – "The curtains of the land of Midian" – in an early biblical source (Hab. 3:7). In addition to Kushu and Shutu we know of the Shusu – the name for desert nomads which became accepted particularly during the New Kingdom; it is not inconceivable that its origin lies in the Egyptian word for "nomad", later borowed by Canaanite and Hebrew (*shosé*) in the sense of a brigand.[21]

E. Egyptian Influence in Western Asia

A great deal is to be learnt about Canaan from Twelfth Dynasty sources in Egypt (1990–1778).[22] A realistic picture of conditions in the country during this dynasty, in the middle of the 20th century, unfolds in the scroll of Si-nuhe — which relates the deeds of an Egyptian official who fled his country, made his way to Byblos and to the *Land of Kedem* arriving finally in Upper Reṭenu, viz. Canaan, where he settled down. In the course of time Si-nuhe became the protégé and son-in-law of Ammi-enshi, a very influential ruler in Reṭenu, who administered various territorial and political units as well as settled and nomadic populations. Si-nuhe succeeded in becoming the head of a tribe in one of the border provinces which was rich in field crops, fruit trees and cattle; when the need arose he went off to combat nomadic tribes and even to fight a duel with a Reṭenu hero. But in his old age Si-nuhe returned to Egypt so as to die in his native land.[23]

From the Si-nuhe story and from other documents it becomes clear that there were conflicts in political and social spheres as well as a certain amount of cultural exchange between the patriarchal, tribal regime of the nomads and semi-nomads and the urban political regime which began to crystallize at the beginning of the Twelfth Dynasty and had developed considerably during the 19th and 18th centuries. In the 19th century mercantile and political intercourse between Egypt and the Syrian coast increased greatly. This fact emerges from the Egyptian documents and is supported also by the results of archeological research which attest sustained political and trade connections between the two countries. This is clearly demonstrated by the important harbor town of Byblos whose kings ruled under the protection of the Egyptian rulers and enjoyed a wide range of barter trade on the coastal road to Egypt.[24] No less remarkable are the sphinxes and statuettes of the Egyptian kings and their officials which were found on the coastal roads and in important Syrian and Canaanite centers, such as Ugarit, Byblos, Beirut, Qaṭna, Megiddo and Gezer. During this period many Egyptians came to the courts of

Reṭenu's rulers on political and economic business, while many inhabitants of the latter country settled in Egypt as traders or craftsmen and particularly as slaves.[25] Quite obviously the Egyptian kings made repeated attempts to subjugate Reṭenu, particularly those areas which were of vital strategic and economic importance to them. The inscription of Sebek-Khu gives an account of one such campaign against the Asiatics in Upper Reṭenu, and describes the conquest of the province of Shechem at the time of Sen-Usert III (middle of the 19th century).[26]

The two groups of Egyptian Execration Texts are of tantamount importance for understanding the political and ethnographic background of the country and its neighbors in this period. These inscriptions contain long lists of foreign governors of cities and countries, whom the Egyptians considered hostile to Pharaoh's rule; many of them were rulers in Reṭenu, particularly in densely inhabited areas, including some fortified cities. The first group of Execration Texts, written on pottery which was purposedly broken immediately after completion, may date from the time of Amen-hotep III or IV; while the second group of similar, though much more detailed texts written on clay figurines, seems to date from the middle of the 18th century.[27] The first group mentions the rulers of political centers like Ashkelon, Jerusalem, Rehob, etc., as well as larger political units and provinces which were ruled by heads of various tribal confederacies. The number of rulers in each one of the political and tribal units was not fixed. It sometimes rose to three or even four people who were probably the heads of the most distinguished families. The second group mentions only one ruler for each of the political centers or the various provinces, or of the "countries." These documents give some indication of the process of large-scale urbanization, which is confirmed by archeological evidence also. In the later Execration Texts the first place in the list of urban centers is occupied by the important harbor towns on the eastern Mediterranean seaboard, which at that time achieved great prosperity and cultivated maritime trade with Egypt; they also acted as middlemen in the trade between Cyprus and the Aegean Islands and between Canaan and Egypt. There were also a great many principal cities in the country's lowlands, in southern Syria, in the Jordan Valley and in the Land of Bashan. Mention is also made of two political centers in the heart of the hill-country of western Canaan. These are Shechem and Jerusalem which according to archeological evidence also were fortified towns at that time.[28]

From these documents we know that Egypt's influence in Asia, at least towards the end of the Twelfth Dynasty, extended along the Mediterranean

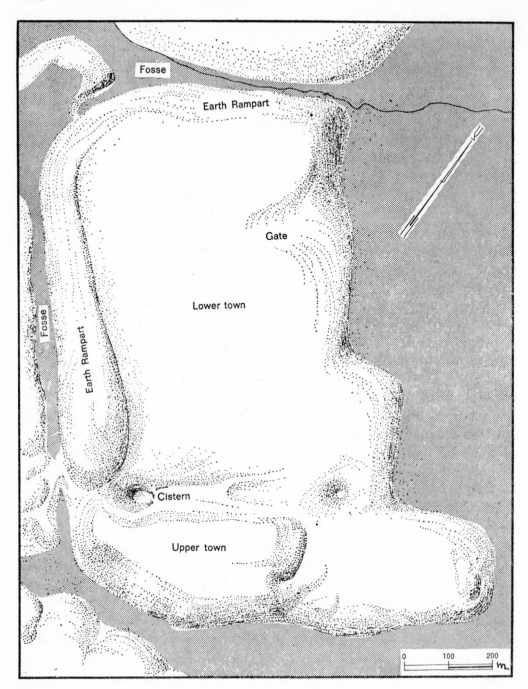

Fig. 25.
Hazor, relief plan of the city mound.
Drawing by Carta, Jerusalem.

seaboard and inland reached as far as the borders of the kingdom of Qaṭanum, which comprised a considerable part of central Syria. The archeological remains of this period discovered in the important harbor town of Byblos and in various other tells bear irrefutable witness to the intensive development which is apparent in all spheres of material culture. Megiddo, which may well have been an Egyptian stronghold in this period, provides a striking example with the remains of its reinforced, mighty wall, its indirect access gate, and its tombs rich in finds which include articles imported from Egypt as well as from the Mediterranean seaboard. As regards the country's inhabitants, their personal names, and also the names of geographical and ethnic elements, it seems that they were for most part speakers of West Semitic dialects, and their close ethnic and linguistic relationship to the Amurrū in Mesopotamia in this period seems certain.

When the Thirteenth Dynasty succeeded the powerful Twelfth Dynasty (1778) Egypt's prestige seems to have been definitely on the decline in the countries of Asia though her contact with the cities of southern Canaan and especially her strong connections with the coastal cities, notably Byblos, did not cease. Yantin the governor of Byblos is known as Pharaoh's vasal even in the reign of Nefer-hotep I (ca. 1750). There has been an attempt to identify this Yantin with the Yantin-hammu of Byblos, a contemporary of Zimri-lim King of Mari, mentioned in one of the Mari Letters.[29] In contrast with the waning of Egyptian influence, this era marks the political and economic strengthening of ties between the Amorite kingdoms in Mesopotamia and those in Syria and Canaan as transpires from the Mari Letters. Apart from Yamhad and Qaṭanum an important place in documents dealing with diplomatic and trade relations is also occupied by the land of Amurru, a region in Syria, south of Qaṭanum, which is described in one of the Mari Letters as the country from which horses were imported, and which became famous in a later period.[30] Apu (Damascus and its neighborhood) Ugarit and Byblos on the coast are also mentioned, and of special interest is Hazor in Upper Galilee which is mentioned in the Execration Texts among the rest of the important political centers. The active diplomatic relations between Hammurabi King of Babylon, Zimri-lim King of Mari and the King of Hazor, which were accompanied by barter trade, lead to the conclusion that Hazor had attained the status of an independent royal city, on the pattern of Qaṭanum in central Syria, and occupied an important place in international relations.[31] This is also supported by archeological finds in Hazor.[32] From the excavations at that site it is apparent that from the 18th century onwards Hazor developed and prospered. The excavated site reveals the plan of an urban center extending over a large area (ca. 185.325 acres) containing an upper town, the king's citadel on the tell proper and a large lower town. The lower town was built in the shape of a rectangle, adjacent to the king's citadel, and protected by large ramparts of beaten earth which served as a foundation for brick walls. As in the case of the fortifications in Qaṭanum and Carchemish, there was a massive gatehouse. There existed no doubt, a connection between the erection of such mighty fortifications and the introduction of the perfected battering-ram in warfare, since we possess equally detailed information about the one and the other from the Mari Letters. Needless to say the lower town contained a large population which, doubtlessly, included merchants, craftsmen and the common people. Maybe that is also where the horses and chariots were kept. Their military function even at this early date is attested in documents from Mari and Alalakh.[33]

F. The "Hyksos" Period

Already at the end of the 18th century the political situation in the Near East was shaken following the downfall of the Middle Kingdom of Egypt and the developments and changes which were growing apparent in Western Asia. Egyptian traditions concerning the new era, the Second Intermediate or "Hyksos" period, are related by the Egyptian-Hellenistic priest Manetho in the form of an historical account, fragments of which are preserved in the writings of Josephus.[34] According to him the "Hyksos" were an unknown people who invaded Egypt from the east, subjugated the country and set up a king, Salitis, who ruled in Memphis. This entire

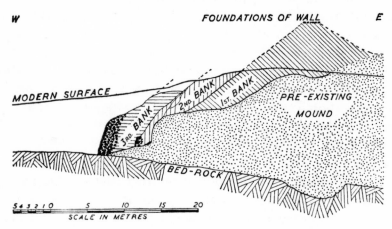

Fig. 26.
Jericho, reconstructed section of the Middle Bronze II Period mound.
Prof. K. M. Kenyon, London.

"nation" was called "Hyksos" viz. Shepherd Kings, "and some say that these people were Arabs." Manetho attributes the founding of the city of Avaris, viz. Egyptian Tanis and its becoming a Hyksos fortress, to Salitis; he even enumerates the names of five kings who reigned after him, including two Jannas (or Aunas) and Apophis, whom the Egyptian sources also consider to have been strong rulers (Khyan and Apopi). Finally, Manetho describes the uprising of the native kings of Thebes who succeeded in capturing Avaris and in expelling the Hyksos from Egypt.

The term "Hyksos", to which Manetho tried to give a popular explanation has a clear parallel from the time of the Middle Kingdom, namely, the ḥqꜣwḫꜣswt, "rulers of foreign countries", the Egyptian term which was currently used for the rulers of Asian countries and which is

Fig. 27.
Model of the "camp" at Tell al-Yahūdiyya.
Drawing by "Carta", Jerusalem.

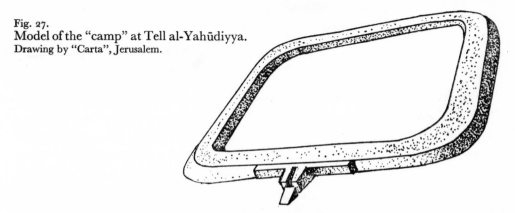

also the accepted title of foreign rulers in Egypt during the Second Intermediate Period. This period, which extended from the end of the 18th century B.C.E. to the establishment of the New Kingdom (ca. 1760 B.C.E.), is one of the haziest in Egyptian history.[35] The following generations considered it a period of weakness and oppression under foreign rule. Queen Hat-shepsut (beginning of the 15th century) boasts that she was responsible for the restoration of the sanctuaries which had been destroyed when the strangers dwelt in Avaris, while a folk tale of later date names Apophis as the ruler of Avaris, maintaining that the whole country was subject to him and that it was he who elevated Seth the chief god of the Hyksos above all the gods of Egypt.[36] Another important document enables us to give an even more exact date for the establishment of Tanis as the Hyksos center. This is the "Stele of the Year 400," put up by Ramses II, which contains a representation of Seth in Eastern garb and an inscription which mentions an event that had taken place at the end of Hor-em-heb's rule (ca. 1320). This is the arrival in Tanis of Seti, father

of Ramses II, when he was a vizier of Hor-em-heb, for the celebration of
the four hundreth anniversary of the founding of the cult of Seth, a date
which is undoubtedly identical with the establishment of Hyksos rule in
Tanis, viz. Avaris. It is not inconceivable that the year when Tanis was
founded is alluded to also in the Bible: "Now Hebron was built seven
years before Zoan [Tanis] in Egypt" (Num. 13:22).[37]

The beginning of the Hyksos period in Egypt was marked by the dis-
integration of centralised rule following the decline of the Middle Kingdom,
and the penetration of a large number of West Semitic tribes who wandered

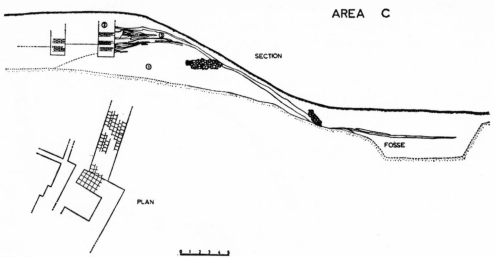

Fig. 28.
Tell Nagila, plan and section of wall and glacis, Middle Bronze II Period.
Mrs. Ruth Amiram, Jerusalem.

from Canaan and adjacent areas to the interior of the Delta region. In the
course of time the Hyksos succeeded in establishing themselves in Lower
Egypt and extending their authority over large areas. The few contemporary sources mention several rulers who were called "rulers of foreign
lands" and generally had West Semitic names, such as 'nthr, Smqn, Bbnm,
Y'qbhr. It would seem that even then Tanis was one of the fortresses
of the foreign rulers. Is is to this period that one must apparently attribute
the large camp, fortified by huge sand and beaten earth ramparts, which
was discovered at Tell al-Yahūdiyya. These ramparts are similar to the type
of fortification which characterizes Canaan during the period under
discussion; a similar one was also found at Heliopolis.[38]

Hyksos rule in Egypt was most strongly established during the period
which the Egyptian historiographers have named the Fifteenth Dynasty
and which lasted ca. 108 years (ca. 1675-1565). The West Semitic tribes,

masses of which settled in various parts of Lower Egypt, particularly in the neighborhood of Tanis (viz. the biblical Land of Goshen) were no doubt firm supporters of the Hyksos rule. It seems logical that these new-comers cultivated close relations with the West Semitic population of Canaan and its border areas, who were closely related to them by origin and country, and that they encouraged them to participate in the economic exploitation of Egypt. A stream of Egyptian goods reached Canaan not only by way of trade, but also as a result of raids and plunder, a develop-ment which doubtlessly expedited the impoverishment of Egypt and the economic reinforcement of the Canaanite cities. As for the ruling Hyksos class, it struck roots in Egypt's cultural life and adapted to the country's regime. An important contribution to the power of their rule was brought by the introduction of warfare systems and weapons from the East, which had so far been unknown in Egypt. These included the chariot drawn by a team of horses and the composite bow.[39] In the middle of the Fifteenth Dynasty the Hyksos rulers managed to extend their political and economic influence southwards as far as Nubia, and northwards as far as the northern reaches of the Eastern Mediterranean. Vast international connections are attested by ornamental articles bearing the name of the great Hyksos King Khyan, which were found in places as far from Egypt as Knossos in Crete, Hattusa the Hittite capital in Anatolia, or Babylon.[40]

G. Urbanization and Fortifications in Canaan

As has been noted, so far only meager and fragmentary information has come to light from Egyptian sources concerning historical and cultural development in the Second Intermediate Period. On the other hand, archeological excavations in Palestine have yielded a wealth of evidence dealing with every aspect of life in the Hyksos period. It first of all dem-onstrates the large scale development in the building of towns and fortresses, from the first half of the 18th century onwards. Settlements fortified with ramparts made of beaten earth or sandwiched layers of crushed and pressed stone and brick topped by a brick wall, sometimes surrounded by a moat, were discovered all over the country. However the greatest concentration was found on the coast and the coastal plain — as far south as settlement extended. Fortifications of this type were erected in already existing places of settlement, and in new ones too. It transpires that in this period the process of urbanization had reached its zenith. The great progress in defensive technique resulted also in a modification of the city gate structure throughout the western Fertile Crescent. The angular narrow entrance protected by a tower which was typical of the preceding period was replaced by the composite gatehouse with a straight entrance, wide enough for a chariot to pass, and to which were attached three artistically executed passages which could be barred by wooden doors; occasionally the gate was fortified by towers.[41] It stands to reason that by then horses and chariots already played an important role in the armies and were kept inside the fortified towns.

Alongside the innovations in fortification technique, there was considerable development in the building of houses for rulers and nobles, in the equipment of their graves, which were rich in funerary objects, and in the manufacture of improved pottery and artistic work. All this points to a high cultural level and to reciprocal contact with the Eastern Mediterranean countries. However, the imports from Egypt were particularly numerous. They included thousands of scarabs, ornaments of gold and other precious metals, vessels and other articles of alabaster. An interesting example of a large city, protected by a mighty glacis and an artificial moat, with palaces and graves rich in locally produced articles and objects imported from Egypt, is Beth Eglaim (Tell al-'Ajjūl) south of Gaza, which was no doubt an important center on the main route to Egypt. The same applies to Sharuhen (Tell al-Far'ah) on the brook of Besor. This city was an important Hyksos stronghold until the campaign to Canaan of Ah-mose, founder of the Eighteenth Dynasty, after the routing of the Hyksos from Tanis. Here too, the huge glacis topped by a brick wall and the broad fosse, indicate an important stronghold on the border of the western Negev, which is the biblical Land of Gerar.[42]

H.   RISE OF INDO–ARIAN POWER IN WESTERN ASIA

In the middle of the 17th century when the Hyksos empire of the Fifteenth Dynasty had reached its zenith, the West Semitic empires in Western Asia were still prosperous, particularly the "great" kingdom of Aleppo (Yamhad) in northern Syria and the Babylonian empire, which continued to be ruled by Hammurabi's descendants. At this time their political position, however, began to weaken and the pressure of the non-Semitic peoples on the countries of the Fertile Crescent continued to grow. There was a particularly sharp increase in the pressure of the Hurrians, who, as early as the Mari period, constituted an important ethnic element in northern Mesopotamia and who moved as far as the regions of the Middle Euphrates and the area north of the kingdom of Aleppo. The same applies to Kassite pressure which threatened the Babylonian empire from

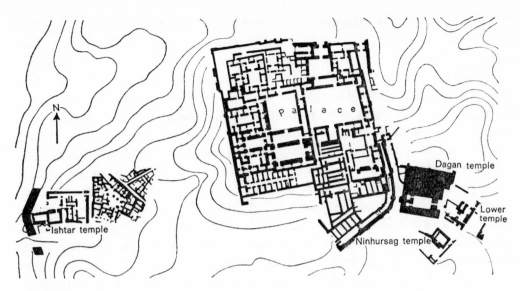

Fig. 29.
Mari, plan of excavated palace and temples.
Encyclopaedie Biblica IV, figs. 561-562.
Drawing by Carta, Jerusalem.

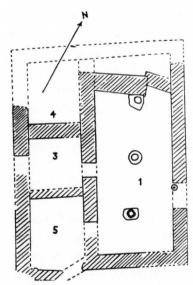

Fig. 30.
Tell Beit Mirsim, plan of a commoner's house, in the Middle Bronze II Period.
Prof. W. F. Albright, Chicago.

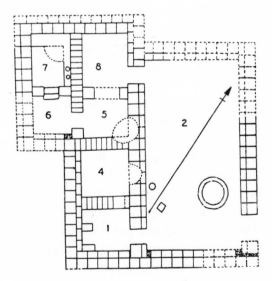

Fig. 31.
Tell Beit Mirsim, plan of patrician house in the Middle Bronze II Period.
Prof. W. F. Albright, Chicago.

the east and grew continually in the days of Hammurabi's successors.[43] An additional important factor was the Hittite empire in Anatolia which had consolidated to such a degree by the middle of the 17th century, that Hattusilis I was able to attack the kingdom of Aleppo and to destroy Alalakh. His successor Mursilis I conquered Aleppo in his great campaign to northern Syria and utterly destroyed the kingdom of Yamhad (ca. 1620).[44] The collapse of this great West Semitic kingdom brought about changes in the ethnic and political geography of the Near East, a process which ended with the conquest and sacking of Babylon by Mursilis I (ca. 1595). Following the destruction of the capital of the Babylonian empire and the end of Hammurabi's dynasty, the Kassites gained control of the entire land of Babylon and founded their empire which endured for a long time. At that time the Indo–Iranian invaders' pressure on northern Mesopotamia had reached its peak; they controlled vast areas of pre-dominantly Hurrian population. These invaders, who appear to be none other than the Ummān–Manda of the Akkadian sources, are first mentioned at the time of Ammizaduqa King of Babylon (middle of the 17th century). It would seem that they were the cause of the mass immigration of Hurrians including Indo–Iranian elements to Syria and Canaan — there existing at that time no power in the political arena to stem the tide. It transpires that the weakening and reduction of the Hyksos empire in Egypt upon the decline of the Fifteenth Dynasty, which was under heavy pressure from the national rulers in Thebes, were the direct result of events in Syria and Canaan. Moreover, already in the second third of the 16th century an Indo–Iranian–Hurrian empire, the kingdom of Mitanni, was established in northern Mesopotamia. This empire was to play an important part in subsequent historical developments and to become a political factor in the western part of the Fertile Crescent also.

As a result of these charges Syria and Canaan became an area of settlement for peoples differing in origin, language and cultural traditions. The Hurrians and the Indo–Iranian element which had joined then, with the addition of emigrants from Anatolia, began to outweigh the auto-chthonous West Semitic inhabitants in most provinces of Syria and Canaan which had a settled population. From this stratum of invaders, who in the course of time intermingled with the country's earlier inhabitants, grew a ruling class with fortified towns, chariots and troops at its command, and a wealth of property and slaves at its disposal. It was the military aristocracy, called Maryannu in the Indo–Iranian sources, which at this time set its mark on the political-military regime and ruled for many generations the subjugated population with its many ethnic and social divisions, in spite of the political changes which took place in the course of the 16th and 15th centuries B.C.E.

The important events which occurred in the last third of the 17th century B.C.E. left their mark on the cultural life also, and their traces are clearly visible at the various sites that have been excavated in Canaan. The rampart type of fortification, predominant in the preceding period, now disappears (the new period constituting the third phase of Middle Bronze II). The excavations at Shechem, Beth-el, Lachish, and Tell Beit Mirsim revealed strong fortifications from this period. Of particular interest is the massive, battered wall at Shechem. It was erected on an earth-work rampart and was built of large blocks of unhewn stones set in straight courses. The so-called "cyclopic" masonry which characterises this wall, was no doubt introduced by the foreign invaders.[45] The same applies to the fortified sanctuary discovered in Shechem, which was built at the same time. It is a compact building with very thick walls. It consists of only one hall with the fortified gate facing the courtyard, and which was protected by two towers. A similar sanctuary was discovered at Megiddo, and there too the first phases of its building can be traced back to the end of the 17th or the beginning of the 16th centuries B.C.E. These two buildings underwent a series of repairs until finally destroyed in the 12th century. It is not inconceivable that the structure in Shechem is the House of Baal-berith (Jud. 9).[46] The sanctuary discovered in the lower town of Hazor also resembles these buildings.

The cultural level as represented by craftsmanship and manufacture would seem to have declined when compared with the preceding period, as a result of the political upheavals of that time and the many changes that took place in the life of the population. It was only when the turmoil of the nations died down that Canaan entered a new phase of cultural development. This is the Late Bronze Period, which began in the middle of the 15th century B.C.E. This new development came in the wake of the decline of the Sixteenth Dynasty Hyksos empire. Around 1565 Ahmose, the founder of the Eighteenth Dynasty from Thebes, vanquished the foreign rulers in the Delta region and conquered Tanis–Avaris their capital; he even undertook a military campaign to southern Canaan and conquered the stronghold of Sharuhen. Egypt entered a new phase of her history – the period of the New Kingdom – and became a decisive political factor in the western Fertile Crescent. This same era witnessed the rise to greatness of the Mitannian empire, whose influence extended in the east beyond Assyria, and in the west over Syria as a result of collision and competition with Egypt.

CHAPTER X

ḤAB/PIRU AND HEBREWS

by M. Greenberg

A. Introductory Remarks

MODERN STUDENTS of Israelite history have shown an interest in the hapiru[1] ever since the first letters from Tell el-Amarna were published in 1888–9. Among these letters, which were eagerly scanned for new light on biblical Canaan, were a half-dozen from the governor of Jerusalem imploring the aid of the Egyptian court against the attacks of the hapiru. The assonance of hab/piru and 'ivri and the apparent concurrence in time, place, and activity between the hapiru and the Hebrew invaders of Palestine seemed sufficient in the eyes of many scholars to justify identifying the two. Thus, it was claimed, there was available at long last "monumental notice of Hebrew victories."[2] When later it was established that the ideogram SA. GAZ, occurring frequently in the Amarna letters to denote hapiru-like groups throughout Syria and Palestine, was, in fact, interchangeable with hapiru, the identification appeared to be confirmed.[3] In spite of many demurrers that have since been put in against it, it has had advocates to the present time. The study of ancient Israel must, accordingly, give consideration to the hapiru and to the possibility of their connection with Hebrew origins.

While our present materials do not tell us all we should like to know about the hapiru they are sufficient to form a general hypothesis which may reasonably be expected to survive the test of new evidence. The material comes from, and is restricted to, cuneiform and Egyptian sources of the 2nd millennium B.C.E.[4] We shall begin by surveying this evidence and drawing what conclusions it allows concerning the nature of the hapiru. We shall then be in a position to compare these conclusions with the biblical data on the Hebrews.

B. The Hab/Piru in the 2nd Millennium B.C.E.

1. Occurrences of SA. GAZ as a verbal or nominal element are available from the Ur III period (2050–1930). The texts in question are primarily

court records. In each case SA.GAZ appears in a context suggesting illegal-ity; a reference to SA.GAZ activity in a passage of the Lipit-Ishtar code (1860) seems also to involve unauthorized action.

2. The earliest passage in which hapiru occurs, phonetically spelled, is in a letter from the Old Assyrian merchant colony of Alishar in Asia Minor (first half of the 18th century). Reference is made to the "ḫabiru of the palace of Shalaḫshuwe" — an unidentified neighbor of Alishar — who are to be ransomed from custody. At the beginning of the 2nd millennium, then, the hapiru appear in the dependent status in which we find them through-out their history.

3. From contemporary Larsa, under the reign of Warad-Sin, seven texts record the receipt by the state treasurers of small cattle "as rations for the SA.GAZ." A text of the first year of Rim-Sin records the allocation of clothing to "ḫapiru sergeants" from a temple treasury. Evidently these SA.GAZ/hapiru were organized military contingents of the Larsa kings.

4. Texts of the Old Babylonian period show the hapiru in a dual role. As we know from the Mari letters, this was a time of considerable turbulence in Mesopotamia, brought about by intense interdynastic rivalries, indi-vidual adventurers, and nomadic incursions. In these letters the hapiru appear as military auxiliaries of the rival king and chiefs: 2,000 are with the Yapah-Adad; Izinabu, a Yamutbalite, has 30 Yamutbalite hapiru under his charge; another contingent are in the service of Ashkur-Adad. At the same time we learn from a letter to Hammurabi that, like his predecessor Rim-Sin, he, too, maintained a SA.GAZ contingent in Larsa, which had its own overseer. A list of the names of eight members of one such military group from the end of this period shows most of the names to be Akkadian, a few West Semitic. An Elamite list of sheep allocated to cantonments of "Amorite (i.e. West Semitic) soldiers" names one such location *Ha-BI-ri*ki, possibly after the "Amorite" hapiru who were there quartered.[5]

But alongside these dependent groups of military auxiliaries appear in-dependent bands of hapiru freebooters. Their activity is usually directed against the towns: they "seize," "raid" (*išḫitū*), or "constantly raid" (*ištanaḫḫitū*) them. One text has them participating in a raid by the men of one town against a neighboring town, a good instance of the anarchic conditions in which the independent hapiru bands thrived.

Thus our sources depict the SA.GAZ/hapiru of the Old Babylonian period as fighting men, either in the service of kings or as independent raiders. Their origins are diverse: some are "Amorite," some "Yamutbalite"; some are foreigners ("Amorites" in Elam), some are "of the land" or have names which connect them with the area in which they are found. Yet, although they may be settled in cantonments they do not seem to have roots in any given locality.

5. Among the Alalakh texts are one of the 18th century and a dozen of the 15th in which the SA. GAZ/hapiru are mentioned. The date formula of an 18th century sale document reads: "The year Irkabtum the king, Shemuba, and the ḫapiru soldiers made peace." While nothing is known concerning this event it may reflect hostility between the Alalakhian king and an independent group of hapiru which was finally ended by a treaty. It was an important event, as shown by its mention in a date formula.

The 15th century texts are, for the most part, military registers of SA. GAZ soldiers belonging to various localities under the control of Alalakh. Following the heading "SA. GAZ soldiers, bearing arms, of the town X" are the name, place of origin, and occasionally the calling, of the individuals of the contingent. Two summary tablets give the total of SA. GAZ as 1,436. They seem to have had their own holdings, called *bīt^lu* SA. GAZ, where they were quartered.

Most of the names are non-Semitic, some are recognizable as Hurrian; scarcely a half-dozen out of the more than a hundred names are Semitic. This distribution accords with the ethnic make-up of the area, and is in agreement with the fact that the towns mentioned as the SA. GAZ's places of origin are presumably scattered in the vicinity of Alalakh. Occasionally a more distant location is mentioned, such as Emar or Canaan. Here again, then, the evidence indicates diversity in ethnic composition and in places of origin, a mixture of local and foreign elements.

It is significant that in nearly every case the SA. GAZ's place of origin is other than the town in which he is found.[6] One feature common to members of the SA. GAZ group was thus the status of strangers. An episode in the life of Idrimi, a king of Alalakh, provides an excellent illustration of why men left home to join the SA. GAZ. Fleeing from a rebellion, the king lodged a night among the Shutu nomads; continuing southward he reached the coastal town of Ammiya, where he was recognized by former subjects of his father. It was with the SA. GAZ that he finally found refuge for seven years, during which time he prepared to regain control of his throne. Such hospitality to fugitives on the part of the SA. GAZ suggests that they were composed, at least in part, of similar elements. The alien and refugee character of the SA. GAZ was doubtless a determining factor in their generally dependent status. It is of importance to emphasize the Alalakh evidence for the urban origins of the SA. GAZ. They do not come from the desert but from the towns; they are not nomadic encroachers upon the settled, but outcasts from civilized society.[7]

6. Material from the 15th century Hurrian principality of Nuzi throws light on a different aspect of the social-legal status of the hapiru. For here we have, in addition to state documents, material from the private archives of prominent citizens who contracted for the service of individual hapiru.

The public documents are similar to the Larsa texts: they relate to the allocation of food and clothing to individuals and groups of hapiru and, in some cases, for the horses of hapiru.[8]

The significant contribution to our information on the hapiru is made by the private documents. These record the voluntary agreement of men and women called hapiru to enter as servants into the households of prominent Nuzians. The terms of the agreement usually bind the hapiru to serve his master as long as the latter lives; occasionally he is permitted to break the agreement upon furnishing a replacement. In return the hapiru receives food and clothing; the relationship may be compared to that of client and patron in Roman law.

Most of the hapiru at Nuzi appear to be foreigners. This is clear, in the first place, from the unusually high percentage of Akkadian names they bear amidst the predominantly Hurrian population. Several are explicitly said to come from Ashur, from Akkad, and from Zarimena. Their client status is evidently an outcome of their foreignness and lack of means: indigent migrants, having come to Nuzi individually and in families, they were constrained to exchange their person for sustenance and protection.

Roughly a third of the hapiru names are non-Semitic, primarily Hurrian. Their presence is sufficient to show that in Nuzi, as elsewhere, the hapiru were ethnically heterogeneous. They had in common neither ethnic nor geographic origins; it was a common social status which identified them and set them apart from the rest of society.

7. The largest single group of texts relating to the SA. GAZ/ḥapiru is found among the Tell el-Amarna letters. These letters date from the reigns of Amen-hotep III and Amen-hotep IV (Akh-en-Aton), and reflect vividly the disturbances which wracked the Syrian and Palestinian provinces of Egypt during this period. In the ensuing anarchy the SA. GAZ/hapiru, available to all as mercenary troops, played a decisive role.

The prime mover of sedition in the north was 'Abd-Ashirti, prince of Amurru, who organized and directed the war against the royal governors. We can follow the success of 'Abd-Ashirti and his sons in the correspondence of Rib-Addi, the loyalist governor of Byblos. Rib-Addi complains constantly of the attacks of 'Abd-Ashirti, his allies, and the SA. GAZ.

The SA. GAZ are not an independent group, but are under the command of 'Abd-Ashirti: he assembles them and stations them where he wishes; they are "his auxiliaries." However, it is impossible to identify the SA. GAZ as a separate element among the anti-Egyptian forces from the letters of Rib-Addi, for it is his custom indiscriminately to lump all his enemies under this rubric.[9]

That the SA. GAZ were a group apart from the rebelling natives is evident from a passage in a letter of a royal deputy in Syria. Among the forces under his command he counts a contingent of SA. GAZ alongside one of the nomadic Shutu. It is thus clear that the SA. GAZ were a separate element; they could ally themselves either with the natives or with the Egyptians. As a rule they were to be found on the side of the natives because these, rather than the Egyptians, were in dire need of auxiliaries. Moreover, from the fact that the term SA. GAZ could cover all those in revolt, it is evident that the group comprised a considerable number of persons who had defected from the Egyptian cause.

The SA. GAZ of the Syrian letters are characteristically affiliated with towns; from them they receive food, equipment, and quarters in return for their military services. A typical relationship is well illustrated in the following letter concerning Amanhatbi, Prince of Tushulti, and his private army of the SA. GAZ. It is interesting not only for its picture of the part the SA. GAZ played in the petty warfare of the towns, but also for the light it throws on the way in which accretions were made to their ranks. The writer is Mayarzana of Hazi, an injured and outraged neighbor of Amanhatbi.

> May the king, my lord, my god, my sun, take note of the deed that Amanhatbi, Prince of Tushulti, has done against the cities of the king, my lord, when the SA. GAZ army made a war on me and seized the cities of the king, my lord . . .
>
> The SA. GAZ seized Mahzibti, a city of the king, my lord, and looted and set it afire. Then to Amanhatbi the SA. GAZ came back.
>
> And the SA. GAZ seized Gilûni, a city of the king, my lord, and looted and set it afire, so that scarcely a single house escaped destruction in Gilûni. Then to Amanhatbi the SA. GAZ came back.
>
> [The letter goes on to describe how two more cities were similarly dealt with.]
>
> Now see: the SA. GAZ raided Hazi, a city of the king, my lord. But we did battle with the SA. GAZ, and we killed them . . .
>
> And when we heard that the SA. GAZ were with Amanhatbi, my brothers and my sons, your servants, [*mounted* (?)] their chariots to

come before Amanḥatbi. And my brothers said to Amanḥatbi, "Surrender the SA.GAZ, the enemies of the king, our lord! We would ask them what they spoke of with you, [*these* (?)] SA.GAZ, wherefore did they seize the cities of the king, my lord, and set them afire?"

And he agreed to surrender the SA.GAZ; but he took them *to free* (?) [*them* (?)]. Then he fled to the SA.GAZ!...[10]

The letters from Palestine depict a wholly analogous situation. Here the foe of Egyptian authority is Lab'ayu, a prince of the central hill country, but there are also other individual adventurers who exploit the weakness of the central government to pillage and harass their neighbors. Here too the correspondents to the court are in the custom of calling all their enemies SA.GAZ — 'Abdū-Heba of Jerusalem uses the term hapiru. But there is abundant evidence here as well that the SA.GAZ/hapiru proper were a distinct element whose ranks were, to be sure, constantly swelled by rebels against Egypt. The SA.GAZ are in the service of Lab'ayu: he gives them Shechem, and his sons hire them to fight against the prince of Megiddo. The townsmen of Lachish, after having slain the local representative of Egypt, are said to have become hapiru.[11]

As before, we find the SA.GAZ/hapiru supported in the main by the towns: Gezer, Ashkelon and Lachish are — it would seem — accused of provisioning them; a deserter to them enters the town of Muḫḫazu to join the SA.GAZ there; all the cities of the king, in fact, are said to be falling away to them. Alongside mercenary bands, however, we hear — particularly in letters from southern Palestine — of what appear to be independent bands of raiders, ravaging the countryside on their own initiative. One text mentions the SA.GAZ alongside the Shutu nomads as plunderers. The cave-filled terrain of the south was apparently found as congenial a refuge by the freebooters of el-Amarna times, as it was by the guerrillas and outlaws of later ages.

In sum, then, the SA.GAZ/hapiru in Syria-Palestine emerge as one of several elements in the population that throve on the disordered circumstances of the Amarna period. While occasionally they are found as independent raiders, their preferred role appears to have been as dependents of the local authorities. They serve as auxiliaries in the forces of both native and Egyptian governors. As at Alalakh and Nuzi they seem to be a mobile group, composed of persons raked together from various places. They welcome fugitive and renegade elements. There is no indication of a tribal consciousness uniting the SA.GAZ bands, nor does their activity, associated as they were with any and all who could hire them, reveal signs of an invasion for conquest of the land. They appear rather as outcasts, banded together from diverse origins, often subsisting on the razzia, but preferably in alliance with towns. Excellent parallels in the society of premonarchic Israel are available.[12]

8. After the Alishar text (B, 2, above), the presence of SA. GAZ/hapiru in Asia Minor is attested by a few Hittite Old Kingdom texts (16th–15th centuries), in which they appear as sizable military contingents subject to the king. One text refers to certain obligations that the king pledged himself to fulfill toward them.[13]

The bulk of the Hittite references to the SA. GAZ/hapiru date from the period of the Empire (14th–13th centuries). The largest number occurs in the formula "gods of the Lulaḫḫu, gods of the ḫapiru" which appears in the lists of divine witnesses at the close of thirteen state treaties. This alone is sufficient to attest that the hapiru were a recognized class of Hittite society; that they were an entity apart, having gods other than those of the official pantheon; and that they were probably foreigners, like the Lulaḫḫu with whom they are paired. Further evidence of their status is offered by an exorcism text countering quarrels among the classes of Hittite society. Ranked between the free-born citizens and the slaves are the Lulaḫḫu and the hapiru.

Among the other references in Hittite texts are two which deserve mention: the one speaks of a hapiru settlement — that is, probably a cantonment, the other applies the epithet SA. GAZ to one Tette, a Syrian prince. Tette appears to be unique among the SA. GAZ in having attained such an exalted station.[14]

9. Extraordinary light is shed on the hapiru in general and on those of the Hittite empire in particular from the Ra's Shamrā texts. The most significant text is a Hittite-Ugaritic state treaty — bearing the seals of Hattusilis III (1275–1250) and Pudu-hepas — concerning the extradition of fugitives. It reads:

> Seal of Tabarna Hattusilis, the great king.
>
> If a servant of a king of Ugarit, or a man of Ugarit, or the servant of a servant of the king of Ugarit should rise up and come into the territory of the SA. GAZ of the Sun [= the Hittite king], I, the great king, shall not receive him; I shall return him to the king of Ugarit.
>
> If the people of Ugarit shall purchase someone of another land with their money, who from the land of Ugarit flees and enters among the SA. GAZ, I, the great king, shall not receive him; I shall return him to the king of Ugarit.[15]

This is the only one of the several Hittite treaties which deal with the extradition of fugitives that specifies the "territory of the SA. GAZ" (*eqli^{lu} SA. GAZ) as the goal of flight. It offers official recognition, so to speak, of the SA. GAZ groups as fugitive havens, attests to the importance of the refugee element in their composition, and shows how men of all conditions were apt to join their ranks. Moreover, the proprietary phrase "SA. GAZ of the Sun" suggests that the Hittite SA. GAZ were directly dependent on the throne, that is, were state dependents. Finally, the fact that these SA. GAZ have a definable "territory" is additional evidence of their recognized status in Hittite society. They are uprooted aliens who live together as clients of the king.

Other Ugaritic texts add further details to the picture. Tax lists in Akkadian and Ugaritic mention a "(quarter of the city) Halab of the hapiru," furnishing the equation Akkadian SAG. GAZ (*sic*) = Ugaritic '*prm*.[16] A clause in a royal grant of property exempts the grantee from having to quarter SA. GAZ or an *ubru* (a foreign dignitary[17]) in his house: both classes could be put up at the state's bidding.[18] There are, finally, two references to the predatory nature of the group: one is a school vocabulary in which the series "robber", SA. GAZ, "criminal" is found; the other concerns an altercation between two cities in which a SA. GAZ attack is involved.[19]

This brings to an end the significant cuneiform material on the hapiru. There are a few omen texts — in which the SA. GAZ play a menacing role, occupation lists — in which they appear among hired and agricultural laborers, and lexical lists — which gloss SA. GAZ with *habbātu*.[20] But there is little additional information that can be gleaned from them.[21]

10. The Egyptian references to the 'pr. w remain to be considered. The 'pr. w are first evidenced in Egypt at the beginning of the 15th century, when they appear as workers in a winepress in the eastern Delta. They continue to appear in a consistently menial status — as quarry workers and stone haulers — up to the time of Ramses IV (1164–1157). That they are foreigners is at times indicated by a foreigner-determinative written with 'pr. w. How they came to Egypt is seen in a list of captives of Amen-hotep II's second Asiatic campaign (ca. 1430): "127 princes of Retenu [Syria-Palestine]; 179 brothers of princes; 3,600 'pr. w; 15,200 living Shasu [nomads]; 36,300 Kharu [settled population of Syria-Palestine]; 15,070 living Neges [north Syrians]." The 'pr. w were thus properly a Syro-Palestinian element; their small number and their position — immediately following the nobility and preceding the natives — recalls their similar status in the Hittite class listing. Can one see here an indication of their

direct dependence on the nobility? At any rate, the 'pr. w are captives in Egypt; hence their position there tells nothing concerning their original status.

Egyptian records mention two encounters with the 'pr. w in Palestine, in the 15th and 14th centuries: in both cases they appear as a disturbing element, in full accord with the picture derived from the Amarna letters.

The SA. GAZ/hapiru, then, are a recognized part of the society of the Near East throughout the 2nd millennium. They usually appear as dependents, serving states and towns in a military capacity, and individuals as household servants. Independent bands appear in 18th century Mesopotamia and 15th-14th century Syria-Palestine. In both instances local conditions are in disorder, so that the outlawry of the SA. GAZ/hapiru seems to be a correlative of local instability. It must be noted however, that, as the omen texts testify, this aspect of the group was prominent in the contemporary conception of them.

The individuals who make up this class are generally foreigners to the localities in which they are found. When their places of origin are specified they are, nearly without exception, towns; to become a hapiru, then, meant to break one's ties, to leave — at times to flee — one's native land, and to exchange a settled for an unsettled, migrant existence.

The composition of the class was diversified: members of military groups, such as are found in Alalakh, derived from many different localities; among them were men of different callings; and — what is particularly significant for us — their names betray a similar ethnic mixture. It was not in their origins that the hapiru were united, but in their foreignness, and their peculiar manner of subsistence. That the hapiru were ethnically or tribally structured seems to be excluded by our present evidence.

How and when the class first came into being cannot as yet be ascertained. Some indications point to the West Semitic infiltration of Mesopotamia at the start of the 2nd millennium as the occasion of its coming into being. Moreover, it would appear that both *hab/piru*, the cuneiform representation of an original *'ab/piru*, and SA. GAZ, best taken as a pseudo-ideogram for *šaggāšu*,[22] are West Semitic derivatives. The etymology of *'ab/piru* is uncertain; the Egyptian and Ugaritic spelling favor *$*p\ r$ as the base, without excluding absolutely *$*b\ r$.[23] For *šaggāšu* the meaning "disturber, restive one," from West Semitic *$*š\ g\ š$, may be suggested.[24] However this may be, the hapiru absorbed vagrant elements of all stocks, so that in the earliest times the terms SA. GAZ and hapiru had already become international coin.

C. The Relation of the Hapiru to the Hebrews

We are now in a position to consider what relation, if any, the hapiru bear to the biblical Hebrews.

Philologically *'ab/piru* and *'ivri* though not transparently related are not irreconcilable, even if the former should derive from **p̄ r* — as present evidence suggests. For it is possible to muster a few instances in which Hebrew *b* appears as *p* in Egyptian and Ugaritic. In form, *'ab/pir* — is a *qatil* stative, *'ivri* a gentilic of the base *'ever;* but the latter, in turn, may go back to *'avir,* so that it is theoretically possible to derive both from a common base.[25]

The usage of *'ab/piru* and *'ivri,* however, is more difficult to harmonize, for while the former is a social classification, with no ethnic implications whatsoever, the latter is a gentilic, designating the Israelites and their ancestors as descendants of Eber — though this interpretation is implied rather than stated explicitly in the Bible.[26] Since the gentilic meaning of *'ivri* in biblical Hebrew has been questioned — usually by the advocates of combining it with hapiru[27] — a review of its occurrences will not be out of order.

Occurrences of *'ivri* cluster in two situations: the Israelite-Egyptian episodes in the Pentateuch (the Joseph story [Gen. 39:14 – 43:32] and the Exodus story [Ex. 1:15 – 9:1]) and the Israelite-Philistine episodes in I Sam. The normative sense of the term in biblical Hebrew must be determined from these contexts. From the contrast of *'ivri-mizri* in Gen. 43:32; Ex. 1:19; 2:11, it follows that, like *mizri* "Egyptian," *'ivri* is an ethnicon denoting Jacobites/Israelites. The same is indicated by the alternation of "YHWH God of the *'ivrim*" (Ex. 5:3) and "YHWH God of Israel" (Ex. 5:1). One notes that *'ivri* is employed a) by foreigners (Gen. 39:14, 17; 41:12; Ex. 1:16; 2:6; and all save one of the I Sam. passages: 4:6, 9; 13:3,[28] 19; 14:11; 29:3); b) by Israelites when speaking of themselves to foreigners (Gen. 40:15[29]; Ex. 1:19; 2:7); c) or by the narrator, when he wants a gentilic to set off Israelites in a foreign environment from their surroundings (Gen. 43:32; Ex. 1:15; 2:11, 13; I Sam. 14:21[30]). In sum: *'ivri* serves the only available ethnicon for the proto-Israelites in the patriarchal narratives, and thereafter, when used as an ethnicon — bereft of the honorific associations of "Israel" — to set off Israelites from foreigners.

Three occurrences remain. Jonah 1:9 — the prophet's "I am an *'ivri,*" responding to the sailors' query, "And of what people art thou?" — falls clearly in b. Gen. 14:13, "Abram the *'ivri,*" belongs to c, its use due evidently to the interest of this author in identifying everyone (and every place) by some qualification (in this verse "Abram the Hebrew" is contrasted with "Mamre the Amorite").

How is it with the law of the "Hebrew slave" (*'eved 'ivri*)? While the earliest occurrence (Ex. 21:2) is not self-explanatory, the deuteronomic restatement of the law (Deut. 15:12) with the addition of *aḥika* "thy brother" all but precludes any interpretation of *'ivri* other than "Israelite." That this is how Jeremiah understood the law is proved by his citation of it (Jer. 34:9) with the gloss *yᵉhudi aḥihu* "his Judean brother." Whether the *'ivri* of the Exodus law ever meant anything else has indeed been argued,[31] but usually on the prior assumption that *'ivri = 'ab/piru*.

No scriptural passage gives explicit ground for extending the scope of *'ivri* beyond Israelites.[32] On the plausible assumption that it is intended to mean, literally, "Eberide," *'ivri* ought logically to apply to many Arab and Aramean peoples as well (Gen. 10:21–25; 11:14–26; I Chron. 1: 17–27).[33] But the fact is that none but the line of Abraham-Isaac-Jacob is ever called *'ivrim*. That biblical writers knew a sense of *'ivri* that could include non-Semites, or that, like *'ab/piru*, denoted a social class, embracing elements of diverse ethnic origins, goes well beyond the evidence.

From the fact that no extra-biblical source ever refers to the people of Israel or Judah as *'ivrim*, it may be inferred that the term is peculiar to biblical Hebrew. Presumably it was an archaic term, utilized in the first place in traditions of the earliest ancestors of Israel, when the gentilics "Israelite" or "Judahite" were not yet available, and later as an outsider's term, in contexts where a bare gentilic was wanted, without any of the proud associations of "Israelite."

The traditional etymologies of the term are not quite satisfying.[34] The derivation from Eber leaves unexplained the peculiar restriction to Israelites: the alternative, from *'ever (ha-nahar)* "beyond (the River [Euphrates])" — (cf. Josh. 24:2) — seems artificial. It is this difficulty of accounting for the origin of *'ivri* with Hebrew resources alone that makes recourse to a combination with *'ab/piru* perennially attractive, though a simple identification of the two would do violence to the distinctive sense of each term. "Abram the Hebrew" offers a point of departure for such a combination, as will be suggested in the sequel.

The attractiveness of the hapiru–Hebrew combination has always been its historical dividend. If the hapiru disturbances of Amarna Palestine could be equated with the Hebrew invasion, a fixed chronological point in early Israelite history would become available, as well as an extra-biblical control to check the biblical record of this event. To be sure, the scope of

Israelite activity is too limited to permit its outright combination with the far-flung SA.GAZ/hapiru. At the most, the Israelite tribes could have been only one element of this widespread group. One must further assume a 15th century stage of Israelite invasion, war, and settlement, prior to the archeologically established 13th century wave of war and settlement. With this assumed earlier wave it has been proposed to identify the activity of (at least part of) the Amarna hapiru.[35]

Our present purpose does not require us to examine the chronology and the stages of the Israelite settlement. For however long and gradual one assumes the process to have been, its distinctive features remain unaltered: it was an ethnic movement, a purposeful invasion of land-hungry tribes intent upon seizing territory for settlement. The tribes first occupied the highlands, where the density of the native population was least; their weakness and ignorance of chariot warfare made the conquest of the plains impossible. Their official policy toward the natives was uncompromisingly hostile. While some instances of assimilation may have occurred, the fundamental antagonism of Israel toward, and its isolation from, the Canaanite population is evidenced in the development of its political and religious institutions: both are in striking opposition to those of the natives.

Beyond the fact that the hapiru and the Israelites were both militant groups, the two differ in every way. The hapiru are not ethnically homogeneous, nor is there any indication that they were tribally structured. Their activity is not informed with a discernable common purpose, but is sporadic and dissociated. There is no more a purpose uniting the many hapiru groups than there is uniting the various petty rulers whom they serve. As a rule the hapiru are subordinates; it is upon the initiative of others that they act, only occasionally — and then merely as raiders — on their own.

There are no grounds for seeing in the hapiru an invading, desert element. Almost all of those whose provenance is known originate among the settled population of the towns; they migrate as individuals or as families. They are, to be sure, foreigners, but the members of a given ḫapiru group hardly ever have a common place of origin.

The hapiru have their own cantonments and occupy areas that are assigned to them. But that, on their own, they ever seize a town, depopulate it and then settle it permanently, is never indicated. Their tactics are to hit and run; a city "looted and burned so that scarcely a house was left standing" is their mark.

The activity of the hapiru is not restricted to the highlands. Megiddo and Aijalon, for example, are no less accessible to them than Shechem. Moreover, they are adepts in chariot warfare.

The close association of the hapiru with the native townsmen, their frequent support of the native rebellion against Egypt, the supply of provisions and equipment which they receive from the cities, above all the wholesale desertions of the natives to the hapiru — all these are irreconcilable with the biblical picture of Israel's long drawn out warfare against the Canaanite cities. The total involvement of the hapiru in the political upheavals of the Amarna age is equally at variance with Israel's isolationist policy. Finally, it is to be noted that the background of Egyptian hegemony is absent from the biblical narratives. The great discrepancy between the Amarna hapiru and the invading Israelite tribes leaves little room for combining the two.

The possibility — and it is no more than that — remains that the Patriarchs — as individuals and families — may have been hapiru. Uprooted from their native place, migrant, having the status of protected clients (*ger wᵉ-toshav*) in the land of their sojourn, they bear the earmarks of the class. Perhaps a reminiscence of their hapiru status is to be seen in the peculiar restriction of *'ivri* (if *'ivri* is a Hebrew adaptation of *'ab/piru*) to the migrant Patriarchs — for example, so as to apply to Abraham,[36] but not to his settled kinsman Lot. If that is indeed the case, the biblical writers recast the term as a gentilic — unless we assume that it had already lost its original meaning before reaching them.[37]

With this speculation we have reached what would seem to be the limits of the justifiable combination of hapiru and Hebrews. To go further is to run the risk of obscuring the proper features of each group. The two may have met in the "wandering Aramean" who was Israel's ancestor. But in all else each pursued its independent historical way.

CHAPTER XI

THE PATRIARCHS IN THE LAND OF CANAAN

by S. Yeivin

A. Habitat and Chronological Considerations

WITH THE ARRIVAL of the family of the Patriarchs in the neighborhood of Shechem there ends the biblical account of their wandering from Ur of the Chaldees by way of Haran to the Land of Canaan, which was destined to become the Promised Land (Gen. 11:31–12:6).

There they found three regions, comparatively restricted but suitable to their semi-nomadic, pastoral economy, in which they could wander about without encroaching on anyone's rights and without moving too far from permanently settled urban centers where they could dispose of their produce and obtain such necessities of life as they were unable to produce themselves.

These three regions were the Jordan rift, with its southern continuation, the Arabah; the mountainous backbone of western Canaan (Judah and Samaria); and the northwestern Negev centered on Gerar. The Lotite clan chose the *kikkar hay-Yarden* (the Jordan rift). The Patriarchs thus lived in the area between the wilderness of Shur (Gen. 16:7), to the south and west of Kadesh, and the Valley of Dothan in Samaria (Gen. 37:17).

Though biblical sources do not mention seasonal wanderings, it may be assumed that the Patriarchs spent the rainy season and spring in the Negev, where the climate is warmer than in the north and where there is no lack of pasturage throughout December-April. During the summer and autumn months however they took refuge from the heat in the cooler highlands, where grazing lands were available in these seasons, for the region was still sparsely populated in the first half of the 2nd millennium B.C.E.

The Patriarchs always chose to camp in the immediate neighborhood of, or not far from towns, for wherever the biblical account speaks of their camping, it invariably mentions a nearby town. Thus Abraham's first station in Canaan is described as "the place of Shechem ... the terebinth of Moreh" (Gen. 12:6). Later he traveled southward "unto the place where his tent had been at the beginning, between Beth-el and Ai" (Gen. 13:3). After a time we find him "by the terebinths of Mamre, which are in Hebron" (Gen. 13:18). Other biblical passages state that Abraham "sojourned in Gerar" (Gen. 20:1),[1] that he "dwelt at Beer-sheba" (Gen. 22:19), that Sarah died at Hebron.

Isaac lived mainly in the Negev: it is explicitly stated that "he dwelt in the land of the South" [= Negev] (Gen. 24 : 62). During a drought he went to Gerar. From the Valley (naḥal) of Gerar he went to Beer-sheba, where he successively and successfully dug for water. Finally he lived at Hebron, where he died.

It is from Beer-sheba that Jacob started on his flight to Paddan-aram (in northern Mesopotamia).[2]   His way led through "the land of Bene-Qedem [the children of the east]." The biblical narrative of Jacob's life mentions all the places, west of the Jordan, where his grandfather Abraham had camped: Shechem, Beth-el,[3] Hebron, Beer-sheba. In addition, Jacob encamped near Ephrath and "beyond Migdal-eder" (Gen. 35:21), while his sons grazed his flocks in Dothan, in the far north. He is also the first Patriarch whom the biblical narrative associates with Transjordan, specifically with Mizpah, Mahanaim, Penuel, and Succoth, all of them in the "mountain of Gilead," the earliest Israelite territory in Transjordan.

The Lotite clan, too, chose to stay in the vicinity of urban settlements, first near the "Pentapolis," as far as Sodom (Gen. 13:12),[4] then at Zoar, and only later, after a natural catastrophe had struck that neighborhood, did it move to the wooded and sparsely populated mountainous region of southern Transjordan. There the earlier separation from the Abrahamite clan became a complete rift, aetiologically justified in later Hebrew tradition by the bastardly origin of the Moabites and Ammonites (Gen. 19:30 ff.)[5]

Members of the patriarchal families tried their hand, at least in the days of Isaac, at agriculture (a typical occupation of semi-nomadic Negev tribes to this very day), and in rainy years they seem to have reaped quite bountiful harvests (Gen. 26:12). One can almost sense the gradual acclimatization of these wandering families to an agricultural life, and the beginnings of a process of their settlement on the land and of their becoming tied to a more restricted area, that is, to the semi-arid neighborhood between Gerar and Beer-sheba, with which the name of Isaac in particular is associated in the biblical tradition.

At all events, in times of drought the inhabitants of the Negev had to take refuge in regions less affected by such calamities.[6] The way to the north into the more fertile areas of the coastal plain was presumably barred by petty city-states, strong enough to prevent the influx of the starving semi-nomads but doubtless apprehensive that they would be unable to get rid of them again, especially since it is likely that they, too, were affected by the same droughts. On the other hand, there was always open for these nomads the way to the southwest, to Egypt, the land of permanent plenty, at least in the eyes of the hungry "Dwellers-on-the-Sand."

The Bible records that "there was a famine in the land; and Abram went down into Egypt to sojourn there; for the famine was sore in the land" [of Canaan] (Gen. 12:10). But as soon as the threat of starvation in the Negev had passed, he returned. Such periodical wanderings to and from Egypt were not rare. The accidental survival of part of an official Egyptian journal of a frontier post in the eastern Delta affords us a welcome glimpse into such occasions, and although some six hundred years later than the days of Abraham, it must reflect the customary procedure. In the eighth year of Mer-ne-Ptah, the journal notes:

> . . . Another communication to my [lord], to [wit: We] have finished letting the Bedouin tribes of Edom pass the Fortress [of] Mer-ne-Ptah Hotep-hir-Maat — life, prosperity, health! — which is [in] Tjeku [Succoth], to the pools of Per-Atum . . . which are [in] Tjeku, to keep them alive and to keep their cattle alive . . .[7]

Under similar circumstances Isaac set out (from the mountains of Judah?) for Egypt, but on reaching Gerar he was commanded in a vision to remain there (Gen. 26:1–6). This change of plans may have been due to a variety of reasons. However, Jacob's behaviour on the occasion of a severe famine (Gen. 42:1 ff.) suggests that Isaac changed his mind as a result of altered political conditions.

If we accept the assumption that the Patriarchs' wandering in the Land of Israel took place in the 18th–16th centuries B.C.E.,[8] the major part of its duration coincides with the period of the Hyksos invasion and domination of Egypt. It has been suggested[9] that the first dynasty of Hyksos rulers (the Fifteenth Dynasty of Egypt) retained its foreign character and probably welcomed additional kindred immigrants, who would naturally tend to strengthen their hold on Egypt. Consequently, no restrictions were placed on the entry and exit of semi-nomadic groups. This situation changed in the days of the pharaohs of the Sixteenth Dynasty who had become more Egyptianized,[10] and who in their attempts both to appease their Egyptian subjects as well as to enforce law and order in the country introduced frontier control and special permission for entry. Learning of this and finding conditions in Gerar favorable, Isaac stayed there. Biblical tradition, although preserving the kernel of actual historical conditions, ascribed the fact, in keeping with its general trend, to divine intervention. Thus Jacob, fully aware of the position, did not even attempt to emigrate with his family to Egypt, but instead sent his sons to purchase food there, and only after he had been officially invited did he go to Egypt.[11]

B. Customs and Ethnic Connections

Although fully intending to settle in the land to which they had newly come, the patriarchal clans kept up their seasonal wanderings, and at first, at least, preserved the consciousness of their origin. They took pride in the purity of their ethnic connections, and to maintain them sent to Paddan-aram, to tribes closely related to them, for wives for their sons. Thus Abraham sent his steward to Nahor to find a wife for his son Isaac, who was to succeed him. As for Ishmael, the son of his concubine Hagar, his mother chose for him an Egyptian wife. Nor apparently did Abraham protest. This, too, happened with Isaac and his sons: when Esau took unto himself wives from the daughters of the land, it was apparently one of the factors responsible for the loss of his birthright; but Jacob's parents saw to it that he should marry a wife from his mother's clan. Esau later tried to mend his ways by marrying the daughter of Ishmael, his uncle. Only after the definite break between Jacob and Laban, expressed by the symbolic partition of Transjordan between them, did intermarriage between the Abrahamites and the Nahorites cease (Gen. 31:45 ff.). The biblical narrative does not dwell on the marriages of Jacob's sons as it does on those of Isaac and Jacob, so that it is only incidentally that we learn that Joseph married an aristocratic Egyptian, that Judah and his sons married Canaanites,[12] that Simeon's sons included "Shaul the son of a Canaanitish woman" (Gen. 46:10).

The history of the Patriarchs makes indeed no further mention of marriages. However, in the course of time Moses the Lawgiver married a Cushite woman, to the displeasure of members of his family (Num. 12:1).[13] The genealogical lists in the Book of Chronicles give here and there some particulars of the marriages of the more immediate descendants of Jacob's sons. Thus, for example, Caleb's third wife was Ephrath (I Chron.2:19),[14] a name obviously connected with a pre-Israelite settlement mentioned in the account of Rachel's death.[15] Jerahmeel's second wife, too, judging by her son's name, was apparently a Canaanite (I Chron. 2:26). Caleb's concubine, Ephah, was most probably a non-Israelite, both by name and status (I Chron. 2:46), and so was another of Caleb's concubines, Ma-

Fig. 32.

Middle Bronze I and II pottery (fig. 1–12 and 13–42 respectively).
M. Avigad, *Biblical Encyclopedia* III, fig. 165
Drawn by '*Carta*', Jerusalem.

acah,[16] while Mered, a descendant of Caleb, married Bithiah, the daughter of Pharaoh (I Chron. 4:18).[17] The same genealogies attribute to Manasseh himself an Aramean concubine, the mother of two clans (I Chron. 7:14–15).[18] Nun, the father of Joshua, was a descendant of Ephraim. This name, probably in its original pronunciation of Nawen (or something similar) occurs in the list of places conquered by Thut-mose III and was apparently situated in the western foothills of Samaria, in the vicinity of Joshua's reputed burial site.[19] This, too, seems to point to intermarriage with autochthonous pre-Israelite families. At least two Benjaminite clans, Ard (Gen. 46:21) and Mikloth (I Chron. 8:32; 9:37–38), also seem to appear in the above mentioned lists of Thut-mose III,[20] with the same implications.[21] Before we discuss the Patriarchs' way of life in Canaan, it would be pertinent to describe first the conditions prevailing there at the time, as these emerge from a study of archeological remains and contemporary extra-biblical documents.

Archeological research has revealed a cultural revolution in the country during the 21st–19th centuries B.C.E., expressed in various aspects of archeological finds dating from this period, which is the first and the beginning of the second phase of the Middle Canaanite (or Middle Bronze) period. There is a marked deterioration in permanent settlements.[22] These facts can be explained by reference to the written records of the time, which testify to an influx into the region known as the countries of the Fertile Crescent of nomadic or semi-nomadic elements of Western Semitic affiliation, who gradually settled there,[23] partly assimilating the autochthonous population and partly exterminating it.

The patriarchal families arrived in Israel toward the end of the 18th century, when this process of new settlement and assimilation was nearing its end, and the most suitable areas in the country were already settled by the West Semites who had preceded them. The Patriarchs therefore had perforce to content themselves with either the wooded mountains in the central, western and southern regions of the country or the less developed areas of the Negev.

While thus taking root in their new surroundings, they continued to preserve their familiar manners and customs. The account of the Patriarchs in Genesis is concerned with one object, namely, to show how through the will, the choice, and the proper guidance of the Almighty a certain stock of common ancestry was gradually whittled down by the elimination of undesirable subsidiary clans to one main stem, from which there finally issued the twelve tribes of Israel. Hence the Bible deals only with family interrelations and squabbles against a very faint background of an economic and cultural *milieu* while omitting every detail which is not absolutely essential to the narrative.

And yet, even with these limitations, it is possible to perceive the existence of a society based on a definite code of customs, if not of actual law, very different from what was later to become the basis of biblical law.

Marriage is strictly endogamous, to such an extent that even half-brother-sister marriages were permitted, though explicitly prohibited by later law (Lev. 18:9; 20:17; Deut. 27:22). Jacob married two sisters, again in explicit contravention of the subsequent biblical law (Lev. 18:18). The father of a dead son (the father-in-law of the widow) was also expected to fulfill the obligation of levirate marriage, in complete opposition to later biblical law (Lev. 18:15; 20:12). Judah himself admitted that his daughter-in-law Tamar was in the right (Gen. 38:26). Moreover, it was he who, believing her to be an adulteress, sentenced Tamar to be burnt, a sentence contrary to biblical law, which prescribes burning only in the case of a daughter of a priest taken in adultery (Lev. 21:9).[24]

The biblical law of inheritance is very explicit and straightforward. A father cannot ignore the rights of a firstborn (Deut. 21:15–17). But in the narratives of the Patriarchs there is a constant disregard of this principle. Esau's rights as the firstborn were transferred to Jacob, who by a ruse took even the blessing which was Esau's due. Reuben's status as the first-born was annulled by his father, apparently on account of his transgression, and transferred to Joseph. This is a clear-cut case of preferring the son of the favorite to that of the unloved wife. Jacob did this with his grand-children, too, giving to Ephraim the right of the firstborn that belonged to his elder brother Manasseh.[25]

Such practices do not reflect the customs and manners of semi-nomadic clans, as the Patriarchs were, nor of settled agricultural communities, as the Canaanites must then have been or as the Israelites later became. They suit a business society, the interests of which are not confined to immovable property. And indeed in the legal documents from Nuzi in Arrapkha we find adoption practices that are aimed at disregarding and by-passing the usages of an agricultural life, enabling a father to upset and even to sell the right of seniority.[26] Hence the Patriarchs were conversant with the laws of Mesopotamia, from whence they had come, and applied them when necessary.

Then again, biblical law does not recognize concubinage, though its existence is mentioned several times in post-patriarchal times,[27] and is also attested in extra-biblical sources.[28] It is only Mesopotamian law that makes it possible to understand various practices of the Patriarchs in this connection.[29]

There is a point which stands out quite clearly, for example, in the account of Jacob's flight from Laban: the latter insists that "the daughters are my daughters, and the children are my children, and the flocks are my flocks, and all that thou seest is mine; and what can I do this day for these my daughters, or for their children which they have borne?" (Gen. 31:43; cf. also verses 26 ff.). Jacob did not dispute this, but claimed that he had rightfully acquired all that he possessed, although Laban had several times tried to cheat him. Biblical law knows only one kind of marriage, whereby a man acquired a wife by paying a marriage gift to her father, after which she comes to live with him in his or in his father's home.[30] But Middle-Assyrian law recognizes a marriage in which the wife remains in her father's home, where she is visited by her husband. In such a case the husband has no right to any of the property in his father-in-law's house.[31]

It is not to be wondered at that personal status (marriage, levirate, inheritance) is almost the sole socio-legal subject on which light is shed in the patriarchal narratives. For the whole purpose of these traditions is to explain how the Israelite nation was born and descended from the Patriarchs by the gradual elimination of kindred units, which likewise developed into separate national entities.

C. CULTIC PRACTICES

The second focal point in these traditions is God's election of the Patriarchs and their descendants, and the covenant He made with them. Hence these traditions illuminate another feature in the life of the Patriarchs, namely, their religious outlook and practice.[32]

Their Deity is a family patron, whose different appellations are connected with the names of the individual Patriarchs. Thus Jacob, in speaking to Laban, refers to "the God of Abraham, and the Fear of Isaac" (Gen. 31: 42). Elsewhere his Deity is called "the Mighty One of Jacob" (Gen. 49:24), and in the covenant between Jacob and Laban, the latter's God is acknowledged as "the God of Nahor," in contradistinction to Jacob's "the God of Abraham" (Gen. 31:53). True, the patriarchal narratives continually mention the Deity under His subsequent tetragrammaton YHWH, but this is undoubtedly to be ascribed to the later compiler or editor of these traditions.[33] Although their Deity was regarded by the Patriarchs as one God, supreme and mighty, so that He could promise them a land not theirs and make a covenant with them about this, there is a great deal of religious tolerance in their attitude to strangers. When Jacob prepared himself for the ceremony of sanctification at Beth-el, he instructed his household: "Put away the strange gods that are among you" (Gen. 35:2–4). From the wording of the passage and from the circumstances it is evident that Jacob did not regard the presence of strange gods in his household as sinful. He merely asked that they be removed in preparation of the purification and sanctification, as can be seen from the end of that same verse: "And purify yourselves, and change your garments." The "strange gods" were neither broken nor destroyed but were respectfully hidden "under the terebinth which was by Shechem," with the intention apparently of removing them and the ornaments, likewise concealed there, when a suitable opportunity arose. Moses, too, spoke to Pharaoh of "the God of the Hebrews,"[34] thus implying the existence of other, Egyptian, gods. There is no sign as yet of the later stubborn and fanatical fight of the prophets and the reforming kings against any manifestation of foreign rites of worship and strange gods, who are "vanity and things wherein there is no profit," whose very existence is denied.[35]

The Deity of the Patriarchs was associated with no specific country or place, but was omnipresent. Wherever the Patriarchs encamped they could erect an altar to Him and call upon the name of the Lord. Thus Abraham in his wanderings built such altars at Shechem, between Beth-el and Ai, at the terebinths of Mamre near Hebron, and at Beer-sheba. Isaac, too, built an altar at Beer-sheba. Jacob erected a pillar (*mazzeva*) and later an altar at Beth-el, another *mazzeva* of a religious character at Gilead, altars at Shechem and Beer-sheba, a second *mazzeva* at Beth-el, and another on Rachel's tomb on the way to Ephrath. In one instance (Gen. 46:1 ff.) the Bible refers to the offering of sacrifices and to visions of the night without mentioning the building of an altar. The account of Jacob's return to Beth-el (Gen. 35:1 ff.) also reveals a glimpse of the rites connected with such altars: these included purification, the removal of the images of other gods, physical cleansing, undoubtedly by lustration, perhaps the wearing of special clothes, and humility in the presence of the Deity, symbolized by the removal of all ornaments that might be considered an expression of pride and ostentation.

Jacob seems to have initiated the practice of assigning names to the altars that he built, though the exact significance of this custom is still not clear. Thus he called the place where he erected his first *mazzeva* Beth-el, renaming it later, when he built an altar there, El-beth-el. The *mazzeva* erected in Gilead as a sign of his covenant with Laban was called Jegar-sahadutha (Aramaic for "the cairn of witness"), while the altar at Shechem was named El-elohe-Israel. In this there is no evidence to support the

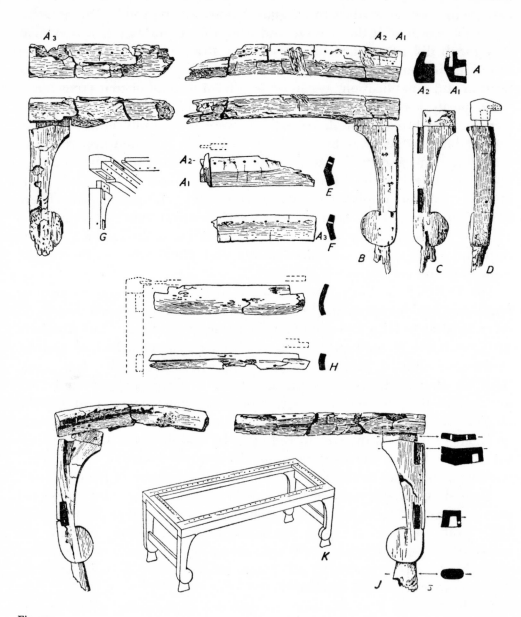

Fig. 33.
Fragments of wooden furniture and reconstruction of a stool
found in a Middle Bronze II tomb at Jericho.
Prof. K. M. Kenyon, London.

view that Jacob considered the altars themselves to be divine objects. The practice may be merely an additional means of "calling upon the name of the Lord," as Abraham had previously done (Gen. 12:8), the altar being named after the Deity in whose honor it had been built (Gen. 21:33 — "the Everlasting God"). The Patriarchs also erected *mazzevot*, explicitly stated to be anointed or unanointed stones, and planted "holy" trees

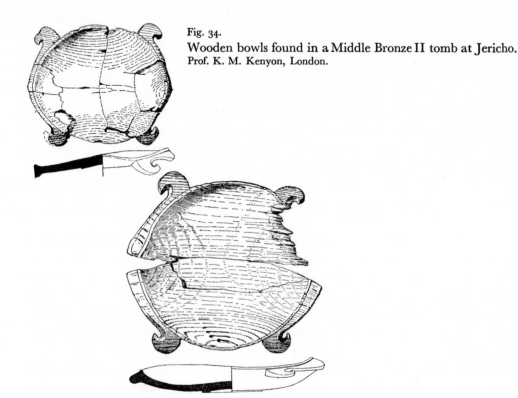

Fig. 34.
Wooden bowls found in a Middle Bronze II tomb at Jericho.
Prof. K. M. Kenyon, London.

at those places where they called upon their Deity. Thus Abraham planted a tamarisk-tree at such a place. In later biblical law both practices were categorically forbidden as pagan rites (Deut. 16:21–22; 7:5; 12:3–4).

One last characteristic feature should be mentioned with regard to patriarchal "holy places." Some of them were Canaanite places of worship. Thus Shechem was later known as a religious center, in which there was a temple to Baal-berith (= "lord of a covenant": Jud. 9:4), and remains of a sanctuary going apparently back to the Middle Bronze Period were actually uncovered in the excavation of Tell Balāṭa, the site of ancient

Shechem.[36] There is no definite evidence that Mahanaim ("And Jacob said when he saw them: 'This is God's camp.' And he called the name of that place Mahanaim": Gen. 32:2) and Penuel (Gen. 32:25–31) in Transjordan may have been associated with some pre-Israelite cultic practices. Nor is there the slightest evidence for associating the other places of worship mentioned in the narratives of the Patriarchs, namely, Beth-el, Hebron, Beer-sheba, and possibly the burial place of Rachel on the way to Ephrath, with non-Israelite religious rites. They all seem to be genuine Israelite centers, later sanctified through their association with patriarchal traditions, although the cult and rites practiced there contained elements borrowed from the Canaanites. Even the one clear case of a pagan religious center at Shechem, mentioned above, may stem from early patriarchal traditions in view of the obviously mixed character of the population, which contained Israelite strains ever since the time of Jacob.[37] Thus even in their choice of cultic centers the Patriarchs seem to have initiated an epoch in the history of the country.[38]

D. Economic and Environmental Conditions

The clan of Terah was originally, so it would seem, engaged in animal husbandry, principally asses for the needs of merchant caravans. They also probably served as caravaneers along the trade routes; hence their strong ties from the very beginning with Ur (of the Third Dynasty). On their arrival in the land of Canaan, the growing disruption of the trade routes in the 18th century tended to make large and small cattle breeding an increasingly important element in their economy.[39]

This is also reflected in such passages as have occasion to mention their staple food.[40] They had naturally to buy from the sedentary population corn for making flour and baking bread (cf. Gen. 42:3). Pulse and fruit[41] were probably obtained in the same way. They may have collected wild honey, if such is meant and not the sweet substance extracted from carobs, dates, or figs by boiling them.

A more fundamental analysis of the narratives concerning the Patriarchs suggests that the life history of each one represents a particular stage in the development of the conditions of their stay in the Land of Israel. Abraham still apparently tried to maintain the tradition of caravaneering between Canaan and Egypt: "And Abraham . . . dwelt between Kadesh and Shur; and he sojourned in Gerar" (Gen. 20:1). In the course of time however (see above) he turned increasingly to animal husbandry, and this may have been the reason for Lot's separation from him. This stage of patriarchal settlement in the land of Canaan may be dated approximately 1750–1680 B.C.E.

Isaac tried his hand at agriculture, but this is mentioned only once (Gen. 26:12 ff.), and nothing much is heard about such attempts afterwards. This "aberration" of Isaac may be partly responsible for the secondary place assigned to him as compared to the larger importance ascribed to Abraham and Jacob. Isaac is also the only Patriarch in connection with whom game is mentioned as a source of food (Gen. 27:3–4). But on the whole hunting is looked upon as an inferior occupation pursued by desert nomads, such as the Ishmaelites or Edomites. This stage may be assigned to 1700–1620 B.C.E.

In the days of Jacob there was a serious breach between the Abrahamites (the Israelites) and the Nahorites (the Arameans), which is reflected in the account of Jacob's flight from Laban and of the covenant made between them for defining the limits of their respective areas of wanderings (Gen. 31). This breach may have been due to economic reasons. With the consolidation of the Hyksos rule in Egypt and Canaan on the one hand, and the rise of the great powers in the Euphrates and Tigris Valleys on the other, all of which took place in the 17th century B.C.E., the semi-nomadic tribes (such as the clans of Abraham and Nahor) were increasingly thrust into the frontier regions bordering on the Syrian-Arabian Desert. There Jacob attempted to extend the area of his activities (during his stay at Paddan-aram). This necessarily assumes that there was a rivalry, with all its implications, for pasturage.

The Jacobites now naturally turned to intermarriage with Canaanite women, which of necessity also led to renewed attempts to adapt themselves to a settled agricultural life. Hence apparently the settlement called Jacob-El which is mentioned among the very earliest conquests of the pharaohs of the Eighteenth and Nineteenth Dynasties. Nevertheless it seems that there was opposition among the Jacobite clans to this intermarriage with the autochthonous population, expressed in the change of Jacob's name to Israel, which emphasized their adherence to the worship of one God. This stage ends with the emigration of Jacob and his sons to Egypt, and is apparently to be dated about 1650–1580 B.C.E.[42]

From the narrative concerning Abraham it is evident that in his days relations between him and the inhabitants of the land were on the whole peaceful and friendly. Objection was raised neither to the Patriarchs' camping in the vicinity of settlements nor to their seasonal wanderings from one area to another. Jacob had no misgivings about setting out alone on his journey to Paddan-aram. Joseph wandered by himself in the mountains of Judah and Samaria and did not hesitate to speak to a stranger whom he met in an isolated place and who directed him on the right way. When the Patriarchs needed some land, they bought it. Thus when Sarah died at Hebron, Abraham paid the full price for a burial cave which he bought from one of the local inhabitants (Gen. 23:3 ff.). In this connection we are given a lively and characteristic picture of bargaining, as also an illustration of the friendly relations between the people of Hebron on the one hand and Abraham and his household on the other. In time this cave became the burial place of all the Patriarchs and their families (Gen. 25: 9–10; 49:31; 50:13). Jacob, too, acquired a camping ground near Shechem, for which he paid the full value.

And yet there was a general feeling of insecurity and mutual distrust in the country, giving rise to outbursts of enmity and bloody clashes. That Abraham and Isaac felt compelled to pass their wives off as their sisters is significant. In two instances Sarah was taken from Abraham — not only by the mighty Pharaoh (Gen. 12:10 ff.) but even by the petty kinglet of Gerar (Gen. 20:1 ff.). This local ruler remarked that Isaac's wife was likely to be violated by one of the people (Gen. 26:7 ff.). And this actually took place in the case of Jacob's daughter, Dinah. In all these instances there obviously existed no way of legal redress, for since they were "strangers and sojourners" in the land (Gen. 23:4), they were considered by the settled population as being outside the pale of established law.[43] The same applied to water rights. Patriarchs wronged by the inhabitants of Gerar did not even attempt to complain, but left the disputed wells and went elsewhere. Abimelech, King of Gerar, did indeed justify himself to Abraham by saying: "I know not who hath done this thing; neither didst thou tell me, neither yet heard I of it, but today" (Gen. 21:26), but there is no reference to his restoring to Abraham the well which his men had dug. The same "outsideness" is evident in the case of Lot. When he sought to prevent the men of Sodom from abusing his guests, they threateningly replied: "Stand back . . . This one fellow came in to sojourn, and he will needs play the judge" (Gen. 19:9). The same fear of enmity and insecurity is also reflected in Jacob's reaction to his sons' raid on Shechem: "Ye have troubled me, to make me odious unto the inhabitants of the land . . . and, I being few in number, they will . . . smite me" (Gen. 34:30).

And yet these wanderers, seemingly downtrodden and legally helpless sojourners, or possibly just because they had no recourse to the protection of the law, were sometimes vaguely feared and mistrusted by the settled population. Thus Abimelech asked Isaac to leave his territory in order to avoid trouble. And the action of Simeon and Levi against Shechem shows

that such misgivings were not imaginary. For when these sojourners suffered any injury, they were apt to take the law into their own hands and
cause irreparable damage. It is not to be wondered at, therefore, that in
certain instances local rulers sought to conclude treaties with them and to
ensure their amity and help in case of need (Gen. 21:22 ff.; 26:26 ff.). Even
the readiness of Hamor, the prince of Shechem, to accept the conditions of
Jacob's sons for a covenant of friendship reveals the same anxiety on the
part of that local kinglet.

E. The Episode of Genesis

In the case of Abraham, his help was apparently sought by local rulers
against a powerful external foe (Gen. 14). Although it appears from the
biblical narrative that Abraham pursued Chedorlaomer and his allies on
his own initiative with the sole purpose of freeing his kinsman Lot, one
could read between the lines an appeal by the pentapolitan confederacy
to come to their assistance, for the one who escaped and informed Abraham
of the defeat of the allies is nowhere stated to be of Lot's household, nor is
there any mention of his actual message. Lot's capture may have been
only an additional incentive for action on Abraham's part. Then again,
on his victorious return, Abraham is met by the King of Sodom, who
wishes to reward him for his share in the campaign.

This account of a battle between a coalition of four Mesopotamian
kings and a confederation of five city-states from south of the Dead Sea
is the only episode of political history, with definite names of states and
rulers, that is connected with the lives of the Patriarchs. Unfortunately, no
extra-biblical information has thus far been found about any of these
kings or about the campaign itself.[44]

Yet the narrative itself seems to have been substantiated by the discoveries of recent years. Coming to the onomasticon of the episode, one
notes that Chedorlaomer, though unknown either as an Elamite king or
as a proper noun, is a plausible Elamite theophoric name, such as Kutir-
lagamar (comparable to Kutir-naḫḫunte and other similar names). The
city-state of Ellasar has been identified as Illassura or Illanssura in Mari,
and even the namesake of its king, the biblical Arioch, has been found in
the Mari archives as Arriwuk, the son of Zimri-lim, the last king of Mari
(at the end of the 18th century B.C.E.). It has been suggested that the
city-state of Shinar is to be identified with Shankhar (Egyptian: Sangara)
in the region of Jabal Sinjār in northern Mesopotamia. The term Goiim
(= "nations") has been compared to Ummān-manda, a miscellany of

northeastern invaders who began to appear at this time in Mesopotamia, while the name of Tidal, the king of these Goiim, is the Hittite Tudhaliya.[45]

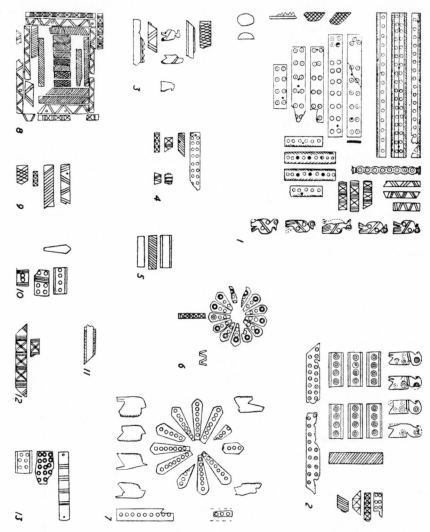

Fig. 35.
Bone inlay from disintegrated wood boxes found in a Middle Bronze II tomb at Jericho.
Prof. K. M. Kenyon, London.

Moreover, in a letter to Zimri-lim, King of Mari, an envoy of his reports that some ten to twelve kings side with Hammurabi, King of Babylon, and a similar number with his adversaries.[46] It is probably in precisely such a situation that a small coalition led by an Elamite king, who enlisted the help of his satellite allies, set out on a military campaign southward. It should be noted that the list of Chedorlaomer's allies includes only potential adversaries of Zimri-lim, who still supported Elam's greatest enemy, Hammurabi of Babylon. Might it not, then, be suggested that Chedorlaomer (= Kutir-lagamar) may perhaps be an Elamite version of the name of the Elamite king of Larsa, the great adversary of Hammurabi, known by his Akkadian name of Rim-Sin, or his predecessor Warad-Sin?

A question that poses itself is what would an Elamite-led coalition of Mesopotamian kings be wanting at the southeastern end of the Fertile Crescent? The archeological investigations of Glueck[47] have shown that numerous settlements along the king's highway that ran the length of Transjordan were destroyed at about the beginning of the 18th century B.C.E., some for ever, others to be resuscitated only about 500 years later. The invasion of nomadic or semi-nomadic tribes responsible for this catastrophe could not immediately have stopped all traffic along this ancient route. Commerce, like all daily occupations, has always been conservative, and caravans of merchants undoubtedly continued to use the highway despite increasing dangers. Since commerce was on the whole a state monopoly, it may be assumed that the states took steps to safeguard the principal routes. There may have been yet another reason for Chedorlaomer's southward campaign, namely, to ensure control by the Elamite allies of this vital highway and prevent its exploitation by the rival Babylonian confederacy.[48] In this connection it is highly interesting to examine the names of Chedorlaomer's foes defeated in this campaign. They are, from the northeast to the southwest, the Rephaim (in Ashteroth-karnaim), the Zuzim (in Ham), the Emim (in Shaveh-kiriathaim), the Horites (in the mountains of Seir). Furthermore, the invaders "smote all the country of the Amalekites, and also the Amorites, that dwelt in Hazazon-tamar" (Gen. 14:5-7). Until they encountered the kings of the Pentapolis in the plain of the Jordan, their only adversaries had been tribes or peoples, whose location is given by mentioning ancient cities. Hence Chedorlaomer's raid took place after the catastrophe which overwhelmed the central and southern regions of Transjordan, but near enough to it for the commercial highway there to be still in use. If the theory of the international constellation propounded above is correct, the Elamite campaign took place in the last quarter of the 18th century B.C.E., that is, in the days of Hammurabi but before he conquered Larsa (ca. 1696 B.C.E., according to the lower chronology). These two chronological pointers agree with each other.

F. The Patriarchs and the Habiru

Following this account of the way of life and of the period of the Patriarchs, the question arises whether theirs was an extraordinary phenomenon
in the general history of that period and region, or whether there were
similar or fragmentary groups living under analogous conditions.

Ever since the period of the Third Dynasty of Ur cuneiform documents
from both halves of the Fertile Crescent mention people called Habiru.[49]

One feels almost compelled to adopt the view of scholars who maintain
that the Israelites (chiefly in post-patriarchal times) were included within
the larger body known as the Habiru. In view of the characteristic features
of patriarchal life, as described above, it must be concluded that the
narratives in Genesis afford a glimpse into the life of the Habiru group from
the *inside*, in contrast to the other documents of the Ancient East which
speak of the Habiru from the *outside* and mostly in hostile terms. It should
however be emphasized that the early Israelite tribes are not *the* Habiru
but rather *a part* of them, a section of a much larger group in that ancient
region at the end of the 3rd and during the whole of the 2nd millennium
B.C.E.[50]

Contemporaneously with the arrival of the patriarchal clans in Canaan,
or possibly slightly earlier, the Hyksos began to invade the Fertile Crescent
from the north.[51] At first it doubtless did not greatly affect such semi-
nomadic clans, especially those living in the mountainous districts of Transjordan. But with the consolidation of Hyksos rule, which assumed a quasi-
feudal form,[52] wandering pastoral clans could find no place within their
socio-political system. Gradually they began to be pushed back into the
desert frontier region on the fringes of the permanently settled areas. Such
a fate would probably have been reserved for the Patriarchs too, had not
lean years constrained them to emigrate to Egypt.

Whether some parts of these clans remained on the desert borders of
Canaan, or in the less accessible wooded regions of Samaria, is disputed,[53]
but according to biblical tradition, concerned as it was with the majority
of the tribes of Israel, "Jacob and his children went down into Egypt"
(Josh. 24:4).

CHAPTER XII

THE RELIGION OF THE PATRIARCHS: BELIEFS AND PRACTICES

by M. Haran

A. The Beliefs of the Patriarchs and Monotheism

THE BIBLE ASSUMES that the Patriarchs were monotheists, their God being the same God in whom the historical People of Israel believed — despite the fact that He made Himself known or revealed Himself to the Patriarchs under other names. The assumption lying at the basis of all the pentateuchal stories is that the religion practised by the writers of these texts was the same the Patriarchs practised. Moreover, the belief in the unity of God was a legacy of the earliest forefathers, from Adam onwards, while idolatry resulted from the corruption of the faith of mankind. This view is characteristic of talmudic literature also. Talmudic legend presents Abraham as a champion of the religion of the One God, depicting him as tormented in a furnace for his beliefs.[1] Christianity took over this idea from Judaism. Paul, for example, accepts as self evident the assumption that Abraham belonged among the true believers, and represents him as the spiritual father of all Israel, the symbol of absolute faith in God (Romans 4: 1–3; Galatians 3:6–16).

During the Middle Ages this idea became an unchallenged principle that affected strongly enough — though indirectly — even modern scholarship. Such influence appears in different ways and found expression in various schools of thought, though some scholars arrived at a similar opinion on their own for what seemed to them objective reasons.

Towards the end of the 19th, and during the 20th century a number of scholars, among whom ethnologists and Catholic theologians, sought to prove by scientific research the existence of an ancient and primitive monotheism, that "degenerated" into idolatry only in the course of man's history. They hoped to find traces of it among the remains of early man, in the concepts of contemporary wild and primitive tribes, in the ancient pagan religions (particularly in the Sumerian religion), and to a certain extent also by examining man's innate spiritual inclinations.[2] Other scholars were of the opinion that the primary religion of all Semitic peoples was monotheistic, or that they were at least inclined toward such a belief. According to them, such an inclination existed mainly among the Western Semites, for whom the word *El* designated a proper name at first, but which in the course of time extended its meaning, until it became an *appellativum*. This is the *Monotheism of El* which scholars have discussed in various manners.[3] Other scholars tried to explain the predisposition of the Semitic peoples toward monotheism by their nomadic life in the desert, which made them ascribe little importance to the cult, but the simplicity of which increased their aspiration toward abstraction, to a synthesis of the divine powers, resulting in the creation of perfectly simple concepts.[4]

The great archeological discoveries of the Semitic civilizations, in the Euphrates Valley, completely invalidated the theory of Semitic monotheism. However, it was precisely these discoveries that were responsible for the formation of another school, which tried to explain in a diametrically opposite manner the apparition of monotheism in the period preceding Moses. This is the Pan-Babylonian school, according to which the monotheistic idea could not have originated in a primitive society, but is the creation of a developed and complex culture. The ancient Babylonian culture therefore cannot have been entirely pagan, but must have contained some monotheistic trends. Abraham, who absorbed something of these trends is portrayed as the first Israelite monotheist, and his move to Canaan — a religious and spiritual awakening — is represented as a reaction against the pagan degeneration and corruption of his time and place. These scholars were obliged to devote considerable energy to the distinction between Babylonian and Israelite monotheism, the latter beginning, according to their theory, with Abraham. The former they tended to imagine as a detached scientific-astrological speculation which did not invalidate paganism but derived from it, while considering God as a natural force or abstract being; the latter they saw as a vital religious message that finally became the inheritance of a whole community and conceived of God as a moral being. They also had to differentiate between the monotheism of Abraham and that of Moses or of the period of the Settlement — the former having been free of cultic practices or priesthood — and distinguished for the direct contact between the believer and his God, which in this respect brought it close to the classical prophetic belief. Others thought that Abraham's monotheism was absorbed on Canaanite soil, and that later on when the Israelite conquerors appeared with their rought religious concepts, they found its remnants in Canaan and with its help elevated their own belief in God to a monotheistic level.[5] The views of the Pan-Babylonian school can be now considered as outdated though their traces can still be found in the works of a number of scholars.[6] Yet other scholars considered Abraham as the first believer in the oneness of God and as the father of the Israelite-biblical faith, without being prompted by adherence to any particular school of thought, but from a fundamental confidence in the biblical evidence and a pronounced conservatism, characteristic of their approach.[7]

However, all such conceptions have remained at the periphery of research and cannot serve as a point of departure today. Anthropology does not, on the whole, accept the hypothesis of an ancient, primitive monotheism, and critical research of the Bible does not generally agree with the assumption that the faith of the Patriarchs was monotheistic, since beyond the tradition and legends portraying the Patriarchs as such, the biblical testimony itself contains decisive evidence suggesting that they were not monotheists.

The portrayal of the Patriarchs as believing in the One God is only a reflection of the specific conditions in which these traditions were projected on the past. People simply wished to perceive the history of the Patriarchs monotheistically and to comprehend it in the same way. However, the analysis of the biblical traditions and the elucidation of their meaning tend to show that the monotheistic parlance conceals an entirely different historical reality.

Monotheistic faith was linked in Israel to the specific divine name — YHWH. True, several other names have been preserved that were considered its synonyms, yet the message of the oneness of God has always been bound up with that name alone. The pentateuchal sources themselves generally admit that the Patriarchs did not know that name or, at all events, it did not occupy in their lives the position it was vouchsafed after Moses' time. Only one source, namely J, uses it in its narrative of the period preceding Moses (Gen. 2:4 ff.). All the other pentateuchal sources admit that the Patriarchs knew God by all kinds of other names, but not necessarily by this one. YHWH was revealed to Moses only (Ex. 3:13–15; 6:2–3) and since then it has been used as the exclusive name of the God of Israel. Moreover, even J, which does not refrain from relating that the Patriarchs and the generations preceding them had already called God by the name YHWH, emphasizes its special revelation to Moses (Ex. 3), which represents a turning point and the beginning of a new period in Israel's history. This constitutes reliable evidence for the historical fact that the monotheistic revolution connected with the name YHWH did not precede Moses and that the Patriarchs had not been monotheists. Furthermore, during the period of the Patriarchs there is no mention of a conflict with idolatry. There is hardly any religious barrier between the Patriarchs and their neighbors — at least, there is no contradictory tension or hatred between their belief and the idolatrous beliefs of their surroundings. Such violent tension and hatred of idolatry is expressed only in legends and traditions appertaining to the times following Moses. Thereafter it constitutes a typical phenomenon throughout the Bible, testifying to the historicity of the monotheistic revolution which took place only with the appearance of Moses.[8]

To these pieces of evidence might be added, as we shall see below, that this belief was not held only by Israel's Patriarchs. According to the Bible itself the Patriarchs were not the ancestors of the Israelite tribes only, but also of other national groups ethnically close to Israel and parallel to it, such as the Ishmaelite, Edomite, Amalekite, Midianite tribes and the *People of Kedem*. They wander in separate, rather small families and as strangers through the lands of the Canaanites and the Amorites. However, their ethnic background is not determined by these foreign nations, but by the Hebrew-Aramean tribes, a part of which had remained in their country of origin, in the north-western corner of Mesopotamia, while part of them had already crossed the Euphrates westwards. Their cultural horizon is pretty uniform. Moreover, there are sufficient indications to warrant the assumption that prior to their final settlement in the lands west of the Euphrates the religious culture of all these peoples was basically similar. Now if we were to claim that the Patriarchs were monotheists, it would imply that the forefathers of the other peoples related by blood ties and by common origin to the Israelites — that is to say, the whole ethnic group made up of the Hebrew tribes and the *Children of Kedem* — were monotheists too. However, this is an unacceptable premise and far from representing historical truth.

Hence it is indisputable that the Patriarchs' veritable historical belief was not monotheistic. However, when we try to deal with the nature of this belief in a positive manner, the problem proves itself even more difficult and complicated. If the Patriarchs' belief had been one of the forms of idolatry, what could have been its distinctive typical character, and on what could a definition of it be based? Any attempt at providing an answer to these questions inevitably entails groping in the dark, since the religious concepts peculiar to that distant period are already surrounded by a dense fog.

B. THE VALUE OF THE BIBLICAL TRADITIONS AS HISTORICAL EVIDENCE

The Wellhausen school considered all the religious aspects of the Patriarchs' stories as a complete and precise projection of Israel's historical religion after the conquest of Canaan. It was considered that these stories do not contain anything that would testify to the faith of the Hebrew tribes before Moses, and that all they can teach is the belief prevailing a long time after the Settlement (actually, only after the period of the Judges). Scholars speculated a great deal on the actual historical existence of the Patriarchs and they devoted much thought to the true nature of these figures, endeavoring to ascertain whether they are a poetic invention, a personification of ethnic groups, or debased mythological figures. Inasmuch as they endeavored to elicit what was the belief held by the tribes before the conquest of Canaan, their starting-point was invariably the crystallized, historical religion of Israel in its country. The method employed was to search in this religion traces of beliefs and customs which might indicate earlier historical stages, residues of the primitive faith from before the Yahwistic revolution. Some scholars drew indeed comparisons with the religious concepts of the pre-Islamic Arabs and occasionally also with the concepts of present-day primitive tribes. This did not, however, alter the principle lying at the basis of their method, which was precise and critical examination of the actual Yahwistic faith. The result was — a varied and colorful kaleidoscope of primitive religions, beginning with fetishism and totemism and ending with various forms of polydemonism, though some scholars occasionally did admit the possibility that the Hebrew tribes might have already approached the level permitting a theistic concept before Moses.[9]

One should not reject this method out of hand, but remember that the way is hard and liable to lead to erroneous views. Traces of primitive beliefs can be discovered in all the developed and historical religions, even in the great religions of our time. This method makes it very difficult to discern whether the remnant we discover in a given historical religion can really serve as evidence for a certain stage in its formation, or whether it is a concept from a distant forgotten world that persisted. According to this method we might conclude, for example, that the historical phase preceding the formation of Christianity was primitive — but in this instance we know perfectly well that the world of concepts into which Christianity was born was anything but primitive.[10] Indeed the polydemonic stage of religious development had been left far behind by all Semitic peoples.

The assumptions of this school were undermined from two sides. On the one hand, a study of the Bible itself made it increasingly obvious that the traditional material upon which the Book of Genesis is based is much more important than used to be thought. True, the material was given a literary form much later than the period with which it deals, but recognition grew of its very early traditional roots and of origins much older than the conquest of Canaan.[11] Scientific research then began to recognize that the general framework of these traditions is reliable. They include many historical and ethnographic data which cannot be explained from the relationship among the peoples in the late period. They contain legal details of family relationships and concepts of property which appear meaningless in the context of a later period or even clearly contradict the laws laid down in the Pentateuch.[12] In short, the traditions dealing with the Patriarchs reflect a specific society the legal and social conditions of which, as well as the historical perspective, differ considerably from those prevailing among the Israelite tribes after the Settlement. On the other hand, the archeological discoveries, particularly those made at Mari and Nuzi, have thrown light on the background of this society. It transpires that a number of legal and social concepts contained in the documents found in those places, as well as legal principles contained in the cuneiform literature of other places, match amazingly well the concepts of the Patriarchs as preserved in the biblical traditions.[13] It has finally grown clear that the traditions concerning the Patriarchs are not to be regarded as an artificial projection of the historical and social reality of Israel in the Iron Age, but as treasures of reliable memories about the second millennium West Semites.

This recognition has correspondingly raised the value of the traditions as evidence for the religious concepts of the Patriarchs. Hence there is an increasing chance that taking the monotheistic wraps off these traditions, the true historical faith of Israel's forefathers will be revealed.

C. SOME FEATURES TOWARD A DESCRIPTION OF THE PATRIARCHS' RELIGION

There are three features specific of the Patriarchs' period which can be used to identify their historical belief. These are: 1) the several names of God (including *El Shaddai* of P), 2) the idiom *God of my father*, and 3) the name YHWH as a vestige from the period preceding Moses.

1. An investigation of the stories in Genesis led scholars to notice long ago that the tales about the Patriarchs employ divine appellations consisting of some name with *El* in the construct, or in the form of an adjective accompanying *El*. Such appellations are found in all the sources and they

are generally connected, according to the contents of the story, with a certain place. Thus J mentions *El ro'i* in speaking of the well Beer-lahai-roi near Kadesh (Gen. 16:13–14). E mentions *El 'Olam* near Beer-sheba (Gen. 21:33), *El-'elohey-Israel* in the neighborhood of Shechem (Gen. 33:20)[14] and *El Beth-el* in speaking of Beth-el (Gen. 31:13; 35:7). P is most consistent in its outlook, assuming that God was known to the Patriarchs only by the name *El Shaddai* (Gen. 17:1; 28:3; 35:11; 48:3; Ex. 6:3), but it does not connect this name with any definite place. *El Shaddai* occurs twice in J and neither is it connected there with any place (Gen. 43:14; 49:25).[15] In Gen. 14 we find *El 'Elyon* quoted by the king of the city of Salem, which is Jerusalem (14:18–22). This is a unique phenomenon which does not occur except in the stories of the Patriarchs.[16] The sources naturally identify all these *Els* with YHWH, the God of the monotheistic faith. The names are regarded simply as His special attributes or revelations and, no doubt, thus were they sunk in the nation's consciousness in post-Mosaic times. But in fact, they actually allude to a historic-religious stage which preceded the Yahwistic religion. In older research these names were considered vestiges of another monotheism, existent before Moses' time (cf. above). The Wellhausen school used to see in all these different *Els* an expression of local demon spirits, remainders of a polydemonic conception which was absorbed by the historical Israelite religion. Through the influence of the school of Gunkel they arrived at the conclusion that these names are merely traces of a special theistic religion, *The religion of Els*, which was widespread in the period preceding the conquest of Canaan and from which the Israelite tribes absorbed something. It was, however, difficult to establish whether this religion from which the Israelite tribes adopted a number of terms and names was Canaanite, or whether this was the original Hebraic legacy of those tribes which had come from beyond the Euphrates.[17] Opinions differed since there was evidence enabling to support either alternative.

There are several important indications denoting a Canaanite atmosphere, first and foremost the close connection of many of these *Els* with definite places. On the face of it this link does not fit in very well with the semi-nomadic character of the Hebrew clans who had arrived in Canaan from far away, and were regarded as strangers tolerated. Of particular interest is the evidence supplied by 14 Gen. which describes Salem, a small kingdom-city, and Melchizedek who is the typical image of a small Canaanite king, such as we read about in the Tell el-Amarna Letters. As a priest of *El 'Elyon*, he blesses Abraham and tithes him, while Abraham in his turn raises his hand and takes his oath by the same *El*. The special appellation of *El 'Elyon*, "Possessor of heaven and earth" (Gen. 14:19–22) – the term *possessor* being used here for *creator* – bears a ressemblance to the syntactical usages of the Ugaritic as well as Phoenician writings.[18] Moreover, extra-biblical documents present *'Elyon* as belonging to the Canaanite

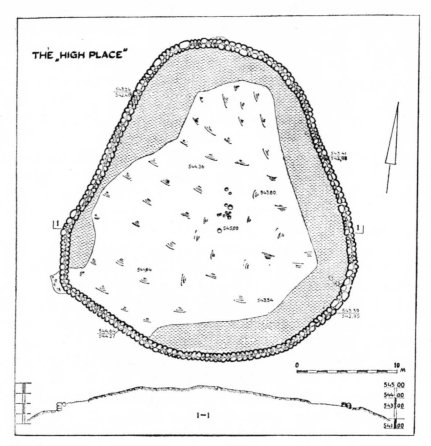

Fig. 36.
Har Jeruḥam, the "High place."
Dr. M. Kochavi, Tel Aviv.

pantheon and it seems probable that *'Olam* and *Beth-El* belonged to the same.[19] Similarly, several theophoric place-names existent in the country and including the element *El* (e.g. Jabneel, Jezreel, Jokteel) may be relics from the period preceding the settlement of the Israelite tribes.

On the other hand, there are a number of decisive pieces of evidence in favor of the hypothesis that several of the names of the gods are connected with the faith the ancient Hebrew tribes practised before the emergence of Yahwism and which are not all of them connected with localities. *El Beth-el* was also revealed to Jacob in Haran, beyond the Euphrates

(Gen. 31:13) and he watches over him during his wanderings. *El Shaddai* is altogether unconnected with any place. It is difficult to think of *Shaddai* as a Canaanite divinity, nor is there any support for it. Its original Hebrew character may well be the most outstanding impression we gather from the traditions preceding the period of Moses, but this can also serve as evidence for the nature of the other *Els*. Even the places linked by tradition

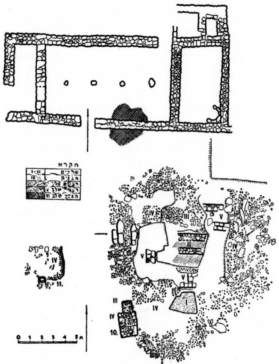

Fig. 37.
Nahariya, plan of the Middle Bronze II temple and "High place."
M. Dothan, *Eretz Israel* IV, (1956) 42, fig. 1.

with *Els* are not generally Canaanite. Beer-lahai-roi is situated in the desert, on the way to Egypt, and the various places in Beer-sheba, Shechem and Beth-el with which the names of *Els* are connected were not even included within the limits of those Canaanite cities, but outside them. Abraham called on *El 'Olam* by the tamarisk in the neighborhood of Beer-sheba (Gen. 21:33), the altar of *El-'elohey-Israel* was erected in a field before the city of Shechem (Gen. 33:18–20); the altar of *El beth-el* is in the open country outside the city, at some distance from Allon-bacuth (Gen. 28:19; 35:7–8). The Patriarchs practically never set foot inside Canaanite cities. They pass them by, camping in their neighborhood near trees and wells — fit resting places for nomads and their flocks.[20]

Additional proof against the Canaanite origin of the *El* religion is the significant fact that no *Baals* are mentioned next to them. In Canaanite concepts the figure of *Baal* is no less prominent than that of *El*. After the Settlement *Baals* occur quite frequently in the life of Israel and occasionally even form elements in the composition of personal names, but there is no mention of them in the whole Genesis. Moreover, theophoric names with *El* are common with the Hebrew tribes even in the period before Moses — the most striking being the very name *Israel*. Just as common are names from the same period which contain the construct *Shaddai* ('Ammishaddai, Zurishaddai, Sheddeur).[21] It appears that even the names Jacob, Joseph, perhaps Isaac too, are only abbreviations of theophoric names in the form of *Jacobel* and *Josephel* similar to Ishmael. Like names have been found in extra-biblical sources also. Such theophoric compounds can be found mainly among the Western Semites, in Babylonian sources from Hammurabi's time.[22]

The second possibility appears to be the correct one, namely that all the divine names containing the component *El* as a construct must not be attributed to Canaanite influence, but considered as echoes from a Hebrew pantheon. The points of contact with the Canaanite area should not mislead us, for the term *El* is to be found in all Semitic languages. In this respect, it is quite possible that the names by which the Hebrew tribes and the Canaanites called their divinities had something in common. After all we find the term *ilāni* used for Canaanite kings as well as among the Habiru. Moreover, any idolatrous conception of the world is remarkably tolerant since a pagan background allows a measure of *recognition* to gods actually belonging to another pantheon. What is more, the pagan world knows *migrations* of divinities from one region to another so that a number of gods from near and far could be amalgamated in a given ethno-religious framework. This is an accepted and well known phenomenon in the ancient world. It is therefore natural that there should be a few points of contact between vestiges of the faith the Hebrew tribes adhered to before Moses' time, and what we know of the world of Canaanite religions. These points of contact should not, however, blind us to the fact that we have here two different ethno-religious cycles, the central concepts of which do not coincide. The religion of the *Els* as it is recorded in the stories in Genesis seems to have been an original Hebrew legacy. Possibly only *El ʽElyon* belongs mainly to the Canaanite cycle. Alone among all the *Els* of the Patriarchs he bears indications of a Canaanite origin – and that, in the Bible story itself. In contrast to all the rest of the Patriarchs' *Els*, Abraham does not "call upon his name," nor does he build him an altar; instead he appears only to recognize him.

2. A distinction must be made between the phrase "God of my father," (and in the second person: "God of thy father," etc.) and the phrase the "God of your fathers," which is a different matter and will be discussed further on. The special feature of the phrase "The God of my father" (*Elohey Avi*) is that the declined construct occurs in the singular. However, this form, in the singular, appears in several places in the stories of the Patriarchs where the subject matter does not seem to fit it, or occasionally it seems almost meaningless. Hence, it can be understood only as an anachronism, common in speech, but which reflects a religious concept characteristic of a different period.

The expression occurs frequently in the stories in J and E, but not in P — perhaps on account of its dogmatic rigor or, because the chapters about the Patriarchs contain limited material from this source. In Jacob's blessing "the God of thy father" appears as a parallel to *El Shaddai* (Gen. 49:25).[23] In the Song of the Sea we find the parallelism "My *El* — My father's God" (not "the God of my fathers"! Ex. 15:2). On his way to Egypt Jacob hears God calling him with the words "I am the *El*, God of thy father" (Gen. 46:3) — that phrase is a kind of synthesis of the names given to the *Els* and "the God of thy father" (for the construct form cf. Gen. 31:13). At the establishment of the covenant between Jacob and Laban we come across the amazing formula: "The God of Abraham, and the God of Nahor, the God of their father, judge betwixt us" (*their father* — in the singular! Gen. 31:53). In the conflict which preceded this covenant both sides repeatedly mention "his father's [Jacob's] God" (Gen. 31:5, 29, cf. 42). Joseph uses this formula in speaking to his brothers (Gen. 43:23) just as they used it when talking to him (Gen. 50:17). The last time it appears is with Moses before the Exodus and again linked with a singular pronoun: its conspicuous oddity obliges us to assume that this is an obsolete expression (Ex. 18:4). At the revelation of the Burning Bush we seem to hear the fusion of two formulas in one utterance: "I am the God of thy father — the God of Abraham, the God of Isaac, and the God of Jacob" (Ex. 3:6), otherwise it would have to be "your fathers" in the plural, as indeed the Samaritan version reads here. A like fusion or partial coalescence with the other formula ("The God of Abraham, the God of Isaac . . .") seems to exist in other passages (Gen. 31:42; 46:1; cf. also 26:24; 28:13). This phenomenon is also characteristic of the patriarchal period and is not encountered in the traditions after the Sinaitic Covenant.

It is doubtless that the biblical sources and the story tellers see in this a mere form of speech expressing one of the names given to the God of Israel. Yet, the fact that this formula is limited to a certain historical period, and precisely to that preceding the Sinaitic Covenant, proves that we have here an actual vestige of a religious concept from that period. After the adoption of monotheism this concept lost its significance, and the biblical tradition considered it as a descriptive title of the One God, just as it regarded the Patriarchs as believers in the One God; however, the tradition reserved the use of this expression for its particular historical limits.

Presumably the term was essentially destined to the household gods — not for the clan or tribal gods in the wider sense — but for the narrow circle of the blood kindred. Every man expelled from the "house" or uprooted from his close family circle, is able to turn to "the God of his father," who bears no special name and probably does not belong among the gods of the pantheon. We should imagine him as a divinity of the lowest order, whose relationship with man bears a stamp of intimacy. He protects a man from his enemies and from harm, he looks after his material well-being; he helps a man when in trouble, guides him on his wanderings and is perhaps mainly called upon by the man who is far from his homeland and his father's house — Jacob in Haran, on his way home or to Egypt, Joseph and his brothers in Egypt, Moses in Midian. Such expressions (*ilī, abīka, abiya, abīni*) are also found in the Assyrian texts from Cappadocia where their meaning might approximate this concept.[24] So far the concept "The God of thy father" has been found also in the Mari Letters, possibly also in the neo-Hittite inscription from Toppadeh.[25]

3. As for the name YHWH — we shall not go far wrong in assuming that it was taken from the ancient Hebrew faith, except that with the ancient Hebrew tribes this was a god amongst many belonging to their pantheon, while with Moses the name underwent a comprehensive conceptual change which raised it above all other names.[26] It is perhaps useless trying to explain why this name was chosen from among all the other names of the ancient Hebrew gods to become the bearer of the new message. However, it is beyond doubt that it originates from the period preceding Moses, the actual name, which is clearly a personal name, suffices to prove this assertion. For the same reason it cannot be explained according to the concepts of monotheism. Its meaning was already unclear in the historical period and the preservers of tradition could understand it only by way of popular etymology. There is no doubt either that the explanation given to it in Ex. 3:14, "I Am That I Am," is nothing but a homiletical interpretation of this type, based solely on a similarity of sound. Modern attempts to interpret the origin of the name YHWH by scientific-etymological means have not so far given satisfactory results. In any case it appears that the religious content embodied in this name

during the pagan period was completely different from the content it has in the biblical sources. This fact, and the fact that even the pronunciation of the name was forgotten (perhaps as early as the biblical period), make its correct interpretation impossible.

An interesting hint that this name was not created by Moses can be found in the biblical sources themselves. True, according to all the sources the name YHWH performed its main historical function and became the name of the One God of Israel only after Moses' message. At the same time, it should not be forgotten that Moses does not introduce Him as a new God, but as the God of Israel's forefathers. It is this affirmation that the God he speaks of is the God of their forefathers that lends authority and validity to his message. It seems as if only on the strength of this can he win the people's attention and sympathy. Two characteristic descriptions distinguish YHWH, both of which point in the same direction: He is the "God of your fathers" and He is the "God of Abraham, of Isaac and of Jacob." It is not surprising that both these descriptions are found in J (Ex. 3:16, and cf. Gen. 26:24; 28:13; 32:9), since according to its conceptions this name was already known to the Patriarchs. It is interesting to note however, that these appellations are strongly emphasized in E when narrating the first revelation to Moses (Ex. 3:6, 13, 15; and cf. Gen. 31:42). The phrase "The Lord [YHWH], the God of your fathers" occurs frequently in the style of D (Dt. 1:11; 26:7, etc.),[27] and it would seem that as far as linguistic usages are concerned D is no less important than the evidence contained in the other sources of the Pentateuch. The style of these titles was transferred to the later parts of the Bible where they became usual.[28] In actual fact, they refer to the promises made to the Patriarchs. YHWH is "The God of the Fathers" since He made covenants with them and swore to let their descendants inherit the land. This is the point that D intends to convey (cf. Dt. 6:23; 26:3, 9). Indeed with D, YHWH signifies "The God of the Fathers" mainly because of the association with the Promised Land (Dt. 1:21; 4:1; 6:3; 12:1; 27:3). Now the very fact that the biblical traditions did not hesitate to introduce the name of YHWH even before the time of Moses constitutes clear evidence that it was not first made known at the Sinaitic Covenant but was produced from the very ancient Hebrew fund, that preceded the monotheistic revolution. The very fact that the biblical sources connected it with the Patriarchs proves that this name enjoyed a certain prominence in the pantheon of the Patriarchs.

P has its own special approach, in which the name YHWH occupies no position whatsoever in the period preceding Moses. It separates the period of the Patriarchs from that following it: so far God revealed Himself regularly only by the name *El Shaddai* — henceforth He is known only by the name of YHWH (Ex. 6:2–3). It is amazing with what consistency all the conclusions were drawn from this point of view, even to setting its seal on the style. In the language of P one never finds the formula "YHWH the God of your fathers." The version typical for its style is "I am the Lord," or "I am the Lord your God" (The first time: Ex. 3:2; later on frequently, particularly in the Holiness Code and in a borrowed form also in Ezekiel). Of course also P tells of the covenant made with the Patriarchs — only according to its system God still hid His identity behind His former name; it identifies *El Shaddai* of the Patriarchs with YHWH of the period following Moses. This identification was not historical, of course, for it is completely inconceivable to change the name of one's god in such a decisive manner, even more so if we assume (as the Bible does) that the Patriarchs were monotheists anyway. The reality concealed behind this identification is that the Patriarchs did worship *other gods*, or at least one *other* god beside YHWH. From this point of view the evidence of P cannot be rejected nor disregarded, since it too is based on traditions no less faithful than those of the other sources. P gives the impression that *El Shaddai* might have been the supreme deity of the Patriarchs, or at least one of the most important in their pantheon. However, P is stricter and more dogmatic than the other sources — its "adaptation" of tradition and summarization being much more schematic and rigid.

In principle all the sources attempted to consider the patriarchal period in a monotheistic perspective, but each one of them from a different angle of vision. The only way of achieving a true description of the faith of that period is to combine the evidence of all the sources. J and E imposed only YHWH or Elohim on this period, though they retained allusions to several other *Els* and used the special concept of "The God of the father." P avoids the use of the name YHWH for that period and imposes only the name *El Shaddai*. In actual fact, all these elements coexisted in the faith of that period. *El Shaddai*, a few more *Els*, "The God of the father", as well as YHWH (prior to Moses' revelation) doubtlessly occupied definite places in the divine complex.

These are therefore the three main premises for a description of the Patriarchs' faith. Apart from these it is difficult to establish whether various other details represent an actual legacy of that same faith, since they are mentioned casually and in few places. Unusual and amazing is the name *The Fear of Isaac* by which Jacob swears (Gen. 31:42, 53); it may reflect a particular concept of the Patriarchs. The name *The Mighty One of Jacob* is mentioned once in Genesis (49:24), also in poetic passages and in Psalms (Isa. 49:26; 60:17; Ps. 132: 2, 5; and cf. Isa. 1:24), and it is impossible to know whether it is a relic from the patriarchal period or, on the contrary, it was a term belonging to the historical period that was retrojected. We find in the biblical poetry that the word *Zur* (rock) and its synonyms (e.g. *Sela'*, *Mezuda*) are sometimes used as appellations of God. On the other hand, the same term is frequently used as an element in the composition of personal names, while it can easily be exchanged for the word *El*. In the same manner many personal names contain elements such as *'Am* (nation), *Av* (father), *'Ah* (brother). Hence (as well as from the etymological explanation of *Shaddai*) it was assumed[29] that the ancient Hebrews worshiped divinities of the mountains and that in addition their gods were conceived as closely connected with the family unit, of which they were considered an integral part. But again it is hard to say to what stage of religious development facts such as these attest: are they a meaningless convention, a relic from a very distant historical past, or do they represent evidence for the period of the Patriarchs itself?

D. THE FAITH OF THE PATRIARCHS WITHIN THE FRAMEWORK OF THE ANCIENT HEBREW TRIBES.

1. As we know, the Patriarchs are portrayed in the traditions of the Book of Genesis within the narrow familial framework, not against the background of national life. They pass through the land of Canaan, camp there in a number of places, but keep apart from the local population, their contacts being limited to a few instances and only to the extent of their needs. At the same time they do not actually lack a national background — except that it is to be found far from Canaan, among the Hebrew-Aramean tribes from which they separated. In Canaan they are considered strangers who came from outside, their "homeland" being in Haran and its neighborhood. The Patriarchs belong to the ethnic framework which is called in the Bible "all the children of Eber" (Gen. 10:21). Within this framework belong: the sons of Joktan (Gen. 10:26—30); the children of Nahor (Gen. 22:20—24); the children of Lot (Moab and Ammon) before they settled in their countries. Of course this framework included also the peoples which were considered Abraham's actual descendants — the people of Ishmael (Gen. 25:12—16), the children of Keturah (Gen. 25:1—4) and the children of Esau (i.e. Edom) (Gen. 36:1—19), before their separation into various tribes. Some of them united as the *people of Kedem* and the country in which they lived a semi-nomadic life is called the *Land of Kedem*

or the *Mountain of Kedem* (Gen. 10:30; 25:6; 29:1, etc.). At the time of the Patriarchs all these units constituted a fairly homogeneous group with a basically similar material and spiritual culture. At times the members of these tribes preferred to marry women from among their blood relations seeking to avoid intermarriage with the inhabitants of their countries of abode who were foreigners to them, even if this entailed journeys to distant places. Isaac and Jacob married women from among the children of Nahor (and cf. Gen. 34). Esau married Hittite women; however, since his father disapproved of them he married Ishmaelite women (Gen. 26:34–35; 28:8–9). The Bible moreover recognizes a number of persons outside the stories of Genesis who are also portrayed against the special ethnic and cultural background of the Hebrew tribes. To these belong Job and his companions, Balaam the son of Beor, Agur the son of Jakeh (Prov. 30:1) and Lemuel (Prov. 31:1).[30] They also bring their contribution towards completing the picture of the special social and historical circumstances in which the Patriarchs acted.

From the beginning of its formation the People of Israel believed that the best of the ethnic heritage of those ancient Hebrew tribes was realized in it. The promise that they would inherit Canaan was in their opinion given to the Hebrew Patriarchs before the national concept *Israel* appeared in the world. The Israelite tribes considered themselves the active ingredient, as it were, among all Abraham's descendants. However, when we try to understand historical reality as is was, we are obliged to disregard the belief in the Chosen People. It is quite clear that in the light of historical reality the religion of the ancestors of the Israelite people did not fundamentally differ from the religion of that whole group of tribes to which they belonged. The biblical traditions actually show that the traits that characterized the Patriarchs' religion were to be found among other Hebrew peoples. They point to a common religious fund of all that ethnic group. This tends to confirm the outline the Bible gives of patriarchal religion and the genuineness of the biblical traditions in general.

Theophoric names with *El* are found among all the ethnic units which belong to the children of Eber.[31] Moreover, the names of *Els*, so characteristic of the patriarchal period, occur against an early Hebrew background, outside Israel also. *El ro'i* was revealed to Ishmael's mother, and was probably revered by his tribes, for the place connected with it — Beer-lahai-roi in the desert, beyond Kadesh (Gen. 16:13–14) — was situated within their area of expansion (cf. 21:20–21; 25:18). The name most often found against such a background is *El Shaddai* — the main *El* of the patriarchal period — and also *El 'Elyon* (God Almighty). Apart from Genesis they appear occasionally in abbreviated adjectival form only (*Shaddai*, *'Elyon*), and occasionally in their complete form, with the word *El* in the second part of the parallelism. Balaam the son of Beor, the prophetic Hebrew seer from Pethor on the Euphrates, mentions *Shaddai* twice in his poems, both times as a parallelism with *El* — once even in a triple parallelism: *El, 'Elyon, Shaddai* (Num. 24:4,16). Job and his companions, who belong to various peoples of the Hebrews and the *Children of Kedem*, mention *Shaddai* no less than thirty-one times, of these fourteen times in a parallelism with *El*,[32] nine with Eloha and eight times without parallelism to any other divine name. This is the decisive section in the use of the name *Shaddai* throughout the Bible. Job and his companions never mention *'Elyon* but this name as well as *Shaddai* were included in the style of the biblic poetry which (in the way of all poetry) preserved ancient linguistic usages.[33] *'Elyon* is mentioned frequently in the psalms, once in a parallelism with *Shaddai* (Ps. 91:1). The poetry of Job as well as the psalms preserved the most ancient shade of meaning of the word *El*. As we know, this word has only a general appellative value in the Bible, however in the poetry of Job (always) and in the style of the psalms (frequently), and to a certain extent in other poetic passages it indicates the One True God, the God of Israel — and in this respect it fulfills to a certain degree the function of a personal name. It is worth noting that the singular form *Eloha* is also characteristic of the poetic language of the Bible, occurring most frequently in Job where it plays in fact the same role as the word *El;* it transpires that it was also taken over by the biblical literature from the ancient Hebrew heritage.

The external sign of the religious communion of the Hebrew tribes was the custom of circumcision. According to the story of P — on the day when Abraham circumcised himself and all the men of his house, Ishmael was also circumcised (Gen. 17:23–27). As a matter of fact, according to the Bible, circumcision was practised among many Hebrew peoples, apart from Israel. In addition to Ishmael and his tribes, the following can be included: the Edomites, the children of Ammon, the Moabites, and "all that have the corners of their hair polled, that dwell in the wilderness" (Jer. 9:24–25; for Edom cf. Ezek. 32:29). Those that have the "corners of their hair polled" are mentioned in one breath with Tema (Jer. 25:23) and Kedar (Jer. 49:28, 32), who according to the genealogical tradition were Ishmael's descendants (Gen. 25:13–15). From the action of Midianite Zipporah who cut off her son's foreskin on her own initiative (Ex. 4:25) we can deduce that circumcision was customary with the Midianites. Indeed, they were considered as descendants of Abraham's concubine

(Gen. 25:2). It can be actually established that in the biblical period all the peoples tracing their descent from Abraham and even those who were considered by the genealogical traditions as children of his concubines, practiced circumcision. Additional proof is supplied by the fact that in the associations of poetic speech and in the biblical narratives the children of Keturah are frequently substituted for the Ishmaelites or are reckoned together with them.[34] The Philistines, on the other hand, were uncircumcised as we learn from the Bible. The same applies to the people of Ashur and Elam (Ezek. 32:21–25), who are placed outside the framework of the Hebrew group despite their being considered descendants of Shem. The Bible mentions also Meshech and Tubal the Japhethites (Ezek. 32:26) as being uncircumcised, as well as the people of Tyre (Ezek. 28:10), the Hivites (Gen. 34:14, ff.) and also the Canaanites and Perizzites (Gen. 34:30). In this respect there was no difference among the seven Canaanite peoples against whom the Israelites waged a war of annihilation. It is interesting that the Egyptians differed from all the Canaanite nations in that they were circumcised (Jer. 9:25; Ezek. 31:18; 32:19, 28, 32; and cf. Josh. 5:9). Hence circumcision was not specific to the group of Hebrew tribes (or to the peoples tracing their genealogy to Abraham and Lot). It is well known that this custom was widespread among various cultures in all parts of the world. However, circumcision differentiated the Hebrew tribes from their surroundings and increased their distinctiveness as against the inhabitants of the countries in which they dwelt.

2. The religion of the Patriarchs, to which belonged a number of other peoples, apart from the direct forefathers of the Israelites, contained something of an innovation when compared to the preceding historical phase. Various allusions in the traditions of Genesis tend to confirm the assumption that at the beginning of the patriarchal period a certain change took place among the Hebrew tribes or some of them,[35] raising them to a new level of religious development. The Bible concentrates this change in the figure of Abraham, the personality felt to have initiated a new period, except that this change recurred and renewed itself occasionally in the lives of Isaac and Jacob.

It is a remarkable fact that all the identifying marks of the religion of the Patriarchs begin with Abraham or one of the other Patriarchs. The biblical tradition does not display complete continuity, between the period preceding Abraham and that following him – there is a sudden break (just as between the period before the Sinaitic Covenant and after it). Wherever the religious qualities specific to the patriarchal period appear embodied in Abraham (and the other Patriarchs), they invariably bear the seal of innovation. The names of the different *Els* are revealed with the Patriarchs, and they had not been known before them. *El ro'i, El 'Olam, El Beth-el* and the like were all first made known to them, or it was the Patriarchs who invested certain places with these names. As usual the clearest and most schematic in this matter is P; the name *El Shaddai* signifies according to it, a specific stage in the divine revelations to mankind — this being the name which indicates precisely the period beginning with Abraham and ending with the appearance of Moses, just as the name *Elohim* represents the period between Adam and Abraham, and YHWH the completed and *absolute* period after the Sinatic Covenant. *El 'Elyon*, as we have said, is the only one of the *Els* not introduced by the Patriarchs' constituting in this regard an exception. We have also seen that the Patriarchs called various places in the country by theophoric names containing the element *El*. Thus Jacob introduced the name Penuel (Gen. 32:30–31) and he changed the name of the city of Luz to Beth-el (Gen. 28:19; 35:6, 15; cf. Jud. 1:23). Even this Patriarch's name was changed by the Bible from Jacob to Israel as we are told by both J (Gen. 32:21–29) and P (Gen. 35:9–10). It is interesting to note how this was understood by the traditions themselves. The change of a person's name — whether he was proclaimed king (without his having been predestinated for it), or appointed to a mission, or he adopted a new religion — invariably symbolized with the ancients a new spiritual life, which permeated his very being.[36] Something of "proselytization" and of this spiritual renewal echoes in the traditions concerning Jacob's change of name to Israel. Thus we have here, as well as in the other pieces of evidence concerning the *Els*, an actual allusion to the fact that belief in the different *Els* did indeed begin with those Hebrew tribes which were moving west of the Euphrates Valley, and that it was apparently this belief which distinguished them from the generations preceding them on that side of the river. Similarly, the term "The God of the Father" occurs for the first time with Abraham (Gen. 31:53) and only from that moment onwards it is employed by the following generations until the revelation at Sinai.

The same applies to the physical mark of identification of the ancient Hebrew religion — circumcision. According to P this mark was first accepted by Abraham and it was he who began to practice it on the people in his house and on his descendents. Certainly there is some rigid historical schematization in this formulation. However, other sources show also that among the peoples and tribes in Western Asia this custom was practiced actually by the group of peoples considered to be descendants of Abraham and Lot. Therefore it seems reasonable to assume that the group of Hebrew tribes which left Aram Naharaim — and which is symbolized in the sources by the figures of Abraham and Lot — adopted the custom of circumcision, fitting it into their new mode of religious life.

It can be said that as a rule the sources do not portray Abraham as a purely ethnographic figure, a fact that a number of scholars noted a long time ago. Abraham is not what is called a *Stammvater* and no nation in the world is called for him. And even if a certain ethnical group is embodied in his personality, yet he and his deeds are no less remarkable for their religious character; he is the protagonist of a certain spiritual awakening.[37] All the sources represent him as having broken away from the background of his childhood, and as he goes to a new country he also begins a new religious life. That is also how he is portrayed outside the Pentateuch, namely in the well known historical survey given in Josh. 24. It speaks of the distant forefathers Terah and his household who lived beyond the river and served other gods. God uprooted Abraham from these surroundings, led him westwards, and starting with him there began a new era which the observer tries to perceive as uninterrupted until the conquest of Canaan.[38]

The fact that some religious innovation took place with the appearance of the Patriarchs is clearly indicated in the traditions of Genesis itself. In all the sources except P, The Lord God of Israel does not gain His historical-national hold with Moses, nor with any other figure prior to the Patriarchs, but was revealed as precisely "The God of Abraham, of Isaac, and of Jacob." According to all the sources a covenant was made with each one of the Patriarchs — and at the basis of these covenants doubtlessly lay a religious concept. Every covenant normally implies commitments binding on both parties. Here, the commitments of one side are clear, namely: to multiply the descendants of the Patriarchs and to give them the Land of Canaan as an inheritance. It is difficult to establish from the stories what obligations the Patriarchs undertook on that occasion, since the sources endowed the whole matter with a decisively monotheistic character, trying to express it in the concepts of the historical Israelite religion. As a result, the specific religious-historical innovation which characterized the beginning of the patriarchal period almost faded from their text. At the same time, it can be recognized that they made an effort to describe the obligations placed upon the Patriarchs in the form of certain religious values. It is only natural that they chose the same values which were consecrated in the Yahwistic religion.

To sum up: The beginning of the patriarchal period witnessed a certain religious change in the life of the Hebrew tribes, the nature of which can be understood only by implication. There is no dearth of historical parallels for this phenomenon of a great awakening resulting in wanderings, accompanied by a spiritual renewal which crystallizes in a religious framework. We are entitled to assume that at the time when the Hebrew tribes left the Euphrates Valley something changed also in their spiritual life, an upheaval which led them towards a new religious framework. Such a change is clearly expressed in the biblical traditions which portray Abraham as a religious hero and show the deep breach between the Patriarchs and that which preceded them. The Bible cannot, of course, clearly delineate the nature of the change, since everything in it assumed a monotheistic form or at least was expressed in the language of a later period. This might have misled earlier scholars (mainly of the Pan-Babylonian school), and made them think that the change which began with Abraham had a monotheistic character. They were, nevertheless, well aware of the existence of a religious change. The true nature of this change is demonstrated by the fact that the specific traits of the Patriarchs' religion begin to be marked from Abraham onward. It therefore seems that they held onto the belief in various *Els* (principally *El Shaddai*), clung to the term "The God of the Father" and accepted the usage of circumcision. Furthermore there may have been something in the content of the ancient Hebrew religion which led towards historical Yahwism. Though we cannot define the former as a monotheistic religion, it possibly contained elements that encouraged and hastened the acceptance of the religion of YHWH by the Israelite tribes.[39] It is, after all, a fact that even after Yahwism was adopted, the Israelite tribes continued at times to use the divine names that had come down to them from the early Hebrew tribes, just as they absorbed the custom of circumcision from that same religion — and as they, no doubt, inherited many a usage and institution. It is this that helps us to understand why the promise of the Land of Canaan was connected with the Patriarchs and none but them. It is, after all, astounding that the real impetus to conquer Canaan began only after Moses' message and was implemented some time after him. Nevertheless, the claim of mastery over the country and the feeling of ownership are not connected in the consciousness of the Israelite tribes with Moses, nor with his message, but precisely with the promises made to Abraham, Isaac and Jacob.

E. SOME FEATURES OF THE CULT

In describing the cultic manifestations of the Patriarchs' religion we are obliged to differentiate between its specific traits and the aspects attributed to it and which are projections from the historical Yahwistic religion.

It is characteristic of the religion of the Patriarchs that, similarly to many other religions practiced by nomads, it has no temples, that is "houses of God" – its entire cultic world being located outside, in the open. All the pentateuchal sources assume that the erection of sanctuaries began only after the settlement in Canaan (P alone dates the establishment of the

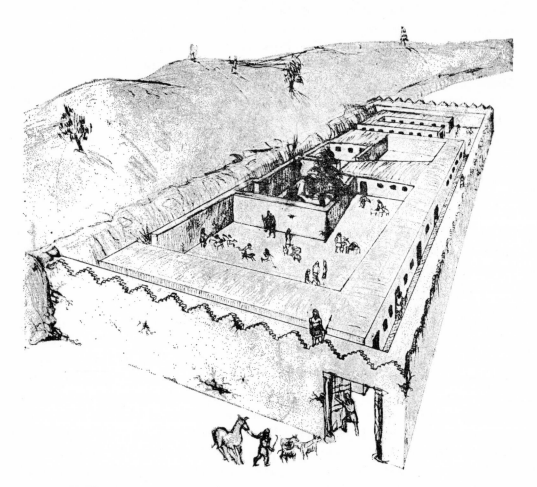

Fig. 38.
Shechem, attempted reconstruction of the "fortress temple" from the
Middle Bronze II Period, as drawn by Daniel S. Wright.

sanctuary i.e. the tabernacle a little earlier, linking it to the revelation at Sinai). However, the Patriarchs' religion knew the altar and the various rites of sacrifices connected with it. Only P does not admit the existence of altars in the period of the Patriarchs — but this is due to its severely hierocentric outlook which cannot accept the existence of altars unconnected with a temple. As to the actual position during the period, we consider the evidence of all the other sources reliable. It is characteristic of the period of the Patriarchs that it contains numerous stories about the *building* of altars. Wherever the Patriarchs encamp with their household and their flocks, they generally erect an altar, as though it were an essential institution without which no proper life was possible. It transpires that in the early Hebrew tribal society the possibility of a secular slaughtering of animals was actually unknown. The various stories relating the Patriarchs' altar building also bear the definite stamp of a "beginning." It appears that these altars erected close to the large towns of Canaan were revered by the people in the historical period, and it was related that they had been put up by the Patriarchs. At the same time the stories about that period presume that temporary altars could be built, to answer some transient need. Balaam the son of Beor had seven temporary altars erected each time, so as to be worthy of a divine revelation (Num. 23:1, 14, 29). Incidentally, this close relationship between cultic ceremonial details and prophetic visions is unique in the Bible. We can notice here the influence exerted by the Babylonian Bārū priests on the Hebrew tribes in the region of the Upper Euphrates.[40]

Among the different types of sacrifice the peace-offering which existed in the early Hebrew ritual (Gen. 31:54; 46:1; Num. 22:40), was the basic sacrifice permitting the consumption of an animal's meat. In addition, the burnt-offering was prevalent (Gen. 22:13). Among the ancients the burnt-offering fulfilled at times the task of purification from defilement or atonement for transgression (Job. 1:5; 42:7—8, no doubt the same applies to the burnt-offering which Balaam brought before his "meeting" with God — Num. 23:15) — somewhat similar to the function of the sin-offering in the priestly law of later times.

In complete accord with the absence of temples, the ancient Hebrew religion did not know priests, which are not mentioned among the Patriarchs.[41] The function of the priest was filled by the head of the family. It was he who brought the sacrifices (like all the Patriarchs, Balak, Balaam, Job and his companions) and it was he who blessed the members of his household (Gen. 26:1—40; 28:1—4; 48:9—20; 49:20—28; and cf. 24:60). In the historical period the blessing was one of the tasks of the priest (Num. 6:22—27; Dt. 10:8; 21:5 and cf. Gen. 14:18—20). The sacrifice of the firstborn animal was an important offering with the early Hebrews, for it was one of the most ancient offerings. We are also entitled to assume that the cultic vow was current amongst them, not just because the Bible alludes to it against the background of the period (Gen. 28:20—22; 31:13), but because of its extreme ancienty and practice by almost every cult civilization. Similarly, stories about that period mention the custom of bowing and prostrating before God or in His honor (Gen. 17:3; 24:26, 48; Num. 22:31; Job. 1:20), which was a common and widespread practice in every popular cult. This is not the case, however, with the unique cultic act of "calling upon the name of the Lord" (Gen. 12:8; 13:4; 21:33; 26:25). The stories endeavor to emphasize through it the inherent religious value of the Patriarchs' deeds, the decisive turning-point represented by their appearance in different parts of Canaan. Every "call upon the name of the Lord" is accompanied by the erection of an altar or the planting of a tamarisk, which were perhaps considered part of the sacral-cultic activities

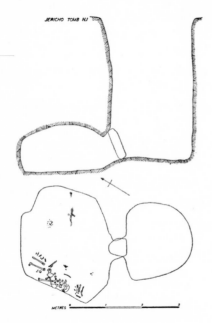

Fig. 39.
Jericho, large shaft tomb from the
Middle Bronze I Period.
Prof. K. M. Kenyon, London.

connected with covenants. But in this case they introduced into their narrative about the patriarchal period a custom prevailing in the historical Jahwistic religion (cf. I Kings 18:24; II Kings 5:11; Zeph. 3:9; Ps. 116:17 etc.).

Similar to other religions of nomadic peoples, that of the Hebrew tribes apparently, knew only holy sites instead of temples. Quite possibly the word *maqōm* (place) occasionally bears a sacral-cultic meaning in the stories of the Patriarchs, meaning a definite locality where sacred objects and cultic accessories were kept.[42] That is the manner in which are mentioned *the place* of Shechem (Gen. 12:6), *the place* between Beth-el and Ai

(Gen. 13:3), the *place of* Beth-el (Gen. 28:11, 16–19). No information has come down to us about places considered holy at that time by the Hebrew tribes themselves. The Bible only mentions places considered holy by the people in the historical period, and it was only their establishment that was attributed to the Patriarchs. In any case those too seem to have been made on the ancient pattern, so that it is not hard to imagine what such a place contained. Naturally, there would be an altar and sometimes

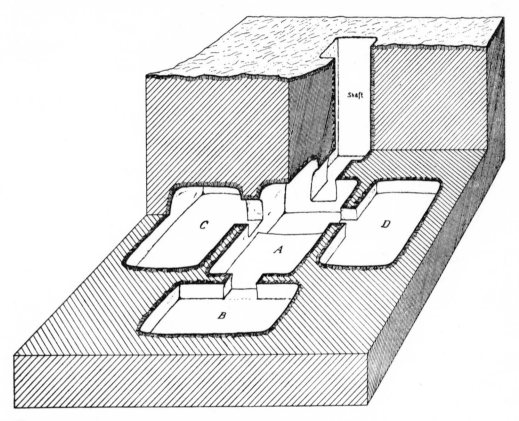

Fig. 40.
Megiddo, plan of shaft-tomb from the Middle Bronze II Period
Guy–Engberg, *Megiddo Tombs*, Chicago, 1938, fig. 168.

sacred trees would stand beside it. Such trees are mentioned in several passages about the days of the Patriarchs — the terebinths of Mamre outside Hebron (Gen. 13:18; 14:13; 18:1, etc.), the terebinth of Moreh in the *place* of Shechem (Gen. 12:6). The place of Shechem which included a tree and an altar within its compass, and which is related by J to memories from Abraham's days, resembles another place, also opposite the town of Shechem where there are also a tree (terebinth) and an altar — except that E relates this latter place to memories from Jacob's time (Gen. 33:18–20;[43] 35:4). This may be one and the same place, but each tradition attributed its founding to a different Patriarch. Similarly it seems possible that two sources handed down two parallel traditions about the same place in the Beer-sheba neighborhood which contained a tamarisk and

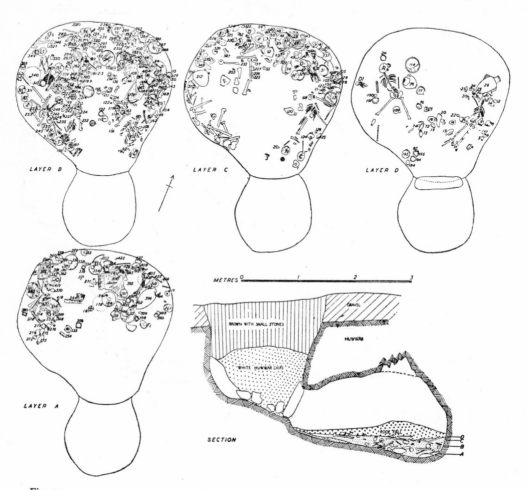

Fig. 41.
Jericho, plan and section of a Middle Bronze II shaft tomb.
Prof. K. M. Kenyon, London

an altar. However, E merely mentions the tamarisk adding that Abraham had planted it (Gen. 21:33), while J only mentions the altar, attributing its building to Isaac (Gen. 26:25).

The pillar, *mazzeva*, could serve as a kind of substitute for the sacred tree, and as a sort of parallel to it, and its place was generally by the altar.

It symbolized the concentration of the divine holiness within the compass of that site. The sacred place near Beth-el, the founding of which the traditions attribute to Jacob, included probably both a pillar and an altar, (Gen. 28:18, 22; 31:13; 35:1, 7, 14), though each one of the stories emphasized a different object and centered the legend around it. One of the places in Gilead, the founding of which was also attributed to Jacob, contained a pillar as well as a heap of stones which served as an altar (Gen. 31:45–48, 51–52, 54). According to the Bible twelve pillars stood by the altar that Moses built in the neighborhood of Mount Sinai (Ex. 42:4). Similarly, in Gilgal there stood twelve stones which were, no doubt, considered pillars (Josh. 4), and most probably an altar was not missing either. The popular religion in the historical period did certainly not forbid the pillars which were essentially sanctified to the God of Israel. In many places in the land of Israel and for the greatest part of the First Temple period it was a regular phenomenon that a pillar stood beside the altar. The pillar (and the same applies to the holy tree), as a sacral-cultic object, was common in various religions, and archeological excavations have brought them to light in many places.

In certain instances the pillar itself served as a place of libation. This custom is mentioned only with the Patriarchs—Jacob pours libations on the pillar of Beth-el and also pours oil on the top of it (Gen. 28:18; 35:14). These may have been customs specific to the early period. Famous trees were also found without altars next to them; they stood isolated and acted as funerary memorials. *Allon-bacuth* (the oak of weeping) near Beth-el indicated the burial place of Rebekah's nurse Deborah (Gen. 35:8); and a special pillar, considered to be "the pillar of Rachel's grave" stood until late times on the border of the tribe of Benjamin (I Sam. 10:2; Jer. 31:14), on the way down to Bethlehem (Gen. 35:19–20; 48:7). It would seem that these were also popular usages from the earliest period to which the masses conservatively clung. Peculiar to the patriarchal period is the story of the divine revelation by the fountain in the wilderness (Gen. 16:7–14), which also appears to have been a holy place, and which can also be considered a characteristic trait of nomadic religion.

NOTES AND BIBLIOGRAPHY

NOTES

CHAPTER I

HISTORIOGRAPHY AND HISTORICAL SOURCES IN ANCIENT MESOPOTAMIA

1 The present chapter is a condensation of my essay "The Idea of History in Ancient Mesopotamia" which appeared in *The Idea of History in the Ancient Near East*, ed. by R. C. Dentan, New Haven, 1955, pp. 37–76, 361–2.

2 T. Jacobsen, *JNES*, 2 (1943), 159 ff.

3 Cf. Epic of Eatna, trans. by E. A. Speiser, *ANET*, p. 114, lines 11–13.

4 Cf. H. G. Güterbock, *ZA*, 42 (1934), 1–91.

5 See A. Goetze, *JCS*, 1 (1947), 253–66.

6 For such "distanzangaben," cf. E. Weidner, *AfO*, 15 (1945–51), 87 ff.; A. Poebel, *JNES*, 1 (1942), 289 ff.

7 Cf. B. Landsberger and K. Balkan, *Belleten*, 14 (1950), 224 ff.

8 *Cuneiform Texts from Babylonian Tablets etc. in the British Museum*, XXII, no. 1.

9 Cf. Güterbock, *loc. cit.*, 13 ff.

10 *ARM*, I, no. 3, line 6.

1 E. Ebeling, *Mitteilungen der altorientalichen Gesellschaft*, 12/2, IV, 20.

2 *Ibid.*, 27

13 Güterbock, *loc. cit.*, 47 ff.

14 Obv. 27.

15 Stele of Nabonidus, 16, 36.

16 A. T. E. Olmstead, *Assyrian Historiography*, Columbia, Missouri, 1916, p. 62.

17 Cf. Epic of Gilgamesh, X, vi, lines 26 ff. (trans. by E. A. Speiser, *ANET*, pp. 92 f.).

18 H. Frankfort, *Kingship and the Gods*, Chicago, 1948, pp. 263 f.

19 See W. G. Lambert and O. R. Gurney, *Anatolian Studies*, 4 (1954), 65 ff.

20 B. Landsberger, *ZA*, 43 (1936), 32–76.

21 See J. Nougayrol, *RB*, 59 (1952), 239–50.

22 Cf. Goetze, *loc. cit.*, 256 ff.

23 See S. N. Kramer, *JCS*, 1 (1947), 33 note 208; cf. *Keilschrifttexte aus Assur religiösen Inhalts*, no. 27.

24 Akkadian *šumma ḫaṭṭitam izīr ilšu ittišu ittanallak*: see *ZA*, 43 (1936), 98, line 31. For close biblical parallels of the second half of this verse, cf. E. A. Speiser, *JAOS*, 75 (1955), 120.

CHAPTER II

UGARITIC WRITINGS

1   Philo's account has not been preserved in its entirety, being known only from quotations in Eusebius, *Praeparationis Evangelicae*, I, 9, 22–10, 46; I, 10, 48; IV, 16, 6. Of the literature on this subject, see C. Clement, "Die Phönikische Religion nach Philo von Byblos," *MVAG*, 42 (1939); O. Eissfeldt, *Taautos und Sanchunjaton*, Berlin, 1952.

2   Most scholars regard them as Canaanite; see, for example, A. Jirku, *JBL*, 52 (1933), 108–20. However, W. F. Albright, *JEA*, 23 (1937), 196–201, has rejected this view and has shown that they are Egyptian in origin. This nevertheless leaves room for doubting whether the texts were translated directly into Akkadian from the Egyptian or whether there was a Canaanite version between the Egyptian original and the Akkadian rendering. The latter alternative allows of the suggestion that Israelite literature was influenced by that of Egypt *via* ancient Canaanite literature.

3   W. F. Albright and W. L. Moran, *JCS*, 4 (1950), 163–8.

4   B. Landsberger, *JCS*, 8 (1954), 56, 129 ff.; M. Noth, *ZDPV*, 65 (1942), 34–63.

5   Wiseman, *Alalakh; idem, JCS*, 8 (1954), 1 ff.

6   *Idem, Alalakh*, no. 136.

7   M. Birot, *RA*, 47 (1953), 172.

8   The Proto-Semitic root of *yqr* is *wqr*. The change of an initial *waw* to *yod* is characteristic of Northwestern Semitic languages.

9   J. Nougayrol, *PRU*, III, 1955, X–XLIII.

10   Wiseman, *Alalakh*, no. 358; *idem, JCS*, 8 (1954), 27.

11   C. F. A. Schaeffer, *Ugaritica*, I, Paris, 1939, pp. 15 f. On this document and two others which apparently attest to contacts between Mari and Ugarit, see F. M. Tocci, *La Siria nell'età di Mari*, Rome, 1960, pp. 69–71.

12   Schaeffer, *op. cit.*, pp. 20 ff. On the Egyptian finds in northern Syria in general and in Ugarit in particular dating from the Twelfth Dynasty, see also W. A. Ward,

Orientalia (n.s.), 30 (1961), 129–36, who correctly points out that they do not constitute evidence of an Egyptian conquest.

13   Schaeffer, *op. cit.*, pp. 53 ff.; cf., however, A. Furumark, *Opuscula Archaeologica*, 6, Lund, 1950, who denies any Cretan influence in Asia, and even the identification of Caphtor with Crete.

14   Gordon, *UM*, 'nt, VI, line 14. And cf. *idem, JNES*, 7 (1948), 263.

15   C. F. A. Schaeffer, *Syria*, 31 (1954), 33–4.

16   Nougayrol, *PRU*, IV, 1956.

17   Schaeffer, *loc. cit.*, 41.

18   *Idem, Ugaritica*, III, Paris, 1956, pp. 163 ff.; Ch. Desroches-Noblecourt, *ibid.*, pp. 180 ff. Mention should also be made here of Amen-hotep II's inscription on his campaigns in Canaan. On whether Ugarit is referred to in this document, see J. A. Wilson, *ANET*, p. 246 note 18.

19   Schaeffer, *Syria*, 31 (1954), 16–23, 42–51.

20   That clay tables were found in an oven ready for baking shows that the enemy came upon Ugarit like a bolt from the blue; see C. F. A. Schaeffer, *CRAI*, 1955, 254–6. The destruction did not affect Ugarit's neighbors Ushnatu and Siyanu; see Nougayrol, *op. cit.*, pp. 15–8. All these data support the widespread conjecture that Ugarit was destroyed by the "Sea Peoples" who, having burnt and sacked the city, proceeded on their way; cf. the *Odyssey*, 10, lines 38–41. The exact date of the destruction is unknown. The latest object from Ugarit that helps in fixing the chronology is a sword on which appears the name of Mer-ne-Ptah (1237–1229 B.C.E.). See Schaeffer, *Ugaritica*, III, pp. 169–77. The last Hittite king mentioned in Ugaritic documents is Tudhaliya IV who, according to the low dating, reigned 1250–1220 B.C.E. He was a contemporary of the Ugaritic king Ammishtamru II, who was succeeded on the throne of Ugarit by Hiranu, Niqmadd III, and 'Ammurapi, in whose days the city was destroyed. Each of these last kings reigned apparently for only a short

time, as is shown from the synchronism between Ammishtamru II king of Ugarit and Ini-Teshub king of Carchemish, and between ʿAmmurapi king of Ugarit and Talmi-Teshub the son of Ini-Teshub king of Carchemish. On these synchronisms, see Nougayrol, *op. cit.*, pp. 7, 8. M. Liverani, *Storia di Ugarit*, Rome, 1962, p. 135, is probably right in linking the destruction of Ugarit with the assault of the Sea Peoples on Anatolia and Syria and their attack in ca. 1200 B.C.E., in the days of Ramses III, on the frontier of Egypt.

21   Schaeffer, *Syria*, 31 (1954), 16–23.

22   *Ibid.*, 16 ff., 50; W. F. Albright, *Festschrift A. Bertholet*, Tübingen, 1950, pp. 1–14.

23   *Idem, BASOR*, 130 (1953), 26 ff.

24   Gordon, *UM*, Krt, lines 201–2.

25   *Ibid.*, text 51 VI, lines 18–21.

26   *Ibid.*, text 76 II, line 9.

27   *Ibid.*, text 128 III, lines 18–9.

28   W. F. Albright, "The Proto-Sinaitic Inscriptions and their decipherment" *Harvard theological Studies* 22), Cambridge, Mass., 1966.

29   F. M. Gross, Jr., *BASOR*, 134 (1954), 15–24.

30   On the problems of this alphabet, see S. E. Loewenstamn, *BIES* (Hebrew), 16 (1952), 32–6, and the literature quoted there. It has recently been shown that in Ugarit, alongside the usual alphabet of thirty letters, a shorter one was also used; see Ch. Virolleaud, *CRAI*, 1960, 85–90. On account of the paucity and brevity of texts in the shorter alphabet, the number of its letters cannot at present be determined. It is only known that the two letters *ṭ* and *š* were replaced by one new letter, and the two letters *ḥ* and *h* invariably by *h*. Virolleaud has suggested that this Ugaritic alphabet is the twenty-two letter Phoenician-Hebrew alphabet. But whereas the shorter Ugaritic alphabet dropped the letter *ḥ* and retained *ḫ*, the opposite occurred in the Phoenician-Hebrew alphabet. The antiquity of the order of the letters of the alphabet also implies the antiquity of their names; see F. M. Cross, Jr., and T. O. Lambdin, *BASOR*, 160 (1960), 21–6.

31   Gordon, *UM*, text 95, lines 8, 9; cf., for example, Ps. 92:14.

32   For example Gordon, *UM*, text 49 VI, lines 30–1; cf. Isa. 41:23. Cf. also J. C. Greenfield, *HUCA*, 29 (1958), 226–8.

33   Gordon, *UM*, ʿnt, II, lines 7, 8.

34   *Ibid.*, text 51 V, lines 65, 66.

35   *Ibid.*, text 128, lines 26, 27.

36   *Ibid.*, ʿnt, V, lines 33–5.

37   *Ibid.*, text 51 III, lines 17–8.

38   *Ibid.*, text 68, lines 8, 9.

39   R. Samuel b. Meir's commentary on Ex. 15:6. For details of this structure, see S. E. Loewenstamm, *Lᵉshonenu*, 27–28 (1963–4), 111–26.

40   Gordon, *UM*, 2 Aqht V, lines 7–8.

41   *Ibid.*, text 127, lines 33–4.

42   F. Thureau-Dangin, *Syria*, 18 (1937), 249 ff.

43   Gordon, *UM*, 2 Aqht I, line 31–2; II, lines 5–6, 19–20.

44   See note 34, above.

45   Gordon, *UM*, text 126 IV, line 3.

46   *Ibid.*, text 51 V, line 46.

47   *Ibid.*, 2 Aqht I, lines 26–7.

48   *Ibid.*, text 126 V, lines 8–29. The description of the creation of the angel of healing is fragmentary. However, two words — *yqrṣ* and *rṭ* — are discernible in it. The verb *qrṣ* is corresponds to the Akkadian verb *karāṣu*, which in the creation narrative denotes the pinching off of a lump of clay by the fingers of the deity, an operation which precedes the actual creation from that lump of clay. Cf., for example, the Epic of Gilgamesh, tablet I, p. 3, line 34, and the laconic statement in the Bible: "I also am formed (*qoraẓti*) out of the clay" (Job. 33 : 6). The noun *rṭ* corresponds to the Akkadian noun *rušum* which in an old Babylonian text denotes the dirt which Ea picked from under his nails and which he used for the purpose of creation. Cf. *CAD*, vol. 16, 251 b.

49   Gordon, *UM*, ʿnt, V.

50   *Ibid.*, text 49 I. On the other hand, this story also indicates that El always retained a certain measure of supreme authority over the world. It is impossible to accept the suggestion of M. D. (U.) Cassuto, *The Goddess Anath* (Hebrew), Jerusalem, 1951, pp. 43, 44, that the sons of El — Baal, the Prince of the Sea, and Mot — forcibly

dethroned their father, exiled him, and divided the world among them. This suggestion is based principally on an analogy with the Greek and Hurrian-Hittite myth. It is indeed possible to identify El with Kronos of the Greek myth and with Kumarbi of the Hurrian-Hittite myth, in both of which the sons of these gods deposed their fathers after a battle. But there are no grounds for assuming that El of the Canaanite myth shared their fate, since Philo of Byblos relates that it was in accordance with El's wishes that Hadad reigned (Eusebius, *Praeparationis Evangelicae* I, 10, 31). M. H. Pope, *El in the Ugaritic Texts*, Leiden, 1955, pp. 27–32, 61–72, has, with the addition of rather weak arguments, repeated Cassuto's suggestion. For an opposing view, cf. R. Follet, *Verbum Domini*, 34 (1956), 280–9.

51   P. W. Skehan, *BASOR*, 136 (1954), 12 ff.

52   Gordon, *UM*, text 51 V, lines 70–1.

53   *Ibid.*, lines 68–9. And cf. M. D. (U.) Cassuto, *From Adam to Noah* (transl. from the Hebrew by I. Abrahams), Jerusalem, 1961, on Gen. 2:8.

54   Gordon, *UM*, text 49 III, lines 6–9.

55   *Ibid.*, text 67 I, lines 1–3.

56   *Ibid*, lines 7–8.

57   For example, Th. H. Gaster, *Thespis* (2nd ed.), New York, 1961, holds that there is a seasonal pattern common to every Ancient Eastern myth which in the pre-epic stage crystallized in a cultic drama. In this seasonal pattern Gaster even includes the myth of Baal's war against the sea and the rivers, a war which, according to him, is renewed annually with the resurrection of Baal when the sea and the rivers strive to flood the earth, the domain of Baal. But it is difficult to understand why this process should take place precisely at the beginning of the rainy season.

58   See, for example, V. and I. R. Jacobs, *HTR*, 38 (1945), 77–109; and, more recently, A. S. Kapelrud, *IEJ*, 13 (1963), 127–9.

59   M. D. (U.) Cassuto, *BIES*, 9 (1942), 45–51; S. E. Lowenstamm, *IEJ*, 12 (1962), 87 ff.; 13 (1963), 130–2.

60   C. H. Gordon, *Ugaritic Literature*, Rome, 1949, p. 4.

61   Cassuto, *loc. cit.*, Gordon, *op. cit.*, pp. 4 ff.

62   On the manner in which through a comparison with the Ugaritic material, the myth is reflected in God's war on the sea and the rivers, see M. D. (U.) Cassuto, *Kᵉnesset* (Hebrew), 8, 3 (1943–4), 127–38. Despite the remarkable similarity between the Ugaritic epic and the mythological allusions in the Bible, the fact that the background of the biblical myth is broader than that of the Ugaritic myth should not be overlooked. In the Ugaritic epic the battle against the forces of the water takes place only in the existing world. In the myth as reflected in biblical passages the battle is, as in the Babylonian epic, at times connected with the creation of the world, as, for example, in Ps. 104:5–9. In Ugarit the Prince of the Sea and the Judge of the River are always mentioned together, which suggests that they may be one deity. In the Bible the sea is at times, as for example in Job 7:12, mentioned by itself, as in the Babylonian epic, and at others with the rivers, as for example in Nahum 1:4, as in the Ugaritic epic. In the Ugaritic epic Baal's enemies are in every instance personified, whereas in the Bible any personification, as in Ps. 74:14, is rare. Generally, the sea and the rivers are depicted as actual water which the Lord dries up, as in Isa. 50:2.

CHAPTER III

THE CANAANITE INSCRIPTIONS AND THE STORY OF THE ALPHABET

1 *Corpus Inscriptionum Semiticarum ab Academia Inscriptionum et Litterarum Humaniorum conditum atque digestum*, Paris, 1881 ff.

2 *Répertoire d'épigraphie sémitique*, publié par la commission du Corpus Inscriptionum Semiticarum, Paris, 1900 ff.

3 The main periodicals concerned with Semitic epigraphy are *Revue des études sémitiques*, now published (since 1948) as *Semitica; Zeitschrift für Semitistik und verwandte Gebiete* (defunct since 1935 ?); *Journal of Semitic Studies: Sefarad;* formerly also *Ephemeris für semitische Epigraphik* (published by M. Lidzbarski); and *Proceedings of the Society of Biblical Archaeology*. Articles dealing with these subjects appear from time to time also in other periodicals concerned with the history, philology, and archeology of the ancient Middle East.

4 M. Lidzbarski apparently dated it to the 10th century B.C.E. (cf. *Ephemeris*, I, p. 111), for he considered it older than the Mesha stele; cf. *idem, Handbuch der nordsemitischen Epigraphik*, Weimar, 1898, I, pp. 118, 176, 419; II, pl. II, a–c. It is now generally agreed that it should be dated to the 8th century B.C.E.; cf. S. Yeivin, *The History of the Jewish Script* (Hebrew), Jerusalem, 1939, I, pp. 120–1.

5 Cf., for example, D. Diringer, *L'alfabeto nella storia della civiltà*, Florence, 1937, pp. 238 ff.

6 It may be an exercise of an unpracticed student of a school of scribes (cf. W. F. Albright, *BASOR*, 92 [1943], 16 ff., and especially 21–2), or a note scratched by a half-educated peasant for his own use. For the date and bibliography, see M. D. (U.) Cassuto, *Encyclopaedia Biblica* (Hebrew), II, Jerusalem, 1954, cols. 471–4, s.v. Gezer, The Gezer Calendar.

7 W. M. F. Petrie, *Researches in Sinai* (2nd ed.), London, 1906, pp. 129 ff., and figs. 138, 139, 141.

8 A. H. Gardiner and T. E. Peet, *The Inscriptions of Sinai*, I, London, 1917, pls. LXXXII–LXXXIII.

9 A. H. Gardiner, *JEA*, 3 (1916), 1 ff.; A. E. Cowley, *ibid.*, 17 ff.; cf. also A. H. Gardiner, *ZDMG*, 77 (1923), 92 ff.

10 K. H. Sethe, *Nachrichten der kaiserlichen Gesellschaft der Wissenschaften zu Göttingen*, 1916, pp. 88 ff.; 1917, pp. 437 ff. For summaries of the earlier theories on the derivation of the Hebrew-Phoenician alphabet, see Diringer, *op. cit.*, pp. 238 ff.; Yeivin, *op. cit.*, pp. 31–50.

11 K. Lake and R. P. Blake, *HTR*, 21 (1928), 1 ff.; R. F. Butin, *ibid.*, 9 ff.

12 No report has, as far as is known, ever been published of this expedition, but it seems that the material found was included in the publications mentioned in note 13, below.

13 K. Lake, A. Barrois, Silva New, and R. F. Butin, *HTR*, 25 (1932), 95 ff.; cf. also R. F. S. Staar and R. F. Butin, *Studies and Documents*, VI, London, 1936.

14 J. Leibovitch, *Les inscriptions proto-sinaïtiques*, Cairo, 1934; Ch. Jean, *Syria*, 9 (1928), 279 ff.; cf. Diringer, *op. cit.*, pp. 250 ff. Leibovitch was the first to use the term Proto-Sinaitic for these inscriptions and their signary in order to differentiate them from the late Semitic inscriptions at Wadi al-Mukattab in Sinai, known as the Sinaitic inscriptions.

15 H. Grimme, *Althebräische Inschriften vom Sinai*, Darmstadt, 1923; *idem, Die altsinaitischen Buchstaben-inschriften*, Berlin, 1929; *idem, Altsinaitische Forschungen*, Paderborn, 1937.

16 W. F. Albright, *BASOR*, 109 (1948), 14; 110 (1948), 6 ff.

17 W. M. F. Petrie, *Kahun, Gurob, and Hawara*, London, 1890, pls. XXVII–XXVIII; cf. also the enigmatic inscription from Karnak recorded by W. M. Mueller, *Egyptological Researches*, I, Washington, 1906, pp. 37–8, and pl. 43.

18 W. R. Taylor, *JPOS*, 10 (1930), 17 ff. For additional bibliography, see G. R. Driver, *Semitic Writing* (2nd ed.), London, 1954, p. 98 note 4.

19   Cf. S. Yeivin, *PEQ*, 1937, 186 note 19; *idem*, *BIES* (Hebrew), 5 (1937–8), 2 note 5.

20   F. M. Th. Böhl, *ZDPV*, 61 (1938), 1 ff., figs. 3–4, and pl. I A–B; cf. P. Kahane, *BIES*, 12 (1945–6), 30 ff., and fig. 1; B. Maisler (Mazar), *ibid.*, 7 (1939–40), 90 ff., and fig. 1; S. Yeivin, *ibid.*, 8 (1940–1), 82 ff.

21   J. L. Starkey, *PEQ*, 1937, 239–40, and pl. VIII, 1; Yeivin, *BIES*, 5 (1937–8), 8 ff., and fig. 6; cf. also Driver, *op. cit.*, pp. 98–9, and fig. 43.

22   Lachish 1 (on a shoulder of a large jar): O. Tufnell et alii, *Lachish*, II, London, 1940, pp. 49 ff., and frontispiece, pl. LX (with bibliography); Lachish 2 (on a bowl from a Late Canaanite II tomb): Yeivin, *PEQ*, 1937, 180 ff., and pls. III–IV; Tufnell et alii, *op. cit.*, IV, London, 1958, pls. XLIII, XLIV, 2; Lachish 3 (on the cover of an incense bowl): Yeivin, *PEQ*, 1937, 193; *idem*, *BIES*, 5 (1937–8), 3 ff., and fig. 3; Tufnell et alii, *op. cit.*, IV, pls. XLIV, 1, XLV, 4; cf. also Driver, *op. cit.*, p. 101, and figs. 49 A–C; Lachish 4 (on a fragment of a bowl found in the debris near the temple): Tufnell et alii, *op. cit.*, II, pp. 55 ff., and pl. XXIX, 12.

23   E. Grant and G. E. Wright, *Ain-Shems Excavations*, V (text), Haverford, 1939, pp. 46–7 (and see the bibliography cited there); E. Grant, *op. cit.*, II, Haverford, 1932, p. 30, and pl. X. For a possible rendering, see Yeivin, *PEQ*, 1937, 187 ff., and pl. V; *idem*, *BIES*, 5 (1937–8), 5–6, and fig. 4 (with bibliography).

24   R. A. Bowman, *apud* P. L. O. Guy, *Megiddo Tombs*, Chicago, 1938, pp. 173 ff., fig. 177, and pl. 128, 15; S. Yeivin, *Kedem* (Hebrew), 2 (1945), 34–5.

25   F. J. Bliss, *A Mound of Many Cities*, London, 1894, pp. 88 ff., and fig. 194. Found near the top of city IV, Late Canaanite II by its assemblage; cf. Yeivin, *History of the Jewish Script*, I, pp. 100–1, and fig. 19.

26   For the graffito on the bowl, see W. M. F. Petrie, *Ancient Gaza*, II, London, 1932, pl. XXX, no. 1109; cf. Yeivin, *op. cit.*, p. 110, and fig. 23; Driver, *op. cit.*, p. 100 (name of site wrong), and fig. 46. For the graffito on the handle, see Petrie, *op. cit.*, pl. XL, 30; F. M. Cross, Jr., *BASOR*, 134

(1954), 24 fig. 13. Both undoubtedly Late Canaanite II.

27   Ruth B. Kallner (Amiran), *Kedem*, 2 (1945), 11, and pl. II, 1; E. L. Sukenik, *ibid.*, 15, and fig. 1.

28   W. F. Albright, *The Excavation of Tell Beit Mirsim*, III, New Haven, 1943 (= *AASOR*, 21–22 [1941–3]), 30–1, and pl. 60, 1; Cross, Jr., *loc cit.*

29   Y. Yadin, *BIES*, 20 (1956–7), 58, and pl. XIV, 4; *idem*, *Hazor*, I, Jerusalem, 1958, p. 107, and pls. CLX, 2, XCIX, 20.

30   R. Amiran and A. Eitan, *BIES*, 28 (1964–5), 198, and pl. 18, 5. The proposed reading is improbable, besides being meaningless. The only similar signs are found in Lachish 4 (on the obverse at the bottom), which is much later.

31   Similar material was acquired from dealers also outside Israel. Thus Gaster mentions a scaraboid seal from Asia Minor (?) published by A. A. Zakharov, *Archiv Orientální*, 7 (1935), 36, and pl. VI, 7; a cylinder seal, with an inscription in similar characters (apparently engraved on it at some later date?), is in the Louvre Museum (L. Delaporte, *Catalogue des cylindres, cachets et pierres gravées de style oriental*, Paris, 1923, pl. 95, 6 [no. A 878]), of unknown provenance; another prismatic seal, which was in the possession of a dealer in Jerusalem (published by S. Yeivin, *JPOS*, 20 [1946], pl. XXX), is probably to be connected with the Byblian hieroglyphic signary; see below. — At various times attempts have been made to summarize and classify the available material. See T. H. Gaster, *PEFQS*, 1935, 128 ff.; *idem*, *PEQ*, 1937, 43 ff.; Yeivin, *ibid.*, 180 ff.; B. Maisler (Mazar), *JPOS*, 18 (1938), 278 ff.; Yeivin, *BIES*, 5 (1937–8), 1 ff.; *idem*, *History of the Jewish Script*, I, pp. 89 ff.; D. Diringer, *Antiquity*, 17 (1943), 82 ff.; Driver, *op. cit.*, pp. 87 ff. But in view of recent progress in the study of the development of the alphabet, a survey of the whole material now available has yet to be written.

32   See notes 22 and 30, above.

33   Cf. S. Yeivin, *RSO*, 38 (1963), 284–5; *idem*, *History of the Jewish Script*, I, pp. 114–5. It was also later noted by D. Diringer, *The Alphabet* (2nd ed.), London, 1949,

p. 211, who however drew no conclusions from this fact.

34 For the date of this inscription, see B. Maisler (Mazar), *Lᵉshonenu*, 14 (1945–6), 177 ff., and the bibliography cited there; cf. M. Dunand, *Byblia Grammata*, Beirut, 1945, pp. 197 ff. Some scholars however maintain that the Ahiram inscription dates from the 10th century: cf., for example, Cross, Jr., *loc. cit.*, 15 ff.

35 Ch. Virolleaud, *Syria*, 10 (1929), 304 ff.; 11 (1930), 200; 12 (1931), 15 ff.; H. Bauer, *Die Entzifferung der keilschrifttafeln von Ras Schamra*, Halle a/S, 1930; E. Dhorme, *RB*, 39 (1930), 32 ff., 571 ff.

36 M. Dunand, *Syria*, 11 (1930), 1 ff., and pl. I. For the later announcement at the 19th International Congress of Orientalists at Rome, cf. W. F. Albright, *BASOR*, 60 (1935), 3 ff.; cf. also J. Leibovitch, *Bulletin de l'institut français d'archéologie orientale*, 32 (1932), 23 ff., and pls. II–III.

37 Dunand, *Byblia Grammata*, pp. 71 ff., and pls. VIII–XIV.

38 Cf. J. Friedrich, *Entzifferung verschollener Schriften und Sprachen*, Berlin-Göttingen-Heidelberg, 1945, p. 112 (with greater reservation in the English translation, 1957); and cf. M. Dunand, *Mélanges Maspéro*, I, Cairo, 1935–1938, p. 569; and see below.

39 E. Dhorme, *Syria*, 25 (1946–8), 1 ff.

40 M. F. Martin, *Orientalia* (n.s.), 30 (1961), 46 ff.

41 *Ibid.*, 31 (1962), 250 ff., 339 ff.

42 L. H. Vincent, *RB*, 41 (1932), 417 ff. Cf. C. H. Gordon, *Antiquity*, 31 (1957), 124 ff., for an attempt to decipher the Linear A script, which may perhaps be applicable in this case too.

43 W. A. Ward and M. F. Martin, *Annual of the Department of Antiquities of Jordan*, 8–9 (1964), 5 ff., and pls. I–VI.

44 But is not unknown, even in Canaan: cf. A. Rowe, *The Topography and History of Beth-Shan*, I, Philadelphia, 1930, pl. 42.

45 H. J. Franken, *VT*, 14 (1964), 377 ff., and pl. I.

46 The present writer intends to deal soon with these inscriptions in a more detailed study; and cf. H. Cazelles, *Semitica*, 15 (1965), 5 ff.

47 A. van den Branden, *VT*, 15 (1965), 129 ff. For a conflicting view, see H. J. Franken, *ibid.*, 150 ff. And cf. note 46, above.

48 Cf. note 46, above.

49 Cf. also the Azarbaal spatula, which is apparently somewhat earlier; and see Dunand, *Byblia Grammata*, pp. 155 ff.; N. H. Torczyner (Tur-Sinai), *Lᵉshonenu*, 14 (1945–6), 158 ff.; Maisler (Mazar), *ibid.*, 169 fig. 2; S. Yeivin, *RB*, 65 (1958), 585 ff.

50 Cf., for example, B. Rosenkranz, *ZDMG*, 92 (1938), 178 ff.; Yeivin, *History of the Jewish Script*, I, pp. 64 ff.; cf. also Diringer, *The Alphabet*, p. 204.

51 M. D. (U.) Cassuto, *The Goddess Anath* (Hebrew), Jerusalem, 1951, p. 11.

52 That this order goes back as far as the 8th century B.C.E., at least, has been proved by the discovery of a graffito scribbled on the steps of the 8th century government building at Lachish. It gives the first five letters of the Hebrew-Phoenician alphabet in their proper order: see Tufnell et alii, *Lachish*, III, London, 1953, pp. 85, 118, fig. 10, and pl. XLVIII B, 3. The Ugaritic abecedary is about 600 years earlier than this graffito.

53 Thus, for example, only one *aleph* sign appears at the beginning of the tablet (namely, *'a*), while the other two *aleph* signs (*'i* and *'u*) appear in the 28th and 29th places respectively; *ḥ* is inserted between *gimmel* and *daleth* (in the 4th place), pushing *daleth* to the 5th place; and thus also the other additional phonemes.

54 The same inventiveness is manifest also in another group of writings: the Phaestus disk, the Linear A and B of Crete and the Mycenean Greek mainland, and the syllabic Cypriot. Syllabic Cypriot was long ago deciphered as Greek. Lately M. Ventris and J. Chadwick have also deciphered Linear B as early Greek (*Journal of Hellenistic Studies*, 73 [1953], 84 ff.). These facts seem to suggest that the Phaestus disk and Linear A may also be Greek or at least some form of a pre-Greek (Pelasgic) Mediterranean. Cf. note 42, above.

The Hittite hieroglyphic script is another attempt to form a national script. It seems that "all indications point toward the Aegean cultural area as its source of origin" (I. J. Gelb, *A Study of Writing*, London, 1952, p. 83).

For other examples of clay tablets incised with hitherto undeciphered inscriptions in an alphabetic (?) script acquired at Istanbul (from a dealer), now in the Leiden Museum, cf. F. M. Th. Böhl, *AfO*, 8 (1932–3), 173–4, and pl. II. These may possibly represent an early (?) attempt to adapt the Hebrew-Phoenician script for the writing of Greek (or some other Asia Minor language).

55   Such seem to be the inscriptions in Leibovitch, *Les inscriptions proto-sinaïtiques*, nos. 345–8, 351, etc.

56   *Ibid.*, no. 349.

57   The Gezer ostracon and the Lachish dagger seem to bear names, while the Shechem stele remains undeciphered.

58   Dunand, *Byblia Grammata*, pp. 19–20.

59   Yeivin, *RSO*, 38 (1963), 284–5.

60   *Idem*, *Archiv Orientální*, 4 (1932), 71 ff.; *idem*, *History of the Jewish Script*, I, pp. 78 ff.

61   *Ibid.*, *pp.* 79 ff.; Gelb, *op. cit.*, pp. 147 ff.

62   Cf., for example, S. Yeivin, *Lᵉshonenu*,

63   *Idem*, *History of the Jewish Script*, I, pp. 17 (1950–1), 70–1.

86–7; Gelb, *op. cit.*, pp. 182 ff.

64   Yeivin, *Archiv Orientální*, 4 (1932), 75–6; *idem*, *History of the Jewish Script*, I, pp. 79-80.

65   See note 37, above.

66   Dunand, *op. cit.*, pp. 145–6.

67   S. Yeivin, *Proceedings of the World Congress of Jewish Studies I* (Hebrew), Jerusalem, 1952, p. 53 (= *Lᵉshonenu*, 17 [1950–1], 68); *idem*, *JPOS*, 20 (1946), 166–7.

68   G. Daressy, *Catalogue général du musée du Caire*, Cairo, 1902, ostraca nos. 24, 105–8, pp. 64–5, and pl. XVIII.

69   Dunand, *op. cit.*, pp. 135 ff., fig. 47, and pl. XIV b. For attempts at decipherment, see H. Grimme, *Muséon*, 49 (1936), 85 ff.; W. F. Albright, *BASOR*, 116 (1949), 12 ff.; Yeivin, *History of the Jewish Script*, I, pp. 63–4, and fig. 13.

70   M.D. (U.) Cassuto, *Orientalia* (n.s.), 16 (1947), 466 ff.; *idem*, *Lᵉshonenu*, 17 (1950–1), 123 ff.

71   Late Canaanite, middle phase: see E. Grant, *Ain-Shems Excavations*, III, Haverford, 1934, p. 27 (§ 12), fig. 2A, and pl. XX (bottom), and the bibliography cited there; cf. also Yeivin, *op. cit.*, I, pp. 71–2, and fig. 15.

72   *Idem*, *Kedem*, 2 (1945), 32 ff., and pl. III, 2 (English summary, p. viii). The knife blade is in the Rockefeller Museum in Jerusalem. For a third inscription recently uncovered at Taanach see D. R. Hillers, *BASOR*, 173 (1964), 45 ff.

73   Cf. Wen-Amon's information on the export of the papyrus from Egypt to Byblos.

74   Cf. also note 59, above.

75   On the 11th century B.C.E. inscriptions from Byblos, see above. On Dunand's impossibly early dating of Shaphatbaal's and Abda's inscriptions (*Byblia Grammata*, pp. 146 ff., and pl. XV), see Maisler (Mazar), *Lᵉshonenu*, 14 (1945–6), 166 ff.; and see below.

76   Cf. also Diringer, *The Alphabet*, pp. 235 ff.; Driver, *op. cit.*, pp. 104 ff.; Yeivin, *History of the Jewish Script*, I, pp. 123 ff.; Cross, Jr., *BASOR*, 134 (1954), 15 ff.; Yeivin, *RB*, 65 (1958), 585 ff.

77   J. T. Milik and F. M. Cross, Jr., *BASOR*, 134 (1954), 5 ff., and figs. 1–2; and see the last two references in note 76.

78   J. T. Milik, *BASOR*, 143 (1956), 3 ff., and fig. 1; and cf. Yeivin, *loc. cit.*

79   Dunand, *op. cit.*, pp. 155 ff., fig. 51, and pl. XIII, 2; on the dating, see the suggestion of Milik, *loc. cit.*; cf. also N. H. Tur-Sinai, *The Language and the Book* (Hebrew), I, Jerusalem, 1948, pp. 32 ff. See also notes 49 and 78, above.

80   At present in the Istanbul Museum. See the latest discussion by Cassuto, *Encyclopaedia Biblica*, II, cols. 471–4, and the full bibliography there. Cf. also D. Diringer, *Le isscrizioni antico-ebraiche palestinesi*, Florence, 1934, pp. 1 ff.; S. Moscati, *Epigrafia ebraica antica*, 1935–1950, Rome, 1951, pp. 8 ff.

CHAPTER IV

THE BIBLE AND ITS HISTORICAL SOURCES

1 Wellhausen gave definitive form to his Documentary theory in his *Prolegomena zur Geschichte Israels*, Berlin, 1883, and gave an account of Israel's history based on his theory in his *Israelitische und jüdische Geschichte*, Berlin, 1894.

2 On the history of critical research of the Bible see, in particular, M. Soloweitchik and S. Rubascheff, *The History of Bible Criticism* (Hebrew), Berlin, 1925; H. F. Hahn, *The OT in Modern Research*, Philadelphia, 1954; H. J. Kraus, *Geschichte der historisch-kritischen Erforschung des AT*, Neukirchen, 1956.

3 The symbols used to denote these Documents are derived from the divine names Jahweh and Elohim in the Book of Genesis, these names being regarded by the Documentary school as the chief means of distinguishing the sources. See C. R. North in *The OT and Modern Study*, ed. by H. H. Rowley, Oxford, 1951, pp. 79 f.; A. Bentzen, *Introduction to the OT* (2nd ed.), Copenhagen, 1952, pp. 27 f.

4 Among these are adherents of the Documentary school, such as G. Hölscher, "Komposition und Ursprung des Deuteronomiums," *ZAW*, 40 (1922), 161–255, who assigns the date of the composition of the Book of Deuteronomy to the period of the Return, while O. Oestreicher, *Das Deuteronomische Grundgesetz*, Gütersloh, 1923, and A. C. Welch, *The Code of Deuteronomy*, London, 1924, as well as others contend that it was composed much earlier than the days of Josiah.

5 In his *A History of the Israelite Faith* (Hebrew), I–IV, Tel-Aviv, 1937 ff.; and in his commentaries on Joshua, Jerusalem, 1959, and Judges, Jerusalem, 1962.

6 That the Priestly Document preceded the Book of Deuteronomy was a view prevalent among biblical critics before Wellhausen, and maintained by several scholars even after his theory was widely accepted. Cf. Kraus, *op. cit.*, p. 262.

7 H. Gunkel wrote neither a comprehensive introduction to the Bible nor a work devoted to an exhaustive statement of his method, the main points of which are set out in the introduction to his commentary on Genesis (*Genesis*, Göttingen, 1910) and in several articles; cf. idem, "Die Grundprobleme der israelitischen Literaturgeschichte," *Reden und Aufsätze*, Göttingen, 1913, pp. 29–38. See also W. Baumgartner, *Zum Alten Testament*, Leiden, 1959, pp. 371 ff.; K. Koch, *Was ist Formgeschichte? Neue Wege der Bibelexegese*, Neukirchen, 1964, *passim*.

8 His most important articles in this field are to be found in his collected studies: A. Alt, *Kleine Schriften*, I–III, Munich, 1953–1959.

9 See M. Noth, *Überlieferungsgeschichtliche Studien*, I, Halle a/S, 1943; idem, *Überlieferungsgeschichte des Pentateuch*, Stuttgart, 1948; idem, *Geschichte Israels* (3rd ed.), Göttingen, 1956; idem, *Gesammelte Studien zum AT*, Munich, 1960; idem, *Die Ursprünge des Alten Israel im Lichte neuer Quellen*, Cologne and Opladen, 1961. Among the scholars of this school is to be included Von Rad who in several instances even influenced Noth's work: see G. von Rad, *Das Formgeschichtliche Problem des Hexateuch*, Stuttgart, 1938; idem, *Theologie des AT*, I: *Die Theologie der geschichtlichen Überlieferungen Israels*, Munich, 1957. See also Hahn, *op. cit.*, pp. 130 ff., 153 ff.

10 The main studies of this school are written in the Scandinavian languages. See the reviews of this theory by G. W. Anderson, "Some Aspects of the Uppsala School of OT Study," *HTR*, 43 (1950), 239–56; North, *op. cit.*, pp. 59 ff.; Bentzen, *op. cit.*, pp. 19 ff.; E. Nielsen, *Oral Tradition*, London, 1954; I. Engnell, "Methodological Aspects of OT Study," *VTS*, 7 (1960), 21 ff. For criticism of the various aspects of the theories of the Scandinavian school, cf. the survey by North, *op. cit.*; and G. Widengren "Oral Tradition and Written Literature," *Acta Orientalia*, 23 (1958), 201 ff.

11 See Kittel, *GVI* 5/6; W. F. Albright, *From the Stone Age to Christianity*, Baltimore,

1940; *idem, The Biblical Period*, New York, 1963; and J. Bright, *A History of Israel*, London, 1960, who is also an adherent of the Albright school.

12 On oral tradition, see Albright, *From the Stone Age to Christianity*, pp. 33–43; E. Jacob, *La tradition historique en Israël*, Montpellier, 1946, pp. 16–43; R. C. Culley, "An Approach to the Problem of Oral Tradition," *VT*, 13 (1963), 113–25; and especially the works of scholars belonging to the Uppsala school. See Nielsen, *op. cit.*, which has additional bibliography. Serious reservations must however be entertained regarding the exaggerated importance attributed by this school to oral tradition in the formation of biblical literature. Cf. Widengren, *loc. cit.*; A. H. J. Gunneweg, *Mündliche und schriftliche Tradition*, Göttingen, 1959.

13 See Gunkel, *Genesis*, pp. XV ff.; Bentzen, *op. cit.*, pp. 235 ff.; O. Eissfeldt, *Einleitung in das AT* (3rd ed.), Tübingen, 1964, pp. 50 ff.; J. L. Seeligmann, "Aetiological Elements in Biblical Historiography" (Hebrew), *Zion*, 26 (1961), 141–69.

14 So, for example, A. Alt, "Josua", *BZAW*, 66 (1936), 13–29; M. Noth, *Das Buch Joshua* (2nd ed.), Tübingen, 1953; Noth later moderated to some extent his approach; cf. M. Noth, "Der Beitrag der Archäologie zur Geschichte Israels," *VTS*, 7 (1960), 278 ff. For a critical study of this approach, see W. F. Albright, *BASOR*, 74 (1939), 12 ff.; Y. Kaufmann, *The Biblical Account of the Conquest of Palestine* (trans. from the Hebrew), Jerusalem, 1953, pp. 64 ff., 70 ff.; J. Bright, *Early Israel in Recent History Writing*, London, 1956, pp. 79 ff.; and cf. also B. S. Childs, *JBL*, 82 (1963), 279–92.

15 Cf. Isa. 27:1; 51:9–10; Hab. 3; Ps. 74:13–15; 89:10–11; Job. 7:12; etc. See M. D. (U.) Cassuto, "The Epic in Israel" (Hebrew), *Kᵉnesset*, 8 (1944), 121–42.

16 Cassuto attempted to prove, on the basis of fragmentary mythological elements and stylistic criteria in the pentateuchal stories, that Israel also had a national-historical epic in comprehensive compositions. Cassuto based his argument in particular on the passages dealing with the

Exodus: see his "The Rise of Historiography in Israel" (Hebrew), *Eretz Israel*, 1 (1951), 85 ff.

17 Solomon's words at the consecration of the Temple: "The Lord hath said that He would dwell in the thick darkness. I have surely built thee a house of habitation, a place for thee to dwell in for ever" (I Kings 8:12–13) are followed in the Septuagint by the sentence: "Is not this written in the book of the Song?" (*ha-Shir*), a sentence which does not, however, occur in the Masoretic text. Some scholars have suggested that "the book of the Song" is none other than the book of Jashar (so, for example, in *Biblia Hebraica* [3rd ed.], *ad loc.*, and that accordingly the book of Jashar also contained a psalm on the consecration of the Temple from the days of Solomon. It seems more probable that the book of Jashar and the book of the Song (if the addition in the Septuagint is indeed based on a Hebrew text that was at the disposal of the translator) are two different compositions, especially since the book of Jashar had as its theme war and heroic exploits, whereas the book of the Song contained psalms and hymns.

18 On Ps. 83, see B. Maisler (Mazar), "The Historical Background of Psalm 83" (Hebrew), *BIES*, 4 (1937), 47–51; on Ps. 68, see M. D. (U.) Cassuto, "Psalm 68" (Hebrew), *Tarbiz*, 12 (1941), 1–27; Albright has sought to explain this psalm as a collection of the opening passages of some thirty ancient psalms and hymns: see W. F. Albright, "A Catalogue of Early Hebrew Lyric Poems [Psalm 68]," *HUCA*, 23 (1951), 1–40.

19 These psalms are also important in elucidating the processes of the oral transmission of biblical stories, since the schemata of the Exodus and of the Israelites' wandering in the wilderness, imbedded in these psalms, are independent of the pentateuchal account. Cf. A. Jirku, *Die älteste Geschichte Israels im Rahmen lehrhafter Darstellungen*, Leipzig, 1917, pp. 104 ff.; S. E. Loewenstamm, *The Tradition of the Exodus in its Development* (Hebrew), Jerusalem, 1965. On the date of Ps. 78, see also O. Eissfeldt, *Das Lied Moses . . . und das Lehr-*

gedicht Asaphs, Berlin, 1958; Loewenstamm, *op. cit.*, pp. 26–30. Ps. 81 and Ps. 95 probably belong to this type of psalm (see S. E. Loewenstamm, "The Bearing of Psalm 81 upon the Problem of Exodus" [Hebrew], *Eretz Israel*, 5 [1959], 80–2) since they also mention events connected with the Exodus as evidence of God's loving-kindness towards His people, and likewise ascribe the nation's moral deterioration to its rebelliousness against God's command-ments. All these psalms have, therefore, to be considered as independent sources, alongside the pentateuchal stories, of the popular tradition on these events.

20 On the genealogical lists in general see the chapter "The Israelite Tribes", sections F ff., in the next volume of this series.

21 See A. Alt, "Das System der Stam-mesgrenzen im Buche Josua," *Kleine Schrif-ten*, I, pp. 193–202; and see the chapter "The Settlement of the Israelite Tribes," in the next volume of this series.

22 See Kaufmann, *op. cit.*, pp. 40 ff.; *idem*, Commentary on Joshua, pp. 270 ff.

23 Scholars nevertheless differ on the exact significance and date of these lists. On the lists in Josh. 13–19, see A. Alt, "Judas Gaue unter Josia," *Kleine Schriften*, II, pp. 276–88; F. M. Cross and G. E. Wright, "The Boundary and Province lists of the Kingdom of Judah," *JBL*, 75 (1956), 202–26; Z. Kallai-Kleinman, "The Town Lists of Judah, Simeon, Benjamin and Dan," *VT*, 8 (1958), 134–60; Y. Aharoni, "The Province-List of Judah," *ibid.*, 9 (1959), 225–40. On the lists of the priestly and levitical cities in Josh. 21, see S. Klein, "The Cities of the Priests and Levites and the Cities of Refuge" (Hebrew), *Journal of the Jewish Palestine Exploration Society*, Jeru-salem, 1934–35, pp. 81–107; M. Haran, "The Levitical Cities: Utopia and Historical Reality" (Hebrew), *Tarbiz*, 27 (1958) 421–39; W. F. Albright, "List of Levitic Cities," *L. Ginzberg Jubilee Volume*, New York, 1945, pp. 49–73; B. Mazar, "The Cities of the Priests and the Levites," *VTS*, 7 (1960), 193–205.

24 On this list, see also B. Mazar, *Encyclo-paedia Biblica* (Hebrew), II, Jerusalem, 1954, cols. 144–5, "Numbers 33."

25 This pragmatic historical conception is also found in the schema of the beginnings of Israelite history in Ps. 78 and Ps. 106, which likewise originated in the period of the Judges. See section F, above. Such a conception found emphatic expression in Deut. 32, which, as its contents suggest, was composed at a time of oppression for Israel. This is also to be assigned to the days of the Judges, to a time of Canaanite oppression before the war of Deborah, according to M. D. (U.) Cassuto (*Encyclopaedia Biblica*, II, cols. 615–7, s.v. Deuteronomy 32), or of Philistine oppression, according to Eissfeldt (*op. cit.*).

CHAPTER V

THE CHRONOLOGY OF THE ANCIENT NEAR EAST IN THE SECOND MILLENNIUM B.C.E.

[1] F. X. Kugler, *Sternkunde und Sterndienst in Babylonien*, II/2, Münster, 1912, pp. 255 ff.; S. Langdon and J. K. Fotheringham, *The Venus Tablets of Ammizaduqa*, Oxford, 1928; O. Neugebauer, *OLZ*, 32 (1929), 913 ff.; 42 (1939), 407 ff.; *JAOS*, 61 (1941), 58 ff.

[2] For a detailed survey of the discoveries and different views (up to 1950), see A. Parrot, *Archéologie mésopotamienne*, II, Paris, 1953, pp. 333–451.

[3] H. Ranke, *The Babylonian Expedition of the University of Pennsylvania*, Series A, VI, I, Philadelphia, 1906, no. 26 (= M. Schorr, *Urkunden des Altbabylonischen Zivil — und Prozessrechts*, Leipzig, 1913, no. 284). The chronological significance of the date was correctly appreciated by Ed. Meyer, *Geschichte des Altertums*, 2 Aufl., 1 Bd., pp. 563. Cf. also E. Weidner, *MVAG* 1915, no. 4, 20–21; and J. Lewy, *ZA* 37 (1929), 97, 100.

[4] See E. Sollberger, *AfO*, 17 (1954/6), 48.

[5] The suggestions in the order of publication are as follows: W. F. Albright, *BASOR*, 77 (1940); A. Ungnad, *AfO*, 13 (1940), 145 ff.; F. Thureau-Dangin, *Mémoires de l'Académie des Inscriptions et Belles-Lettres*, 43 (1942), 229 ff.; W. F. Albright, *BASOR*, 88 (1942), 28 ff.; 99 (1945), 9 ff.; F. Cornelius, *Klio*, 35 (1942), 1 ff.; F. M. Th. de Liagre Böhl, *King Hammurabi of Babylon in the Setting of his Time*, [= *Med. der Kon. Ned. Akad. van Wetensch*, Niew Reeks, 9, no. 10], Amsterdam, 1946; E. Weidner, *AfO*, 15 (1945–1951), 85 ff.; K. Schubert, *WZKM*, 51 (1952), 21 ff.; A. Goetze, *BASOR*, 122 (1951), 18 ff.; B. Landsberger, *JCS*, 8 (1954), 31 ff.; 47 ff.; 106 ff.; and see note 2, above.

[6] These fragments were published by O. Schroeder and edited by E. Weidner, *MVAG*, 20 (1915), no. 4; 26 (1921), no. 2. The list *KAV* 14 has been treated by B. Landsberger (*JCS*, 8 [1954], 31), who has shown that it derived from a different

tradition, independent of the canonical king-list *KAV* 216 (re-publication: E. Weidner, *AfO*, 3 [1926], 70–1), is of a different type. Its compilers recorded the Assyrian and opposite them the Babylonian kings, without indicating their regnal years. This list is valuable for the several synchronisms between the kings of Assyria and Babylonia, particularly during the "dark ages" (in the 16th-15th centuries). For the "Nassouhi king-list", copied in the days of Ashurdan II (934–912), see Essad Nassouhi, *AfO*, 4 (1928), 1 ff.; E. Weidner, *ibid.*, 11 ff.

[7] A. Poebel, *JNES*, 1 (1942), 247 ff.; 460 ff.; 2 (1943), 56 ff.; I. J. Gelb, *ibid.*, 13 (1954), 209 ff.

[8] See Th. Jacobsen, *The Sumerian King List*, Chicago, 1939 (= *Assyriological Studies*, 11), p. 192; A. Poebel, *JNES*, 2 (1943), 71 ff.; M.B. Rowton, *Iraq*, 9 (1946), 98 ff.; *JNES*, 18 (1959), 220.

[9] For the view that the chronicles, rather than the eponym lists, were the main source of the Assyrian king-list, see B. Landsberger, *JCS*, 8 (1954), 33–35; 109–111.

[10] These fragments are: 1) VAT 13056 published by E. Weidner in *AfO*, 20 (1963), 115–116, describing the war between Enlil-nirari (no. 74 in the Assyrian king-list) and Kurigalzu II of Babylon; 2) VAT 10281 published by E. Weidner in *AfO*, 4 (1927), 213–217, describing the wars between Ashur-resh-ishi (no. 86) and Ninurta-nadin-shumi of Babylon; 3) VAT 10453 + 10465 published by E. Weidner in *AfO*, 17 (1954–56), 384 and edited by H. Tadmor in *JNES*, 17 (1958), 133–134, relating events in Assyria and Babylonia during the reign of Tiglath-pileser I (no. 87). Though essentially Assyrian in origin and spirit, these chronicles also relate the major events in Babylonia, and therefore should rather be called the "Synchronistic Chronicles."

11   B. Landsberger, *JCS*, 8 (1954), 34–35; I. J. Gelb, *JNES*, 13 (1954), 224.

12   Gelb, *ibid.*, p. 226.

13   Cf. the "Enlil-nirari Chronicle" (above, note 10) which apparently dates the war between Assyria and Babylonia to a *limmu*-year of Șilli-Adad.

14   E.g. the "Tiglath-pileser I Chronicle," line 9 (above, note 10): "Marduk-nadin-ahhe reigned for 18 years."

15   Evidence to support the suggestion that the chronicles served as a source for the Assyrian royal annals in the 14th–11th centuries is presented by the writer in a paper read before the 5th World Congress of Jewish Studies in Jerusalem, July 1965: "The Beginnings of Assyrian Historiography" (to be published).

16   For the meaning of *țuppu* in the king-list, see B. Landsberger, *JNES*, 8 (1949), 265 ff.; *JCS*, 8 (1954), 111–4; M.B. Rowton, *JNES*, 10 (1951), 197 ff.; *ibid.*, 18 (1959), 213 ff.

17   On fragment KAV 15, see details in Landsberger, *JCS*, 8 (1954), 31, 36; H. Lewy, *Mélanges Isidore Lévy*, Brussels, 1955, p. 264, note 2.

18   E. Weidner, *AfO*, 15 (1945–51), 96 ff.; Landsberger, *JCS*, 8 (1954), 31 ff.; H. Lewy, *loc. cit.*

19   According to Landsberger (*JCS*, 8 [1954], 43, 106, note 190 [b]); W. F. Albright (in *BASOR*, 88 [1942], 31) restores [24] years. The conjecture of A. Poebel (*JNES*, 1 [1942], 293), that $x = 0$, is improbable.

20   E. Ebeling, B. Meissner and E. Weidner, *Die Inschriften der alt-assyrischen Könige*, Leipzig, 1926, p. 120, lines 33 ff. (= D. D. Luckenbill, *Ancient Records of Assyria and Babylonia*, I, § 119), p. 162, lines 5 ff.

21   E. Weidner, *Die Inschriften Tukulti-Ninurtas I* (*AfO*, Beiheft 12), Graz, 1959, no. 7, lines 21 ff. (= Luckenbill, *op. cit.*, § 186), and cf. A. Poebel, *JNES*, 2 (1943), 299, and E. Weidner, *AfO*, 15 (1945–1951), 94.

22   E. A. W. Budge and L. W. King, *Annals of the Kings of Assyria*, London, 1902, p. 95, lines 60 ff. (= Luckenbill, *op. cit.*, §§ 259–60).

23   There is no reason to accept only Tiglath-pileser's evidence and to reject the statement of Shalmaneser (so, for example, M. B. Rowton, *JNES*, 17 [1958], 108–9). Rowton's assumption that the scribes of Tiglath-pileser I had at their disposal a continuous and complete *limmu*-list — from the days of Shamshi-Adad I onwards — on which they based their exact calculations, is not likely. It does not tally with the fact that in the canonical Assyrian king-list, which according to Rowton was excerpted from the very same continuous and complete *limmu*-list, there is a gap (which is z; see A 2, above), for the period after Shamshi-Adad. One must admit that the exact nature of the sources for the chronological statements in the inscriptions of the Middle Assyrian kings is, as yet, incompletely known.

24   E. Borger, *Die Inschriften Asarhaddons* (*AfO*, Beiheft no. 9), 1956, p. 3, col. III, 16 ff. (= Luckenbill, *op. cit.*, II, § 706).

25   See Landsberger, *JCS*, 8 (1954), 40–1; and cf. J. Lewy, *ZA*, 37 (1929), 103–5; Rowton, *JNES*, 17 (1958), 109.

26   King-list A: C. J. Gadd, *Cuneiform Texts etc. in the British Museum*, London, 1931, p. 36, pls. 24–5. The list has been cleaned in the British Museum laboratories, and several numbers — in the defective parts of the list — can be read somewhat differently from Gadd. (See now A. K. Grayson, *lišān mitḫurti* [W. von Soden Festschrift] Neukirchen–Vluyn, 1969, 106 ff.) King-list B: for a reproduction, see P. Rost, *MVAG*, 2 (1987), no. 2, pl. I. For an explanation of the exaggerated number of regnal years attributed to the kings of the Second Dynasty, see A. Poebel, *Miscellaneous Studies* (*Assyriological Studies*, 14), Chicago, 1947, pp. 110 ff. King-list C: A. Poebel, *The Second Dynasty of Isin according to a New King-List Tablet* (*Assyriological Studies*, 15), Chicago, 1955.

27   See, for example, W. F. Albright, *BASOR*, 69 (1938), 19; and cf. Landsberger, *JCS*, 8 (1954), 45, note 65; 70, note 181.

28   Cf. Rowton, *JNES*, 17 (1958), 100.

29   F. Thureau-Dangin, *Journal asiatique*, 1909/II, 154 ff.; *idem*, *RA*, 33 (1936), 53 ff.; Goetze, *JCS*, 11 (1957), 63–4.

30   According to Landsberger (*JCS*, 8 [1954), 65, note 160), this inscription is apocryphal, but see Rowton, *JNES*, 17 (1958), 103. See also Goetze, *JCS*, 11 (1957), 65.

31   H. G. Güterbock, *ZA*, 42 (1934), 79 ff.; W. F. Albright, *BASOR*, 126 (1952), 25, note 3; Goetze, *JCS*, 18 (1964), 98.

32   Gulkishar (see B 6) may have reigned several years in the city of Babylon after the end of the First Dynasty and before the Kassite Agum II seized control of it (Goetze, *JCS*, 11 [1957,] 66).

33   *The Babylonian Expedition of the University of Pennsylvania*, I, no. 83; cf. Landsberger, *JCS*, 8 (1954), 70, note 181; Goetze, *ibid.*, 11 (1957), 66, note 130.

34   S. Langdon, *Die Neubabylonische Königsinschriften* (= *Vorderasiatische Bibliothek*, 4), Leipzig, 1912, pp. 228, 238. On these traditions, see F. Schmidtke, *Die Welt des Orients*, 1 (1947), 51 ff.

35   G. Dossin, *Syria*, 32 (1955), 1 ff.; *ARM*, I, no. 3.

36   *Idem*, in *Studia Mariana*, Leiden, 1950, pp. 51–61; and see Landsberger, *JCS*, 8 (1954), 39, note 44.

37   For the present state of the problem, see W. Röllig in *La civilisation de Mari* (ed. J. R. Kupper) (= *Compte Rendu de la XVᵉ Rencontre Assyriologique Internationale* [= *Bibliothèque de la Faculté de Philosophie et Lettres de l'Université de Liège*, CLXXXII]), Paris, 1967, pp. 97–102 (cf. also H. Lewy, *ibid.*, pp. 25–26).

38   T. Baqir, *Sumer*, 5 (1948), 84–6.

39   Landsberger, *loc. cit.;* H. Lewy, *Die Welt des Orients*, 2 (1959), 438 ff.; W. F. Leemans, in *Foreign Trade in the Old Babylonian Period*, Leiden, 1960, pp. 176–181, tends to lower the date of Shamshi-Adad's death to Hammurabi's 14th year, but the earlier date seems historically preferable.

40   D. J. Wiseman, *The Alalakh Tablets*, London, 1953, pp. 2–3.

41   The existence of two kings by the name of Ammitaqum is suggested by F. Cornelius, *Revue hittite et asianique*, 66 (1960), 22.

42   See Landsberger, *JCS*, 8 (1954), 51 ff.; Goetze, *BASOR*, 146 (1957), 20 ff.; *JCS*, 11 (1957), 68 ff.; W. F. Albright, *BASOR*, 146 (1957), 27; W. Nagel and E. Strommenger,

JCS, 12 (1958), 109 ff.; M. B. Rowton, *CAH* (rev. ed.), I, chap. VI, p. 43; and especially the very detailed and sound discussion of H. Klengel, *Geschichte Syriens im 2. Jahrtausend v. u. Z.* Teil I, *Nordsyrien*, Berlin, 1965, pp. 102–174; 203–218. It is impossible to accept the complicated and radically different theory proposed by S. Smith (*Alalakh and Chronology*, London, 1940, pp. 31 f.; *Anatolian Studies*, 6 [1957], 173 ff.), and followed by D. J. Wiseman (see above, note 40) and L. Woolley (*A Forgotten Kingdom*, Harmondsworth, 1953, pp. 66 ff.), that stratum VII at Alalakh was contemporaneous with the Mari Age: that is, the days of Yarim-lim I and Hammurabi I, kings of Yamhad, Shamshi-Adad I of Assyria, and Hammurabi I of Babylon.

43   Wiseman, *Alalakh*, no. 6, line 27; Landsberger, *JCS*, 8 (1954), 52; O. R. Gurney, *CAH* (rev. ed.), I, chap. 6, (= fasc. no. 11), 1962, pp. 18–19.

44   Goetze, *JCS*, 11 (1957), 70, notes 185–186; Gurney, *op. cit.*, p. 19.

45   Rowton, *op. cit.*, p. 44. Alalakh was destroyed by Hattusilis I (H. Otten, *MDOG*, 91 [1958], 78); however, Aleppo was not captured by him but by Mursilis, his successor, some dozen years later; and cf. Gurney, *op. cit., loc. cit.*

46   No contemporary documents concerning this major historical synchronism have been discovered. A later text — "The Proclamation of Telepinus" (a fifth king after Mursilis) – describes it in the following manner "And he (i.e. Mursilis) went to Aleppo and destroyed Aleppo and brought captives and goods of Aleppo to Ḫattushash. But afterwards he went to Babylon and destroyed Babylon. Also the Hurrians he defeated and he kept captives and goods of Babylon in Ḫattushash" (translation by H. G. Güterbock, *Journal of World History*, 2 [1954], 385).

47   H. Otten, *MDOG*, 83 (1951), 62 ff.; K. A. Kitchen, *Suppiluliuma and the Amarna Pharaohs*, Liverpool, 1962, pp. 52 ff. It should be noted that the evidence provided by these lists is often puzzling. Sometimes the lists contradict each other and in some instances they omit one or several kings known from other sources. On the

other hand, the lists also mention princes who never reigned; cf. next note.

48   A. Goetze, *BASOR*, 122 (1951), 18 ff.; *JCS*, 11 (1957), 55 ff.; a more critical opinion on the chronological value of these lists was recently expressed by H. Otten, "Die hethitischen historischen Quellen und die altorientalische Chronologie", *Abhandlungen der Akademie der Wissenschaften und der Literatur, Geistes- und sozialwissenschaftlichen Klasse*, Jahrgang 1968, no. 3, 101 ff. According to Otten, the evidence of the offering lists tallies with the lower chronology (cf. also Otten, *MDOG*, 83 [1951], 60). The same opinion was for a time held by Rowton, *BASOR*, 126 (1952), 20 ff. Cf. also F. Cornelius, *AfO*, 17 (1956), 302 ff., but see the critical remarks of A. Goetze, in *JCS*, 22 (1968), 46 ff.

49   M. B. Rowton, *JNES*, 17 (1958), 105–7.

50   M. E. L. Mallowan, *Iraq*, 4 (1937), 29 ff.; 9 (1947), 20 ff.

51   Helene J. Kantor, *JNES*, 15 (1956), 158a, note 22.

52   Cf. W. Nagel–Eva Strommenger, *JCS*, 12 (1958), 119 ff.

53   S. Smith, *American Journal of Archaeology*, 49 (1945), 1 ff.; F. Matz, *Historia*, 1 (1950), 182; W. F. Albright, *BASOR*, 127 (1952), 30; A. Parrot, *Archéologie mésopotamienne*, II, pp. 397 ff.; Rowton, *JNES*, 17 (1958), 99.

54   See Albright, *BASOR*, 127 (1952), 30, note 9: Landsberger, *JCS*, 8 (1954), 119.

55   G. Dossin, *Syria*, 20 (1939), 109.

56   See J. Wilson, *The Burden of Egypt*, Chicago, 1951, p. 134; and W. A. Ward, *Orientalia* (n.s.), 30 (1961), 22 ff., 129 ff.; J. van Seters, *The Hyksos: A New Investigation*, New Haven-London, 1966, pp. 73–81. In support of the lower chronology it has been suggested that *'ntn*, a Byblos prince of the period of Nefer-hotep I, who according to Albright's system reigned from 1740–1730, be identified with Yantin-hammu of Byblos who is known from the Mari Letters (W. F. Albright, *BASOR*, 99 [1945], 9 ff.; 176 [1964], 38–44). But since the Mari Letters which mention this king have not been published yet, one does not know exactly whether Yantin-hammu lived in the days of Shamshi-Adad or in those of Zimri-lim. There are also divergent views as regards the date of Nefer-hotep I, some scholars assigning him to 1750–1740 or even earlier; see for example H. Stock, *Studien zur Geschichte und Archaeologie der 13. bis 17. Dynastie Ägyptens*, Glückstadt, 1942, p. 62; T. Säve-Söderbergh, *JEA*, 37 (1951), 54, note 1; but cf. note 61 below. If Albright is correct in his identification and in the date he assigns to Nefer-hotep I, then Yantin-hammu reigned for at least 35 years, that is, from ca. 1765 to 1730. He was apparently preceded by Yakin-ilu prince of Byblos, who is known from the days of the king Sehetibre of the Thirteenth Dynasty (Albright, *BASOR*, 99 [1945] 11, note 5); W. C. Hayes, *CAH*, (rev. ed.), II, chap. 2, p. 6. Cf. now also B. Mazar, *IEJ*, 18 (1968), 85 ff.

57   G. Farina, *Il papiro dei re; restaurato*, Roma, 1938; A. H. Gardiner, *The Royal Canon of Turin*, Oxford, 1959.

58   Ed. Meyer, *Ägyptische Chronologie*, Berlin, 1904, pp. 57 f.; W. G. Wadell, *Manetho* (Loeb Classical Library), London, 1940, pp. 67 ff.; and note 64, below.

59   R. A. Parker, *The Calendars of Ancient Egypt*, Chicago, 1950, pp. 63 ff. For the reigns of its individual kings — some of them coregents in their fathers' lifetimes — see W. F. Edgerton, *JNES*, 1 (1942), 307 ff.; and Parker, *op. cit.*, p. 89.

60   See note 56, above. On the Thirteenth Dynasty, see Hayes, *op. cit.*, pp. 5 ff.; and for details J. von Beckerath, *Untersuchungen zur politischen Geschichte der zweiten Zwischenzeit in Ägypten*, Glückstadt, 1964. According to von Beckerath, Nefer-hotep reigned from 1741 to 1730.

61   See J. A. Wilson, in *ANET*, pp. 252–253; T. Säve-Söderbergh, *JEA*, 37 (1951), 62–63; van Seters, *The Hyksos*, pp. 97–103; and most recently H. Goedicke, *Chronique d'Egypte*, 41 (1966), 23–39; W. Helck, *ibid.*, 234–241; G. A. Gabela – K. A. Kitchen, *ibid.*, 43 (1962), 259–263.

On the relation between Avaris, Tanis and Pi-Ramses see now: van Seters, *The Hyksos*, pp. 127 ff.; E. Uphill *JNES* 27 (1968), 291 ff.; 28 (1969), 15 ff.

62   See L. Habachi, *Annales du Service des*

Antiquités, 53 (1955), 195 ff.; W. Helck, *Die Beziehungen Ägyptens zu Vorderasien im 3. und 2. Jahrtausend v. Chr.*, Wiesbaden, 1962, p. 113; T. G. H. James, *CAH* (rev. ed.), II, chap. 7 (= fasc. no. 34), 1965, pp. 3–8.

63   On the chronology of the Hyksos kings of Egypt (the Fifteenth-Sixteenth Dynasties), see Sir Alan Gardiner, *Egypt of the Pharaohs*, Oxford, 1961, pp. 155 ff.; Hayes, *CAH* (rev. ed.), I, chap. 6 (= fasc. no. 4), 1962, pp. 15 ff.; II, chap. 2 (= fasc. no. 6), 1962, pp. 19 ff.; von Beckerath, *op. cit.* (see above, note 60), pp. 218–224, dates the Fifteenth Dynasty to 1652–1544 and the Sixteenth Dynasty to 1650–1550. These dates, however, as well as that of Ka-mose (according to his system: 1560–1554), are based on the lower set of dates for the Eighteenth Dynasty; and see in detail section B 1 below.

64   For a comprehensive discussion of the astronomical data and the evidence from Manetho, see Ed. Meyer, *Ägyptische Chronologie*, Berlin, 1904, pp. 45–68; 88–103. A new analysis of the evidence from Manetho relating to the Eighteenth-Twentieth Dynasties and its comparison with the data contained in the documents themselves has been made by Helck, *Untersuchungen zu Manetho und den ägyptischen Königslisten*, Berlin, 1956, pp. 65 ff. (hereafter: Helck, *Unt. Man.*).

65 *Iraq*, 8 (1946), 94 ff.; *JEA*, 34 (1948), 57 ff.; *JNES*, 18 (1959), 213 ff.; *JCS*, 13 (1959), 1 ff.; *JNES*, 19 (1960), 15 ff.; 25 (1966), 240 ff.

66   L. Borchardt and P. V. Neugebauer, *OLZ*, 30 (1929), 445 ff.; L. Borchardt, *Die Mittel zur zeitlichen Festlegung von Punkten der ägyptischen Geschichte und ihre Anwendung*, Cairo, 1935, pp. 19–29. Borchardt preferred 1537, the lowest date, and is followed in it by W. C. Hayes in *CAH* (rev. ed.), I, ch. 6 (fasc. no. 4), p. 17; and II, ch. IX (fasc. no. 10, pt. 1), p. 5. But see W. F. Edgerton, *AJSL*, 53 (1937), 188 ff.; R. A. Parker, *Calendars of Ancient Egypt*, p. 76, n. 85; and *Revue d'Égyptologie*, 9 (1952), 101 ff., suggests 1540/42. Sir Alan Gardiner (*Egypt of the Pharaohs*, Oxford, 1961, p. 443) seems to have accepted this latter and assigns Amen-hotep I to 1550–1528.

67   This possibility, which is still far from being proven, has recently been suggested by a number of German Egyptologists — most of them protagonists of the lower chronology for the Old Babylonian period and of the lower dating of the Eighteenth and Nineteenth Dynasties (see table V): W. Helck, *Die Beziehungen Ägyptens zu Vorderasien im 3. und 2. Jahrtausend v. Chr.*, Wiesbaden, 1962, p. 224; H. Stock, *MDOG*, 94 (1963), 78–80; E. Hornung, *Untersuchungen zur Chronologie und Geschichte des neuen Reiches*, Wiesbaden, 1964, pp. 15–23. See, however, the critical remarks of K. A. Kitchen, *Chronique d'Égypte*, 40 (1965), 310 ff.; and E. Uphill, *Bibliotheca Orientalis*, 23 (1966), 33 ff. See also R. A. Parker, quoted by W. F. Albright, *Bibliotheca Orientalis*, 21 (1964), note 1; D. N. Redford, *JNES*, 25 (1966), 124.

68   For the evidence on the length of reign of Ah-mose and Amen-hotep I, see recently Hornung, *op. cit.*, pp. 31 ff.; and Redford, *op. cit.*, pp. 114–119. The regnal years of the first two Thut-moses are problematic. The highest known regnal year of Thut-mose I is his 9th, and of Thut-mose II, his 18th. The authenticity, however, of this latter has been challenged by a number of scholars; see Redford, *ibid.*, p. 117. If Thut-mose I is identified with Manetho's "Mephres" and Thut-mose II with his "Chebron" (Josephus, *Contra Apionem*, I, 15 = Wadell, *op. cit.*, p. 101), then these two kings should be credited with 12 years and 9 months, and 13 years, respectively, though Helck and Hornung (*op. cit.*, p. 33) emend "13" to "3"; Redford, on the basis of some new evidence (*op. cit.*, p. 118), suggests a reign of 11 years for Thut-mose II.

69   *JEA*, 28 (1942), 4 ff.

70   *JNES*, 16 (1957), 40–42. However, Hayes in *CAH* (rev. ed.), I, chap. 6 (= fasc. no. 4), p. 17, note 5, suggests that "source errors of equal gravity have to be assumed in the case of either date" (i.e. also in the case of the second lunar date), and therefore he does not accept Parker's verdict against 1504.

71   For the evidence on the length of their reigns, see Kitchen, *op. cit.* (see above,

note 67), pp. 5 ff.; Hornung, *Untersuchungen, etc.,* pp. 33 ff.; and the literature quoted by Redford, *JNES,* 25 (1966), 119–122.

72   See. A. H. Gardiner, *JEA,* 31 (1945), 27; Helck, *Unt. Man.,* p. 66. The hypothesis of the coregency solves the contradiction between the dates of Amada and the Memphis stelae; see Wilson, *ANET,* p. 245, note 1; and S. Yeivin, *JARCE,* 6 (1967), 119–120. On the whole problem in detail, see Redford, *JEA,* 51 (1965), 107–122. Most recently, a new lunar date for the 19th year of Amen-hotep II was brought to attention by Hornung (*ZDMG,* 111 [1967], 11–16), followed by von Beckerath (*ZDMG,* 118 [1968], 18–21). Accordingly, Amen-hotep II came to the throne either in 1439 (= after a coregency of two years and 4 months) or in 1437 (= after a coregency of 4 months). Both scholars follow the lower date for Thut-mose III.

73   C. Aldred, *ZÄS,* 94 (1967), 1–6; *idem, Akhenaten,* 1967, pp. 100 ff. Aldred suggests that coregency was the normal practice in the Eighteenth Dynasty, and that it existed in every reign, with the possible exceptions of Thut-mose IV and Tut-ankh-Amon.

74   See K, Seele, *JNES,* 14 (1955), 172 f.; C. Aldred, *Akhenaten,* p. 244. An independent three-year reign for Smekh-ka-Re is assumed by Sir Alan Gardiner, *op. cit.,* pp. 232–233; 443; and see the detailed discussion of D. N. Redford, *History and Chronology of the Eighteenth Dynasty of Egypt,* Toronto, 1967, pp. 170 ff.

75   For a critical analysis of the conflicting views, see E. F. Campbell Jr., *The Chronology of the Amarna Letters,* Baltimore, 1964 (which gives the bibliography). If it could be proven that Tut-ankh-Amon — who reigned 10 years, and died as a young man (at any rate, before reaching 20) — was indeed a son of Amen-hotep III, as suggested by Aldred (*Akhenaten,* p. 98), the case for a coregency would here have a decisive argument. A strong case for the coregency has been presented by K. A. Kitchen, *Suppiluliuma and the Amarna Pharaohs,* Liverpool, 1962, and Aldred, *Akhenaten,* pp. 104–116 (see also Kitchen, *Chronique d'Égypte,* 40 [1965], 319; 43 [1968], 315–

320; *JEA,* 53 [1967], 128–182). Against the coregency are Hornung, *Untersuchungen,* pp. 71 ff.; and especially Redford, *op. cit.* (see above, note 73), pp. 88 ff. (but cf. now E. F. Wente, *JNES,* 28 [1969] 273 ff.).

76   K. Seele, *JNES,* 14 (1955), 175, suggests that Akh-en-Aton reigned 21 years, but see H. W. Fairman, *JEA,* 46 (1960), 108; and Redford, *JNES,* 25 (1966), 121.

77   K. A. Kitchen, *Suppiluliuma and the Amarna Pharaohs,* Liverpool, 1962.

78   Cf. Redford, *JNES,* 25 (1966), 122–123. Redford assigns to Hor-em-heb the ostraca from el-Amarna bearing the dates of the 28th and 30th years of an unknown ruler.

79   A. H. Gardiner, *The inscription of Mes,* Leipzig, 1905, p. 122, note 72; Borchardt, *Mittel, etc.,* p. 85, note 5, suggested to read "58th" year, but Gardiner, and recently Redford (*JNES,* 25 [1966], 123), reaffirmed the reading "59th".

80   Cf. A. R. Schulman, *JARCE,* 3 (1964), 68–69.

81   *JEA,* 54 (1968), 95–99.

82   It is not impossible that the scribe of that particular Akkadian letter (for which see B. Landsberger's remark, *apud* K. Balkan, *Belleten,* 12 [1948], 749) wrote Niphururia instead of the correct Naphururia — Akh-en-aton's regular name in the el-Amarna correspondence with Burnaburiash. Completely different a problem is the identity of the addressee of El-Amarna Letter no. 9 with "Niphururiaš" — a late contemporary of Shuppiluliuma I, according to Hittite documents — see E. Edel, *JNES,* 7 (1947), 14 f.; J. Vergote, *Toutankh-amoun dans les archives hittites,* Istanbul, 1961; but cf. Campbell, *op. cit.,* pp. 56 ff.; Redford, *History and Chronology of the Eighteenth Dynasty,* pp. 158 ff.

83   R. Parker, *JNES,* 16 (1957), 42–43.

84   Hornung, *Untersuchungen,* pp. 50–51; Redford, *op. cit.,* pp. 183 ff. — both in favor of 1290. However, Rowton's arguments in favor of 1304 (*JNES,* 19 [1960], 15 ff.; 25 [1966], 240 ff.) have been accepted by some Egyptologists, e.g. Hayes, *CAH* (rev. ed.), I, chap. 6 (fasc. no. 4), p. 19; Aldred, *Akhenaten,* p. 261; Harris, *JEA,* 54 (1968), 99. In this connection, it should

be noted that the low dates given by Helck for the Eighteenth-Nineteenth Dynasties (in *Beziehungen*), followed by several other scholars, are based on Rowton's earlier studies (*JEA*, 34 [1948], 57 ff.), the conclusions of which for the chronology of the Nineteenth Dynasty have subsequently been revised by him.

85 The letter found at Bogazköy was published in *Keilschrifttexte aus Boghazköi* (= *KBo*), I, no. 10; translated by D. D. Luckenbill, *AJSL*, 37 (1924/5), pp. 200 ff.

86 M. B. Rowton, *JEA*, 34 (1948), 67–70; H. Tadmor, *JNES*, 17 (1958), 139; and E. Edel, *JCS*, 12 (1958), 130 ff., where the pertinent lines are translated.

87 Rowton (*JNES*, 19 [1960], 16–18; 25 [1966], 243–249) — where a different translation of the passage in question is proposed. Cf. now also Redford, *op. cit.*, pp. 195 ff., and the critical remarks of Kitchen against Redford, in *Chronique d'Égypte*, 43 (1968), 231 ff.

88 *KBo* 14; edited and translated by A. Goetze, *Kizzuwatna and the Problem of Hittite Geography*, New Haven, 1940 (*Yale Oriental Series, Researches*, XXI), pp. 27 ff.; M. B. Rowton, *JCS*, 13 (1959), 5 ff.

89 Published in *Keilschrifturkunden aus Boghazköi* (= *KUB*), XXXVI, no. 70; edited by H. Otten in E. Weidner, *Die Inschriften Tukulti-Ninurtas I* (= *AfO*, Beiheft 12), p. 67.

90 Hornung, *Untersuchungen*, pp. 51–53. But see the critical remarks of Kitchen, *Chronique d'Égypte*, 40 (1965), 315 ff.; and especially those of Rowton, *JNES*, 25 (1966), 249 ff. Cf. more recently Redford, *History and Chronology of the Eighteenth Dynasty*, pp. 199 ff.

91 On the identification of Menophres with Seti I, see W. Struve, *Ägyptische Zeitschrift*, 63 (1927), 45 ff.; K. Sethe, *ibid.*, 66 (1931), 1 ff.; with Ramses I, see J. Černý, *JEA*, 47 (1961), 150 ff.; Hornung, *Untersuchungen*, p. 61, note 39, and pp. 61–62. The identification of Menophres with Memphis (cf. Rowton, *Iraq*, 8 [1946], 109; Redford, *op. cit.*, p. 214) raises considerable philological difficulties and is hardly tenable (oral communication from

Prof. H. J. Polotsky); see Hornung, *Untersuchungen*, pp. 61–62.

92 Meyer, *Ägyptische Chronologie*, pp. 28 ff. See also G. H. Wheeler, *JEA*, 9 (1923), 196 ff.; R. Parker, *Revue d'Égyptologie*, 9 (1952), 101 ff.; F. Cornelius, *AfO*, 17 (1956), 304.

93 See K. Sethe, *Die Zeitrechnung der alten Ägypter, etc.*, Göttingen, 1920, p. 308; Sewell, in S. R. K. Glanville (ed.), *The Legacy of Egypt*, Oxford, 1942, p. 7; R. Parker, *The Calendars of Ancient Egypt*, pp. 39, 198; von Beckerath, *Tanis und Theben*, Hamburg, 1951, p. 105. The method of reckoning the beginning of the cycle depends on the angle of vision from which the ancient Egyptians observed the rising of the star Sothis; and see W. F. Edgerton, *AJSL*, 53 (1937), 192.

94 Hornung, *Untersuchungen*, pp. 40–41.

95 See J. Černý in *Le fonti indirette della storia Egiziana* (ed. by S. Donadoni, Studi Sem., 7), Roma, 1963, p. 39 (cf. however Rowton, *JEA*, [1968], p. 73). As regards the "year 10" in the Sallier Papyrus I, which has often been attributed to Mer-ne-Ptah, Prof. Černý kindly pointed out to me that H. Gauthier (*Le Livre des rois d'Égypte*, II, Cairo, 1912, p. 113, note 4) has shown that this should be attributed most probably to Ramses II (and also that it should be read "year 9" and not "year 10"); and cf. Černý, *op. cit.*, note 31. For the suggestion of higher dates for Mer-ne-Ptah's reign, see von Beckerath, *op. cit.*, p. 107, note 579; Hayes, *CAH* (rev. ed.), I, chap. 4 (fasc. no. 4), p. 20. Both of them assign about 12 regnal years to Mer-ne-Ptah; while Rowton (*JEA*, 34 [1948], 73), and now Helck (*Materialen zur Aegypt. Wirtschaftsgeschichte d. Neuen Reiches*, IV, 1963, pp. 732 ff.), accept Manetho's tradition as regards Mer-ne-Ptah's 19 regnal years; see also Hornung, *Untersuchungen*, pp. 95–96.

96 See Helck, *Unt. Man.*, p. 70; Hornung, *Untersuchungen*, pp. 96–97. On the last kings of the Nineteenth Dynasty, see A. H. Gardiner, *JEA*, 44 (1958), 12; L. H. Lesko, *JARCE*, 5 (1966), 29–32.

97 On the alleged Asiatic "ruler" Irsu who is said to have usurped the throne during the assumed gap between the Nine-

teenth and Twentieth Dynasties, see for details W. Helck, *ZDMG*, 105 (1955), 44; J. von Beckerath, *ibid.*, 106 (1956), 249; *idem*, *JEA*, 48 (1962), 74; J. Vandier, *L'Egypte* (4th ed.), Paris, 1962, pp. 655–7; L.H. Lesko, *JARCE*, 5 (1966), 30.

98　Ramses III died in his 32nd year (Černý, *Le fonti indirette*, p. 45; Hornung, *Untersuchungen*, p. 97).

99　J. Černý, *CAH* (rev. ed.), II, chap. 35 (= fasc. no. 27), p. 4. This total will be somewhat higher should R. A. Parker's suggestion (*Révue d'Egyptologie*, 11 [1957], 163–4) that Ramses X reigned 10 years be confirmed.

100　T. E. Peet, *JEA*, 14 (1928), 65. J. Černý, *op. cit.*; Hornung, *Untersuchungen*, pp. 97–100; Gardiner (*Egypt of the Pharaohs*, p. 446) allots only 97 years to the Twentieth Dynasty.

101　Černý, in *Le fonti indirette*, pp. 62–65; S. Wenig, *ZÄS*, 94 (1967), 134–39. Wen-Amon's expedition to Palestine took place in the year 5 of Heri-hor's era. Černý (*loc. cit.*) suggests that there are indications that Wen-Amon returned to Egypt in the year 7 of the new "era", which was the year of Heri-hor's death. W. F. Albright, *Studies Presented to David Moore Robinson*, I, St. Louis, 1951, pp. 223 ff. has suggested a date for Wen-Amon's journey which is 30 years lower, but that date (1060) is founded on the lower alternative for Ramses II (1290) and the extension of Mer-ne-Ptah's reign to 19 years.

102　Sir Alan Gardiner, *op. cit.*, p. 447; E. Young, *JARCE*, 2 (1963), 99–111; J. Černý, *CAH* (rev. ed.), II, chap. 35 (= fasc. no. 27), 1965, pp. 40 ff. Cf. however, E. Hornung, *OLZ* 61 (1966), 438–442, and more recently E. F. Wente, *JNES*, 26 (1967), 155–176.

103　George Smith, *The Assyrian Eponym Canon*, London, 1875, p. 83; A. Ungnad, in *Reallexikon der Assyriologie*, II, Berlin-Leipzig, 1938, p. 414.

104　E.g. Ashur-nadin-apli (no. 79), and Tiglath-pileser II (no. 97), are given 3 and 32 years respectively in the Khorsabad list, as against 4 and [3]3 years in the Nassouhi list. Ashur-uballit I (no. 73), and Adad-nirari I (no. 76) are given 36 and

32 years respectively in the Khorsabad list against 35 and [3]3 years in the fragment *KAV* 9. See M. B. Rowton, *Iraq*, 8 (1946), 99; H. Tadmor, *JNES*, 17 (1958), 135. (See now A. K. Grayson, in *lišan mithurti*, [von Soden Festschrift)], Neukirchen-Vluyn, 1969, p. 119).

105　Tadmor, *op. cit.*, pp. 135–136.

106　E. Weidner, *AfO*, 10 (1935), 27 ff.; 15 (1945–51), 86.

107　Rowton, *JCS*, 13 (1959), 6–7; J. A. Brinkman, *A Political History of Post-Kassite Babylonia*, Rome, 1968, pp. 68 ff.

108　A. Peobel, *The Second Dynasty of Isin according to a New King-list Tablet*, Chicago, 1955 (= *Assyriological Studies*, 15).

109　See F. Thureau-Dangin, *RA*, 24 (1927), 197; the number of Kurigalzu's regnal years in the king-list is defective. The most probable restoration is 2[5], though a most recent collation of the tablet by Grayson (*op. cit.* [above, note 104], p. 108), suggests the reading of 45 or 55 years, which is far too high on the basis of the historical synchronisms between Babylonia, Assyria and Egypt in the Amarna period.

110　For this complex historical problem see W. Röllig, *Heidelberger Studien zum alten Orient*, Heidelberg, 1967 (*A. Falkenstein Festschrift*), pp. 173–177. (Now also J. A. Brinkman, *Orientalia*, 38 [1969], 320 ff.).

111　K. Balkan, *Belleten*, 12 (1948), 753; Rowton, *JCS*, 13 (1959), 5. Kudur-Enlil's father Kadashman-Enlil II reigned most probably 15 years. The figure in King-list A is broken off but could be restored as 1[5]. The highest recorded year in the economic documents is his 15th (Balkan, *op. cit.*, p. 752; Rowton, *loc. cit.*).

112　K. Jaritz, *Mitteilungen des Instituts für Orientforschung*, 6 (1958), 200; Hornung, *Untersuchungen*, p. 47, note 38; Rowton, *JNES*, 25 (1966), 243, and especially pp. 255–256, where an explanation on the nature of the "year 18" is offered.

113　This can be inferred (a) from a document published by F. E. Peiser (*Urkunden aus der Zeit der dritten Babylonischen Dynastie*, Berlin, 1905, no. 32), which deals with a loan given in the 12th year of Shagarakti-Shuriash until the accession year (*reš šarruti*) of Kashtiliash his son; the loan could hardly have been given for 6 years; and (b) from an unpublished Nippur tablet (no. 7113 — Rowton, *op. cit.*, p. 225) which mentions years 9, 10, 11 and 12 of Shagarakti-Shuriash and the accession year of the following king, probably his successor.

114 See in detail H. Tadmor, *JNES*, 17 (1958), 136–137. The proposed 7–year gap has been accepted by Rowton in *CAH* (rev. ed.), I, chap. 6 (fasc. no. 4), 1962; p. 35, and, with reservations, in *JNES*, 25 (1966), 257–258. See also D. J. Wiseman, *CAH* (rev. ed.), II, chap. 31 (fasc. no. 41), 1965, p. 3. For a different opinion, see J. M. Munn-Rankin, *CAH* (rev. ed.), II, chap. 35 (= fasc. no. 49), 1967, pp. 16–18; and Brinkman, *Political History of Post-Kassite Babylonia*, pp. 64–67.

115 Rowton, *JNES*, 19 (1960), 19.

116 Tadmor, *JNES*, 17 (1958), 137–138.

117 A possible astronomical datum has been suggested by Rowton in *Iraq*, 8 (1946), 106–107. But see Brinkman, *op. cit.*, p. 68, note 345.

118 E.g. Rowton, *Iraq*, 8 (1946), 94–95.

119 Tadmor, *JNES*, 17 (1958), 131–132.

120 *CAH* (rev. ed.), II, chap. 6 (= fasc. no. 4), 1962, pp. 34–35.

121 There is no longer doubt as to the attribution of the "Broken Obelisk" to Ashur-bel-kala. See K. Jaritz, *Journal of Semitic Studies*, 4 (1959), 204 ff.; R. Borger, *Einleitung in die assyrischen Königsinschriften*, I, Leiden, 1961, pp. 134 ff.

122 Submitted in the Hebrew version of the present chapter on chronology — *The World History of the Jewish People*, First Series, II, *The Patriarchs and Judges*, Tel Aviv, 1967, p. 58.

123 The same date for the accession of Adad-apla-iddina has recently been suggested — though on quite different grounds — by J. A. Brinkman (*Political History of Post-Kassite Babylonia*, pp. 74–77), with a margin of error of ± 5 years.

124 The exceptions are Mursilis II, who reigned about 30 years (A. Goetze, "Die Annalen des Muršiliš," *MVAG*, 38 [1933], 8–9); Urhi-Teshub, his grandson, who reigned 7 years — possibly a round or even typological figure (E. H. Sturtevant —

G. Bechtel, *A Hittite Chrestomathy*, Philadelphia, 1938, p. 77, col. III, 63); Shuppiluliuma, who reigned about 40 years (Kitchen, *Suppiluliuma and the Amarna Pharaohs*, p. 23).

125 A. Goetze (*Kleinasiatische Forschungen*, I, pp. 115 ff., 401 ff.) may be correct in his criticism that the Hittite word in question does not mean an eclipse but only an "omen," "portent." Yet it is difficult to explain a solar "portent" as anything other than an eclipse; and see F. Cornelius, *AfO*, 17 (1956), 11 ff.; and H.G. Güterbock, *apud* Rowton, *CAH* (rev. ed.), I, chap. 6 (= fasc. no. 4), 1962, p. 46, note 2.

126 E. Forrer, *Forschungen*, II/I, Berlin, pp. 1 ff.

127 See E. Edel, *JNES*, 7 (1948), 11 ff.; J. Vergote, *Tout-ankh-amoun dans les archives hittites*, Istambul, 1961, pp. 4 ff; U. G. Güterbock, *JCS*. 10 (1956), 94 note *e*; cf. also H. J. Houwink Ten Cate, *Bibliotheca Orientalis*, 20 (1963), 276; 22 (1965), 153.

128 The problem of the exact filiation of Shuppiluliuma's predecessors and their exact order has not yet been solved finally. A. Goetze's solution has been adopted here — *JCS*, 11 (1957), 59; and see recently *JCS* 22 (1968), 46 ff. For the deeds of Tudhaliya II (sometimes referred to as Tudhaliya I), see O. R. Gurney, *CAH* (rev. ed.), II, chap. 15 (a) (= fasc. no. 44), 1966, pp. 16–22. For a different reconstruction of Shuppiluliuma's genealogy, see H. Otten, *op. cit.* (above, note 48), pp. 108 ff.

129 See Goetze, *JCS*, 11 (1957), 73; Gurney, *op. cit.*, p. 8.

130 See E. Laroche, *Anadolu*, 2 (1935), 13; H. Otten, *apud* E. Weidner, *Die Inschriften Tukulti-Ninurtas I* (*AfO*, Beiheft 12), 1959, p. 64–65; A. Goetze, *CAH* (rev. ed.), II, chap. 24 (= fasc. no. 37), 1965, pp. 45 ff.

131 E. Laroche, *RA*, 47 (1953), 70 ff.; *idem*, *Anadolu*, 2 (1955), 8; Goetze, *op. cit.* (above, note 129), pp. 53–54; H. Otten, *MDOG*, 94 (1963), 1 ff.

132 D. J. Wiseman, *The Alalakh Tablets*, London, 1953, pp. 5–8.

133 S. Smith, *The Statue of Idri-mi*, Ankara, London, 1949. The scribe Sharuwa who wrote the inscription is mentioned in the tablets from the time of Niqmepa.

¹³⁴ Smith, *ibid.*, p. 17; Goetze, *JCS*, 11 (1957), 67. King Barattarna is also mentioned in the treaty between Idrimi and Pilliya of Kizzuwadna (Wiseman, *Alalakh*, no. 3). On Barattarna, see W. F. Albright, *BASOR*, 118 (1950), 17, note 27; Landsberger, *JCS*, 8 (1954), 55, note 101; Goetze, *JCS*, 11 (1957), 67, note 149. On Pilliya, see Goetze, *ibid.*, p. 72. For the possibility that a distinction should be made between Pilliya I — an early contemporary of Idrimi — and a later king Pilliya II, see Gurney, *CAH* (rev. ed.), II, chap. 15 (a) (= fasc. no. 44), 1966, pp. 5, 14–15.

¹³⁵ Wiseman, *op. cit.*, nos. 13, 14.

¹³⁶ See in detail B. Landsberger, *JCS*, 8 (1954), 54, followed by M. B. Rowton, *CAH* (rev. ed.), I, chap. 6 (= fasc. no. 4), 1962, p. 60, who revised his previous, late dating for Saushshatar (*BASOR*, 126 [1952], 23).

¹³⁷ See Gelb, *Hurrians and Subarians*, Chicago, 1946, pp. 76 ff.; and cf. Goetze, *JCS*,

11 (1957), 66–68; *idem*, *CAH* (rev. ed.), II, chap. 17 (= fasc. no. 37), 1965, pp. 3 ff.; J. M. Munn-Rankin, *CAH* (rev. ed.), II, chap. 25 (= fasc. no. 49), 1967, pp. 3–10.

¹³⁸ The evidence on Syria during this period has recently been treated in detail by H. Klengel, *Geschichte Syriens im 2. Jahrtausend v. u. Z.*, I, *Nordsyrien;* II, *Mittel- und Südsyrien*, Berlin, 1965–69. See also Helck, *Beziehungen;* M. Liverani, *Storia di Ugarit*, Roma, 1962; E. Cassin, H. Otten, A. Malamat, J. Yoyotte and J. Černý, in *Fischer Weltgeschichte*, 3, *Die altorientalischen Reiche*, II, Frankfurt, 1966; M. Drower, *CAH* (rev. ed.), II, chap. 10 (= fasc. 64, parts 1–2), 1969–70 (includes bibliography).

¹³⁹ This English version is a complete revision of the original Hebrew (published in 1967), brought up to date through 1968/69. The author wishes to express his thanks to Prof. A. R. Schulman and Aharon Kempinsky for their critical remarks on the Egyptian and Hittite sections respectively.

CHAPTER VI

THE NORTHWEST SEMITIC LANGUAGES

1   N. Slouschz, *Ozar ha-Kᵉtovot ha-Feniqiyyot* (*Thesaurus of Phoenician Inscriptions*), Tel-Aviv, 1942, p. 20; H. Donner and W. Röllig, *Kanaanäische und aramäische Inschriften*, I, Wiesbaden, 1962, p. 3, no. 14.

2   *Ibid.*, p. 5, no. 24.

3   *Ibid.*, p. 5, no. 26, line 20.

4   It is not only the *h* of the pronominal suffix *-him* that became *n* in intervocalic position. Similarly, original *'alōhīm* "gods" — with vowel *a* in the first syllable as in Syriac — became *'alōnīm*. The singular *'alōn*, which (like the Hebrew *'elōah*) is rare, is doubtless backformed from *'alōnim*.

5   Donner and Röllig, *op. cit.*, p. 23, no. 124, line 2.

6   Slouschz, *op. cit.*, p. 10; Donner and Röllig, *op. cit.*, p. 2, no. 10.

7   Slouschz, *op. cit.*, p. 16, lines 6, 7; Donner and Röllig, *op. cit.*, p. 3, no. 13, lines 6, 7.

8   It will be seen that all of the four Hebrew verbs refer to present time; but because of the complicated rules of biblical Hebrew, this present time is expressed first by a participle, then by a perfect consecutive, then by an imperfect, and then again by a perfect consecutive.

9   That this well-known feature of Common Aramaic was also present in Samalian is vouched for by *hrpy* "he set free," Donner and Röllig, *op. cit.*, p. 39, no. 215, line 8 (bis), which cannot very well be read otherwise than as *harpī*.

10   For the spelling *ymy*, cf. Heb. **yam* (epigraphic *ym;* and the masoretic plural *yāmīm, ymē*).

11   Donner and Röllig, *op. cit.*, p. 39, no. 214.

12   At least according to the criterion of resemblance; for the resemblance of Samalian to Common Aramaic appears very considerable once one eliminates the features that have been attributed to it on the basis of false interpretations of the texts. True, a common feature (isogloss) does not necessarily indicate genetic relationship, but languages whose past history is unknown can only be classified on the basis of resemblances.

13   Among these, the Pentateuch Targum which is extant in a manuscript in the Neofiti Library, Rome, is of great importance.

CHAPTER VII

WARFARE IN THE SECOND MILLENNIUM B.C.E.

[1] Y. Yadin, "Hyksos Fortifications and the Battering-Ram," *BASOR*, 137 (1955), 23.

[2] Ch. F. Jean, "L'Armée du royaume de Mari" *RA*, 42 (1948), 135 ff.

[3] Ch. Virolleaud, "Les villes et les corporations du royaume d'Ugarit," *Syria*, 21 (1940), 135 ff.; *idem. PRU*, II.

[4] Knudtzon, *EA*; Mercer, *AT*.

[5] A. Goetze, *Kulturgeschichte des alten Orients* (*Kleinasien*), Munich, 1933, p. 114, bibliography; *ANET*, pp. 318 ff.; 353, 354.

[6] *ARE*.

[7] H. Bonnet, *Die Waffen der Völker des alten Orients*, Leipzig, 1926, "*Bogen*."

[8] W. F. Albright and G.E. Mendenhall, "The Creation of the Composite Bow in Canaanite Mythology," *JNES*, 1 (1942), 227 ff.; Y. Yadin (Sukenik), "The Composite Bow of the Canaanite Goddess Anath," *BASOR*, 107 (1947), 11 ff.

[9] *ANEP*, fig. 309.

[10] Cf. note 8, above.

[11] E. R. Lacheman, "Epigraphic Evidences of the Material Culture of the Nuzians," *apud* R.F.S. Starr, *Nuzi*, I, text, Harvard University Press 1939, Appendix D (pp. 528 ff.); Y. Yadin, *BASOR*, 107 (1947), 13. (It seems that this is how the document which speaks of sending 7,200 green canes of different measurements [two ells, three ells and four ells] is to be understood). Cf. L.W. King: *The Letters and Inscriptions of Hammurabi*, III, London, 1900, XXII.

[12] A. Alt, "Neues aus der Pharaonenzeit Palästinas," *PJB*, 32 (1936), 31 ff.

[13] F. Thureau–Dangin, "Kabâbu, Arîtu, Tuksu," *RA*, 36 (1939), 57 ff.

[14] Ch. Virolleaud, *PRU*, II, nos. 123, 154; Y. Yadin, *ibid.* 13 note 8; and cf. Knudtzon, *EA*, no. 184. According to it the three quivers contained ninety bows (H. Ehelolf, *ZA* [NF], 11 [1939], 70).

[15] For the different types of this sword see R. Maxwell–Hyslop, "Daggers and Swords in Western Asia," *Iraq*, 8 (1946), 1 ff.

[16] See Y. Yadin, "*The Scroll of the War of the Sons of Light against the Sons of Darkness*" (transl. from the Hebrew) Oxford, 1962, p. 125 note 2.

[17] *ANEP*, fig. 161; N. Davies, *The Tomb of Ken-Amun at Thebes*, New York, 1930, pl. XXIV.

[18] *ANEP*, 268, no. 161; Lacheman, "Epigraphic Evidences," *ibid.* 540.

[19] Lacheman, *ibid.* 541.

[20] R. Maxwell–Hyslop, "Western Asiatic Shaft–Hole Axes," *Iraq*, 9 (1949), 90 ff.; K. Kenyon, "A Crescentic Axehead from Jericho and a Group of Weapons from Tel-el-Hesi," *Annual Report of the Institute of Archaeology, University of London*, 11 (1955), 1 ff.

[21] R. Mawwell–Hyslop, *loc. cit.*

[22] *ANEP*, figs. 160, 300, 302, 303.

[23] See note 21, above.

[24] *Ibid.*

[25] R. Maxwell–Hyslop, "Bronze Lugged Axe or Adze-blades from Asia," *Iraq*, 15 (1953), 69 ff.

[26] J.R.Kupper, "Notes Lexicographiques," *RA*, 45 (1951), 125–128; Y. Yadin, "Hyksos Fortifications etc.," *BASOR*, 137 (1955), 30.

[27] See note 26, above.

[28] Cf. O. R. Gurney, *The Hittites*, London, 1952, pp. 178–179; Y. Yadin, *loc. cit.*

[29] J. Weisner, "Fahren und Reiten in Alteuropa und im Alten Orient," *AO*, vol. 38, nos. 2–4, Leipzig, 1939.

[30] A. Salonen, *Der Abschnitt "Wagen" der 5. Tafel der Serie ḪAR-RA-ḫubullu*, Helsinki, 1945; W. F. Albright, *BASOR*, 77 (1940), 31; *idem*, *JPOS*, 15 (1935), 224 note 97; Ch. F. Jean, *loc. cit.*; *ARM*, XV, 1954, 295 s.v. Char; Chariot; Cheval.

[31] A. Salonen, *op. cit.*; A. Moortgat, "Der Kampf zu Wagen in der Kunst des Alten Orients," *OLZ*, 33 (1930), 841 ff.; idem: *Vorderasiatische Rollsiegel*, Berlin, 1940.

[32] Y. Yadin (Sukenik), "A Note on the TLT SSWM in Ugarit," *JCS*, 2 (1948), 11 ff.

[33] Y. Yadin, "Goliath's Javelin etc.," *PEQ*, 87 (1955), 67.

34   A.Moortgat, *Vorderasiatische Rollsiegel.*
35   See note 34, above.
36   *ANEP*, figs. 183, 314.
37   *Ibid.* fig. 314.
38   G. Loud, *The Megiddo Ivories*, Chicago, 1939, pl. XXXIII.
39   H. Carter and P. E. Newberry, *Tomb of Thout-môsis IV*, London, 1904; W. F. Albright, "A Prince of Taanach in the Fifteenth Century B.C." *BASOR*, 94 (1944), 22; B. Maisler, *Luḥot Ta'anak*, "Klausner Volume" (1937), 44 ff. According to these documents there were also a number of places in Palestine which supplied the different kinds of timber for chariot parts.
40   A. Salonen, *op. cit.*
41   See note 39 above.
42   Ch. Virolleaud, *PRU*, II, p. 152. note 121.
43   The meaning of *"trm"* seems to be the harness on the heads of the horses as can be seen from Cant. 1:10: "Thy cheeks are comely with circlets" (when comparing the beloved to a steed drawing one of Pharaoh's chariots).
44   Most of the material given below is to be found in Ch. F. Jean, *RA*, 42 (1948), 135 ff.; and see *ARM*, XV, 1954: "Armée" (289), "Dawidûm," (299), "Homme" (311), "Razziarezzou" (328), "Ruse de guerre" (332), "Soldat" (334), "Troupes" (338).
45   See the following notes and cf. I Sam. 24:2.
46   Ch. F. Jean, "Autres lettres de Mari," *Revue des études Sémitiques et Babyloniaca*, 1942–1945, (1944), no. 131.
47   G. Dossin, "Benjaminites dans les textes de Mari," *Mélanges Syriens*, II, Paris, 1939, pp. 981–996.
48   S. Tolkowsky, "Gideon's 300" *JPOS*, 5 (1925), 69 ff.
49   A. Goetze, *BASOR*, 95 (1944), 18.
50   All of it according to Breasted's calculations, and cf. J. H. Breasted, *The Battle of Kadesh*, Chicago, 1903; *ARE* III § 335. However, according to different calculations the army consisted of 3,500 chariots and 17,000 infantry; cf. also A. Goetze, *Kulturgeschichte des alten Orients (Kleinasien)*, p. 118.
51   The Hebrew word *na'arim* appears here and in other contexts meaning selected warriors. W. F. Albright, "Mitannian Maryannu, 'Chariot Warrior', and the Canaanite and Egyptian Equivalents," *AFO*, 6 (1930–31), 220; *idem*, "The Seal of Eliakim, etc.," *JBL*, 51 (1932), 82 ff. As for the Egyptian word "young warriors" – *d mw* – cf. R. O. Faulkner, "Egyptian Military Organization," *JEA*, 39 (1953), 32 ff.
52   *ANET*, p. 476.
53   Mercer, *AT*, I, no. 132, line 56. In another letter we read of an escort force of 3,000 men which arrived with Pharaoh's messengers *idem, ibidem*, no. 11, line 24.
54   See note 50 above.
55   H. H. Nelson, *The Battle of Megiddo*, Chicago, 1913; *ANET*, p. 237.
56   *ANET*, p. 246, and cf. E. Edel, "Die Stelen Amenophis' II aus Karnak usw," *ZDPV*, 69 (1953), 98 ff.
57   Mercer *AT*, II, 290a, line 25.
58   *Ibid.* I, 127, line 37.
59   *Ibid.* 3, line 32; 19, line 84.
60   *Ibid.*, 9, line 37, etc.
61   Goetze, *AM*, p. 17.
62   H. G. Gueterbock, "Die historische Tradition.... bei Babyloniern und Hethitern," *ZA*, (NF) 10 (1937), 121.
63   H. Lewy, "Gleanings from a New Volume of Nuzi texts," *Orientalia* (NS), 10 (1941), 201.
64   R. O. Faulkner, *ibid.*, 45–46.
65   Cf. *ibid.*, 43.
66   W. F. Albright, "Mitannian maryannu, etc.," *AfO*, 6 (1930–31), 217 ff.
67   M. S. F. Hood, "Mycenaean Cavalryman," *The Annual of the British School of Archaeology at Athens*, 48 (1953), 84–93; A. R. Schulman, "Egyptian Representations of Horsemen and Riding in the New-Kingdom," *JNES*, 16 (1957), 263 ff.
68   Lacheman, *loc. cit.*; Ch. F. Jean, *Syria*, 28 (1951), 282 ff.; Ch. Virolleaud, "Les Villes etc.," *Syria*, 21 (1940), 135 ff.
69   *ANET*, p. 476.
70   *Ibid.*, p. 238.
71   Mercer, *AT*, II, p. 141, lines 19–30.
72   R. O. Faulkner, *ibid.*, 32 ff.
73   A. H. Gardiner, "The Ancient Military Road between Egypt and Palestine," *JEA*, 6 (1920), 99 ff.
74   Mercer, *AT*, I, p. 85, lines 51 ff.
75   *ANET*, p. 236.

76 Krt. lines 80—85, 172—175.

77 *ARM*, I, 43, lines 4—12.

78 *Ibid.* II, 13.

79 And cf. the law concerning booty which David made: I Sam. 30:23—25.

80 Ch. F. Jean, "L'Armée, etc.," *RA*, 42 (1948), 135 ff.

81 R. O. Faulkner, *loc. cit.*

82 Ch. Virolleaud, *loc. cit.*

83 The whole of the following introduction comes from R. O. Faulkner, *loc. cit.*; H. W. Helck, *Der Einfluss der Militärführer in der* 18. *ägyptischen Dynastie*, Leipzig, 1939.

84 Y. Yadin, "Hyksos Fortifications etc.," *BASOR*, 137 (1955), 30; W. von Soden, *Orientalia* (NS), 22 (1953), 195.

85 R. O. Faulkner, "The Euphrates Compaign of Thutmosis III," *JEA*, 32 (1946), 40 ff.

86 *ANET*, p. 240.

87 *ARM*, II, 24, lines 25—26; 30, lines 20—21; Ch. F. Jean, *loc. cit.*; idem., "Les lettres de Mari," *Revue des études Sémitiques et Babyloniaca*, 1 (1941), 82.

88 *ARE*, III, § 473.

89 All the material presented below is taken from: G. Dossin, "Signaux lumineux au pays de Mari," *RA*, 35 (1938), 174—186.

90 *ANET*, p. 483.

91 G. Dossin, *ibid.* 180.

92 *Ibid.* p. 182.

93 N. H. Torcyner (Tur-Sinai), *Te'udot Lachish*, Jerusalem (1940), 115 ff., for a detailed discussion.

94 Cf. Peneiǀ 'olam ha-miqra, I, Jerusalem, 1958, 207, and notes *ibid.*

95 *ARM*, II, 55 line 5.

96 *ARE*, III § 334. Cf. also M. S. F. Hood, *loc. cit.*; A. R. Schulman, *loc. cit.*

97 Mercer, *AT*, I, no. 88.

98 *ANET*, p. 482; *ARM*, II, 22.

99 *ARM*, I, 10, line 14; 29, line 6.

100 G. Dossin, "Benjaminites etc.," *Mélanges Syriens*, II, 985.

101 Idem., *ibidem.*

102 G. Dossin, "Signaux lumineux etc.," *RA*, 35 (1938), 178.

103 Ch. F. Jean, *loc. cit.*, 122.

104 J. H. Breasted, *The Battle of Kadesh.*

105 *ARE*, III, § 330.

106 *Ibid.* § 321.

107 *ANEP*, figs. 179—180.

108 *ANET*, p. 143.

109 J. H. Breasted, *op. cit.*

110 *ANET*, p. 235.

111 Goetze, *AM*, 55.

112 *Ibid.* 133.

113 *ANET*, p. 236.

114 It is interesting that both in the battle of Megiddo and in the battle of Kadesh the neglect of this principle cost the attacking armies a heavy defeat. The Egyptian army, after its initial victory over the Canaanites near Megiddo, was in a hurry to lay hands on the booty and this enabled the Canaanites to flee from the city. "Now if only his majesty's army had not given up their hearts to capturing the possessions of the enemy, they would [have captured] Megiddo at this time," *loc. cit.*

115 H. Burne, *The Art of War on Land*, Harrisburg, 1947.

116 *ANEP*, figs. 314—316.

117 *Ibid.* figs. 318—319.

118 *Ibid.* fig. 322.

119 *ARE*, III, § 336.

120 *ARE*, II, § 589, p. 233 n.d.

121 *ANET*, p. 236.

122 P. Kraus, "Altbabylonische Briefe," *MVAG*, 35 (1931), 19 ff. And cf. Gideon's Battle (Jud. 7).

123 Goetze, *AM*, 133.

124 W. F. Albright, *BASOR*, 94 (1944), 21, and cf. also: Maisler, "*Luḥot Ta'anak*," Klausner Volume, 44 ff.

125 *ANET*, p. 477.

126 Cf. Y. Yadin (Sukenik), "Let the Young Men, I Pray Thee, Arise and Play before us," *JPOS*, 21 (1948), 110 ff.

127 According to the names of the towns: *Lachish*, III, 35; J. Garstang, *Joshua-Judges*, London, 1931; and cf. A. G. Barrois, *Manuel d'archéologie biblique*, I, Paris, 1939, 127 ff. (la fortification).

128 J. Garstang, *op. cit.*, 167.

129 Y. Yadin, "Hyksos Fortifications etc.," *BASOR*, 137 (1955), 25; T. Säve Söderbergh, "The Hyksos Rule in Egypt," *JEA*, 37 (1951), 53 ff.

130 Y. Yadin, *ibid.*, 23 ff.

131 Boghazköy, Alishar, Hazor.

132 E.g. *ANEP*, fig. 329.

133 Y. Yadin, *ibid.*, 31.

134   S. Yeivin, "The Date of the Tunnel in the Lachish Glacis," *Eretz Israel* (Hebrew) I, 29 ff., doubts whether this method existed before the first millennium.

135   *ARE*, II, § 13.

136   *ANET*, p. 238.

137   *Ibid.* p. 237.

138   *ANEP*, fig. 344.

139   *The entrance into the city* was apparently the postern gate which was characteristic of the Late Bronze Period. The examples from Alishar, Boghazköy and Ugarit prove that these gates — which enabled citizens to enter and leave the place at a time of emergency when the main gates were kept shut — could also serve as a means of breaking into the town.

140   *ANET*, pp. 22—23.

CHAPTER VIII

THE PATRIARCHS AND THEIR SOCIAL BACKGROUND

1 The Book of Genesis, except for such episodes as that in chap. 14, was never conceived as contemporary history but rather as the prelude to history. Accordingly, central ideas are given precedence over the individual personalities.

2 Cf., for example, W. F. Albright, *From Stone Age to Christianity*, Baltimore, 1940; *idem, The Archaeology of Palestine*, Harmondsworth, 1960.

3 For a lucid and popular treatment of this theme, see M. Burrows, *What mean these Stones?* New York, 1957.

4 The tradition concerning Ur arouses suspicion at the outset by its reference to the *Kasdim*, the "Chaldees," which cannot but be an anachronism in the age of the Patriarchs. The weight of the evidence, internal as well as external, points clearly to the region of Haran as the actual home of Abraham.

5 For Alalakh, see provisionally E. A. Speiser, *JAOS*, 74 (1954), 18 ff.; for Ugarit, cf. *idem, ibid.*, 75 (1955), 154 ff.

6 *ARM*, I, 60 : 6.

7 *Ibid*, II, 37.

8 See G. Dossin, *RA*, 42 (1948), 125 ff.; and cf. A. Malamat, "'Prophecy' in the Mari Documents" (Hebrew), *Eretz-Israel*, 4 (1956), 82 ff.

9 Cf. *Israel Life and Letters*, May–June, 1953, pp. 56 ff.

10 See Wiseman, *Alalakh*, no. 9.

11 Cf. E. A. Speiser, *Journal of World History*, 1 (1953), 311 ff.

12 Cf. *idem, Orientalia* (n.s.), 25 (1956), 13.

13 *Idem, AASOR*, 10 (1928–9), 31 ff.

14 *Idem, JBL*, 74 (1955), 252 ff.

15 *RA*, 23 (1926), 127; for a provisional survey of Nuzi parallels, cf. C. H. Gordon, *RB*, 44 (1935), 34 ff.

16 For a comprehensive statement on Mesopotamian civilization and its relation to religion and society, cf. E. A. Speiser in *The Idea of History in the Ancient Near East*, ed. by R. C. Dentan, New Haven, 1955, pp. 37–76.

CHAPTER IX

CANAAN IN THE PATRIARCHAL AGE

1 For the meaning of this West-Semitic name, apparently 'lmw (the transcription of the semitic *L* or *r* by Egyptian' is common in the Middle Kingdom period), see the different views of A. Reuveni, *Shem, Ham and Japheth*, (Hebrew), Tel-Aviv, 1932, pp. 19 ff.; S. Yeivin, *Atiqot*, (Hebrew), II, 1957, 145; W. Helck, *Die Beziehungen Ägyptens zu Vorderasien im 3. und 2. Jahrtausend*, Wiesbaden, 1962, pp. 18 ff.

2 J. Wilson, *ANET*, pp. 227 ff.

3 W. M. F. Petrie, *Deshasheh*, London, 1898, pl. IV, and for the date of the relief – H. Kees, *WZKM*, 54 (1957), 99.

4 L. Oppenheim, *ANET*, pp. 265 ff.; E. F. Weidner, *AFO*, 16 (1952/3), 1 ff.; C. J. Gadd, *The Dynasty of Agade*, *CAH*, I (rev. ed.), pp. 10 ff.; A. Malamat, in *Western Galilee and the Coast of Galilee* (Hebrew), Jerusalem, 1965, pp. 76 ff.

5 Cf. Gadd, *ibid.*, p. 41.

6 Most remarkable are the descriptions of the Amurrū (MAR–TU) as wild nomads who endanger the peace of the country, in the epic Lugalbanda – En-me-kar (M. Falkenstein, in *Comptes rendus de la seconde rencontre Assyr. inter.*, Paris, 1957, pp. 12 ff.) and in various documents from the Third Dynasty of Ur. See G. Buccellati, *The Amorites of the Ur III Period*, Naples, 1966. The god Amurru appears as a nomadic figure outside civilized society; see J.-R. Kupper, *Mémoires de l'Académie royale de Belgique, classe de lettres*, 55, I, (1961).

7 For this dark period which it was customary to divide into two (Early Bronze IV and Middle Bronze I), and which Miss Kenyon calls the transitional period from the Early Bronze to the Middle Bronze, see K. Kenyon, *PEQ*, 1952, 4 ff.; 62 ff.; 1953, 81 ff.; 1954, 45 ff.; 1955, 108 ff.; idem, *Archaeology in the Holy Land*, London, 1960; pp. 135 ff.; G. E. Wright (ed.), *The Bible and the Ancient Near East*, New York, 1961, pp. 86 ff.; W. F. Albright, *BASOR*, 168 (1962), 36 ff.; R. Amiran, *IEJ*, 10 (1960), 204 ff.

8 It is interesting to note the similarity between the sanctuary containing two rows of menhirs discovered in Tell Ḥuweira (A. Moortgat, *Tell Chuera*, Cologne–Wiesbaden, 1960–1962) on the way from Aleppo to Haran – and the holy places in Ader and in Bab edh-dhra' in Transjordan (for the last named place see W. F. Albright, *BASOR*, 95 [1944], 2 ff.). For the impressions of roll seals from this period see M. W. Prausnitz, in *Eretz Israel*, (Hebrew), 5 (1959), 31 ff.

9 Cf. the summarizing survey of N. Glueck, *Rivers in the desert*, New York, 1959, *passim*; W. F. Albright, *BASOR*, 163 (1961), 36 ff.

10 Cf. M. Kochavi, "Middle Bronze Settlements in the Negev" (Hebrew), "*Madda*," 8, 6 (1963), 8 ff.

11 For the wall against the Amurrū which was called *muriq Tidnim* viz. that which removes the Tidnim (one of the Amurru tribal associations) cf. Maisler, *Untersuchungen*, p. 3; C. J. Gadd, "Babylonia", *CAH* I (rev. ed.) pp. 17 ff. Amen-em-het I, the founder of the Twelfth Dynasty, built a similar wall on Egypt's eastern border as a protection from the nomads.

12 Of the series of volumes in transliteration and French translation so far published: *Archives royales de Mari* (=*ARM*), I–XII, XV, 1946–1964; and cf. A. Malamat, "Mari," *Encyclopaedia Biblica*, (Hebrew) IV, cols. p. 559 ff., (and the bibliography there).

13 For the personal names see Th. Bauer, *Die Ostkanaanäer*, Leipzig, 1926; J. Bottéro – A. Finet, *ARM*, XV, 1954; J. I. Gelb, *JCS*, 15 (1961), 27 ff.; W. F. Albright, *JAOS*, 74 (1954), 222 ff.

14 For the nomadic tribes see J.-R. Kupper, *Les nomades en Mésopotamie au temps des rois de Mari*, Paris, 1957, and for the sons of Nahor – B. Maisler (Mazar), in "*Zion*" (Hebrew) XI (1946), 8 ff.

15 For Yamhad and Qaṭanum see G. Dossin, *Bulletin de l'Académie royale de Belgique*, 1954, 417 ff.; J.-R. Kupper, "Nor-

thern Mesopotamia and Syria," *CAH*, II (rev. ed.), pp. 19 ff.

16   G. Dossin, in *Syria*, 19 (1938), 117.

17   A. Malamat, in *Western Galilee and the Coast of Galilee*, pp. 79 ff.

18   For the main routes and stations see W. W. Halls, *JCS*, 18 (1964), 57 ff.

19   See B. Mazar "*Eretz Israel*", (Hebrew) (1954), 19 ff.; W. F. Albright, *BASOR*, 163 (1961), 40 ff.; and for the documents from Ṣerābīt al-Khadim, J. Černy, in *Archiv Orientali*, 7 (1935), 384 ff.; *idem, The Inscriptions of Sinai*, II, London, 1955.

20   The fresco was published by P. E. Newberry, *Beni Hasan*, London 1893, I, pl. 38 cf. Mazar, *ibid.*, 27. For Seth in the Akkadian documents see J. R. Kupper, *RA*, 55 (1961), 197 ff.

21   For Kushu see B. Mazar "Cushan," *Encyclopaedia Biblica*, IV, cols. 70–71, and on the Shosu – Grdseloff, *Revue de l'histoire juive en Egypte*, 1 (1947), 69 ff.

22   For this period see W. C. Hayes, *JNES*, 12 (1953), 31 ff.; *idem*, "The Middle Kingdom in Egypt", *CAH*, I (rev. ed.).

23   See the translation into English by J. Wilson, *ANET*, pp. 18 ff., and into Hebrew by S. Yeivin, *The Si-nuhe Scroll*, Tel-Aviv, 1930.

24   The material from Byblos was published in the report of M. Dunand, *Fouilles de Byblos*, I–II, Paris, 1939–1958 and W. F. Albright, "Byblos", *Encyclopaedia Biblica*, II, cols. 404 ff.; B. Mazar, in *Western Galilee and the Coast of Galilee*, pp. 4–5, and also S. H. Horn, in *Andrews Univ. Seminary Studies*, I (1963), 52 ff.

25   See Helck, *op. cit.*, 69 pp. ff.

26   T. E. Peet, *The Stela of Sebek-Khu*, Manchester, 1914; Wilson, *ANET*, p. 230.

27   The first group of Execration Texts was published by K. Sethe, *Die Ächtung feindlicher Fürsten, Völker*, etc., Berlin, 1926, and the second by G. Posener, *Princes et pays d'Asie et de Nubie*, Brussels, 1940; and cf. B. Mazar, "*Eretz Israel*," III, (1954), 21 ff. and lastly, Helck, *op. cit.*, pp. 49 ff. A new collection of Execration Texts was discovered at Margissa in Nubia; see M. G. Posener, *Syria* 43 (1966), 277 ff.

28   On Shechem see G. E. Wright, *Shechem*, 1965, pp. 57 ff.; and on Jerusalem see K. M. Kenyon, *PEQ*, 1963, 9 ff.; 1964, 8.

29   See W. F. Albright, *BASOR*, 99 (1945), 9 ff.

30   B. Landsberger, *JCS*, 8 (1954), 56.

31   A. Malamat, in *Isaac Baer Jubilee Volume*, (Hebrew), Jerusalem, 1961, pp. 1 ff.

32   See the detailed report of the Hazor excavations by Y. Yadin and others, *Hazor*, I–III, 1958–1961, *passim*. The influence which the northern regions of Syria exerted at that time on the culture of Canaan is also expressed by the pottery called Khaburian – see R. Amiran, *Ancient Pottery of the Holy Land* (trans. from the Hebrew), Tel Aviv, 1969, p. 102, *passim*.

33   Cf. Y. Yadin, *BASOR*, 137 (1955) 23 ff.; *idem* "*A Military History of Canaan in the Biblic Times*," (Hebrew), Tel-Aviv, 1964, p. 334; and the chapter in this volume.

34   Josephus, *Against Apion*, I, 14 ff.

35   H. Stock, *Studien zur Geschichte und Archäologie der 13 bis 17. Dyn. Ägyptens*, Glückstadt, 1942; W. von Bissing, *AFO*, 11 (1936), 325 ff.; R. M. Engberg, *The Hyksos Reconsidered*, Chicago, 1939; A. Alt, *Die Herkunft der Hyksos in neuer Sicht*, Berlin, 1954; T. Säve–Söderbergh, *JEA*, 37 (1951) 53 ff.; W. C. Hayes, "Egypt: From the Death of Amenemes III to Seqenre II,," *CAH*, II (rev. ed.); Helck, *op. cit.*, pp. 92 ff.

36   Wilson, *ANET*, pp. 231 ff.

37   Cf. P. Montet, *Kemi*, 4 (1933), 191 ff.; K. Sethe, *Zeitschrift für ägyptische Sprache und Altertumskunde*, 65 (1930), 85 ff.; Wilson, *ANET*, p. 253 and for the Biblical source – B. Maisler (Mazar), in *Dinaburg Volume*, (Hebrew), Jerusalem, 1949, p. 313.

38   See W. M. F. Petrie, *Hyksos and Israelite Cities*, London, 1906, pp. 3 ff.; *idem, Heliopolis*, London, 1915, pp. 3 ff., pls. 1–3.

39   See the chapter in this volume.

40   H. Stock, *MDOG*, 94 (1963), 73 ff.

41   For the fortifications of the Hyksos period see W. F. Albright, "The Excavation of Tell Beit Mirsim II," *AASOR*, 17 (1936–1937), 27 ff.; Y. Yadin, *BASOR*, 137 (1955), 23 ff.; Recently, remains of ramparts were discovered in additional sites viz. at Tell Nagila, Jaffa, Akzib, etc.

42   On Beth-Eglaim (W. M. F. Petrie, *Ancient Gaza*, I–IV, London, 1931–4) see

W. F. Albright, *AJSL*, 55 (1938), 337 ff. and on Sharuhen – W. M. F. Petrie, *Beth Pelet*, I, London, 1930, pp. 15 ff.

43   On the Hurrians see I. J. Gelb, *Hurrians and Subarians*, Chicago, 1944; E. A. Speiser, *Cahiers d'histoire mondiale*, 1 (1953), 311 ff.; J.–R. Kupper, "Northern Mesopotamia and Syria," *CAH*, II (rev. ed.), pp. 38 ff.

44   See Kupper, *ibid*, 32 ff.

45   Cf. G. E. Wright, *Shechem*, pp. 62 ff.

46   See B. Mazar, "Migdal," *Encyclopaedia Biblica*, (Hebrew), IV, cols. 633 ff.; G. E. Wright, *op. cit.*, pp. 80 ff. Remains characteristic for this period i.e., Middle Bronze II, 3, were discovered in layer D in Tell Beit Mirsim; see Albright, *AASOR*, 17, 26 ff. Cf. now B. Mazar, *IEJ* 18 (1968) 91 ff.

CHAPTER X

HAB/PIRU AND HEBREWS

1 The labial is ambiguously represented by cuneiform signs which may be read as *bi* or *pi*. On the Egyptian and Ugaritic writing with *p*, see note 23, below.

2 The title of C. R. Conder's article in *PEFQS*, 1890, 326 ff.

3 See the summary of F. M. Th. Böhl, in *Kanaanäer und Hebräer*, Leipzig, 1911, pp. 85 ff.

4 For comprehensive collections and analyses of the available material on the hapiru, see J. Bottéro, *Le problème des Habiru*, Paris, 1954; and M. Greenberg, *The Hab/piru*, New Haven, 1955.

5 On the Babylonian evidence, see the excellent survey of J.-R. Kupper, *Les nomades en Mésopotamie au temps des rois de Mari*, Paris, 1957, pp. 249–59.

6 The one exception in the published texts is Wiseman, *Alalakh*, no. 182:10 (Greenberg, *op. cit.*, no. 26 : 10) where Erata of Anzaqar appears among the SA. GAZ o Anzaqar.

7 This is not to say that no persons of nomad extraction were among the hapiru (cf. the evidence relating some Mari-text hapiru to nomadic tribes collected by J.-R. Kupper, "Sutéens et Hapiru," *RA*, 55 [1961], 197–200); only that the group as a whole cannot be characterized as "desert invaders"; see Greenberg, *op. cit.*, pp. 86–7.

8 Bottéro, *op. cit.*, nos. 67–9; Greenberg, *op. cit.*, nos. 52–7; E. Cassin, "Nouveaux documents sur les Habiru," *Journal asiatique*, 246 (1958), 225–36.

9 For Rib-Addi's letters, see Bottéro, *op. cit.*, nos. 94–124; Greenberg, *op. cit.*, nos. 66–90. On the usage of (SA.) GAZ in these letters, see Greenberg, *op. cit.*, pp. 71 f.

10 Bottéro, *op. cit.*, no. 129; Greenberg, *op. cit.*, no. 95.

11 For the Palestinian letters, see Bottéro, *op. cit.*, nos. 136–53; Greenberg, *op. cit.*, nos. 101–18. On the usage of SA. GAZ and hapiru in these letters, see Greenberg, *op. cit.*, p. 74.

12 For example, the bands of "vain fellows" (*anashim reqim*) that collect around Abi-

melech (Jud. 9:4) and Jephthah (Jud. 11:3); the roving *condottiere* Gaal the son of Ebed (Jud. 9: 26 ff.); and David's roaming band, composed of "every one that was in distress, and every one that was in debt, and every one that was discontented" (I Sam. 22:2). The case of David is most illuminating: note the refugee nature of the group, all of whom are outcasts from civilized society; note their attempts to gain the favor and protection of the cities (I Sam. 23), and their final association with a local Philistine dynast who "gives" them a town as their quarters (I Sam. 27:5–6) precisely, for example, as Lab'ayu "gives" Shechem to the hapiru (Bottéro, *op. cit.*, no. 145; Greenberg, *op. cit.*, no. 112). For this meaning of the oft-repeated accusation that the towns of the king are being "given" to the SA. GAZ/hapiru, see Greenberg, *op. cit.*, note to no. 110 : 31. On these parallels in the society of Amarna Palestine and premonarchic Israel, see also Alt, "Erwägungen über die Landnahme der Israeliten," *Kleine Schriften*, I, p. 170.

13 Bottéro, *op. cit.*, no. 72; Greenberg, *op. cit.*, no. 120; H. Otten, "Zwei althetitische Belege zu den Hapiru (SA. GAZ)," *ZA* (N. F.), 18 (1957), 216–23.

14 Other indications that hapiru attained respectable status: at Nuzi one can infer that some were "decurions" (*emantuḫlu*): see Cassin, *loc. cit.*, 229 ff., who quotes SMN 3242 (*Harvard Semitic Series* xv, 62) and comments thereon; again, at Alalakh a sizable number are charioteers — i.e. highly trained soldiery (Bottéro, *op. cit.*, nos. 43, 46; Greenberg, *op. cit.*, nos. 29–30). Where the hapiru contingents were organized by the state their members could rise to positions of respect and responsibility.

15 Bottéro, *op. cit.*, no. 161; J. Nougayrol, *PRU*, IV/1, 1956, pp. 107 f.

16 Bottéro, *op. cit.*, nos. 154–6; Greenberg, *op. cit.*, nos. 140–2.

17 E. A. Speiser, *AASOR*, 16 (1935–6), 124; idem, *JAOS*, 74 (1954), 162; J. Lewy, *Orientalia* (n.s.), 11 (1942), 32 note 1.

[18] Bottéro, *op. cit.*, no. 159; Nougayrol, *PRU*, III/1, 1955, pp. 102 f.

[19] Bottéro, *op. cit.*, nos. 157, 162; Nougayrol, *op. cit.*, III/1, pp. 213 f.; IV/1, pp. 161 ff.

[20] The meaning of *habbātu* is probably "wanderer, vagrant" (from *ḫabātu ša alāki* = "*habātu* of movement"); see the discussion in Greenberg, *op. cit.*, p. 89, and the comment by J. Lewy *apud* Bottéro, *op. cit.*, p. 203 note to p. 143 (for a dissenting view, favoring "robber," cf. that of B. Landsberger, *apud* in *ibid.*, pp. 203–4).

[21] Or from the *hab/pir*-element in names (collected in Greenberg, *op. cit.*, pp. 57 ff.), or from the god *Hab/piru* (Bottéro, *op. cit.*, nos. 167, 89–90; Greenberg, *op. cit.*, nos. 155–6) — whose connection with the hapiru is at best questionable — if, indeed, the reading is not rather *Hawiru* (*ḫa'iru*) "spouse" (W. von Soden *apud* Bottéro, *op. cit.*, p. 135). Whether the Middle Babylonian gentilic *habirāyu* (Bottéro, *op. cit.*, nos. 165–6; Greenberg, *op. cit.*, nos. 143–4) has anything to do with our problem is doubtful; see, for example, R. Borger, *ZDPV*, 74 (1958), 126.

[22] The phonetically consistent variants SA. GA. AZ and SAG. GAZ. seem to point to this.

[23] West Semitic is regularly represented by cuneiform ḫ. The ambiguity of the cuneiform representation of the middle radical (see note 1, above) compels us to lean on the Egyptian and Ugaritic writings, which are not altogether sure supports themselves; for Egyptian *p*, while regularly corresponding to Semitic *p*, may represent the Semitic *b* when preceded or followed by *r/l* (B. Gunn *apud* E. A. Speiser, *AASOR*, 13 [1931–2], 38 note 93); and Ugaritic can be shown sporadically to have gone its own way in voicing labials (Greenberg, *op. cit.*, p. 90, note 24). Nonetheless the reluctance of Borger, *loc. cit.*, 127–8, to rely on such abnormalities is justified. One may doubt whether any question as to the middle radical would have survived the Egyptian and Ugaritic evidence for *p*, had not a connection with *'ivri* "Hebrew" been at stake.

[24] The appeal to a West Semitic root is based a) on the need of Akkadian lexicographers to gloss SA. GAZ/*šaggāšu* by *habbātu* — unnecessary, had *šaggāšu* carried its normal Akkadian value "murderer"; b) the inappropriateness of the Akkadian value as an appellation for the class as a whole.

[25] Speiser, *loc. cit.*, 40 note 96.

[26] See the ancient discussion in Genesis Rabba 42, 8 (Greenberg, *op. cit.*, p. 5 note 24, where it is also shown that the LXX Τῷ περάτῃ [Gen. 14:13] follows the opinion that derives *'ivri* from *'ever* [hanahar], and has nothing to do with the verb *'avar*).

[27] See, for example, Alt, "Ursprünge des israelitischen Rechts", *Kleine Schriften*, I, pp. 292 ff., who sees in *'ivri* a generally derogatory social classification.

[28] Read: *wa-yishmᵉ'u pᵉlishtim le'mor pashᵉ'u ha-'ivrim;* S. R. Driver, *Notes on Samuel* (2nd ed.), Oxford, 1913, *ad loc.*

[29] To call the land of the patriarchs' sojourning *erez ha-'ivrim* is perhaps no more than an anticipation of the later *erez yisra'el* (which would have been an anachronism here). In itself however the naming of the territory, in which they roam, after nomadic herdsmen is not unparalleled: a Mari text mentions three kings "of town X and the country (*māt*) of Y" — where in each case Y is a nomad tribe (G. Dossin, "L'inscription de fondation de Iaḫdun-Lim, roi de Mari," *Syria*, 32 [1955], 14, col. III, lines 4–9; cf. Kupper, *Les nomades en Mésopotamie*, p. 31). For another view, see Y. M. Grintz in *'Oz lᵉ-David* (Ben-Gurion Volume) (Hebrew), Jerusalem, 1964, pp. 92–102.

[30] This passage is often cited to show that *'ivrim* may refer to non-Israelites. But the very necessity of further qualifying "Israel" in the second part of the verse by the clause "that were with Saul and Jonathan" indicates that the preceding *'ivrim* were their countrymen: if the two were not congruous, what need was there further to qualify the latter? See the apt argumentation of J. Wellhausen, *Der Text der Bücher Samuelis*, Göttingen, 1871, *ad loc.*

[31] See Ibn Ezra's dispute (comment to Ex. 21:2) with those who broadened *'ivri* to include peoples kindred to Israel. The

attempt of J. Lewy, *HUCA*, 14 (1939), 608 ff., to interpret Ex. 21:2 ff. in the light of Nuzi habiru contracts is criticized in Greenberg, *op. cit.*, p. 67 note 28; A. Alt's equation of '*ivri* and hapiru here led him to strike out the then superfluous '*eved* (*Kleine Schriften* I, p. 291 note 2) — which bodes ill for that equation.

32   On I Sam. 14:21, see note 29, above.

33   See Ibn Ezra to Ex. 21:2; and A. Guillaume, *PEQ*, 1946, 64 ff.

34   See note 25, above.

35   See H. H. Rowley, *From Joseph to Joshua*, London, 1950, for a comprehensive review of the entire problem. Rowley's position — including his treatment of the habiru — is criticized pertinently by M. Noth, *VT*, 1 (1951), 74 ff.

36   Gen. 14:13. If this datum is late (see the judicious treatment by H. Gunkel, *Genesis* (3rd ed.), Göttingen, 1910, pp. 288–90) it may be no more than a retrojection of the gentilic '*ivrim* found in the Israel–Egypt stories, in a passage where an ethnic designation for Abraham was needed to set him off from Mamre the Amorite. In that event we should be left with no compelling etymology for '*ivri*. On the other hand, this may be among the authentic data of this singular chapter (see Gunkel, *ibid.*, *loc. cit.*), in which case it may be, on the contrary, the source of the subsequent usage of '*ivri* as an ethnicon. The possibility that "Abram the Hebrew" is a genuinely ancient tradition opens the way to a combination with hapiru.

37   The biblical genealogists will then have combined the fact that the Patriarchs were '*ivrim* with the fact of their kinship with other Aramean and Arabic tribes to create the eponymous ancestor Eber, from whom all descended.

CHAPTER XI

THE PATRIARCHS IN THE LAND OF CANAAN

1   What is meant here is undoubtedly the neighborhood of the royal city of Gerar.

2   See R. T. O'Callaghan, *Aram Naharaim*, Rome, 1948, p. 96.

3   Ai is no longer mentioned in this connection.

4   Since Sodom and Gomorrah are mentioned in Gen. 13:10, and Sodom again in verse 12, it may be assumed that the expression "the cities of the Plain" (עָרֵי הַכִּכָּר) refers to the Petapolis mentioned in Gen. 14:2.

5   For a political reason as the background to this discrimination against the Moabites and the Ammonites, see S. Yeivin, *Sefer Dinaburg* (Hebrew), Jerusalem, 1949, pp. 38–40. See also later in this chapter.

6   Such migrations from the neighborhood of Beer-sheba took place even in Chalcolithic times, though their destinations are unknown. See J. Perrot, *IEJ*, 5 (1955), 183–4

7   *ANET*, p. 259.

8   S. Yeivin, *Studies in the History of the Israelites and their Land* (Hebrew), Jerusalem and Tel-Aviv, 1960, pp. 47 ff., and especially p. 58; *Encyclopaedia Biblica* (Hebrew), I, Jerusalem, 1950, cols. 4 ff.; see also W. F. Albright, *BASOR*, 163 (1961), 41 ff.; S. Yeivin, *Bet Miqra* (Hebrew), 7, 4 (1963), 13 ff.; *idem, RSO*, 38 (1963), 301–2.

9   See E. Drioton and J. Vandier, *L'Égypte* (4th ed.), Paris, 1962, pp. 288 ff.; but cf. *ibid.*, pp. 650–1.

10   So it was originally held.

11   See however the end of the chapter, below.

12   On the attempts of the sages to solve this difficulty, see M. Ben Yashar, *Bet Miqra*, 10, 2–3 (1965), 89 ff.

13   In this connection it makes no difference whether the reference is to Zipporah the Midianite, who is described as a Cushite, or to another wife of Moses, who happened to be a Cushite. The point is that intermarriage with non-Israelites, in preference to endogamous marriage, was frowned upon.

14   Cf. I Chron. 2:24, 50; and see *Encyclopaedia Biblica*, III, Jerusalem, 1958, cols. 487 ff., "Judah."

15   Gen. 35:16. In later times, when this Canaanite settlement had apparently been destroyed and abandoned, Ramah was regarded as the place of Rachel's death (see Jer. 31:14, and David Qimḥi's comment on the verse, based on the Midrashim).

16   I Chron. 2:48; 3:2; 7:15; 8:29; 9:35. On the Canaanite origins of the name Maacah, see S. Yeivin, *Eretz-Israel* (Hebrew), 4 (1956), 38–40, although the name may be basically Aramean (see Gen. 22:24; II Sam. 10:6).

17   Apparently a daughter of one of the late Ramessides of the Twentieth or of one of the Delta kinglets of the early Twenty-First Dynasty.

18   This tradition of course reflects the mixed composition of the population in Transjordan, in the territory of the half tribe of Manasseh.

19   No. 75; see S. Yeivin, *Proceedings of the XXIInd International Congress of Orientalists* II, 1957, p. 592.

20   Nos. 100, 106, both apparently within the territory of the kingdom of Gezer, in its western and eastern parts respectively. This territory was mainly included within Dan's earlier area of settlement. But cf. *Encyclopaedia Biblica*, II, Jerusalem, 1954, cols. 263 ff., "Benjamin," and cols. 677 ff., "Dan."

21   Such intermarriage notices as well as the full genealogies are naturally of very great importance in reconstructing the story of the Israelite conquest, settlement, and amalgamation with the pre-Israelite population of the country.

22   See W. F. Albright, *The Archaeology of Palestine*, Harmondsworth, 1949, p. 88.

23   Yeivin, *Eretz-Israel*, 4 (1956), 37 ff.

24   See the references in note 8, above.

25   For details, see the references in note 8, above.

26   See E. Chiera, *Joint Expedition with the Iraq Museum at Nuzi*, Boston, 1927; E. Chiera and E. A. Speiser, *JAOS*, 47 (1927),

37 ff.; Yeivin, *Studies in the History of the Israelites and their Land*, loc. cit.

27 Apart from the cases already mentioned above, see Jud. 19:1 ff., and especially verse 4, where the concubine's father is called the man's father-in-law; II Sam. 3:7; I Kings 11:3.

28 N. Avigad, *IEJ*, 3 (1953), 143 ff.; *idem*, *PEQ*, 1946, 125 ff.

29 See chapter VII, "The Patriarchs and their Social Background," in this volume. Cf. L. Woolley, *Abraham*, London, 1936, pp. 151 ff.; Yeivin, *op. cit.*, *loc. cit.*; J. Wellhausen, *Israelitische und jüdische Geschichte*, Berlin-Leipzig, 1921, pp. 10 ff. On the episode of Rachel's stealing the teraphim from her father Laban and its interpretation against the background of Mesopotamian customs, see C. J. Gadd, *RA*, 23 (1926), 49 ff.; C. H. Gordon, *RB*, 44 (1935), 34 ff.; *ANET*, pp. 219–20. Incidentally, the true meaning of the term "teraphim" is now known; previously it had been variously explained by different scholars, although all were apparently agreed that they were connected with divine images; see Gen. 31 : 30; and also the comments of Ibn Ezra and Naḥmanides on Gen. 31:19.

30 Cf., for example, such passages as Ex. 22:15; Deut. 20:7 (note: "his house"); 21:12 (note: "to thy house"); 24:1–3 (note: "out of his house"); Jud. 19:2 ff.; Ruth 4:10.

31 See *ANET*, p. 182 (§ 27).

32 For a detailed account of the religion of the Patriarchs, see chapter XII, "The Religion of the Patriarchs etc.," in this volume; cf. Yeivin, *Bet Miqra*, 7, 4 (1963), *loc. cit.*; *idem*, *RSO*, 38 (1936), 285–90.

33 Cf. Ex. 6:2–3. Under the name of *El Shaddai*, God revealed Himself to Abraham (Gen. 17:1). On the latter appellation see S. Yeivin, *Alon Memorial Volume*.

34 Ex. 5:1 ("the Lord, the God of Israel"); 10:3 ("the Lord, the God of the Hebrews").

35 Naturally, the conditions and circumstances were then entirely different.

36 M. Avi-Yonah and S. Yeivin, *The Antiquities of Israel* (Hebrew), I, Tel-Aviv, 1957, pp. 165 ff.; L. E. Toombs and G. E. Wright, *BASOR*, 161 (1961), 11 ff.; and see G. E. Wright, *Shechem*, London, 1965.

37 See S. Yeivin, *Encyclopaedia Biblica*, II, cols. 653–4, "Dinah," *ibid.*, II, cols. 677 ff., "Dan," *ibid*, IV, cols. 79 ff., and especially cols. 92–3, "*kibbush ha-Arez*."

38 See Y. Kaufmann, *A History of the Israelite Faith* (Hebrew), Jerusalem and Tel-Aviv, 1954–7.

39 For the details, see Yeivin, *Bet Miqra*, 7, 4 (1963), 13–4, 38 ff.; *idem*, *RSO*, 38 (1963), 284–5, 290 ff.

40 Gen. 18:8 ("And he took curd, and milk, and the calf"); 27:9 ("two . . . kids of the goats").

41 It was in this manner, too, that were obtained the nuts and the almonds as well as the aromatic herbs and the honey which Jacob's sons took to Egypt (Gen. 43:11).

42 See Yeivin, *Bet Miqra*, 7, 4 (1963), 46–7; *idem*, *RSO*, 38 (1963), 300–2. What is known as the lower chronology is used here.

43 For the details, and for this background to the growth of the religion of the Patriarchs, see Yeivin, *Bet Miqra*, 7, 4 (1963), 25 ff.; *idem*, *RSO*, 38 (1963), 279 ff.

44 See however W. Hallo, *JCS*, 18 (1964), 57 ff.

45 For an investigation into the names, and on the general background of this episode, see Yeivin, *Studies in the History of the Israelites and their land*, pp. 56 ff. (and see the detailed bibliography there).

46 See T. Säve-Söderbergh, *JEA*, 37 (1951), 54.

47 See N. Glueck, "Explorations in Eastern Palestine," *AASOR*, 14 (1933–4), 81 ff.

48 How extensive was the commerce of these Mesopotamian allies in that region can be gauged from the fact that several city-states (as far as Hazor in Galilee) are mentioned in the correspondence uncovered at Mari.

49 See J. Bottéro, *Le problème des Ḥabiru*, Paris, 1954; M. Greenberg, *The Ḥab/piru*, New Haven, 1955; M. P. Gray, *HUCA*, 29 (1958), 135 ff.; see also chapter X, "Hab/piru and Hebrews," in this volume; and see Yeivin, *Bet Miqra*, 7, 4 (1963), 24 ff.; *idem*, *RSO*, 38 (1963), 271 ff.

50 The last trace of the Habiru-Hebrews in the land of Israel is to be found in the days of Saul (I Sam. 13 : 7). On the origin and disappearance of the Habiru, see S.

Yeivin, *Proceedings of the XXVth International Congress of Orientalists*, I, Moscow, 1962, pp. 439 ff.

51 See Drioton and Vandier, *L'Égypte*, (4th. ed) pp. 288 ff.

52 Cf. K. v. Galling, *Biblisches Reallexikon*, Tübingen, 1937, "Hyksos."

53 Cf., for example, H. H. Rowley, *From Joseph to Joshua*, London, 1950, pp. 122 ff. (and the bibliography cited there).

CHAPTER XII

THE RELIGION OF THE PATRIARCHS:
BELIEFS AND PRACTICES

¹ 'Eruv. 53a; Gen. Rabba, sect 38, 13; sect. 42, 4; Tanḥuma, Leḵ leḵa, no. 2 etc. and cf. Jubilees 12:1—14; cf. also Josephus *Ant.* I, 154 ff.

² As there exists a great deal of literature on these matters, only the most important works will be indicated here and in the following footnotes. M.–J. Lagrange, *Etudes sur les religions sémitiques*, (2nd ed.) Paris, 1905; P. W. Schmidt, *Der Ursprung der Gottesidee* (2nd. ed.), Münster, 1926–1937; idem, *Origin and Growth of Religion* (translated by J. J. Rose), New York, 1931, (Schmidt's views are close to those of the ethnologist Andrew Lang who also speaks of primitive monothesim); S.H. Langdon, *Semitic Mythology*, Boston, 1931, pp. 89, 93. For a correct, though not exhaustive criticism of Schmidt's and Langdon's views and a rejection of Marston's (Ch. Marston, *The Bible Comes Alive*, London, 1937), who accepts their views, cf. Th. J. Meek, "Primitive Monotheism and the Religion of Moses," *Review of Religion*, 4 (1940), 286–298. For the refutation of Lang, K.Th. Preuss and Schmidt's views on primitive monotheism, see Y. Kaufmann, *History of Israelite Faith* I (Hebrew), Jerusalem and Tel Aviv, 1954, pp. 287–289, 315–323.

³ Lagrange, *op. cit.*, pp. 70–83; Langdon, *op. cit.*, p. 93; F. Delitzsch, *Babel und Bibel* (5th ed.), Leipzig, 1905, pp. 49, 75. A somewhat similar view is expressed by Kittel, in *GVI*, I ⁵ ᵘ⁻ ⁶, 258, 264–5, 288–290. He speaks of a monistic *El Religion* which is close to monotheism. Trends approaching the monotheistic conception existed in Canaan, symbolised amongst others by the figure of Melchizedek King of Salem, priest of *El 'Elyon*. Abraham himself was no real monotheist, neither did he worship this god, but his belief was close to monotheism.

⁴ E. Renan, *Histoire du peuple d'Israël*, I, Paris, 1887 (in Book I see especially chapters 3, 4).

⁵ H. Winkler, *Abraham als Babylonier*, Leipzig, 1903, pp. 25 ff.; A. Jeremias, *Monotheistische Strömungen innerhalb der babylonischen Religion*, Leipzig, 1904; idem, *Das AT im Lichte des Alten Orients* (3rd ed.), Leipzig, 1916, pp. 257 ff.; 263–276; B. Baentsch, *Altorientalischer und israelitischer Monotheismus*, Tübingen, 1906, pp. 5 ff., 42–54, 62–65; F. M. Th. Böhl, "Das Zeitalter Abrahams," *AO*, vol. 29, fasc. 1, Leipzig (1930) 41–44; and also Delitzsch (see note 3 above).

⁶ See for example L. Wooley, *Abraham: Recent Discoveries and Hebrew Origins*, London, 1936, pp. 188–190, 198, 241–255. And cf. also Kittel, *loc. cit.*

⁷ See for example: E. König, *Geschichte der Alttestamentlichen Religion*, Gütersloh, 1912, pp. 26–34, 124 ff. Cf. also "The Modern Attack on the Historicity of the Religion of the Patriarchs," *JQR*, (NS) 22 (1931–2), 119–142. A number of strong arguments and discerning distinctions are to be found in the detailed article by I. Rabin, "Studien zur vormosaischen Gottesvorstellung," *Festschrift zum 75 jährigen Bestehen des jüdisch-theologischen Seminars*, I, Breslau (1929), 257–356, but it also bears the stamp of fundamentalist treatment.

⁸ On all this cf. Kaufmann, *op. cit.*, I, pp. 726–736, II, pp. 29–30.

⁹ There is no point in giving here the whole vast scientific literature which follows this system. Any bibliographical selection will necessarily be fragmentary. The most systematic and detailed attempt to follow this method is perhaps that of Lods; cf. A. Lods, *Israël des origines au milieu du VIIIe siécle*, Paris, 1930 (particularly part II, vol. II: "The Religion of the Nomadic Hebrews," English translation by S. H. Hooke, London, 1948). Cf. also his article — "The Religion of Israel-Origins," *Record and Revelation*, ed. by H. W. Robinson, Oxford, 1938, pp. 187–202.

¹⁰ This was correctly emphasized by W.W. Graf Baudissin, *Kyrios als Gottesnahme im Judentum*, etc., III, Giessen, 1929, pp. 158–164, but even he was not free of the system

according to which the stories of the Patriarchs only reflect the religious situation of the period following Moses.

11   For detailed discussion see H. Gunkel, *Genesis* (3ʳᵈ ed.), Göttingen, 1910, § 4 and cf. H. Gressmann, "Sage und Geschichte in den Patriarchen-erzählungen," *ZAW*, 30 (1910), 25 ff.; Kittel, *GVI*, I, § 24.

12   Cf. at present: Gressmann, *ibid.* 30—34; Kittel, *op. cit.* § 25; Kaufmann, *op. cit.*, pp. 187—196, 208—210 and see "Avoth" in *Encyclopaedia Biblica*, (Hebrew) I, cols. 7–8.

13   Cf. the summary of this aspect in "The Patriarchs and their Social Background," chap. VII above.

14   *Israel* appears to indicate here the name of the man and not the name of the nation, as was already felt by the traditional commentators (Rashi, Abraham ibn 'Ezra, Samuel ben Meir).

15   Read: *weʾel Shaddai* instead of *weʾet shaddai*, like in the ancient versions, and cf. commentaries. According to this, the name *Shaddai* does not appear by itself in Genesis but only in the complete form of *El Shaddai*.

16   An isolated and unusual instance is "the house of Baal-berith," (Jud. 9:4), which is also called "the house of El-berith" (*ibid.* 46). Several Greek versions read *Baal* for it, in the second verse. It would seem that Baal-berith is here the original name, while El-berith was at most a customary substitute. We must remember that here this name was given to a house, i.e. to a temple, while with the Patriarchs there were no temples (cf. see below). Hence El-berith has no connection whatsoever with the *Els* of the patriarchal period.

17   Cf. Gunkel, *op. cit.* LX, pp. 187, 236, 285, Gressmann, *ibid.* 8 ff.; idem, *Moses und seine Zeit*, Göttingen, 1913, pp. 425—430. To the *Els* mentioned Gressmann adds *El paḥad* in place of the "*paḥad* of Isaac" mentioned in Scripture (Gen. 31:42, 53) and locates him at Mizpah. But this assertion has no basis. Gunkel at first thought that the Israelite tribes adopted the *El Religion* via the Canaanites. Later on he reconsidered his views and accepted Gressmann's opinion that this is an original Hebrew heritage. Baudissin disagreed with

both of them and followed Gunkel's former view, cf. Baudissin, *op. cit.* pp. 124–143; cf. also Kittel, *GVI*, I⁵ ᵘ. ⁶ 264–265, and see also I. Rabin, *op. cit.*, 285–295.

18   See M. D. Cassuto, *From Adam to Noah*, (Hebrew), Jerusalem, 1944, pp. 113—115; idem. *The Goddess Anath*, (Hebrew), Jerusalem, 1951, p. 43 and not as explained by G. Levi della Vida, "El Elyon in Genesis 14: 18–20," *JBL*, 63 (1944), 1 note 1.

19   *'Elyon* is mentioned in the Aramaic inscription of Sujin and in the writings of Philo of Byblos Ἐδιοῦν). Οὐδωμῶς according to Damascius. Beth-el as a specific divinity is mentioned in the contract between Eserhaddon King of Assyria and the King of Tyre, in the words of Philo of Byblos (Βαῖτυδος), in personal names in the Bible (Zech. 7:2), in extra-Biblical sources (Elephantine Papyrus and Aramean inscriptions) and according to some also in the Ugaritic inscriptions, and perhaps in several verses in the Bible (e.g. Jer. 48:13; Hos. 10:15; Am. 3:14); cf. *El beth-el, El 'Olam, El 'Elyon*, in *Biblical Encyclopaedia*, (Hebrew), I, cols. 285–289, and cf. H. G. May, "The Patriarchal Idea of God," *JBL*, 60 (1941), 120—121, and in the literature given there.

20   Occasionally, scholars portray the different *Els* as being attached to these same Canaanite cities, and they use this assumption as a starting-point for explaining their nature. This also applies to Gressmann (see note 17 above). The traditions determine the wanderings of the Patriarchs on the borders and in the interior of the country. But even in these areas they have no contact with the Canaanite walled cities since they only dwell in the open country, within sight of the cities (cf. Gen. 14:17–18; 33:18—20).

21   A similar Hebrew name *Shaddaiammi* is perhaps mentioned in a contemporary Egyptian source, see W. F. Albright, *From the Stone Age to Christianity*, Baltimore, 1940, p. 185.

22   See Ranke *apud* H. Gressmann, *JAW*, 30 (1910), 6—7 and cf. May, *JBL*, 60 (1941) 116—7, note 8.

23   See note 15 above.

24   On the Cappadocian parallels see

J. Lewy, *Revue de l'histoire des religions*, 110 (1934), 50 ff.; and cf. Albright, "The Names Shaddai and Abram," *JBL*, 54 (1935), 188—190. However in the Cappadocian texts no nameless "God of the father" appears. They call by this name at least the God Ilabrat, and perhaps also other gods (according to Albright). For "God of the father" in general, cf. also May, *ibid.*, 60 (1941), 123—126, who adduces some relevant notes. See also J. P. Hyatt, *VT*, 5 (1955), 130 ff. and the literature there. Alt's particular view refers to a different matter. A considerable number of scholars appear to have confused it with the subject discussed by Lewy.

25 See Hyatt, *ibid.*, 131—132.

26 Scholars had noticed quite a time ago that YHWH originated in the period which preceded Moses. See for example B. Stade, *Biblische Theologie des AT*, I, Tübingen, 1905 § 15, 1. This aspect of the Patriarchs' belief is indicated below as it appears to the present writer.

27 Despite the fact that it is D which emphatically proclaims: "YHWH made not this covenant with our fathers, but with us, even us, who are all of us here alive this day" (Dt. 5:3).

28 Compare against this view, that expressed by Alt in *Der Gott der Väter*, Stuttgart, 1929, and which has been accorded much attention in the latest works on the subject. See now Alt, *Kleine Schriften*, I, 1—78.

29 W. F. Albright, *From Stone Age*, etc., pp. 185—187.

30 Cf. B. Mazar (Maisler), "The Genealogy of the Sons of Nahor and the Historical Background of the Book of Job" (Hebrew) Zion, 11 (1946), 1—16; Kaufmann, *The History of Israelite Religion*, (Hebrew), II, 653.

31 Among the children of Joktan: Almodad, Abimael (Gen. 10:26, 28). Among the children of Nahor: Kemuel, Bethuel (Gen. 22:21—22); to Ishmael can be added Adbeel (Gen. 25:13); among Keturah's children: Eldaah (Gen. 25:4); of the children of Edom: Eliphaz, Reuel, et al. Job's companions: Eliphaz, Elihu the son of Barachel; Ithiel (Prov. 30:1); Lemuel (*ibid.* 31:1), and cf. Reuel, priest

of Midian (Ex. 2:18). On the other hand, we do not find such names, for example, among the Horites, the inhabitants of the land of Seir (Gen. 36:20—30). The names Mehujael, Metushael (Gen. 4:18) and Mahalaleel (Gen. 5:15) which refer to people before the Flood, are fictitious or their form was Hebraised. Compare Methuselah in the parallel tradition (Gen. 5:25) with Metushael.

32 One need not necessarily look for such parallelism in two adjacent parts of the same verse. Sometimes it occurs in two adjoining, connected verses. See for example Job. 21:14—15; 22:2—3.

33 Apart from the stories of the Patriarchs the name *Shaddai* occurs twice in Ezekiel (1:24; 10:5) — doubtlessly under the influence of P — and twice in Ruth (1:20—21), spoken in a rhymed, elevated prose by Naomi, on her return from the Field of Moab.

34 The children of Keturah belonged to the *Children of Kedem* (Gen. 25:1), but the latter are mentioned in Jer. 49:28, as a parallel to Kedar. In the story of Gideon we read of "The Midianites and the Amalekites" (who belong to the Children of Edom) and the *Children of Kedem* (Jud. 6:3), but further on they or their kings are called Ishmaelites (ibid. 8:24). Similarly, in the story of the sale of Joseph, the Ishmaelites (Gen. 37:25—28) are changed to Midianites and to M^edanim (ibid. 28, 36) — and even if we were to assume that this proves different sources, it still indicates that these peoples were ethnically and socially close to each other. Isa. 60:6—7 enumerates in one list, Midian, Ephah and Sheba all of which are children of Keturah (Gen. 25:2—4) with Kedar and Nebaioth the Ishmaelites. The Dedanites, who are children of Keturah, are mentioned next to the Ishmaelites Tema and Kedar or interchanged with them (Isa. 21:13—17 [and *ibid.* 11, for Dumah, also an Ishmaelite]; Jer. 25:23). P says nothing of the children of Keturah, while several of the peoples mentioned in JE as the children of Keturah (or the children of Joktan) are considered by P as children of Cush the son of Ham (Gen. 10:6—7). But this does not alter the

possibility that P considered them to be circumcised too, since Mizraim (also one of the circumcised peoples) was descended from Ham.

35 This depends on the answer to the question what is comprised in the ethnic concept *Hebrew* according to the Bible — whether it includes all the nations considered as the *sons* of Eber (Gen. 10:21—25, as stated above), or only the descendants of Abraham, who according to it was the first *Hebrew* (Gen. 14:13). It appears that in the Bible itself there is no decision taken on this subject, but to the extent the biblical tradition mentions a religious innovation, it refers to Abraham's descendants only.

36 For this matter cf. F. M. Th. Böhl, "Das Zeitalter Abrahams," *ibid.*, 32—33. He says these things precisely of the Abram-Abraham change of name, while he does not attribute any proselytizing meaning to the Jacob-Israel change. In our view, it is difficult to attribute a religious value to the first change, since it obviously depends on linguistic-dialectal variations. As against this, Jacob and Israel are completely different names, and the story of their change can only be understood against the background of the religious transformation undergone by the Hebrew tribes.

37 On this point the exponents of the Pan-Babylonian school were right in stressing the religious aspect of Abraham's personality. For a correct presentation of this matter, see for example, Böhl, *ibid.*, 41.

38 In the former research this chapter was used as evidence for the monotheistic turning-point which took place since Abraham. See for example, E. König, *Geschichte der Alttestamentlichen Religion*, pp. 26—28. Actually all that can be concluded is the fact that a certain change did occur. The monotheistic character the Bible attributes to this turning-point is taken from the concepts of the historical Israelite faith, and cf. Josh. 24:14: "And put away the gods which your fathers served beyond the River, *and in Egypt;* and serve ye the Lord." The writer did feel that the Exodus was also connected with a religious turning-point, to which the whole Bible subscribes.

39 In this respect there is some truth in Alt's view that the religion of the Patriarchs was a preparatory stage towards the religion of YHWH and that it was on this account that the latter became the dominant religion of the Israelite tribes. Cf. Alt, *Kleine Schriften*, I, pp. 62 ff. We cannot, however, accept his description of the Patriarchs' religion. For the religion of the Patriarchs as a forerunner of the Yahwistic faith cf. also Kaufmann, *The History of Israelite Religion*, II, p. 31. The Pan-Babylonian school supported, of course, the same point of view.

40 S. Daiches, "Balaam, A Babylonian bārū," in *Hilprecht Anniversary Volume*, London, 1909, pp. 60—70; and cf. J. Liver, "Balaam in the Biblical Tradition," (Hebrew), *Eretz Israel*, 3 (1954), 99—100.

41 Moses' father-in-law who was called *priest of Midian*, (Ex. 2:16; 18:1), maybe according to the late concepts. Nowhere in the Bible is Balaam called a priest. Neither is there any reference to a priesthood in the Book of Job.

42 Close to the meaning of Arabic *maqām*. On this matter cf. A. Lods, *Israel*, pp. 264 ff.

43 The text has: "And he erected [*wayyazev*] there an altar," but since in other passages we find the verb "erect" used for a pillar, it has been suggested to read here: "And he erected there a pillar." But further on we read: "And called it (Hebrew *lo* 3rd person sing. masc.) — which was therefore emended to *lah* (3rd person sing. fem., the word pillar being feminine). But there does not seem to be any real difficulty about the words:" And he erected there an altar," since with the ancients a single stone could serve sometimes as an altar, and the verb "erect" is adequate in this context.

BIBLIOGRAPHY

CHAPTER I

HISTORIOGRAPHY AND HISTORIC SOURCES

Albright, W. F., *From the Stone Age to Christianity* Baltimore, 1940.

Brundage, B.C., "The Birth of Clio: A Résumé and Interpretation of Ancient Near Eastern Historiography," *Teachers of History*, ed. by H. S. Hughes, Ithaca, 1954, 199–230.

Frankfort, H., *Kingship and the Gods*, Chicago, 1948.

Gadd, C. J., *Ideas of Divine Rule in the Ancient Near East*, London, 1948.

Güterbock, H. G., "Die historische Tradition und ihre literarische Gestaltung bei Babyloniern und Hethitern bis 1200," *ZA*, 42(1934), 1–91.

Jacobsen, T., *The Sumerian King List*, Chicago, 1939.
"Mesopotamia", apud H. Frankfort et alii, *The Intellectual Adventure of Ancient Man*, Chicago,1964, 125–222.

Kramer, S. N., "Sumerian Historiography," *IEJ*, 3(1953), 217–232.

Labat, R., *Le caractère religieux de la royauté assyro-babylonienne*, Paris, 1939.

Mowinckel, S., "Die vorderasiatische Königs- und Fürsteninschriften", *H. Gunkel Festschrift* (= Forschungen zur Religion und Literatur Alten und Neuen Testaments, N.F., 19 Heft 1 Teil), Göttingen 1923, 278–322.

Olmstead, A. T., *Assyrian Historiography*, Columbia, Missouri 1917.

Speiser, E. A., "The Idea of History in Ancient Mesopotamia," *The Idea of History in the Ancient Near East*, ed. by R. C. Dentan, New Haven 1955, 37–76, 361–362.

CHAPTER II

UGARITIC WRITINGS

Ginsberg, H. A., *Ugaritic Writings*, Jerusalem, 1936.

Cassuto, M. D., *The Godess Anath*, (Hebrew), Jerusalem, 1951, and see there the author's bibliography accompanying the articles on Ugarit.

Aistleitner, J., *Die mythologischen und kultischen Texte aus Ras Schamra*, Budapest, 1959 *Woerterbuch der Ugaritischen Sprache*, Berlin 1963.

Caquot, A., "le dieu 'Athtar," *Syria*, 35 (1958), 45–60.

Driver, G. R., *Canaanite Myths and Legends*, Edinburgh, 1956.

Fronzaroli, P., *La Fonetica Ugaritica*, Roma 1955.

Gaster, T. H., *Thespis; Ritual Myth and Drama in the Ancient Near East* (rev. ed.), New York 1961, passim.

Ginsberg, H. L., "Ugaritic Myths, Epics, and Legends," *ANET²*, 129–155.

Goeseke, H., "Die Sprache der Semitischen Texte aus Ugarit und ihre Stellung innerhalb des Semitischen," *Wissenschaftliche*

Zeitschrift der Martin-Luther Universitaet Halle-Wittenberg, Gesammelte Sprachwissenschaft VII, 7(1958), 633–652.

Gordon, C. H., *Ugaritic Literature*, Roma 1949.
Ugaritic Textbook, Roma, 1965, (cf. there the bibliography of bibliographies).

Gray, J., *The Krt Text in the Literature of Ras Shamra*, Leiden 1955.
The Legacy of Canaan, The Ras Schamra Texts and their Relevance to the Old Testament, Leiden 1957.

Kapelrud, A. S., *Baal in the Ras Shamra Texts*, Copenhagen, 1952.

Klengel, H., "Zur Geschichte von Ugarit," *OLZ*, 57(1962), 453–462.

Liverani, M., *Storia di Ugarit*, Roma, 1962.

Mendelsohn, I., "Samuel's Denunciation of Kingship in the Light of the Akkadian Documents from Ugarit," *BASOR*, 143 (1956), 17–22.

Nougayrol, J., *Le Palais royal d'Ugarit*, III–IV, Paris, 1955–1956.

Obermann, J., *Ugaritic Mythology*, New Haven 1948.

Pope, M. H., *El in the Ugaritic Texts*, Leiden 1955.

Schaeffer, C. F. A., et alii, *Ugaritica*, I–III, Paris, 1939–1956.

Selms, A., van, *Marriage and Family Life in Ugaritic Literature*, London, 1954.

CHAPTER III

THE CANAANITE INSCRIPTIONS AND THE STORY OF THE ALPHABET

Yeivin, S., *The history of the Jewish script* (Hebrew), I, Jerusalem, 1939.

Diringer, D., *The Alphabet²*, London, 1949.

Driver, G. R., *Semitic Writing: From Pictograph to Alphabet²*, London, 1954.

Dunand, M., *Byblia Grammata*, Beyrouth 1945

S. Yeivin, *JPOS*, 21 (1948), 165 ff., (criticism on the above mentioned).

Friedrich, J., *Entzifferung ferschollener Schriften und Sprachen*, Berlin 1954.

Gelb, I. J., *A Study of Writing*, London, 1952.

Milik, J. T., "An Unpublished Arrow-Head with Phoenician Inscription of the 11th–19th Century B.C.," *BASOR*, 143(1956), 3 ff.

Milik, J. T. — Cross, F. M., Jr., "Inscribed Javelin-Heads from the period of the Judges: A Recent Discovery in Palestine," *BASOR*, 134(1954), 5 ff.

Yevin, S., "Note sur une pointe de flèche inscrite provenant de la Beqaa (Liban)," *RB*, 65(1958), 585 ff.

CHAPTER IV

THE BIBLE AND ITS HISTORICAL SOURCES

"The Beginning of Historiography in Israel", *Eretz Israel I* (1951) 85–88.

Kaufmann, Y., *A History of the Israelite Religion I, IV*, Tel Aviv, 1962.

Albright, W. F., *From the Stone Age to Christianity*, Baltimore, 1940.

Segal, M. Z., *Introduction to the Study of the Bible* (4th ed., Hebrew), Jerusalem, 1956.

Soloweitchik, M., and Rubascheff, S., *The History of Bible Criticism* (Hebrew), Berlin, 1925.

Cassuto, M. D., "The Epic in Israel" (Hebrew) *K^enesset* 8 (1943–4) 121–142.

Bentzen, A., *Introduction to the Old Testament²*, Copenhagen, 1952.

Bright, J., *Early Israel in Recent History Writing*, London, 1956.

Cook, S. A. "Saliant Problems in OT History," *JBL*, 51 (1932), 273–299.

Dentan, R. C. (ed.), *The Idea of History in the Ancient Near East*, New Haven, 1955.

Eissfeldt, O., *Geschichtsschreibung im Alten Testament*, Berlin 1948.
Einleitung in das Alte Testament³, Tübingen 1964.

Hahn, H. F., *The Old Testament in Modern Research*, Philadelphia, 1954.

Jacob, E., *La tradition historique en Israël*, Montpellier, 1946.

Jirku, A., *Die älteste Geschichte Israels im Rahmen lehrhafter Darstellungen*, Leipzig, 1917.

Mowinckel, S., "Hat es ein israelitisches Nationalepos gegeben," *ZAW*, 53 (1935), 130–152.

Nielsen, E., *Oral Tradition*, London, 1954.

Rowley, H. H., (ed), *The Old Testament and Modern Study*, Oxford 1951.

Speiser, E. A., "The Biblical Idea of History in its Common Near Eastern Setting," *IEJ*, 7 (1957), 201–216.

Wright, G. E., "Archaeology and OT Studies," *JBL*, 77 (1958), 39–51.

CHAPTER V

THE CHRONOLOGY OF THE ANCIENT NEAR EAST IN THE SECOND MILLENNIUM B.C.E.

Albright, W. F., "A Third Revision of the Early Chronology of Western Asia," *BASOR*, 88 (1942), 28 ff.
"An Indirect Synchronism between Egypt and Mesopotamia, c. 1730 B. C.," *ibid.*, 99 (1945), 9 ff.
"Stratigraphic Confirmation of the Low Mesopotamian Chronology," *ibid.*, 144 (1956), 26 ff.
"Further Observations on the Chronology of Alalakh," *ibid.*, 146 (1957), 26 ff.

Beckerath, J., von, *Untersuchungen zur politischen Geschichte in der zweiten Zwischenzeit in Ägypten*, Glückstadt, 1964.

Brinkman, J. A., *A Political History of Post-Kassite Babylonia, 1158–722 B.C.*, Rome, 1968.

Campbell, E. F., *The Chronology of the Amarna Letters*, Baltimore, 1964.

Černý, J., "The Contribution of Study of Unofficial and Private Documents to the History of Pharaonic Egypt," *Le fonti indirette della storia Egiziana*, ed. by S. Donadoni (*Studi Sem.*, 7), Roma, 1963, pp. 31 ff.

Cornelius, F., "Die Chronologie des vorderen Orients im 2. Jahrtausend v. Chr." *AfO*, 17 (1956), 294 ff.

Drioton, E. and Vandier, J., *L'Égypte⁴*, Paris, 1962.

Edgerton, W. F., "Chronology of the Twelfth Dynasty," *JNES*, 1 (1942), 307 ff.

Gardiner, Sir Alan H., *Egypt of the Pharaohs*, Oxford, 1961.

Gelb, I. J., "Two Assyrian King Lists", *JNES*, 13 (1954), 209 ff.

Goetze, A., "The Problem of Chronology and Early Hittite History," *BASOR*, 122 (1951), 18 ff.
"On the Chronology of the Second Millennium B.C.," *JCS*, 11 (1957), 53 ff.
"Alalakh and Hittite Chronology," *BASOR*, 146 (1957), 20 ff.
"The Kassite and Near-Eastern Chronology," *ibid.*, 18 (1964), 97 ff.
"The Predecessors of Šuppilulimaš of Hatti and the Chronology of the Ancient Near East," *JCS*, 22 (1968), 46 ff.

Gurney, O. R., *The Hittites*, London, 1961.
"Anatolia," *CAH* (rev. ed.), II, chap. 15(a) (= fasc. no. 44), 1966.

Hayes, W. C., in "Chronology," *CAH* (rev. ed.), I, chap. 6 (= fasc. no. 4), 1962, Section I; and bibliography there.

Helck, H. W., *Untersuchungen zu Manetho und den ägyptischen Königslisten*, Berlin, 1956. *Die Beziehungen Ägyptens zu Vorderasien im 3. und 2. Jahrtausend v. Chr.*, Wiesbaden, 1962.

Hornung, E., *Untersuchungen zur Chronologie und Geschichte des Neuen Reiches*, Wiesbaden, 1964.

Kitchen, K. A., *Suppiluliuma and the Amarna Pharaohs*, Liverpool, *1962*. "On the Chronology and History of the New Kingdom," *Chronique d'Égypte*, 40 (1965), 310 ff. "Further Notes on New Kingdom Chronology and History," *ibid.*, 43 (1968), 313 ff.

Landsberger, B., "Assyrische Königsliste und 'Dunkles Zeitalter'," *JCS*, 8 (1954), 31 ff., 47 ff., 106 ff.

Laroche, E., "Chronologie Hittite: état des questions," *Anadolu*, 2 (1955), 1 ff.

Lewy, H., "On some Problems of Kassite and Assyrian Chronology," *Melanges Isidore Levy*, Brussels, 1955, pp. 241 ff. "The Synchronism Assyrian-Ešnunna-Babylon," *Die Welt des Orients*, 2 (1959), 438 ff.

Otten, H., "Die hettitischen 'Königslisten' und die altorientalische Chronologie," *MDOG*, 83 (1951), 47 ff. Die hethitischen historischen Quellen und die altorientlische Chronologie, Wiesbaden, 1968; *Abhandlungen der Akademie der Wissenschaften und der Literatur, Geistes und Sozialwissenschaftlichen Klasse, Jahrgang 1968, no. 3.*

Parker, R. A., *The Calendars of Ancient Egypt*, Chicago, 1950. "The Lunar Dates of Thutmose III and Ramesses II," *JNES*, 16 (1957), 39 ff.

Parrot, A., *Archéologie mésopotamienne*, II, Paris, 1953, pp. 332 ff.; and bibliography there.

Poebel, A., "The Assyrian King-List from Khorsabad," *JNES*, 1 (1942), 247 ff, 460 ff; 2 (1943), 56 ff.

Redford, D. B., "On the Chronology of the Egyptian Eighteenth Dynasty," *JNES*, 25 (1966), 113 ff. *History and Chronology of the Eighteenth Dynasty of Egypt*, Toronto, 1967.

Rowton, M. B., "The Date of Hammurabi," *JNES*, 17 (1958), 97 ff. "The Background of the Treaty between Ramesses II and Hattusilis III," *JCS*, 13 (1959), 1 ff. "Comparative Chronology at the Time of Dynasty XIX," *JNES*, 19 (1960), 15 ff. "Chronology", *CAH* (rev. ed.), I, chap. 6 (= fasc. No. 4), 1962, Section II; and bibliography there. "The Material from Western Asia and the Chronology of the Nineteenth Dynasty," *JNES*, 25 (1966), 240 ff.

Schmidtke, F., *Der Aufbau der Babylonischen Chronologie* (*Orbis Antiquus*, 7), Münster, 1952.

Smith, S., *Alalakh and Chronology*, London, 1940.

Tadmor, H., "Historical Implications of the Correct Rendering of Akkadian *dâku*," *JNES*, 17 (1958), 129 ff.

Thureau-Dangin, F., "La chronologie de la première dynastie babylonienne," *Mémoires de l'Académie des Inscriptions et Belles-Lettres*, 43 (1942), 229 ff.

Weidner, E., "Bemerkungen zur Königliste aus Khorsabad," *AfO*, 15 (1945-51), 85 ff.

Wente, E. F., "On the Chronology of the Twenty-First Dynasty," *JNES*, 26 (1967), 155 ff.

CHAPTER VI

THE NORTHWEST-SEMITIC LANGUAGES

Ohlendorf, A., "The place of Ugaritic among the Semitic languages" *Tarbiz*, (Hebrew) 24 (1951), 121–125.

Aisleitner, J., "Studien zur Frage der Sprachverwandtschaft des Ugaritischen," *Acta Orientalia*, 7(1957), 251–307; 8 (1958), 51–98.

Brockelmann, C., *Grundriss der vergleichenden Grammatik der semitischen Sprachen*, I–II, Berlin, 1908–13.

Dahood, M., "The Linguistic Position of Ugaritic in the Light of Recent Discoveries," *Sacra Pagina*, I, Paris, Gembloux 1959, 269–279.

Fleisch, H., *Introduction à l'étude des langues sémitiques*, Paris, 1947.

Friedrich, J., "Kanaanäisch und Westsemitisch", *Scientia*, 84 (1949), 220–223.

Garbini, G., *Il semitico di nord-ovest*, Napoli 1960.

Ginsberg, H. L., "Aramaic Studies Today," *JAOS*, 62 (1942), 229–238.

Kramers, J. H., *De semietische talen*, Leiden 1949.
"Langues et écritures sémitiques," *Dictionnaire de la Bible, Supplément*, V, Paris 1957, 257–334.

Moran, W. L., "The Hebrew Language in its Northwest Semitic Background," *The Bible and the Ancient Near East* (Essays in honor of W. F. Albright, ed. by G. E. Wright), London, 1961, 54–72.

Moscati, S., "Il semitico di nord-ovest", *Studi orientalistici in onore di G. Levi Della Vida*, II, Roma 1956, 201–221.
"Sulla posizione linguistica del semitico nord-occidentale", *RSO*, 31 (1956), 229–234.

Moscati, S., (ed.), Spitaler, A. Ullendorff, E., von Soden, W., *An Introduction to the Comparative Grammar of the Semitic Languages: Phonology and Morphology (Porta Linguarum Semiticarum, NS VI)*, Wiesbaden, 1964 (and cf. there the comprehensive bibliography in the publications of the years 1908–1962).

Rinaldi, G., *Le lingue semitiche*, Turin, 1954.

Rosenthal, F., *Die aramäistische Forschung seit Th. Nöldeke's Veröffentlichungen*, Leiden 1939.

CHAPTER VII

WARFARE IN THE SECOND MILLENNIUM B.C.E.

Yeivin, S., "Building" (III "Fortifications") *Encyclopaedia Biblica* II, Jerusalem, 1954, cols. 223 ff.

Albright, W. F., "Mitannian maryannu, 'Chariot-Warrior', and the Canaanite and Egyptian Equivalents," *AfO*, 6 (1930–31), 217 ff.

Albright, W. F. and Mendenhall, G. E., "The Creation of the Composite Bow in Canaanite Mythology," *JNES*, 1 (1942), 277 ff.
Archives royales de Mari, I–XII, XV, Paris 1946–1964.

Barrois, A., *Manuel d'archéologie biblique*, I, Paris, 1939, 127 ff. (La fortification).

Bonnet, H., *Die Waffen der Völker des alten Orients*, Leipzig, 1926.

Breasted, J. H., *The Battle of Kadesh*, Chicago, 1903.

Chenet, G., "Hrb de Ras-Shamra-Ugarit," *Mélanges Syriens (Dussaud)*, I, Paris, 1939, 49 ff.

Cross, F. M. — Milik, J. T., "El Khadr Javelin and Arrow Heads," *Annual of the Department of Antiquities of Jordan*, 3 (1956), 15 ff.

Dossin, G., "Signaux lumineaux au pays de Mari", *RA*, 35 (1938), 174–186.
"Benjaminites dans les textes de Mari," *Mélanges Syriens*, II, Paris 1939, 981–996.

Faulkner, R. O., "The Battle of Megiddo", *JEA*, 28 (1942), 2–15.

"The Battle of Megiddo," *JEA*, 38 (1952), 2 ff.

"Egyptian Military Organization," *JEA*, 39 (1953), 32 ff.

"The Euphrates Campaign of Tuthmosis III," *JEA*, 32 (1946), 40 ff.

Goetze, A., "Die Annalen des Muršiliš," *MVAG*, 38 (1933), 1 ff.

Helck, H. W., *Der Einfluss der Militärführer in der 18. ägytischen Dynastie*, Leipzig 1939.

Hood, M. S. F., "A Mycenaean Cavalryman," *The Annual of the British School at Athens*, 48 (1953), 84–93.

Hrozný, B., "L'Entraînement des Chevaux chez les Anciens Indo-Européens etc," *Archiv Orientální*, 3 (1931), 431–461.

Jean, Ch. F., "L'Armée du Royaume de Mari," *RA*, 42 (1948), 135 ff.

Knudtzon, J. A., *Die El-Amarna Tafeln*, I–II, Leipzig, 1907–1915.

Lacheman, E. R., "Epigraphic Evdences of the Material Culture of the Nuzians," apud R. F. S. Starr, *Nuzi*, I, Text, Harvard University Press, 1939, Appendix D (528 ff.)

Maxwell-Hyslop, R., "Daggers and Swords in Western Asia," *Iraq*, 8 (1946), 1 ff.

"Western Asiatic Shaft-Hole Axes", *Iraq*, (1949), 90 ff.

Moortgat, A., "Der Kampf zu Wagen in der Kunst des Alten Orients," *OLZ*, 33 (1930), 841 ff.

Vorderasiatische Rollsiegel, Berlin, 1940.

Nelson, H. H., *The Battle of Megiddo*, Chicago, 1913.

"The Naval Battle Pictured at Medinet Habu," *JNES*, 2 (1943), 40 ff.

Salonen, A., *Der Abschnitt "Wagen" der 5. Tafel der Serie ḪAR — ra = ḫubullu*, Helsinki, 1945.

Säve-Söderbergh, T., "The Hyksos Rule in Egypt," *JEA*, 37 (1951), 53 ff.

Schulman, A. R., "Egyptian Representations of Horsemen and Riding in the New-Kingdom", *JNES*, 16(1957), 263 ff.

Thureau-Dangin, F., "Textes de Mari," *RA*, 33 (1936), 169–179.

"Kabâbu, Arîtu, Tuksu," *RA*, 36 (1939), 57 ff.

Wiesner, J., "Fahren und Reiten in Alteuropa und im Alten Orient", *AO*, Band 38, Heft 2–4, Leipzig, 1939.

Wilson, J. A., "The Texts of the Battle of Kadesh," *AJSL*, 43 (1927), 266 ff.

Wolf, W., *Die Bewaffnung des altägyptischen Heeres*, Leipzig 1926.

Yadin (Sukenik), Y., "The Composite Bow of the Canaanite Goddess Anath," *BASOR*, 107 (1947), 11 ff.

"A Note on the TLT SSWM in Ugarit," *JCS*, 2 (1948), 11 ff.

"Let the Young men, I Pray Thee, Arise and Play before us," *JPOS*, 21 (1948), 110 ff.

"Hyksos Fortifications and the Battering-Ram," *BASOR*, 137 (1955), 23 ff.

"Goliath's Javelin, etc.," *PEQ*, 87 (1955), 58 ff.

CHAPTER IX

THE PATRIARCHS IN THE LAND OF CANAAN

Yadin, Y., *The Art of Warfare in the countries of the Bible*," Ramat Gan, 1963.

Yeivin, S., *The epos of Shanhet*, Tel Aviv, 1930. *Studies in the History of Israel and his land*, Tel Aviv, Jerusalem, 1960.

Mazar, B., "Canaan on the eve of the Patriarchs' Period," *Eretz Israel* III (1954) 18–32.

Malamat, A., "Hazor head of all those kingdoms in the light of the epigraphic and archeologic descoveries," *Isaac Baer Jubilee Volume*, 1961, p. 1–7.

Albright, W. F., "Abram the Hebrew", *BASOR*, 163 (1961), 36 ff.

Alt, A., *Kleine Schriften zur Geschichte des Volkes Israel*, I, III, München, 1953, 1959. *Archives royals de Mari*, I–XII, XV, Paris 1946–64.

Amiran, R., *Ancient Pottery of the Holy Land* (trans. from the Hebrew), Tel Aviv, 1969.

Bauer, Th., *Die Ostkanaanäer*, Leipzig 1, 926.

Beckerath, J., von, *Untersuchungen zur politichen Geschichte der zweiten Zwischenzeit in Ägyptien*, Glückstadt, 1964.

Dunand, M., *Fouilles de Byblos*, I–II, Paris 1939–1958.

Edzard, D. O., *Die "zweite Zwischenzeit" Babyloniens*, Wiesbaden, 1957.

Gelb, I. J., *Hurrians and Subarians*, Chicago 1944.

Glueck, N., *Rivers in the Desert*, New York 1959.

Hayes, W. C., "The Middle Kingdom in Egypt; Internal History from the Rise of the Heracleopolitans to the death of Ammenemes III," *CAH*, I (rev. ed.), ch. XX.
"Egypt; from the Death of Ammenemes III to Sequenenre II," *ibid.*, II (rev. ed.), ch. II.

Helck, H. W., *Die Beziehungen Ägyptens zu Vorderasien im 3. und 2. Jahrt. vor Chr.*, Wiesbaden, 1962.

Kenyon, K. M., *Excavations at Jericho*, I–II, London, 1960–1965.

Kupper, J. -R., *Les nomades en Mésopotamie au temps des rois de Mari*, Paris, 1957.
"Northern Mesopotamia and Syria," *CAH*, II (rev. ed.) ch. I.

Loud, G., *Megiddo*, II, Chicago, 1948.

Maisler (Mazar), B., *Untersuchungen zur alten Geschichte und Ethnographie Syriens und Palästinas*, Giessen, 1930.

Montet, P., *Byblos et l'Égypte*, Paris, 1928.

Moscati, S., *I predecessori d'Israele*, Roma 1956.

Noth, M., *Die Ursprünge des alten Israel im Lichte neuer Quellen*, Köln, 1961.

Posener, G., *Princes et pays d'Asie et de Nubie* Bruxelles, 1940.

Posener, G.—Bottéro, J.—Kenion, K. M., "Syria and Palestine, c. 2160–1780 B.C.," *CAH*, I (rev. ed.) ch. XXI.

Sturm, J., *Der Hethiterkrieg Ramses II*, Wien 1939.

Tocci, F. M., *La Siria nell'età di Mari*, Roma, 1960.

Wiseman, D. J., *The Alalakh Tablets*, London 1953.

Woolley, L., *Alalakh*, Oxford, 1955.

Wright, G. E., *Shechem*, New York, 1965.

CHAPTER X

CANAAN IN THE PATRIARCHAL AGE

Kaufmann, Y., *A History of the Jewish Religion* II, Tel Aviv, 1942, pp. 7 ff., 328 ff. "The Hebrews in the biblic literature," *'Oz le David* (Ben Gurion Volume), Jerusalem, 1964, pp. 103–113.

Albright, W. F., "The Smaller Beth Shan Stele of Sethos I (1309–1290 B.C.)," *BASOR*, 125 (1952), 24 ff.
"Abram the Hebrew," *ibid.*, 163(1961), 53 f.

Alt, A., "Erwägungen über die Landnahme der Israeliten in Palästina", *PJB*, 35, (1939), 56 ff. (= *Kleine Schriften*, I, München, 1953, 168 ff.).

Bottéro, J., *Le problème des Ḥabiru* (Cahiers de la Société Asiatique, XII), Paris, 1954.

Greenberg, M., *The Ḥab/piru* (American Oriental Series, 39), New Haven, 1955.

Kupper, J. -R., *Les nomades en Mésopotamie au temps des rois de Mari*, Paris 1957.
"Sutéens et Ḥapiru," *RA*, 55 (1961), 197 ff.

Lewy, J., "Ḥābirū and Hebrews," *HUCA*, 14 (1939), 587 ff.

Noth, M., *Geschichte Israels²*, Göttingen, 1954, 38 ff.

Rowley H. H., *From Joseph to Joshua*, London, 1950.

M. Noth, *VT*, 1 (1951), 74 ff. (cf. criticism of the above mentioned).

Vaux, R., de, "Les Partriaches hébreux et les découverts modernes," *RB*, 55 (1948), 337 ff.

CHAPTER XI
HAB/PIRU AND HEBREWS

Albright, W. F., "Abram the Hebrew," *BASOR*, 163 (1961), 36 ff.

Alt, A., *Der Gott der Väter*, Stuttgart, 1929 (= *Kleine Schriften*, I, München, 1953, 1 ff.).

Gordon, C. H., "Abraham and the Merchants of Ura," *JNES*, 17 (1958), 28 ff.

Speiser, E. A., "The Verb SHR in Genesis and Early Hebrew Movements," *BASOR*, 164 (1961), 23 ff.

Wooley, L., *Abraham*, London 1936.

Yeivin, S., "The Age of the Patriarchs," *RSO*, 38 (1963), 277 ff.

Yeivin, S., *Studies in the History of Israel and his Land*, Tel Aviv, Jerusalem, 1960, pp. 25 ff., 45 ff.

"Studies about the period of the Patriarchs," *Bet Miqra* III, 4 (1963), 13 ff.

CHAPTER XII
THE RELIGION OF THE PATRIARCHS:

Alt, A. *Der Gott der Väter*, Stuugart, 1929 (= *Kleine Schriften*, I, München, 1953, 1 ff.).

Cross, F. M., Jr., "Yahweh and the God of Patriarchs," *HTR*, 55 (1962), 225–259.

Eissfeldt, O., "El and Yahweh," *JSS*, 1 (1956), 25–37 (= *Kleine Schriften*, III, Tübingen 1966, 386–397).

Haran, M., "An outline of the Patriarchs's religion" *'Oz l᷎ David* (Ben Gurion Volume) Jerusalem, 1964, pp. 40–20.

Haran, M., "The Religion of the Patriarchs: An Attempt at a Synthesis," *Annual of the Swedish Theological Institute*, 4(1965), 30–55.

Hoftijzer, J., *Die Verheissungen an die drei Erzväter*, Leiden, 1956.

Kaufmann Y., *A History of the Israelite Religion* II, Tel Aviv, 1962, pp. 23–36.

Lods, A., "The Religion of Israel-Origins," *Record and Revelation*, ed. by H. W. Robinson, Oxford, 1938, 187–215.

May, H. G., "The Patriarchal Idea of God," *JBL*, 60 (1941), 113–128.

Weippert, M., "Erwägungen zur Etymologie des Gottesnamen *'El Šaddj*," *ZDMG*, 111 (1961), 42–62.

INDEX OF NAMES AND PLACES

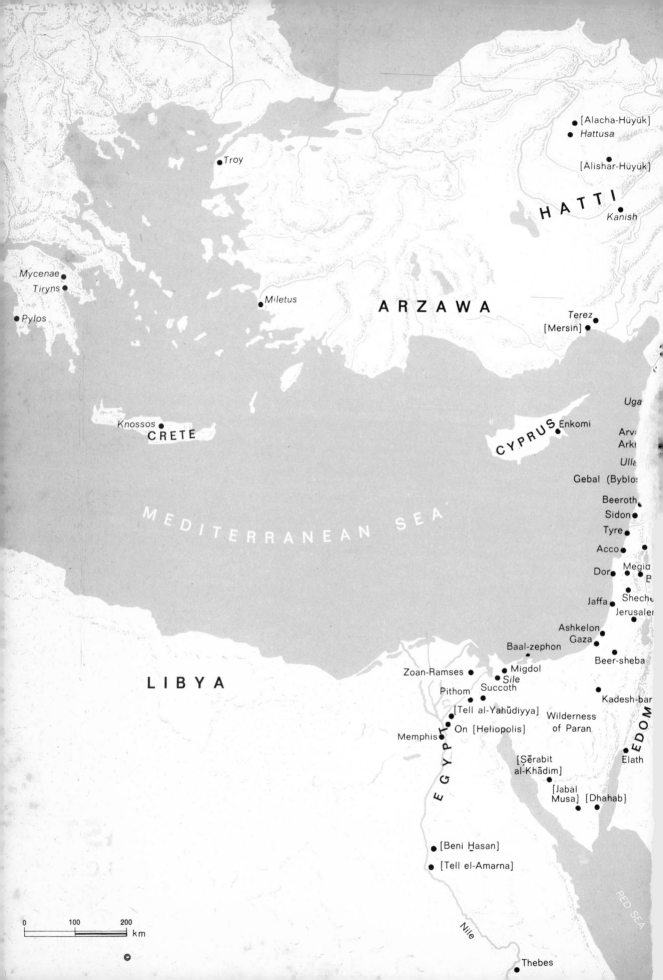

Troy

Mycenae
Tiryns
Pylos

Miletus

[Alacha-Hüyük]
Hattusa

[Alishar-Hüyük]

HATTI

Kanish

ARZAWA

Terez
[Mersin]

Knossos

CRETE

CYPRUS · Enkomi

Uga

Arv
Arkı

Ulla

Gebal (Byblos

Beeroth
Sidon
Tyre
Acco

Dor · Megia
B

Jaffa · Sheche
Jerusaler

Ashkelon
Gaza

Beer-sheba

MEDITERRANEAN SEA

LIBYA

Baal-zephon

Zoan-Ramses · Migdol
Sile
Pithom · Succoth

[Tell al-Yahūdiyya]
On [Heliopolis]

Memphis

EGYPT

Kadesh-bar

Wilderness
of Paran

EDOM

Elath

[Sērabit
al-Khādim]

[Jabal
Musa] [Dhahab]

[Beni Ḥasan]

[Tell el-Amarna]

RED SEA

0   100   200
                km

Nile

Thebes